BEFORE THE SPUD

INDIANS, BUCKAROOS, AND
SHEEPHERDERS IN PIONEER IDAHO

BEFORE THE SPUD

INDIANS, BUCKAROOS, AND SHEEPHERDERS IN PIONEER IDAHO

Evan E. Filby

Sourdough Publishing
Idaho Falls, Idaho

ISBN 978-148-0063112

Before the Spud is produced, upon order placement, by CreateSpace, an amazon.com company. Orders may be placed with the *Before the Spud* eStore at www.createspace.com/4019457 or through www.amazon.com. We will consider bulk orders at special discounts for educational purposes, fund-raising, or corporate gifts. Museums, historical associations, and schools are particularly encouraged to apply. Contact the author through the imprint addresses provided below.

Sourdough Publishing
2184 Channing Way, Suite 437
Idaho Falls, ID 83404
e-mail: Sourdough@Earthlink.net

TABLE OF CONTENTS

ACKNOWLEDGEMENTS

Before the Spud is the book I wrote because I was interested in the history of the cattle industry in Idaho, but there was nothing like it "out there." I found books about a few specific regions in the state, but none that gave a comprehensive view. So I began researching the topic, which led me to broaden the subject to include horses and sheep. During that research, I met many helpful people at libraries and historical museums around the state. To all those who provided that help: Thank you! This book would not have been possible without you.

We should all, writers and readers alike, acknowledge the work of those many dedicated people who are trying, usually with minimal resources, to preserve our history. That obviously includes the Idaho State Historical Society, as well as many small regional and county historical associations. Finally, we must include the Library of Congress, the U. S. National Archives, and the Smithsonian Institution. Thank you all!

My wife, Caroline, has contributed greatly to the project. She encouraged the idea of traveling for on-site research, and to see first-hand many of the locations where key events took place. She read and commented on the entire manuscript, pointing out places where it could be improved. I cannot thank her enough.

Preface: Ground Rules

This narrative presents the early history of stock raising in Idaho. People tend to concede a "cowboy" past to states like Wyoming, Nevada, and Montana. Not so with Idaho. Yet, far more than most outsiders realize, Idaho was, and still is, a cowboy state. My only regret is that I can not tell many more stories of those who made it so.

I have based these accounts on personal memoirs, newspaper articles, various histories, and other resources. Whenever I can, I identify pioneer voices and let them speak for themselves. Thus, I never "make up" conversations. I include the words, thoughts, or feelings of historical figures only if they or a first-hand witness preserved them in some way. Occasionally, specific references are identified within the text. Beyond that, a section at the back of the book lists my sources with a chapter-by-chapter breakdown of where each is used.

Sometimes I describe an event as a "you are there" scene. I want you to feel like you're looking over the shoulders of the participants. Most of these are activities we know happened, just as described. For many events, I set the scene using other sources. For example, one local historian related how stockmen drove small cattle bands through Salmon City in the early 1870s. The author does not say much about what the town looked like at the time. Fortunately, we know that from a contemporary photograph.

A few such scenes are composites, based on multiple descriptions. For example, no buckaroo left a diary, that we know of, describing his daily life. So we do not have an account of how on a certain day, a crew cut out calves for branding and ear-marking. Yet we know such roundups happened on a regular basis. Other observers have described the equipment and techniques used. Plus, we know the locations involved, and the terrain. It is no great trick to put the pieces together. However, as noted above, I draw the line at putting words in the participants' mouths.

To avoid confusion, I use common names for major landscape features like rivers, lakes, and so on. Admittedly, this is a bit of "back-sliding." Pioneers and explorers often gave their own names to landmarks. A few times, I want to quote a source that uses one of those "private" names. In some other cases, a designation has special historical meaning. I try to explain these specific circumstances in the text.

Every quarter century, starting in 1800, I will provide *The Big Picture,* a quick "time-stamp" of U.S. events and status. This should help provide perspective on happenings in Idaho.

CHAPTER ONE: THE FIRST STOCKMEN OF IDAHO

The four white men, burdened with packs and flintlock rifles, tramped along a well-worn Indian trail. They saw nothing of the Shoshone Indian band whose traces they had spotted earlier. The broken terrain provided many hiding spots for an ambush.

The track loosely followed a stream up the increasing slope. At over seven thousand feet elevation, air comes in gasping breaths and thighs burn. Hardened to tough conditions, these men have never been this high before. When the worst of the grade eased, they stopped to rest and quench their thirst from a flow of icy-cold spring water. Substantial peaks crowded in from the north and south, but the way west looked clear.

"After refreshing ourselves, we proceeded on to the top of the dividing ridge, from which I discovered immence ranges of high mountains still to the west of us, with their tops partially covered with snow," wrote Captain Meriwether Lewis in his journal for Monday, August 12, 1805. His advance party of the Corps of Discovery thus became the first Americans to cross the Continental Divide. They were also the first white men to view the future state of Idaho.

However, the Captain had more pressing concerns than the presence of large peaks to the west. They'd seen plenty of tall mountains already from their course up the Missouri River. They could look back at a dozen great peaks, some rising a mile above the river valley: Mount Edith, Bridger, Crow, Big Baldy, Elkhorn, and more.

Unfortunately, deep into the Rocky Mountains, the Missouri splits into three smaller streams. The Gallatin, Madison, and Jefferson rivers therefore contain many more rapids and shallow stretches than the Missouri itself. The Continental Divide looms to the west, a half-mile of vertical rise. They knew they must get help from the Indians, perhaps the Shoshones. Lewis wrote, "If we do not find them or some other nation who have horses, I fear the successful issue of our voyage will be very doubtful."

The Corps had started up the Jefferson-Beaverhead river course, but the swift current and many rocks and riffles slowed progress to a crawl. Finally, Lewis and three men forged ahead: "For, without horses we shall be obliged to leave a great part of our stores, of which it appears to me that we have a stock already sufficiently small for the length of the voyage before us."

Thankfully, the hail and soaking rain of yesterday had blown out. Still, the chill winds cutting through Lemhi Pass on the Continental Divide leached warmth from any exposed skin. They must find shelter. Most of all, however, Lewis needed to find the Shoshones.

The men followed the Indian trail down the steep western slope. After dropping over nine hundred feet from the pass, they came, said Lewis, "to a handsome bold running creek of cold, clear water. Here I first tasted the water of the great Columbia River."

After this refreshment, they continued along the Indian trail to a spring, where they encamped for the night. Greenery nourished by spring water stood out against the drab yellow-browns and grays of the spent hillside vegetation.

In the morning, they followed the trail as it descended toward the Lemhi River plain. After about four miles, they spotted three Indians observing them from a distant hill. The natives watched long enough to get a good look at the strangers, and then disappeared. Undeterred by the apparent rebuff, Lewis and his men continued along the trail. Within "not more than a mile," they stumbled upon three females. A young woman quickly raced away. The other two, an "elderly woman" and a pre-teen, "seated themselves on the ground, holding down their heads as if reconciled to die."

Lewis quickly drew on the sign-language skills of interpreter George Drouillard. With presents and careful words, he gained the old woman's confidence. He then coaxed her into persuading the fugitive girl to return for her own gifts.

They all now headed down the trail toward the valley. Soon enough, a large band of warriors galloped toward them. They brandished bows and arrows and a few trade guns. Fortunately, the presence of the women, happy with their gifts, quickly defused a potentially deadly situation.

Lewis brought forth the customary pipe to smoke and parley with the Indians, especially the chief, "Cameahwait." Finally, they all moved to Cameahwait's campsite, located on the Lemhi River. As best he could via the crude vehicle of sign language, Lewis explained their mission and its peaceful intent. What Lewis saw as the "extreme poverty" of the tribe perhaps magnified the value of what Lewis called "trifles." Later, the Shoshones shared their only provisions, serviceberry and chokecherry cakes, with the hungry white men.

After this "hearty meal," Lewis surveyed the Lemhi, which he found "about 40 yards wide, very rapid, clear, and about 3 feet deep."

The chief said it discharged into the much larger Salmon River about a half-day's march below his camp. Concerning the Salmon, Cameahwait asserted, "that the river was confined between inaccessible mountains, was very rapid and rocky insomuch that it was impossible for us to pass either by land or water down this river."

The chief could hardly have given Lewis worse news. If true, it would stymie the Corps on their most crucial goal, assigned by President Thomas Jefferson. The Missouri had brought them this far. They must find a Pacific Northwest river to complete a "direct & practicable water communication across this continent for the purposes of commerce."

The Big Picture. Five years before this meeting, in 1800, the U.S. had no reason for such an Expedition. President John Adams presided over a nation of 16 states, Vermont, Kentucky, and Tennessee having been added to the original Thirteen. The population was around 5.3 million, roughly double that at the start of the Revolution. In November, Congress met for the first time in the new capital in Washington, D.C., and Adams moved into the new Executive Mansion there.

When Jefferson took office in 1801, the United States ended basically at the Mississippi River. "Westerners" – those living beyond the Appalachian ranges – needed secure access to outside markets through New Orleans. This newfangled federal government had to meet that demand. Otherwise, they might just go off on their own.

British probes in western Canada heightened Jefferson's concerns. Thus, in January 1803, Congress approved two funding requests. They authorized over $9 million to buy New Orleans from France, and twenty-five hundred dollars for the Corps.

Jefferson had already selected Captain Lewis, his personal secretary or "aide de camp," to lead the venture. Lewis, then about twenty-eight years old, had been born in the same "Virginia planter" environment as Jefferson. After a year in the militia, Lewis spent seven or eight years as an Army officer. He thus knew how to lead men. Duty in the west acquainted him with the wild conditions of the frontier. He had also dealt with Indians. Best of all, he had learned much about nature through observation and shrewd reasoning.

Meanwhile, Jefferson had also sent agents off to France to talk about New Orleans. Jefferson's envoys arrived in Paris at a crucial moment. War loomed between France and Great Britain. Napoleon knew he couldn't protect his North American holdings, and he needed money. Thus, his negotiator offered to sell all of Louisiana to the astonished Americans. Naturally, they accepted.

Neither Jefferson nor Lewis knew of this right away, of course. Word did not reach the States until July. Lewis had reviewed what they would need to do. Besides dealing with the natives, they must survey the route and terrain, and record scientific data. They should really have another officer. He selected William Clark as the right man, one whose skills complemented and enhanced his own. Jefferson concurred.

About four years older than Lewis, Clark had also served in the militia and then the Army. He too had been born in Virginia. The family had moved to Kentucky when Clark was about fourteen. He thus knew the frontier and its people – Indians as well as settlers – better than Lewis.

A slow exchange of letters established Captain Clark as co-leader of the Expedition. By then news of the Louisiana Purchase had reached even the western frontier. The Purchase encompassed much of what are now the states north of Texas between the Mississippi River and the Continental Divide. It did not include the Pacific Northwest. That was unclaimed, and therefore disputed, territory.

Right now, fourteen months and around three thousand travel miles into the journey, Captain Lewis faced a make-or-break crisis. If they could not continue down the Salmon River, they absolutely must have horses. On this point, his observations

Salmon River Canyon

offered better news. Lewis recorded a key fact from his first sight of Cameahwait's band. The Indians were "mounted on excellent horses."

He quizzed the chief further about the river and country to the west. Cameahwait responded with an even more graphic portrayal. He told Lewis "that the perpendicular, and even jutting, rocks so closely hemmed in the river that there was no possibility of passing along the shore; that the bed of the river was obstructed by sharp pointed rocks, and the rapidity of the stream such that the whole surface of the river was beaten into perfect foam, as far as the eye could reach." Not only that, but "the mountains were also inaccessible to man or horse."

That sent Lewis back to the issue of getting the Corps and its baggage across the Divide. Drouillard had checked and figured the tribe had about four hundred horses. Scholars generally believe the Shoshones obtained horses as early as 1690 AD. Ten years earlier, the Pueblo Rebellion had chased the Spanish out of New Mexico. The tribes lasted twelve years before the Spanish quashed them again. During that time, the sedentary Pueblos traded horses to their friendlier neighbors to the north and east. Horses vastly improved the mobility of many nomadic peoples. They could now follow and hunt buffalo more effectively. Later, tribes traded south for new stock.

But the wealth of new herds proved irresistible, and horse theft soon became a common "sport." Cameahwait said that recent Blackfeet raids had severely reduced their herd. These better-armed bands claimed the upper Missouri River plains, and often struck across the Divide.

His tribe's urgent need for guns and ammunition surely explains why Cameahwait treated Lewis's appeal seriously. Finally, the chief and a couple dozen tribesmen went with the whites to meet Captain William Clark and the rest of the Corps.

Clark's contingent included the Shoshone girl, Sacagawea, the wife of their French-Canadian interpreter, Toussaint Charbonneau. In large part, the captains had hired Charbonneau so his wife could provide a language bridge to the Shoshones. Coincidentally, she turned out to be Cameahwait's sister.

Through a multi-lingual language chain, Lewis again explained their mission and how the Indians could benefit themselves by helping the Corps. He wanted them "to collect as many horses as were necessary to transport our baggage to their village." There, the Corps would "trade with them at our leisure for such horses as they could spare us."

Later, the captains discussed what to do next. Clark questioned the "gloomy picture" Cameahwait had painted of the Salmon. He wanted to see for himself. They agreed to again split the party. Clark would check out the river. Lewis would haul the rest of their baggage across when the Indians returned with enough horses.

Late the next morning, most of the Shoshones headed back to their camp. Clark, Charbonneau and Sacagawea, and a party of soldiers accompanied them. Nearing the Divide, they experienced the capricious nature of weather in these mountains. Pennsylvanian Patrick Gass, among the oldest members of the Corps at thirty-three, kept his own journal. Although the morning had been fine, Sergeant Gass wrote, "This afternoon there was a violent gust of wind, and some rain fell. In about an hour the weather became clear, and very cold, and continued cold all night."

The day after that, they reached the Shoshone camp, an assemblage of "about 25 lodges made of willow bushes." Gass said, "They are the poorest and most miserable nation I ever beheld; having scarcely any thing to subsist on, except berries and a few fish."

Gass noticed that their only source of wealth also brought trouble. He said, "They have a great many fine horses, and nothing more; and on account of these they are much harassed by other nations."

Captain Clark detailed Charbonneau and Sacagawea to explain what the Corps needed, and to hurry the horses along to Lewis. Then the soldiers procured a guide and followed the river downstream.

At the confluence of the main and north forks of the Salmon, they found "3 lodges of Indians." Gass recorded a key point. He noted that these natives "who are detached in small parties, appear to live better, and to have a larger supply of provisions, than those who live in large villages." Still, Gass opined that the people at the forks "appear to be the most wretched of the human species."

Stripped of Euro-American bias, the sergeant's observations here, and back at the village, captured a rare snapshot of a society struggling to adapt.

The Shoshone subsisted as hunter-gathers, and seasonal fishermen. The Great Basin and its fringes – Nevada, western Utah, southern Idaho, and southeast Oregon – are quite arid. Tribesmen had to move constantly, to allow the plants and small game to recover.

The size of the area exploited depended upon how far they could haul a load on foot. That curbed the formation of large villages. Thus, in the three-lodge party, Gass saw the product of centuries of hunter-gatherer adaptation. It worked very well, under the circumstances.

However, Shoshones like Cameahwait's band had embraced a "new technology" – the horse. When the Corps arrived, these first stockmen of Idaho had become skilled horseback hunters, and quite affluent by Shoshone standards.

But small, old-style hunter-gatherer parties lacked the manpower to deter horse thieves. The tribes responded with the "composite band." These combined several horse-owning family groups into larger villages for mutual protection. Unfortunately, normal hunter-gatherer practices could not provide the required food, forage, and other supplies. Thus, much of the disparity Gass observed arose because Shoshone social and political customs had not yet fully adapted to their new way of life.

In composite bands, family leaders formed a "council of equals." Personal prestige and force of character made Cameahwait the chief. Lewis finally did grasp that point. He said, "He who happens to enjoy the greatest share of confidence is the principal Chief."

From that, Lewis also noted the fact that the position of chief was not hereditary. Still, the lack of structure confounded Lewis. A man became chief, apparently, by general agreement and without ceremony. An experienced politician might possibly have understood, but the captain did not. In fact, the whites never fully appreciated the tenuous nature of Cameahwait's authority.

Corps members also seemed to feel the tribe had horses to spare. That was not the case. Periodically, the whole village had to pick up and move. An equal number of horses hardly sufficed for one hundred warriors plus three hundred women and children.

Over the next few days, Clark's Salmon River command battled some dreadful terrain. Often they had to scale lofty ridges to bypass the dangerous torrents. On August 24th, Gass wrote, "The river at this place is so confined by the mountains that it is not more than 20 yards wide, and very rapid. The mountains on the sides are not less than 1000 feet high and very steep."

Later, Clark pushed ahead with a smaller party, returning after a reconnaissance twelve miles down the river. Gass reported the Captain's conclusion that the Salmon was, indeed, impassable: "The water is so rapid and the bed of the river so rocky, that going by water appeared impracticable; and the mountains so amazingly high, steep and rocky, that it seemed impossible to go along the river by land."

Blocked by the Salmon, the Corps traded for about thirty horses, loaded their supplies and equipment, and pointed north. The Shoshones said the rugged route would lead them around the impassable Salmon wilderness.

The trail proved immensely difficult. Clark wrote, "Proceeded on through thickets in which we were obliged to cut a road, over rocky hillsides where our horses were in perpetual danger of slipping to their certain destruction."

To make matters worse, a classic early-September cold front caught them deep in the mountains. Gass, in his typical matter-of-fact tone wrote, "A considerable quantity of snow fell last night, and the morning was cloudy."

Clark noted ground "covered with snow" and said that they had to take time in the morning "to thaw the covering for the baggage."

Virginian Joseph Whitehouse, a First Infantry private, reported, "The morning clear but verry cold. Our mockersons froze hard." Sergeant John Ordway, from New Hampshire and thus no stranger to wintry weather, wrote "Our fingers aked with the cold."

Several days of such travel brought them into easier country north of Idaho. There, they met a large band of Flathead Indians. Lewis purchased more horses, bringing their total to forty, plus three colts.

Finally, "Old Toby," their Shoshone guide, led them down the Bitterroot Valley. Private Whitehouse noted the "high mountains on the left side of the creek, which are covered with pitch pine. Some of the highest are covered thick with snow."

The Corps turned up Lolo Creek and returned to Idaho on September 13, 1805. The men marched somewhat southeast after crossing the pass, circling a prominence thick with spruce and fir trees. In less than a half mile, they marched onto a marshy meadow, and then followed Pack Creek downstream until "the mountains closed in on either side."

From there, the trail avoided the narrowing valley and mounted to near the ridge top, descending now and then to cross a small stream. The party repeatedly had to scramble over fallen timber.

Hunters had not been very successful. The men had to butcher a colt to supplement the "portable soup," a dried beans and vegetables concoction Lewis had purchased before heading west.

For some reason, Old Toby misread the route and led them downstream along the Lochsa River. Toby finally led them onto the ridges, closer to the proper Lolo Trail. On their fourth day in Idaho, Sergeant Gass wrote, "Last night about 12 o'clock it began to snow. We renewed our march early, though the morning was very disagreeable, and proceeded over the most terrible mountains I ever beheld. ... In the night and during the day the snow fell about 10 inches deep."

Clark took the lead to break trail through the mounting drifts and wrote, "I have been wet and as cold in every part as I ever was in my life, indeed I was at one time fearfull my feet would freeze."

The snow started to melt the next day, but that created new hazards: mud, slippery slopes, and washed-out sections of trail. That evening, they butchered their last colt for dinner. They finished off the meat the next morning.

At this point, Captain Clark led a party of six hunters ahead, hoping to find game. Lewis followed with the rest of the Corps, "being determined to force my march as much as the abilities of our horses would permit."

The day after Clark left, Lewis's column followed a ridge to a high point from which they spied "a large tract of prairie" off in the distance. They still had a way to go, but at last they could see an end. Yet they could not afford a letdown. Further along, one horse fell from their path "and rolled with his load near a hundred yards into the creek." Miraculously, the animal rose unhurt, with its load intact.

The hunting-party strategy paid its first dividend within two days. Clark's hunters had stumbled across a horse. They had breakfast from the butchered animal, then left the rest for the main party. The next day, a member of Clark's advance party met Lewis's band with a supply of dried fish and roots obtained from the Nez Percés Indians. Clark had reached their village two days earlier.

After a much-needed meal, Lewis and the rest of the Corps hurried on. Glad to escape the "dismal and horrible mountains," they didn't much mind the broken, pine-covered foothills they descended into. Finally, they marched onto Weippe Prairie, reaching the Nez Percés village in the late afternoon of September 22nd.

"The Indians belonging to this band received us kindly, appeared pleased to see us, and gave us such provisions as they had," Sergeant Gass noted.

Later that evening, Captain Clark joined them, accompanied by Twisted Hair, an older chief. The younger "great chief" of the band had set out "with all the warriors of the nation to war, on a southwest direction, and would return in fifteen or eighteen days."

Clark sympathized with Lewis and the others – who were, he said, "much fatigued and hungry" – but he quickly got down to business. He asked Twisted Hair to describe the river system leading out of Nez Percés country. The chief sketched a map of the Clearwater-Snake-Columbia river chain on white elk skin. He claimed a two-week voyage would get them to the Pacific Ocean.

However, the captains had to attend to many details before they could go on. To begin with, exhaustion and perhaps the change to a diet of roots and dried fish laid up much of the Corps, including Lewis. Nonetheless, the Corps moved to the Clearwater. They then marched downstream to the confluence of its main and north forks. They stopped at a location known to us as "Canoe Camp."

At Canoe Camp, they observed that the Nez Percés had excellent trade links to the coast. Gass noted that the tribes had "a great many beads and other articles."

Significantly, he also said, "They have a large stock of horses."

On October 1, Sergeant Gass wrote, "This was a fine pleasant warm day. All the men are now able to work; but the greater number are very weak."

Teams scouted the riverbank for suitable trees and selected large ones for their cargo vessels. They also needed a smaller, more maneuverable dugout. Chips flew as carefully placed ax blows felled four trees of roughly three-foot thickness, and one lesser one. Fortunately, mature Ponderosa pines have few limbs on the lower 30-35 feet they needed for their largest canoes. All they had to do was strip off the bark.

Axmen fashioned enough flat surface so the bare timbers could be levered onto a frame. Then two sawyers began the backbreaking task of whipsawing the green, sapped-filled logs into a squat U-shape, 32-34 inches wide and 20-22 inches high. Further axe work gave them a roughly tapered bow and stern.

Next, the men hollowed out the hull. Gass said, "To save them from hard labour, we have adopted the Indian method of burning out the canoes."

Sergeant Ordway explained that they "built fires on some of them to burn them out. Found them to burn verry well."

Marking the area to be removed, they piled hot coals on the surface and let them eat into the log. Periodically, they removed the embers and chopped the charred wood out with an adze. They had to be careful not to ignite wood chips or other tender around the work site. After a week, the canoes had taken shape. Then the best bladesmen finished the surface using a well-sharpened adze or draw-knife. The final transport vessel weighed well over a ton.

Nez Percés in Dugout on the Clearwater

Twisted Hair and a younger chief agreed to act as guides and intermediaries. Twisted Hair also promised to hold their horses until the Expedition returned the following year. Clark had the soldiers brand and crop the forelocks of the horses before turning them over to the chiefs' caretakers.

On October 7th, the soldiers tested their craft for leak-tightness on the aptly named Clearwater – waters so transparent the trout seemed to float in space over the stony bottom. By mid-afternoon, they had balanced the canoe loads.

In his journal, Gass noted, "About 3 o'clock in the afternoon we began our voyage down the river, and found the rapids in some places very dangerous."

Captain Clark reported, "One canoe, that in which I went in front, sprung a leak in passing the third rapid."

Many Indian lodges dotted the shoreline. Along here, the Clearwater flows through a deep valley. Grass and wildflowers carpet the steep slopes, but few pine trees grow. High above, irregular prairie lands stretch off into the distance. They camped 25-30 miles down the river.

They embarked the next morning under cloudy skies. For much of the day, they made good progress. However, later in the day, Sergeant Gass's canoe slammed into a rock, spun, and struck again. The impact split the side of the craft and threw Gass overboard. He scrambled back, but the canoe quickly sank among the rocks.

"I had my canoe stove, and she sunk. Fortunately, the water was not more than waist deep, so our lives and baggage were saved, though the latter was wet," Gass said.

Clark quickly organized a rescue party, which took off the men and cargo and "towed the empty canoe on shore." Gass and three other soldiers carefully repaired the damage. Clark wrote, "At 1 o'clock she was finished, stronger than ever."

Unfortunately, the baggage took much longer to dry. They waited until the next morning to resume their voyage. The travelers encountered several sets of rapids until, Clark said, "We arrived at the head of a very bad riffle, at which place we landed."

They scouted the white water from on shore, then decided to run the canoes through one at a time. The Corps landed again below the "riffle" to repair one damaged canoe and dry its cargo. On October 10, they reached the Snake River and paddled downstream to camp for the night.

The Corps of Discovery finally came in view of the Pacific Ocean on November 7, 1805. Within a month, they picked a spot south and west of present-day Astoria for their winter encampment. The Corps completed their winter quarters and moved in around Christmas. They called it Fort Clatsop after a nearby Indian tribe.

During the interminable, wet winter, the captains recorded long passages about the plants, animals, and Indian tribes they had observed west of the Rockies. Lewis, considered a fine judge of horseflesh, admired the Indians' horses. He wrote, "Their horses appear to be of an excellent race; they are lofty, eligantly formed, active and durable; in short many of them look like the fine English coarsers and would make a figure in any country."

He also clearly described the famed Appaloosa strain, for which the Nez Percés are renowned. "Some of those horses are pied with large spots of white irregularly scattered and intermixed with the black, brown, bay, or some other dark color," he said.

Looking ahead, he suggested that whites could purchase horses for "paltry trinkets which in the U' States would not cost more than one or two dollars."

They returned to Nez Percés country in late April, hoping to hurry across the Bitterroots. However, on May 7, Lewis wrote, "The spurs of the Rocky Mountains which were in view from the high plain today were perfectly covered with snow."

The Nez Percés warned that it might be a month or more before they could cross. The captains finally accepted that the risks of a premature attempt were too great.

When several top-level chiefs joined them, the captains used the opportunity to explain their plans for future commerce with the Indians. This included a request that a Nez Percés representative accompany them on their journey east. Although the Indians seemed to respond favorably, ultimately, nothing happened.

The Nez Percés certainly hoped to obtain a steady supply of guns and ammunition from the whites. However, unlike the Lemhi Shoshone, they probably did not feel a sense of urgency. If the ample bounty of their homeland should falter, the surplus from their great horse herds could be traded for food and other necessities.

Their neighbors feared their power and ferocity. Some years later, a Snake River Shoshone chief ridiculed the notion of making peace with the Nez Percés. He declared, "They are at this moment on our lands, and perhaps before night, my wives and my children will be scalped by them!"

In the end, the rich and powerful Nez Percés would cooperate only on their own terms. Clark noted, "When we had established a trading house on the Missouri as we had promised, they would come over and trade."

Forced to be satisfied with this meager assurance, the Corps retrieved their horses and cached supplies. They then settled in at the "Long Camp" to wait for the snow to melt. For the next few weeks, they tried to enlarge their food supply by hunting and trading with the locals. Captain Clark's medical skills proved to be their most reliable source of provisions and additional horses. As Lewis had put it earlier, "My friend Captain Clark is their favorite physician and has already received many applications."

The Americans found much to like about the Nez Percés, including their horses and horsemanship. Lewis recorded their game of "shooting their arrows at a bowling target made of willow bark" and observed that "they are expert marksmen and good riders."

In mid-May, as they accumulated more horses, Lewis wrote, "These horses are active, strong and well formed. These people have immence numbers of them."

Unfortunately, several of the stallions obtained by the Corps were wild and dangerous. A visiting Nez Percés helped geld them, using an approach where he carefully dissected "the stones" from the surrounding tissues. Lewis noted that the man "assures us that they will do much better in that way."

Lewis had George Drouillard geld one using the normal method practiced by the whites. Nine days later, Lewis observed that the horses castrated by the Indian method "do not swell nor appear to suffer as much as those cut in the common way."

Finally, Lewis recorded his absolute belief that "the Indian method of gelding is preferable to that practiced by ourselves."

May 22nd dawned clear and sunny. In the afternoon, hunters brought in five deer they had killed.

As Sergeant Gass directed the men in some routine camp chores, they noticed a stir on the far side of the river. Soon a swarm of riders twisted and turned through the brush. Sometimes they scaled the bluffs and then turned down again in a wild scramble. The watchers finally spotted a frantic deer, running for its life. Everywhere the animal dodged, a tenacious horse and rider dashed to block it.

At last, the frantic deer plunged into the run-off swollen river. A soldier took careful aim and shot the fugitive. Within minutes, the natives launched a raft and gathered in their prey. After this exhibition, Gass wrote, "These Indians are the most active horsemen I ever saw. They will gallop their horses over precipices that I should not think of riding over."

Despite such diversions, the delay severely tried the patience of the captains and their men. Lewis noted, "We have not now any time to delay if the calculation is to reach the United States this season."

They made one abortive attempt in mid-June, but encountered impossible conditions almost immediately. Lewis wrote, "Here was winter with all its rigors; the air was cold, my hands and feet were benumbed."

Finally, they obtained guides and set out again. Sergeant Gass remarked, "It appeared to me somewhat extraordinary, to be travelling over snow six or eight feet deep in the latter end of June."

They camped at Lolo Hot Springs, in the future Missoula County, Montana, on June 29, 1806. The Corps of Discovery had left Idaho behind.

By August 12th, the Corps was a few days out of Montana on the Missouri River. The captains had again split the party to broaden their explorations. The bow oarsman of Lewis's canoe saw a campsite he thought might belong to some white men. Lewis landed and "found it to be the camp of two hunters from the Illinois by name Joseph Dickson and Forest Hancock."

Dickson and Hancock had been hunting beaver, with little success, but were determined to continue the hunt upstream. They accompanied the Corps down river for a few days, and managed to persuade Private John Colter to join their venture. Of course, Colter was still in the Army, but the captains granted him an early discharge. Clark noted, "We were disposed to be of service to any one of our party who had performed their duty as well as Colter."

Lewis and Clark and most of the Corps reached St. Louis, Missouri on September 23, 1806. They had been gone roughly two years and four months.

Even before they arrived, Captain Lewis had been busy on a draft of his initial report. He first confirmed that they had completed their journey and returned safely. Then he delivered the bad news. There was no "direct & practicable water communication across this continent."

At best, the water route included two major portages – at the Great Falls of the Missouri, and near The Dalles on the Columbia. The mountain streams contained miles of passable, but perilous rapids. Worst of all, a long stretch of rugged country separated the navigable portions of these systems. Some of the gap was impassable in winter,

Despite the negatives, Lewis extolled the commercial potential of the western lands. The watersheds "abound" in fur-bearing animals, he reported. American firms could reap huge profits by gathering furs and shipping them, via the Columbia, to the rich Oriental markets in Canton.

Bulk goods purchased in the Far East would reach the U.S. by sea, but many items could traverse the continent more directly via the route the Expedition had mapped. Lewis envisioned pack trains loaded with valuable furs moving west. Those would pass eastbound trains loaded with spices, exotic Oriental art, and other high-value goods. This part of the plan depended upon the large Shoshone and Nez Percés horse herds. Cheap and readily available Indian horses would reduce "the expences of transportation over this portage to a mere trifle."

American firms could cut the British out of the western fur trade. "If the government will only aid, even in a very limited manner, the enterprize of her Citizens," Lewis asserted, "I am fully convinced that we shall shortly derive the benefits of a most lucrative trade."

The Captains wrapped up their western affairs and made their way to Washington. In early 1807, they and their men received rewards for their amazing results. Most of the enlisted men received grants of land and many received double pay for their time in service.

Lewis and Clark did better, of course. Both received double pay for the duration of the trip, and handsome land grants. Jefferson made Clark a "Brigadier General of Militia." That position paid as well as the same Army rank, but involved limited peacetime duty. The President also appointed him Superintendent of Indian Affairs for the Territory of Upper Louisiana.

Lewis became Territorial Governor. He would be the key figure in the political and commercial development of the new lands. Unfortunately, Lewis would prove ineffective as Governor. Nor would he live to profit from his vision of the western fur trade.

Still, his prophetic words set off a trade war that virtually wrote the early history of Idaho and the Pacific Northwest. The indigenous first stockmen of Idaho would both benefit and suffer from that conflict.

Party of Indian Scouts

Chapter Two: Fur Trade Era – Canadians Dominant

The tiny flotilla edged out into the swirling flow of the Missouri River, leaving St. Charles behind. In March 1811, this village, perhaps a day's journey northwest of St. Louis, was the next-to-last white settlement on the way west. The keelboat's ten pairs of sweeps dipped into the chocolate water as rain pattered on the surface. This Wilson Price Hunt party included John Bradbury, a Scots naturalist. He noted the beat of "the Canadians measuring the strokes of their oars by songs, which were generally responsive betwixt the oarsmen at the bow and those at the stem: sometimes the steersman sung, and was chorused by the men."

Four years in the planning, Hunt's group represented the Pacific Fur Company. The firm was an affiliate of the American Fur Company. Wealthy entrepreneur John Jacob Astor had fostered both companies. He created the PFC to explore the opportunities suggested by the Corps of Discovery reports. Astor, born in the Duchy of Baden, Germany, immigrated to the U.S. in 1784. Historian Hiram Chittenden noted that he had "become the leading fur merchant of the United States and probably the leading authority in the world upon that business."

Fur Magnate John Jacob Astor

Astor began considering a western venture in 1807-1808. Early on, he tried to fashion a partnership with the North West Company (NWC), a British-Canadian fur trade competitor. Suspicious NWC managers eventually let the negotiations die.

Astor found few Americans with the necessary experience. He therefore persuaded three Scots-Canadians to become partners in the PFC. In fact, Wilson Price Hunt was the only native-born U.S. citizen among the original senior partners. Born in rural New Jersey, Hunt gained experience with the fur business as part owner of a store in St. Louis, Missouri. Aged twenty-eight when the expedition began, he had consulted personally with Lewis and Clark, and closely studied the records of their expedition.

Donald Mackenzie, one of the senior Scots-Canadian partners, accompanied Hunt on the overland journey. The same age as Hunt, Mackenzie emigrated from Scotland in 1801. He had spent the intervening years working for the NWC at remote fur-trade outposts. Hunt's rowers chanted their chorus in French because most of the expedition's clerks and trappers were also seasoned Canadians.

In late May, Bradbury noted in his journal, "Whilst at breakfast on a beautiful part of the river, we observed two canoes descending on the opposite side. In one, by the help of our glasses, we ascertained there were two white men, and in the other only one."

They soon identified the canoeists as trappers from the fledgling Missouri Fur Company. The MFC had an exclusive license to trap and trade throughout the Missouri River watershed. Several St. Louis businessmen, including William Clark, founded the company. Territorial Governor Meriwether Lewis signed their license. Historians have assumed that Lewis also had a behind-the-scenes share. Such an arrangement was not uncommon in those times.

If Lewis did own a piece, he did not live to profit from it. In October 1809, fellow travelers at an inn in central Tennessee found him dead from gunshot wounds. Citing his well-known bouts of depression, historians have ruled his death a suicide. Conspiracy proponents think his political enemies had him murdered.

Andrew Henry, a St. Louis businessman with lead mine interests south of the city, was another MFC partner. In 1810, Henry built an outpost near present-day Three Forks, Montana. That was partly at the advice of John Colter. After leaving Lewis and Clark, Colter and his two partners trapped only briefly before they argued and then split up. Colter had joined the MFC and explored extensively, including parts of eastern Idaho.

Constant Indian attacks made the Three Forks post untenable. (And convinced Colter he should get out of the trade.) Henry tried again at a spot about twenty-five miles southwest of where the north branch of the Snake River exits the mountains. There, the party built Henry's Fort on what came to be called Henry's Fork. The Fort was the first U. S. post west of the Continental Divide. Records credit a North West Company trading post on Lake Pend d'Oreill as the first Euro-American structure west of the Divide.

A bitter East Idaho winter persuaded Henry to abandon the post after the spring trapping campaign. Although he still hadn't given up, three of his trappers did call it quits. After walking out of the mountains, they built canoes and glided down the Missouri to where they met Hunt.

Even ordinary trappers knew of the wealthy and influential Astor. The three were no doubt happy to join Hunt's expedition. They also convinced him that they now knew a better route to the mountains. To follow it, however, they all needed horses. After hard trading among the Arikaras in South Dakota, the column departed the villages in mid-July.

Their group of fifty-six men, one man's Indian wife, and two children did not have enough mounts. Subsequent mountain-man experience in the Rockies showed that they should have had a minimum of 120 animals. They started with only eighty-two. Hunt reported that they did begin to add horses along the way. (Bradbury returned to St. Louis from the Arikara villages.) In early August, they dickered with some Cheyenne Indians. Hunt wrote, "I bought thirty-six horses there at a price better than that which I paid the Aricaras."

They finally reached the area that would be called "Jackson's Hole" – a "hole" being a flat plain encircled, or largely surrounded, by high mountain ranges. Thwarted by the narrow Snake River canyon, they engaged Indian guides, who led them over "an easy and much-traveled trail" (Teton Pass) into Idaho on October 5, 1811. Ominously, Hunt recorded that "Snow whitened the summit and the northern slopes of the heights."

Beyond the pass, they dropped down to the plains and marched to Henry's Fort. There, Hunt decided the river would be much easier going. He wrote, "The river is nearly a half mile wide here, and beaver are plentiful."

He assigned a small trapping party to stay at Fort Henry with the horses. The rest built dugout canoes. Hunt said, "With the cargoes loaded into our canoes, we left this place on the 19th. The force of the current hurried us along at a rapid pace."

Despite a few moderately difficult rapids, his Canadian boatmen were far happier on the water than on horseback. The voyage went well until they reached central Idaho. There, they encountered the dangerous whitewater pass known to us as Caldron Linn. Hunt wrote, "Our journey was less fortunate on the 28th; for after passing through several rapids, we came to the entrance of a narrow gorge. Mr. Crook's canoe capsized, one of his companions drowned, and we lost a great deal of merchandise."

Further exploration showed that the river path was impossible. Because they now had no horses, Hunt cached the goods they could not carry. They then split into smaller parties that could live off the land, and tramped west. Hunt's group finally stumbled out of the eastern-Oregon mountains, barely escaping the early winter storms. They reached some Indian villages along the Columbia River in late January 1812.

"They told me of some white men who had built a large house at the mouth of the river, surrounding it with stakes, etc," Hunt said. This news was a huge relief.

In September 1810, long before Hunt departed from St. Charles, Astor's ship *Tonquin* had sailed from New York. The *Tonquin* carried a complement of workers to build and man the firm's Pacific terminus, Astoria. The ship arrived off the Oregon coast on March 1811. They then became some of the first travelers to experience the extremely dangerous turbulence of the Columbia River bar. In the end, their passage cost eight lives and two ship's boats.

While workmen on shore completed Astoria, the *Tonquin* sailed north to trade with the coastal tribes. Tragically, an Indian attack in mid-June led to the destruction of the ship and the deaths of all but one of the crew. At that time, Hunt had not even reached the Arikara villages where he bargained for horses. Hunt's group finally reached Astoria in February 1812.

Donald Mackenzie had led one of the separate bands out of Idaho. They had arrived a month before Hunt. During the spring, Astor's men began exploring and forging ties with the various tribes. Donald Mackenzie voyaged up the Columbia to deal with the Nez Percés.

One of Mackenzie's clerks, Ross Cox, had occasion to observe some tribesmen riding the cliff along the Snake River. The path, he said, "was barely wide enough for one horse at a time. Yet along these dangerous roads the Indians galloped with the utmost composure; while one false step would have hurled them down a precipice of three hundred feet into the torrent below."

Fur Trader Donald Mackenzie

"They have immense bands of wild and tame horses," Cox commented. However, Mackenzie found them a distinctly hard sell. Cox said, "They do not differ much from the Wallah Wallahs in their dress or language, but are not so friendly, and demand higher prices for their horses."

As well they might; they sensed how much the whites needed the animals. Moreover, they were justifiably proud of their prosperity and warrior prowess. Enemies feared their ferocious attacks, while allies welcomed their highly effective help. Historian Francis Haines said, "One can imagine, then, their indignation toward a stranger who asked that they do woman's work for a few gaudy trinkets which did not appeal to them. They could secure guns, ammunition, knives, and blankets in exchange for some of their surplus horses without stooping to do such labor."

While Mackenzie was learning the hard way that not everyone cared to trap beaver to obtain the white man's goods, another member of the firm was having his own troubles.

In late June 1812, Astoria supervisors tasked junior partner Robert Stuart to lead a group carrying dispatches east for transmittal to Astor. Aged twenty-seven, Robert was the nephew of one of the other senior partners. He emigrated from Scotland around 1807, and then gained experience with the North West Company.

Stuart's party entered Idaho by the middle of August. Shortly thereafter, they discovered that their Indian guide, whom they had deemed trustworthy, had made off with two of their horses. In his journal, Stuart wrote, "Concluding from our lesson of yesterday [morning] that no dependence could be placed on the Indians ... we determined to keep a constant guard during the remainder of this voyage, the night to be divided into three watches and one person to stand at a time."

A few days later, the group topped a slight rise and saw the river curving out of sight to the east. Descending the slope, the column rode out onto a level plain, perhaps three miles wide. Towering bluffs crowded the flat's northern border. The southern slope rose much more gradually to an equal height.

They rode more or less parallel to the Snake for a few miles. Their path led past cottonwood and hawthorn stands and through underbrush. Here and there they entered low areas overgrown by tall grass and reeds. Waterfowl swirled overhead, their cries and grunts both familiar and new. Willow thickets lined portions of the bank.

The river course now curved away from the escarpment to form a sinuous S through the middle of the plain, cutting across their line of march. Ready for a cool drink after their trek across the dry uplands, the little caravan approached the water.

To their surprise, they found one of the Henry's Fort trappers fishing from the bank. Before Stuart could question the man's presence, the willows began to thresh about, and three more men emerged. They too were from the Fort.

Five trappers had explored south across East Idaho after Hunt embarked on his ill-fated voyage down the Snake. Disaster then followed disaster. In the midst of repeated Indian forays, the fifth man had deserted with one of their horses. In the end, these four had lost all their horses, supplies, and equipment.

"After regaling our half famished friends with the best our small pittance of luxuries could afford," Stuart wrote, "we proceeded along the banks of the river for 3 miles, to a good fishing and grazing place, where we took up our lodging for the night."

Stuart's party proceeded to where Hunt had cached their surplus goods. Unfortunately, Indians had discovered six of their nine hiding places and emptied them. Three of the four trappers wanted to try again, so Stuart resupplied them from the remnants. They marched off to join an Astorian party sent to trap along the Boise River. In a tragic irony, Indians killed all those trappers a few months later.

Stuart continued east, essentially completing a reverse march along what later became the Oregon Trail through Idaho. However, north of Bear Lake they encountered a band of "insolent" Crow Indians. Stuart dealt with them, but changed his route to avoid any further trouble. Nonetheless, less than a week later the Crows found their camp and ran off all their horses.

Stuart's party walked out of Idaho with what they could carry after destroying the extra. They wintered in a crude camp on the North Platte River about twenty-five miles upstream from Scotts Bluff. They built canoes and resumed travel in early March. In mid-April they learned "The disagreeable news of a war between America & Great Britain."

Stuart and his men arrived in St. Louis at the end of April 1813.

The men at Astoria first learned of the war from a North West Company factor. Mackenzie saw a copy of the Declaration of War in mid-January, 1813. The factor also claimed a British warship would soon arrive to capture their post.

At first the Astorians decided to abandon the post. Had they chosen to move inland, the loss of Astoria might not have ended Astor's venture in the Northwest. One small warship lacked the manpower to search the wilderness. And they had time because the HMS *Racoon* did not arrive until months later. However, Duncan McDougall, the chief Pacific Fur Company partner at Astoria, had other plans. He arranged the sale of that facility to his former employer, the North West Company. Most analysts conclude that he sold out too easily and for a bargain-basement price.

Meanwhile, Robert Stuart had delivered his verbal report in June. Astor deemed it "satisfactory." However, news that his "partners" had sold him out began to filter east by around July 1814. He knew everything by early fall.

For years, he sought compensation from the Federal government for the loss of Astoria. Of course, he had lost far more than that facility. Besides the *Tonquin*, another supply vessel had shipwrecked off Maui. Ultimately, of the 135 to 144 men associated with the Columbia venture, sixty-five died: by drowning, other accidents, or Indian attack. The Pacific Fur Company was formally dissolved in November 1814.

Not quite two years later, Wilson Price Hunt returned to New York by sea and reported directly to Astor. He had protested the sell-out, to no avail. From there, Hunt returned to St. Louis to resume his mercantile business. He also bought land and considered publishing the journal of his overland journey to Astoria.

Hunt's account confirmed Astor's suspicions, but gave no consolation. Diplomacy did offer some cold comfort. In 1818, a new treaty opened the Pacific Northwest to entrepreneurs from both the U. S. and Great Britain. An odd provision declared that Astoria was officially American territory. Of course, the property there belonged to the North West Company. This quirk would later strengthen American territorial claims in the region.

Coincidentally, a different treaty decision played out that same year in the Great Lakes region. During the War, British forces captured Fort Mackinac, located on the vital strait that connects Lake Michigan and Lake Huron. The final peace accord returned the fort to the United States. On July 4, 1818, Robert Stuart, Resident Manager for Astor's American Fur Company, greeted a flotilla of boats at the dock near the Fort.

Unlike most of the other Scots-Canadians, Stuart stayed with Astor's firm. Astor soon rewarded him with the job at the re-established fur trading post on Mackinac Island. The little fleet brought supplies, trade goods, and more men. Stuart ran the post until Astor closed it in 1835.

For a decade after 1814, the North West Company faced no commercial rival in Idaho. Yet, due to other priorities, they did little with their Columbia Division for two years. Then, during the fall of 1816, Donald Mackenzie (now, like McDougall, working for them) led an expedition into Idaho. He returned the following summer with a sizable load of furs.

After unloading and re-equipping the "Snake Brigade" (their term for the large band of trappers and support personnel), Mackenzie marched into Idaho for the 1817-18 season. Their returns were "far beyond expectation." For the next season, the Brigade included around fifty-five men, 300 traps, and nearly 200 horses.

Impressed by the Boise Valley, Mackenzie built a small post there. Unfortunately, inter-tribal conflicts made the area very dangerous. The Indians eventually burned the fort. Aside from that, success followed success. The returns from the 1819-20 season reportedly doubled those of any previous year. The caravan of some seventy trappers, with 154 horses loaded down with pelts, stretched over two miles.

Meanwhile, in central Canada, the North West Company fought a brutal trade war with the Hudson's Bay Company. The HBC held a Royal monopoly in the Hudson's Bay watershed. They saw the NWC as an interloper in "their" rightful expansion territory. In 1821, the British government forced a merger on the two, during which the North West Company's identity was mostly submerged. As part of the shake-up, officials promoted Donald Mackenzie to a chief factor's position in Canada.

Without a strong leader, the Brigade had limited success in and around Idaho. Finally, in 1823, the Company called on Finan McDonald to take over. McDonald had well over a decade of western fur trade experience. For his first campaign, he led the column across Montana to Big Hole Prairie. There, they lost a man to hostile Blackfeet. The Brigade arrived along Idaho's Lemhi River sometime around mid-April. They encamped near a creek gurgling off the mountains where a ridge overlooked the site.

Dawn came late but swiftly here in the shadow of the Divide. A strong wind swirled the smoke from the fires the camp keepers were stoking. Many men still lay wrapped in their furs. Suddenly, a volley of shots sprayed the camp. An eyewitness said, "All hands in confusion sprang up and went out to see what was the matter; some with one shoe on and the other off, others naked, with a gun in one hand and their clothes in the other."

Finan led an immediate counterattack with about thirty men. However, the Indians, identified as Piegans, disappeared into the rough foothills.

McDonald carefully marshaled about forty-five men and issued extra "powder and ball." He assigned about twenty others to guard the camp. Company policy did not encourage proactive measures against the Indians, but such a large-scale assault required a response. The trappers overtook the attackers two ravines from their campsite. The Indians held a strong position, but Finan executed a flanking maneuver, and both sides opened fire.

"As soon as the firing commenced, the Indians began their frantic gestures, and whooped and yelled with a view of intimidating; they fought like deamons."

When about twenty Indians and three trappers had been killed, the Piegans appeared ready to surrender. However, a sudden trapper rush seemed to signal "no quarter," so the survivors fled "into a small coppice of wood."

The Brigade might have decided they'd inflicted enough punishment, but then they found the scalp of the man lost on Big Hole Prairie. Enraged, the trappers stepped up their gunfire. According to the witness, they expended "fifty-six pounds weight" of ball and buckshot. By now their ears rang from the clamor, and shoulders ached from the fierce recoil of fouled barrels.

Unsure how many Indians remained, the trappers were reluctant to dive into the brush for a hand-to-hand clash. The wind and the dryness of the terrain suggested a better idea: burn them out. Within minutes, flames swept through the Indian hiding place. Then, "volleys of buck-shot were again poured into the bush to aid the fire in the work of destruction."

Frantic defenders tried to burst through the blaze, but trapper gunfire felled most of them. Reportedly, "only seven out of the seventy-five which formed the party of unfortunate Piegans returned home to relate the mournful tale."

The trappers had lost a half-dozen men, not enough to seriously hamper their campaign. They garnered a respectable take for the year.

Actually, the Hudson's Bay Company no longer considered high profits their main priority for the Columbia Division. They believed that the Pacific Northwest would eventually become U. S. territory. Thus, a directive from top management stated, "it will be very desirable that the hunters should get as much out of the Snake country as possible for the next few years."

Aside from grabbing what they could, the Brigade might also "trap out" Idaho, making the area unprofitable. That would provide a buffer between American companies and the rich fur country of New Caledonia (essentially, today's British Columbia).

Although American trappers had not yet appeared west of the Rockies, they remained very active to the east. The Missouri Fur Company maintained posts on all the major rivers. Also, Astor's American Fur Company had created a specific Western Department in 1821. Smaller firms and independent operators added to this mix.

In 1823, Alexander Ross replaced MacDonald as Snake Brigade leader. Another Scot who had emigrated to Canada, Ross received his introduction to the fur trade with Astor's Pacific Fur Company. When the PFC went under, he worked for the Canadians and made the transition to the Hudson's Bay Company.

In the summer of 1824, Ross entered new country in the upper Boise River watershed. The terrain was murderous. Ross said, "We had to make our way over a frightful country. In winding among the rocks on the top of one of the mountains, one of our horses was killed, and a child belonging to one of the freemen was within a hair's breadth of sharing the same fate."

"Never did man or beast pass through a country more forbidding or hazardous. The rugged and rocky paths had worn our horses' hoofs to the quick, and we not infrequently stood undecided and hopeless of success," he also observed.

Ridge, Upper Boise River

That fall, they camped on the upper Salmon River. Then, a party of American trappers under Jedediah Smith arrived at his campsite. Smith had provided an armed escort for a band of HBC trappers who had been "robbed and left naked on the plains."

Annoyed, Ross observed, "With these vagabonds arrived twenty American trappers from the Big Horn River but whom I rather take to be spies than trappers."

Smith's band worked for the Rocky Mountain Fur Company, owned by Andrew Henry and General William H. Ashley. After the debacles at Three Forks and in Idaho, Andrew Henry had withdrawn from the fur trade. Then the War of 1812 drew him into the Missouri Territorial Militia. There, he met and became friends with Ashley.

Ashley was born around 1780 and raised near Richmond, Virginia. By 1808 he lived in Missouri, where he invested in mining ventures. Ashley rose to the rank of Lieutenant Colonel in the militia during the War of 1812. (He would become a Brigadier General in 1821.)

After the War, Ashley entered politics. Also, he and Henry seem to have shared some business activities over the next few years. Then, in 1821, a Paris journal published Wilson Price Hunt's account of his trek across the Rocky Mountains to Astoria. Hunt, of course, had long since made a place for himself in St. Louis business and political affairs.

It seems highly probable that Ashley and Henry consulted with Hunt about the fur trade, although the records are unclear on this point. The following year, Ashley published (March 20, 1822), a now-famous job announcement in the *Missouri Republican*: "To enterprising young men. The subscriber wishes to engage one hundred young men to ascend the Missouri river to its source, there to be employed for one, two, or three years."

Not long after that, they obtained licenses to enter Indian country – working through William Clark. They then led their first expedition up the Missouri. That attempt ended badly, thwarted by hostile Arikara Indian attacks. In 1823, Ashley sent Jed Smith to blaze an alternative route into the Rockies.

Thus, American trappers worked the west side of the Continental Divide in the spring of 1824. In June, they met to deliver their pelts to a company factor for transport to St. Louis. The company earned healthy profits from that first season in the west.

After delivering the pelts, Smith and another band stayed in the mountains. They worked their way into southeast Idaho, where they found the pillaged HBC trappers in September 1824.

The band under Jedediah Smith accompanied Ross and his trappers to their Montana base. There, Ross learned that Peter Skene Ogden had replaced him as Snake Brigade leader.

Quebec-born in 1790, Ogden entered the fur trade as a teenager. By 1814, he had charge of a North West Company post in northern Saskatchewan. During the war between the NWC and HBC, Peter earned a reputation for ruthless violence. When the two firms merged, Ogden found himself in serious trouble. However, his deep knowledge of the trade won him a reprieve. Ogden soon proved that his new employers had made a smart business move.

In December, Ogden and Smith marched together toward Idaho. The Brigade included seventy-one men and boys, eighty guns, and over 370 horses. It was, according to Ross, "the most formidable party that has ever set out for the Snakes."

Yet that mattered little. Not until the major fur trade era neared its end would the Canadians regain their monopoly, or near-monopoly, on the business.

The Canadian activities had proven to be a bonanza for the Nez Percés and Cayuse stockmen. Annually, the Company bought around 250 horses for food, and another hundred or so to replace worn out pack animals. Guns, ammunition, knives, blankets, and other goods proliferated among the tribes, even as beaver stocks declined.

In the new, highly competitive future, that boom would exact a dangerous price.

Pack Train in the Wilderness

Chapter Three: Competition Heats Up

The Snake Brigade, led by Peter Skene Ogden, and Jedediah Smith's party of Americans, plodded across Horse Prairie. Snow swirled around them and low clouds hid the peaks to their south and southwest. February brings heavy amounts of snow to these mountains, so they camped until the flurries blew out. Finally, after three days, they tramped through the drifts across Lemhi Pass and dropped into the valley beyond.

"Now that we are among Buffaloe and grass for our poor horses, it is found necessary to remain about this quarter for some time," Ogden's chief clerk, William Kittson, wrote.

In fact, they stayed near the Salmon River for over a month. Then the Americans headed southeast across the plains toward the Snake. Ogden's much larger Brigade trailed behind. Actually, the Canadians would have preferred to "lose" the American to keep them ignorant of the best trapping grounds. However, while Ogden was experienced and clever, he had little luck in avoiding the Americans. The two bands stayed fairly close all the way into southeast Idaho.

Finally, on the Bear River, the Canadians thought they had achieved some distance. However, they could not totally shake the Americans. As Hudson's Bay Company management had feared, the much higher prices offered by the St. Louis traders induced many Canadian trappers to jump ship. Around a third from the 1825 contingent deserted. They took with them detailed knowledge of the beaver country west of the Divide.

The Big Picture. In 1825, the U.S. comprised twenty-four states, Missouri having been admitted four years earlier. John Quincy Adams was President, and the nation's population topped 11 million (more than double what it had been at the turn of the century). That year, the Erie Canal opened for traffic. Partly because of the Canal, the population living beyond the East-coast band of states increased by more than 4 million over the next fifteen years.

While Ogden struggled to retain his men, the Rocky Mountain Fur Company sought to strengthen its grip on the American side of the business. However, despite their improved returns in 1824, Andrew Henry went west only briefly before leaving the mountains completely.

After that season, the RMFC devised a new strategy. Only supplies and furs would travel to and from the mountains, not the entire trapping crew. Thus, as spring turned into summer, William Ashley marched west from St. Louis with a pack train of supplies. His journal entries show it was not an easy trip. He wrote, "This country is almost destitute of grass."

Nearing its destination, the pack train crossed South Pass. Ashley said, "Having found yesterday some grass we moved our camp to day about one mile – where we remained the day for the benefit of our horses."

Ashley brought his loads to what became a defining feature of the Mountain Man era in the Rocky Mountains: the annual rendezvous. At the rendezvous, companies traded guns, ammunition, tools, and other goods for furs accrued by the trappers. The 1825 exchange took place on a tributary of the Green River near present-day McKinnon, Wyoming. Rocky Mountain Fur Company profits from that season were substantial, further rousing competing firms.

One of the sad ironies of the fur trade era involved those company profits. While men like Ashley made fortunes, individual trappers generally did well to break even, despite all their punishing and dangerous labor.

The threat of Indian attacks or serious accidents dictated that trappers travel in larger groups. For the Americans, these might contain twenty or thirty men, plus camp keepers. (The romanticized lone Mountain Man on horseback, trailing a packhorse, came after large parties were no longer profitable.)

After locating an area with beaver sign, they established a central camp. Late in the afternoon, sets of two or three men rode out along tributaries and side streams. Each had a pack animal loaded with traps. Experience, or instinct, guided them to prime beaver habitat. At intervals, each Mountain Man selected an area where he could set his six to ten traps.

The trapper generally searched for a spot close to the bank, in relatively shallow water but with a deeper stretch nearby. Standing in the chill snowmelt, he scraped out a base in the stream bed for the five-pound trap. Then he stretched an attached five-foot chain deeper into the watercourse. This required great care. Numbness in his feet, legs, and hands dogged every motion.

Moving into the deeper current, the trapper inserted a pole through the ring on the end of the chain, then anchored the pole securely in the bottom. He then returned to the bank. After smearing pungent beaver musk – bait – on an overhanging branch, he set the trap. That required prying open the spring-loaded jaws and securing one side with a tab connected to a flat plate in the center.

Trying to sniff the musk, the animal would set off the trap. Its instinctive response to danger was to seek deeper water, where the chain held it to drown.

Satisfied, the trapper slogged to a point where man-smell wouldn't spook his prey and climbed ashore. He returned to the base camp when all his traps were set.

There, trappers would huddle around the fires, hoping their clothes would dry before they had to sleep. Traps were checked in the morning. The trapper quickly removed the pelt, musk gland, and tail. If the camp was low on provisions, he might carve out additional cuts of meat.

They carried the fresh hides back to camp. There, support personnel – trappers' Indian wives (and children) and the less-experienced men or boys – scraped and stretched them. Dried pelts would be folded fur-to-fur and bundled into packs of sixty to eighty count.

Trappers considered beaver tail a delicacy, broiled over a campfire. Living on a diet of lean game meat, Mountain Men knew the value of such a high-energy food source.

Trapping continued through the prime beaver seasons: spring and fall. During the winter, beavers huddle in their lodges, eating food stocked in better weather. In spring, the animals still had their luxurious winter coats. Naturally, the beaver's heavy fur thins out during the summer … the best time for the rendezvous. Ashley again supplied the 1826 gathering in the Cache Valley of Utah.

Emboldened by his profits, Ashley reduced his active participation in the trade. He remained a highly respected authority on the fur business, however. Ambitious businessmen and government officials regularly sought his advice.

Ashley sold the business to the team of Jedediah Smith, David Jackson, and William Sublette. (Records tend to confuse the company designation. Some accounts refer to the firm of Smith, Jackson and Sublette. Historian Hiram Chittenden, and others, used the Rocky Mountain Fur Company name.)

Talks with HBC trappers gave the partners some idea of the fur trade potential of the "Oregon Country." That name basically included our Pacific Northwest with much of today's British Columbia thrown in. They first needed to deploy trappers there to go head-to-head with the Canadians.

However, they knew little about what lay to the south of Oregon Country, between the Rockies and California. For all anyone could tell, the region might contain a vast, untapped fur bonanza, free for the taking.

Thus, in August 1826 Smith's band of trappers pointed southwest from the Great Salt Lake. They barely survived the trek across the arid lands into southern California. Smith's return to the 1827 rendezvous pleased his partners personally, but the trip did nothing for their "bottom line." At a higher level, Smith's journey provided Americans with their first knowledge of previously unknown terrain. On July 17, 1827, Jed sent a long letter report to "Genl. Wm. Clark, Supt. of Indian Affairs."

President James Madison had appointed Clark Governor of Missouri Territory in 1813. He retained that position until Missouri became a state in 1821. Clark campaigned to be the first state governor, but lost. President Monroe made him Superintendent of Indian Affairs in 1822. Clark had Smith's letter printed in the *Missouri Republican.*

Naturally, other ambitious Americans did not concede the rich western profits to the RMFC or to the Canadians. For example, the Western Department of Astor's American Fur Company steadily extended its operations. The Missouri Fur Company even competed for furs at the 1828 rendezvous.

The HBC Snake Brigade trapped all across Idaho south of the Salmon. During this time, Ogden recorded a crucial fact about the fur business. He wrote, "No trapper can do justice to his traps unless he has 4 good horses. My party average this; but the horses [are] too young to endure privations."

Despite American competition, the Brigade did well. Still, the strain had begun to wear on Ogden. His journal entry for New Year's Day, 1829 provides evidence of Ogden's state of mind. Out of all the earliest Snake Bri-

Snake Brigade Leader Peter Skene Ogden

gade members, he wrote, "There remains now only one man."

He was further dismayed to realize that, "All have been killed – with the exception of two who died a natural death – and are scattered over the Snake Country."

The Brigade next trapped the Portneuf River drainage, crossed over to Bear River, and then into Utah. Moving on to the Humboldt River in Nevada, Ogden noted, "The Indians are not numerous in this quarter, but from the number of fires seen on the mountains are fully aware of our presence, and we must look out for our horses."

They crossed back onto the Owyhee River, and then marched over Oregon's Blue Mountains. Nearer to the HBC base, Ogden said, "Thus ends my 5th trip to the Snake Country. We have no cause to complain of our returns."

John Work, "a worthy successor," replaced Ogden the following year. The HBC moved Ogden to a coastal trading post located about seventy miles southeast of today's Ketchikan, Alaska. The Company would reassign him to their Columbia Division many years later.

For his first campaign, John Work's column comprised nearly forty men "able to bear arms," seven male camp workers, plus numerous women and their children. Their column included more than 270 horses. Work said, "The horses are pretty well loaded with provisions, as the journey lies through a country where animals are scarce."

Work still had to contend with severe competition. In November, trapping on the Little Wood River, he wrote, "Americans are encamped within a short distance of us. ... A Mr. Fontenelle, who manages this business, is now at Snake River with 50 men. They have great quantity of goods en cache. They have been hunting on the Upper Snake."

Lucien Fontenelle, highly experienced in the trade, represented the American Fur Company, but other firms also had men in the area.

Work spent the winter on the lower reach of the Portneuf. There, they "found good feeding for horses, and a great many Snakes are encamped around."

However, their troubles continued when trapping resumed in the spring. By the time they returned to base, they had lost nearly a third of their horses – thirty to theft alone. Work attributed this to "a great degree of negligence on the part of the men."

In 1831, two Americans initiated operations that would have significant impacts on the West in general, and Idaho in particular.

First, in August, Captain Benjamin L. E. Bonneville requested and received a leave of absence from the U. S. Army. He planned to set up a fur trade/trapping business. As a bonus, Bonneville could study the "joint occupancy" lands of the Oregon Country. His venture would cost the government nothing.

Bonneville, born in France to bourgeoisie parents, came to the U. S. in 1803, when he was just seven years old. He graduated from the U.S. Military Academy at West Point in 1919. For over a decade, he served at duty stations ranging from the northeast to posts along the Mississippi River. The lands to the west, and the fur trade, intrigued him.

After rounding up backers, Captain Bonneville marched west in May of 1832 with 110 men. Unlike previous leaders, Bonneville had loaded most of his supplies on wagons. The expedition became the first to push wagons across the Continental Divide, at South Pass. Near the Green River, his party met an American Fur Company pack train, led by Fontenelle. The well-known AFC leader had little trouble luring some of Bonneville's most experienced trappers away.

Beyond Green River, the terrain was far too rough for wagons. This forced Bonneville to cache the supplies he could not carry by pack train. The column of horses and mules traversed southeast Idaho and took up a winter camp in the Salmon-Lemhi area.

At the next Green River rendezvous, in July 1833, Bonneville's band returned just twenty-three bundles of pelts. His poor showing makes an interesting contrast with the success of a man who was on his way to becoming a Mountain Man legend: Joseph L. "Joe" Meek. Born in extreme western Virginia in 1810, Joe had signed on with the Rocky Mountain Fur Company in late 1828. His trapping career began in Idaho along the Teton River and Henry's Fork.

Joe attended his first rendezvous the following summer. By the time he arrived at the 1833 gathering, Joe had "graduated" to the status of free trapper. He now gambled on his skill and savvy to earn a better return trapping for himself. He then sold his furs to one of the companies.

The Captain had to deal with the fact that his first year in the fur trade had been a failure. A local American Fur Company manager summed it well in a letter (September 25, 1833) to Astor, "Bonneville, out of all his grand expedition, will have only enough to pay the wages of his men."

Despite that inauspicious start, Bonneville stayed in the intermountain west for two more years. In eastern Idaho, they explored from Henry's Fork all the way south to Bear Lake. Across southern Idaho, he and his men observed many important tributaries of the Snake: the Portneuf, Raft, Bruneau, Malad, Boise, Payette, and numerous smaller creeks.

They also noted American and Salmon Falls. (There is no indication they saw Shoshone Falls). The 1837 publication of Washington Irving's account, *The Adventures of Captain Bonneville,* extolled Bonneville's exploits as a western explorer.

A fine leader, Bonneville had no skill whatsoever as a trader/trapper. His second year in the mountains was a disaster. Returns for the third year were better, but Bonneville and his backers had finally had enough. He returned to Missouri in August 1835.

In an odd coincidence, a second latecomer to the fur trade also decided to cut his losses in late 1835. Like Bonneville, Nathaniel J. Wyeth had decided in 1831 to pursue a venture in the West. The largely uninformed, but eloquent, pamphleteering of Hall J. Kelley inspired Wyeth's ambition. Kelley fervently advocated the American settlement of Oregon.

Born in Cambridge, Massachusetts in 1802, Wyeth briefly managed a lakefront resort. He then took a job in the ice industry, where he made a name for himself. Still, prospects in the West drew him. Some time in 1831 or early 1832, he formed a company to pursue western fur trading and trapping. Sadly, time would show that he had based his plans on limited and hopelessly inaccurate information.

Nathaniel's cousin, John B. Wyeth, eagerly joined the venture. Later, he wrote a scathing account of his experiences. In St. Louis, the flaws in Captain Wyeth's plan became glaringly apparent. But Wyeth finally had his party ready and they proceeded west.

Fortunately, the band of eighteen men attached itself to the column of the experienced trader William Sublette. With the addition of a third group, the column comprised about eighty men and three hundred horses. Such a strong force had no reason to fear hostile Indian attacks. However, they still had to stay alert against horse thieves. In July 1832, the column arrived at the rendezvous site.

"This agreeable valley is called by the trappers Pierre's Hole," John Wyeth wrote in one of his more positive recollections.

Pierre's Hole was the only Idaho location where the fur companies held a full rendezvous. (They *had* staged a limited one there in 1827.) These gatherings attracted huge bands of Indians. Of course, the companies were there to collect furs from their contracted men, pay them, and equip them for another season.

They would also bargain with the Indians and with free trappers. Even as this business proceeded, the trappers pursued what was arguably their main goal ... to have a good time. Good times meant booze, which Chittenden said "flowed like water."

Washington Irving, more of a romantic storyteller, wrote that the trappers "engaged in contests of skill at running, jumping, wrestling, shooting with the rifle, and running horses. ... They drank together, they sang, they laughed, they whooped ... "

Irving freely described all that boyish fun. He passed over the rampant go-for-broke gambling and chasing after Indian women. The gambling, games, and drunken debauchery continued until the trappers were broke, or heavily in debt.

From all accounts, Captain Wyeth's green New Englanders took no part in these "festivities." In his account, John Wyeth claimed that grumbling had started early among the men. A few recognized Wyeth's misinformed preparations. On the trip west, exhaustion from the grueling travel set in. And the danger was more acute than they'd ever imagined. All this they blamed on what they viewed as Wyeth's poor leadership. After an angry confrontation, seven of the eighteen men abandoned his venture.

The younger Wyeth wrote that, to prepare for his foray deeper into Idaho with the remaining men, Captain Wyeth "purchased twenty-five horses from the Indians, who had a great number, and those very fine, and high-spirited. Indeed the Western region seems the native and congenial country for horses."

On July 18th, Captain Wyeth was preparing to march west from Pierre's Hole when the trappers espied a body of Indians approaching. The Gros Ventre Indians, which these were, were allies of the notoriously hostile Blackfeet tribe. Although they shared neither lineage nor language with the Blackfeet, Americans almost invariably lumped the two together.

Entire family groups on the move wanted no trouble, so a chief rode out to parley under signs of peace. Unfortunately, the two who advanced to meet him had grievances. One was a half-Indian member of the Flathead tribe, which had suffered heavily from Blackfeet raids. The other, Antoine Godin, harbored a deep-seated hatred for the death of his Iroquois father at the hands of the Blackfeet.

In the event, while Antoine shook hands with the Gros Ventre, the Flathead shot him dead. They then grabbed the chief's bright red blanket and raced triumphantly back to the trappers' camp.

The Gros Ventre saw before them only a group of around forty men. Nathaniel Wyeth wrote, "The Indians were disposed to give us their usual treatment when they meet us in small bodies."

The location was probably about three miles south of today's Driggs. There, the families hastily built a crude palisades of deadfall timbers. Before the Gros Ventre could organize an attack, reinforcements in the form of more trappers and their Indian allies (Nez Percés and Flatheads) arrived.

"A general fire was immediately opened upon the fort, and was warmly kept up on both sides until dark," Warren A. Ferris wrote. He was one of several Mountain Men who gave accounts of the Battle.

At least once before nightfall, the allies tried to rush the enemy redoubt. They retreated after Gros Ventre gunfire killed one man and wounded several others, including William Sublette. Joe Meek and another man carried Sublette off the battlefield.

Finally, the trappers and their allies returned to their campsites. This allowed the Gros Ventres to flee during the night. Four whites were killed during the battle, along with seven of their allies. They found nine slain warriors inside the fort. The Gros Ventre had also left behind most of their belongings and a couple dozen dead horses. Irving wrote that, "The Blackfeet afterward reported that they had lost twenty-six warriors in this battle."

Afterwards, Captain Wyeth's party headed west. For a while they traveled with Milton G. Sublette, another associate in the Rocky Mountain Fur Company. The joint expedition rode south toward the Portneuf, then west across southern Idaho. When they split up at the end of August, Wyeth's group returned to the Snake River, probably near the mouth of the Owyhee. From there, they continued to Fort Vancouver.

With too few horses, they had to cache the furs they collected, so the venture had nothing to show for its efforts. Then the ship contracted to meet them with supplies foundered in the South Pacific. Finally, Wyeth dissolved the compact among the remaining participants.

Yet, still hopeful, during his overland trip east to St. Louis in 1833 he concluded a deal with Milton Sublette. Wyeth would supply trade gear for the 1834 rendezvous. Back in New England, Wyeth and his backers formed the Columbia River Fishing and Trading Company. This time around, Wyeth knew enough to recruit westerners for his expedition.

He did, however, agree to escort a party of Methodist missionaries from New England across the continent to Oregon. He also allowed two naturalists to join them. Botanist Thomas Nuttall was an experienced western traveler, having explored the plains there twice. The much younger Philadelphia physician John Kirk Townsend knew nothing of the Far West. The column left Independence, Missouri near the end of April. Townsend noted that their caravan included "seventy men, and two hundred and fifty horses."

The Captain had clearly paid attention, and learned his lessons well. The pack train advanced in double file while, Townsend observed, "The band of missionaries, with their horned cattle, rode along the flanks."

Entrepreneur Nathaniel J. Wyeth

About a week later, Milton Sublette, the RMFC associate who had spearheaded Wyeth's contract, grew almost too sick to stay in the saddle. He finally turned back. The deal supposedly obligated the Company itself, but Wyeth must have had his doubts.

As they neared the rendezvous location, Wyeth sent letters ahead reminding the principals of their deal and announcing his impending arrival. It didn't help. The RMFC representatives refused to accept the goods, paying a minimal "penalty" instead.

Wyeth spent no time bemoaning this betrayal. On July 1, 1834, he penned a letter to his backers explaining what he proposed to do: "I shall proceed about 150 miles west of this and establish a fort in order to make sale of the goods which remain on my hands."

Wyeth marched into Idaho and down the Bear River valley. In addition to Wyeth's journal, Osborne Russell, a twenty-year-old employee of his from Maine, kept a detailed record. Before signing on with Wyeth, he had spent a couple years with a midwestern fur company.

Around the 8th, they camped near Soda Springs. Russell remarked, "This place which now looks so lonely, visited only by the rambling Trapper or solitary Savage will doubtless at no distant day be a resort for thousands of the gay and fashionable world, as well as Invalids and spectators."

The column turned north from Soda Springs. On July 15, they located a suitable site for a trading post. Wyeth called it Fort Hall, after one of his backers.

The area particularly impressed John Townsend. He said, "This is a fine large plain on the south side of the Portneuf, with an abundance of excellent grass and rich soil. The opposite side of the river is thickly covered with large timber of the cottonwood and willow, with a dense undergrowth of the same, intermixed with service-berry and currant bushes."

Russell was among those tasked to build Wyeth's fort. "On the 18th we commenced the Fort, which was a stockade 80 ft square built of cotton wood trees, set on end sunk 2 1/2 feet in the ground and standing about 15 feet above, with two bastions 8 ft square at the opposite angles."

At the end of the month, the missionaries went ahead with Thomas McKay, a Hudson's Bay Company leader. Wyeth's party had met McKay's band during the rest stop near Soda Springs. With the Fort ready for operation, Wyeth also continued on to Oregon.

He left behind a dozen men, including Osborne Russell. Russell noted, "I now began to experience the difficulties attending a mountaineer, we being all raw hands. ... Altho the country abounded with game, still it wanted experience to kill it."

Besides the men and the usual horses and mules, Wyeth left behind three cows. These were the first cattle to be set grazing in Idaho. Fort Hall was the third white settlement in the state and far more successful than its predecessors. However, Wyeth was not the beneficiary of that success.

Meanwhile, although smaller groups of HBC trappers hunted in Idaho, the Snake Brigade no longer did. A large force simply couldn't turn a profit on the sparse catch that remained. Nonetheless, they had no intention of conceding even those meager returns to the Americans. To counter Wyeth's post, McKay built Fort Boise on the Snake near the mouth of the Boise River.

In July 1835, new travails hit Wyeth's enterprise. First, a canoe loaded with dried salmon had capsized, and eight of the ten occupants perished. Then one of his best trappers and a companion had been murdered and a valuable load of beaver pelts stolen. On top of that, illness almost killed Wyeth during the summer.

The situation in and around Idaho offered more discouragement. The manager at Fort Hall had recruited additional men, but they had little success in southeast Idaho and southwest Wyoming. After the 1835 rendezvous, a band trapped further north, including parts of western Wyoming and south-central Montana. Disgusted by inept leadership, a half dozen men abandoned the column.

Moreover, successive attack by hostile Indians wounded several men and left them dangerously short of horses. Only aid from an experienced band under Jim Bridger kept their plight from being even worse.

They returned to northeast Idaho in late September. Although Russell was by no means the most experienced in the Wyeth party, their leader tasked him to ride ahead to the Fort and return with more horses. Poor directions soon had Russell wandering in the plains well west of Henry's Fork. Then fortune turned his way.

"Buffaloe were carelessly feeding all over the plain as far as the eye could reach," he wrote in his journal. "I watched the motions of the dust for a few minutes when I saw a body of men on horse back pouring out of the defile among the Buffaloe." The Indians killed huge numbers of buffalo. Russell estimated "upwards of a thousand ... without burning one single grain of gunpowder."

With better directions, Russell finally arrived at Fort Hall. His contract had expired, so when Wyeth got there on December 20th, the trapper "bid adieu to the 'Columbia River Fishing and Trading Company' and started in company with 15 of my old mess-mates to pass the winter ... on Port Neuf, about 40 Mls. SE from Fort Hall."

Russell would stay into the next decade as a free trapper.

Wyeth spent the winter at the Fort. Ever hopeful, he devised yet another scheme and sent a letter to the HBC Chief Factor, John McLoughlin. He proposed to restrict his fur business to areas not generally frequented by HBC parties. Also, if they would meet his supply needs, he would sell his pelts only to them. Although McLoughlin personally liked and admired Wyeth, he refused.

In 1837, the HBC bought Fort Hall for a very nominal fee. The following year they assigned an experienced manager to run the post. They also enlarged and rebuilt the structure using adobe brick. After that, the British-Canadians again had a virtual monopoly on the Idaho fur trade.

Ironically, more or less parallel with the failed attempts of Bonneville and Wyeth, the fur trade had itself begun a slow decline. In 1833, the far-sighted John Jacob Astor envisioned the day. He said, "I very much fear beaver will not sell very soon, unless very fine."

He then began negotiations to sell off his western fur trade interests. In this, he was partially guided by his ongoing correspondence with Wilson Price Hunt. In addition to his own Missouri ventures, the former Astorian often acted for Astor on matters other than the fur trade.

Astor completed the sale of all his western American Fur Company holdings in June 1834. He would close out the last of his fur holdings the following year. By the end of the decade, even ordinary trappers realized that the large-scale fur trade was about over. Silk hats had become the fashion, and beaver prices plummeted.

However, Wyeth's assistance to the Methodist missionaries in 1834 foreshadowed the next stage in Pacific Northwest development. The rendezvous of 1836 reinforced that change. The fact that more missionaries came excited little comment. However, these two Presbyterian churchmen – Marcus Whitman and Henry Harmon Spalding – brought their wives.

Narcissa Whitman rather "set the standard" for pioneer women on the soon-to-be Oregon Trail. Born Narcissa Prentiss in western New York State in 1808, she grew up in an atmosphere of religious fervor. By the time she completed school and began to teach, she longed to perform missionary work. Her marriage to Marcus Whitman in 1836 made that possible. Marcus had already served a year-long mission in northern Idaho and Montana.

Henry Spalding was also born in western New York, around 1803, a year after Marcus. After preparation at an academy in New York, he attended college and a seminary before being ordained as a minister in 1835. Assigned to establish a mission in northern Idaho, Spalding persuaded Whitman to join his party.

Narcissa sent a stream of letters home and also kept a journal. Marcus had tried to take a wagon over the Trail. By the time they reached the Hagerman area, only a cart made from a pair of wheels remained.

Concerning the Three Island Crossing, Narcissa wrote, "Husband had considerable difficulty in crossing the cart. Both cart and mules were turned upside down in the river and entangled in the harness. The mules would have been drowned but for a desperate struggle to get them ashore."

They finally dumped even the cart after Fort Boise. The party spent some time at Fort Vancouver and then split. The Whitmans built a mission five or six miles from today's Walla Walla, Washington. Their venture would end tragically a decade later.

Spalding and his wife settled at Lapwai, on the Clearwater River. Two years later, the Lapwai mission herd included a dozen cattle. Spalding also introduced irrigated farming near the mission. Among other crops, he grew the first potatoes in the future state. Henry even obtained a printing press and published materials in the Nez Percés language, including the Bible.

Missionaries continued to trek across Idaho to Oregon. In 1838, three missionary couples crossed. They left their small herd of nine cattle at Fort Hall. The Company guaranteed replacements in the lower Columbia valley. Not all of the missionaries' cattle ended up in Idaho, but by 1840 the Panhandle stations boasted over thirty head.

Thus, as the major fur trade era closed, the missions and southern Forts laid the foundation for stock raising in Idaho. That enterprise would eventually surpass the horse herds of the indigenous peoples.

Trading pelts for guns, ammunitions, blankets, trinkets, and other goods brought relative prosperity, in their terms, to some. They sold thousands of horses to the whites, for food, and to replace animals lost to crippling injuries, illness, or theft.

But those gains came at some cost. The tribes escaped the wholesale slaughter from the white man's diseases, but individuals and whole families did succumb. Moreover, the white onslaught devastated the stocks of normal food animals they hunted.

In 1841, Osborne Russell was eking out his livelihood along the Portneuf, Blackfoot, and Bear river watersheds. Russell wrote, "In the year 1836, large bands of buffalo could be seen in almost every little valley on the small branches of this stream. At this time, the only traces which could be seen of them were the scattered bones of those that had been killed."

Russell's next sentence is especially poignant with regard to the Indians' plight: "The trappers often remarked to each other as they rode over these lonely plains that it was time for the white man to leave the mountains, as the beaver and game had nearly disappeared."

CHAPTER FOUR: WAGONS ACROSS IDAHO

The line of trapper horses ambled across the grassy plain toward Fort Hall. Unfortunately, the pack string contained few pelts. As Joe Meek said, "beaver were scarce" in the streams of southeast Idaho and southwestern Wyoming.

At least they weren't empty handed. Osborne Russell said they had "killed a fat Grizzly Bear and some antelope. Loaded the meat on our horses and started to the Fort."

Russell respectfully referred to his senior compatriot as "Major Meek." Only thirty years old in September 1840, Meek had trekked the Rockies nearly twice as long as Russell. (Russell was twenty-six.) The small party trailed into the Fort. Russell had been based here since late 1838, the last year he attended a rendezvous. The HBC had, of course, replaced the original cottonwood enclosure with a similar but somewhat larger adobe structure.

Waiting there, they found Mountain Man Robert "Doc" Newell. Meek and Newell had originally come west together. Unlike Meek, Newell had attended the 1840 Green River rendezvous, the last authentic Mountain Man gathering. Newell said, "But times was certainly hard. No beaver and everything dull."

Three missionary couples attended the conclave. The group also included a party of eight settlers, and the Joel Walker family, with five children. (Walker was the brother of Joseph R. Walker, a subleader on Bonneville's 1832-35 expeditions.) Since Newell had already planned to march to Fort Hall, he signed on to guide the emigrants that far.

Meek interviewer/biographer Frances Fuller Victor wrote that Newell said to Meek, "Come, we are done with this life in the mountains – done with wading in beaver-dams, and freezing or starving alternately – done with Indian trading and Indian fighting."

According to Victor, Newell went on, "The talk is that the country is going to be settled up by our people, and that the Hudson's Bay Company are not going to rule this country much longer. ... Shall we turn American settler?"

Newell's journal contains no such high-flown rhetoric. He doesn't even mention that Meek agreed. Newell writes simply that, "On the 27th of September 1840 with two waggons and my family I left Fort Hall for the Columbia."

William Craig, another old-time Mountain Man, brought his family along too. The missionaries and settlers traveled to Oregon separately. Joe Meek claimed land 10-15 miles west of Portland. Irrepressible, he soon became involved in Oregon politics. He helped form the first Provisional Government of Oregon and became first sheriff and then legislator.

Three notable events had occurred in the span of a few months.

First, although Newell admitted having "some difficulty," he had shown that wagons could be pushed through Idaho and on over the Blue Mountains. Second, and equally telling, three diehard trappers moved to Oregon. Their stories virtually defined what it meant to be a Mountain Man, yet they left the mountains.

Finally, a white family with children traveled overland to Oregon for the first time. Previous to this, family groups had only arrived by sea.

The next year, the first ripple of the coming tidal wave entered Idaho. John Bidwell had tried to homestead in Missouri, but that didn't work out. Reluctantly, he went back to teaching school. Then he ran into a Frenchman who had actually been to California. Bidwell later wrote, "His description of California was in the superlative degree favorable, so much so that I resolved if possible to see that wonderful land."

After considerable effort, Bidwell and a party of about sixty people gathered near Westport, Missouri. Although Bidwell had been the driving force, John Bartleson campaigned for, and got, the title of "Captain." Bidwell wrote, "Our ignorance of the route was complete. We knew that California lay west, and that was the extent of our knowledge."

Fortunately, they attached themselves to a Roman Catholic missionary party led by Father Pierre Jean de Smet. Old time Mountain Man Thomas Fitzpatrick guided them. The Bidwell-Bartleson Party remained intact as far as Soda Springs, where de Smet and Fitzpatrick planned to turn north.

Father Pierre Jean de Smet

Fitzpatrick had little direct knowledge of how the Missourians might reach California with their wagons. About half the party decided they'd rather follow the better-known route to the Columbia. That block of thirty-two people was the first large band of non-trappers to cross the Oregon Trail.

The Bidwell faction sent four men to Fort Hall. They hoped Richard Grant, the HBC manager, could advise them on a route. The rest immediately marched south along the Bear River. Amazingly, they all made it to California.

Sources vary somewhat, but it's known that 125-140 emigrants crossed Idaho in 1842. Although they brought wagons,

Grant talked them into continuing with a pack train. No matter the psychological impact, Newell's passage with two lightly loaded wagons hardly proved the route. However, records suggest that wagons did traverse the Idaho portion of the California Trail. That route led southwest toward the Humboldt River in Nevada.

Osborne Russell had hung on in Idaho after Newell and the others left. He was there in late August when, he wrote, "There arrived at the Fort a party of Emigrants from the States on their way to Oregon Territory among whom was Dr. E. White, U. S. sub agent for the Oregon Indians."

Russell too had tired of the meager returns from the hard and dangerous life of a trapper. He hitched up with the wagon train "and arrived at the Falls of the Willamette River on the 26 day of Septr. 1842."

The Hudson's Bay Company consistently underestimated the "draw" of the Pacific Northwest lands for ordinary citizens in the eastern United States. There is no sign that Richard Grant saw the wavelet of 1842 as much to concern him.

By this time, his strategy of trading company vouchers for missionary stock had allowed him to build a respectable herd. Beyond that, his modest farming efforts supplemented the staples shipped in from Vancouver. (The Fort had not yet achieved self-sufficiency in foodstuffs.) Even so, Grant expected better overall profits from emigrants than from the fur trade.

In 1843, an actual wave hit. Over nine hundred emigrants passed through Idaho. Neither Fort Hall nor Fort Boise could handle such a flood, no matter what prices they charged. In mid-August, explorer John C. Fremont sent his guide, Kit Carson, for supplies. Carson said, "Fremont set out to explore Great Salt Lake, while I went on to Fort Hall for a fresh supply of provisions."

Fremont called the results "a scanty but very acceptable supply," and noted that the needs of the emigrants had strained the Fort's resources.

Traffic increased rapidly, reaching over twenty-five hundred travelers in 1845. The influx doubled the number of Americans in Oregon. Mountain Man Stephen Meek, Joe's brother, played a role in that crossing. In March, he obtained letters of recommendations from William Sublette and other prominent traders in St. Louis. These, he wrote "secured me the position as guide to the immense emigrant train of 480 wagons then preparing to go to Oregon."

Travelers typically began their overland journey from Missouri in the spring. They slowly mounted the rising plains to the Rockies while the landscape seemed lush and verdant. Most didn't reach Idaho until the blistering height of summer. By July and August, forage grasses had wilted under the heat and dryness. Dust choked the trails. No one even thought of settling in such a place.

Mrs. Elizabeth Dixon Smith crossed the Trail in the late Forties. The day after they passed Fort Hall, she wrote in her diary, "August 29. ... You in 'the States' know nothing of dust. It will fly so that you can hardly see the horns of your oxen. It often seems that the cattle must die for want of breath ... "

The heat and dust distressed the emigrants, but they were deadly for the stock. Diaries are replete with tales of draft oxen collapsing under the strain.

"We see a great many abandoned, lame and worn out cattle and the air is literally filled with stench from dead oxen," another diarist said of one difficult ridge crossing.

Fortunately, relatively few parties tried to drive large herds of stock over the Trail in the Forties. Those who did met a lot of resistance from travelers with no animals or only a small band. Most emigrants felt that a drive with many cattle posed a much greater risk of a stampede. They also claimed that the cattle milled about and slowed the column.

Clearly, a big drive churned up more dust, which was already a problem. All those loose cattle also reduced the forage available for the draft animals and riding stock.

Some drovers answered by keeping their drive well away from emigrant wagons trains. Thus, in 1843, a group brought "several thousand loose horses and cattle" along the Trail. Their detached "cow column" maintained a steady pace a half-day or so behind the wagon train.

The leader of the column, Captain Jesse Applegate, later wrote a celebrated account of "A Day with the Cow Column of 1843." Describing the morning start, he wrote, "By five o'clock the herders begin to contract the great moving circle, and the well-trained animals move slowly towards camp, clipping here and there a thistle or tempting bunch of grass on the way."

With so many animals passing through, the herds at the two HBC forts grew as pioneers traded failing stock for goods, or a lesser number of fresh animals. The quality of the herds also improved as stockmen culled out "Spanish" cattle in favor of midwestern animals. Those breeds produced more and better beef, milk, cheese, and butter.

Fort Hall, of course, lay three to six weeks further than Fort Boise from the Pacific supply depots. Thus, Richard Grant made a concerted effort to augment his herd and grow local crops. At least he had promising country to support his efforts.

Rufus Sage, a journalist in search of book material, visited the region in November 1842. He wrote, "The country in the neighborhood of Fort Hall affords several extensive valleys upon the Snake river and its tributaries, which are rich, well timbered, and admirably adapted to the growth of grain and vegetables. The adjoining prairies also, to some extent, possess a tolerable soil, and abound in a choice variety of grasses."

A year later, Captain John C. Fremont camped along the Bear River. He wrote in his journal, "The mountains here are covered with a valuable nutritious grass, called bunch grass, from the form in which it grows, which has a second growth in the fall."

By the mid-1840s, Idaho had a nascent cattle industry. Besides the forts in the south, herds at the Protestant and Roman Catholic missions in the Panhandle had also grown. The Nez Percés were also building up stocks by trading along the Trail.

Historian Francis Haines said the Nez Percés "considered ways of diverting the tide of travel, with its accompanying profits, to their own country. They wanted the trains to … follow the old war trail up the Weiser River to the head of the Little Salmon and on down to the Clearwater instead of crossing the Snake River for the steep climb up the Blue Mountains."

Pioneer Joel Palmer, later an Oregon legislator, found the Nez Percés near the Spalding mission eager to deal. He wrote, "The neighboring Indians soon drove in some horses to trade, and before night we had disposed of all but four head of our cattle, one yoke of oxen, one yearling heifer, and a yearling calf."

He also said, "They have made considerable advances in cultivating the soil, and have large droves of horses, and many of them are raising large herds of cattle."

Various records suggest that several hundred head of cattle ranged northern Idaho in the late 1840s. The Lapwai Mission itself owned 92 cattle and 39 horses at the end of 1847. That's when Spalding inventoried the property, after the Whitman Massacre.

Historians have written volumes about the murders of Marcus and Narcissa Whitman and twelve others at their mission near Walla Walla. Reasons for the killing had deep roots. However, the proximate cause was the inability of Marcus to save many Cayuse Indian patients from a measles epidemic. After the massacre, Henry Spalding evacuated to Oregon with his wife. She died there four years later. Henry remarried and eventually returned to Lapwai. He died there in 1874.

The Massacre also brought together two old-timers from the fur trade era. The year before, a treaty with Great Britain settled the U.S. border with Canada in the west. The future Pacific Northwest states were now officially part of the United States. However, Congress lagged in organizing the new holdings. The Provisional Government provided only a minimal political organization in the region.

The HBC assigned former Snake Brigade leader Peter Skene Ogden to the management council for their Columbia District properties. The Indians still held 45-50 white prisoners after the killings. Ogden hurried into Cayuse country, hoping to secure their release. Skillfully applying the prestige of the Company and his own force of personality, the old trader succeeded.

Their helplessness in the Cayuse emergency frustrated Oregon's Provisional Government officials. They sent Joe Meek to Washington D. C. with news of the massacre and a request for action. Joe's western knowledge and perhaps his "gift of gab" led to creation of Oregon Territory in August 1848. The Territory encompassed all the Pacific Northwest, plus area east of the Continental Divide.

Appointed a U. S. Marshal for the new Territory, Meek escorted their new governor west the following spring. Two years later, Marshal Joe Meek supervised the hanging of five Cayuse Indians convicted for the Whitman Massacre. That "lesson" did not end the Cayuse War, however. Joe spent 1855-1856 fighting in that conflict.

The Oregon Country received rather little notice during this general period. In late 1845, the United States annexed Texas as our 28th state. Mexico, of course, never recognized the Republic of Texas. Their troops continued to attack the new state. Thus, in May 1846, the U.S. declared war and Army columns invaded Mexico. Meanwhile, American naval units annexed California. In early 1848, the Treaty of Guadalupe Hildago ended the war. Except for a minor adjustment in 1853, the nation had attained its contiguous continent-spanning borders.

Despite those stirring national milestones, events on the Oregon Trail proceeded rather normally, if there was such a thing. Traffic was still very heavy. Barnet Simpson, a ten-year-old pioneer in 1846, told a reporter, "At Fort Hall my father exchanged all of the bacon and flour and cornmeal he could spare for an order on Dr. McLoughlin for a similar amount at Oregon City. This saved hauling this surplus across the Cascades."

By 1848, Fort Hall dealt mostly with the wagon trains. They still traded for top-quality furs, but the depressed prices relegated that to a minor sideline.

The year before, Richard Grant had retrieved two of his sons from near Montreal. This turned out to have great significance to the history of stock raising in the Rockies. The sons had been living with Richard's mother. His wife had died less than two years after the 1833 birth of John Francis ("Johnny") Grant in Alberta, Canada. When he got time off, Richard took the children east.

Stockman Johnny Grant

Now Richard had remarried, and he worried about his mother's health. Considering that he had grown up in settled country, Johnny adapted well to frontier living.

Outside events again impacted what happened at Fort Hall and in southern Idaho. James Marshall discovered gold in the millrace of John Sutter's California sawmill. The gold rush started in California itself, from stores and farms, and even the ships in San Francisco harbor. By mid-July, an estimated 4,000 prospectors were in the Sierras. The rush from Oregon swelled during the following month. About then, the *New York Herald* printed a story about the discovery. September saw more stories in the East.

In 1849, twenty to twenty-five thousand hopeful prospectors traveled overland to California. Many anxious travelers pushed west from near Soda Springs on the new Hudspeth's Cutoff, rather than turning northwest toward Fort Hall. Oddly enough, this "shortcut" reduced the distance by only about 25 miles. It also ventured through rougher country. Records show that many parties actually made better time going the long way.

Even with this diversion, Fort Hall managed to hang on for a few more years. Naturally, the Oregon-bound traffic dipped severely in 1849. However, it rebounded to around six thousand the following year. All told, over thirty-three thousand pioneers followed the Trail to Oregon from 1850 through 1854. Of course, nearly four times that many went to California.

The Big Picture. In 1850, President Zachary Taylor died of cholera on July 9, and Millard Fillmore was sworn in to succeed him the following day. The U.S. expanded to 31 states when California was admitted to the Union in September. The population was over 23 million, more than double that of a quarter-century earlier. *The Scarlet Letter*, by Nathaniel Hawthorne, was published; its "daring" subject made it an instant best seller.

Also during this time, Johnny Grant laid the foundation for a thriving ranch. In his memoir, he said, "Every summer we went on the road to trade with these newcomers at Soda Springs. I traded for lame cattle and they were always the best, because somehow the best got lame the quickest. ... After some years I had over one thousand head."

Asked to transfer to another post in 1851, Richard Grant resigned instead. "After my father left the fort, he went like the rest of us to trade with the immigrants in the summer and with the Indians in the mountains in the winter," Johnny noted.

The Grants weren't the only ones trading with the natives. Travelers regularly bargained for fresh Indian horses. Others sought guides to help with the route, looking for better forage. They even paid to have tribesmen cut firewood and help remove rocks from the road.

"That such beneficial interactions occurred, frequently and with considerable significance, contradicts the widely disseminated myth of incessant warfare between brave overlanders and treacherous Indians," historian John Unruh wrote in his magistral text, *The Plains Across.*

One of the more dramatic examples involved the noted Three Island Crossing, near today's Glenns Ferry. The travelers faced a crucial decision as they approached this notorious landmark. The route along the south bank was longer, with more stretches that had little water or forage.

Yet the crossing could be deadly, as Marcus and Narcissa Whitman almost discovered. Even the descent presented problems. From the bluffs to the river level, the wagons and oxen had to negotiate a nearly 12 percent grade. (That's double what Federal regulations allow for Interstate highways.)

Slowly, the first emigrant guided the oxen down the rocky, rutted trail. The stout pole jammed through the spokes of a rear wheel as a makeshift brake thumped and grated over the stones, hindering concentration. Dust swirling in the canyon wind obscured the traveler's vision. If the pole snapped, the oxen and wagon would all tumble to destruction. One after another, the wagons inched their way down to the river. The families followed with the loose stock.

Guidebooks and travelers' journals generally advised: "It is best in fording this river to engage a pilot." Well-informed trains almost always followed this advice. For their train of twenty to thirty wagons, the individual cost seemed minimal.

The pioneers considered the first leg to the closest island fairly easy. It proved less troublesome than many streams they had already crossed. From there, the guide led them upstream. Then he had them turn sharply down to the second island. At last they reached the final stage. One pioneer observed, "From [the] second island to main shore is more difficult; it is about three hundred yards wide and the current very rapid."

Guidebooks warned of deeper holes in the bottom, which teams had to swim over. Unwary drivers might have their wagons drift quickly downstream. Hitching four yoke of oxen on a wagon, with two drivers, they prepared to cross this tricky stretch.

The guide led them upstream at a sharp angle for thirty to forty feet. The wagon master followed him, and two outriders flanked the teams. Three additional rigs joined the train. The guide now turned across the main stretch. To spare the teams, the column allowed the current to nudge them downstream somewhat.

A couple times, they hit deeper pockets, but generally only one yoke had to swim while the other three had their hooves on the gravelly bottom. With four yoke, the current did not push the wagon too far downstream.

As they approached the opposite shore, the train again struck upstream into the current. They quartered against it until quite close to shore. Finally, the teams turned almost parallel to the shoreline and mounted a natural ramp onto dry land.

Periodically, the pioneers led the freshest ox teams back across to reinforce those waiting to cross. After a few hours, everything had crossed, including the loose stock.

Contrary to another myth, the overlanders did not obtain services (like the crossing guide) and goods for a mere pittance. After dealing with some Snakes, one pioneer described them as "very sharp traders, not easily cheated."

Occasionally, the moccasin was on the other foot. One emigrant received what appeared to be a stack of 5-dollar gold coins for a "very good rifle." In better light he discovered they were cheap advertising tokens. By then, "The sly Snake had disappeared into the mountains."

Actually, the overlander's major Indian problem was theft. Typical emigrant comments included, "We have had no trouble with the Indians, with the exception of horse and cattle stealing."

Emigrants also had to be alert against constant petty thievery during daytime visits. Sometimes, the natives combined theft and "services." They would steal horses from one wagon train and sell them to one following. Unruh said, "This practice was common enough for the Salt Lake City *Deseret News* to warn overlanders about it."

There were indeed acts of violence. Although these were generally isolated incidents, newspaper accounts routinely sensationalized them. Naturally, the more common violence by travelers against natives seldom made the papers.

In actual fact, Indian attacks claimed few lives compared to deaths due to illness and accidents. Indians killed a few hundred emigrants along the Trail before the Civil War. In contrast, perhaps twenty thousand travelers died in other ways. Many people drowned in the dangerous river crossings. Second to that was mishandling of firearms.

But overall, sickness claimed perhaps ten times as many as did accidents. Cholera was by far the greatest killer. Emigrants also succumbed to "mountain fever" (Rocky Mountain spotted fever or Colorado tick fever), smallpox, mumps, and many others. Of course, stay-at-homes also died at an alarming rate. But the rigors of traveling and camping in the open heightened the risk. Even fairly conservative projections suggest a doubled mortality rate.

More than one diarist commented upon the signs of death. Abigail Scott crossed the Trail as a seventeen-year-old in 1852. Her father made Abigail responsible for keeping a journal of the trip. On May 10th, her entry bemoaned "the sickness and death of our beloved Mother!" She died of cholera.

Emigrants Crossing the Plains

After that, Abigail began noting the many graves they passed. On July 16th, she wrote, "We encamped near the Bear River and find good grass; The mosquitoes are troublesome in the extreme; passed four graves."

A month later, they had just left Idaho. She wrote, "There are two graves near our camp, of a recent date; We have seen several graves every day for the past week ... "

In late August, her youngest brother died. Abigail briefly taught school in Oregon before she married Benjamin Duniway in 1853. Abigail Scott Duniway would gain notoriety as a leader in the Pacific Northwest women's suffrage movement.

The aforementioned Mrs. Elizabeth Smith dealt with death also. Of the one hundred and forty people in their wagon train, they lost seven. Three died in accidents (two drownings, one accidental shooting) and four from sickness. Her own husband had taken sick before they floated down the Columbia. He died two months after they landed in Portland.

The emigrant throngs – ten thousand in 1852 alone – ballooned Oregon's population. An estimated thirty-five thousand people lived in and around the Willamette Valley in 1853. The few thousand pioneers around Puget Sound protested what they perceived as willful neglect by the Territorial government.

To placate demands for more local control, the Congress split the region in March 1853. Washington, the Idaho Panhandle, and Montana became a new Washington Territory. Oregon Territory now included Oregon, most of Idaho, and part of Wyoming.

This influx of whites also aggravated conflicts with the natives. Gold discoveries in southwestern Oregon added prospectors to the mix and increased the friction. These clashes festered across the Pacific Northwest throughout the decade. Sometimes they escalated into all-out war.

What pioneers called the "Snake" actually included Shoshone, Bannock, and Northern Paiute tribes. They ranged across southern Idaho, northern Nevada, and southeast Oregon. The Snakes regularly traded with the northwest tribes, and some had ties through intermarriage. As the years passed, the turmoil further west began to spill over into Idaho.

As many thousands of pioneers trekked across their lands, the natives saw a wider and wider swath of denuded grazing land. White hunters ranged far afield, taking game the Indians needed to survive. Natives still traded with the pioneers, but bands also harassed the trains, especially smaller ones.

Contact was oddly uneven. Many emigrant groups met few Indians, some saw none. Other trains seemed to run a gauntlet of trouble. The small (fourteen "able bodied men") Americus Savage party was an example of the latter. After warnings at Fort Hall, Savage proposed that they establish a night guard. Train members scoffed at the notion, so Savage was left to make occasional turns by himself. A few days from the Fort, he found clear indications that Indians were stalking the train. The next night, warriors stampeded their horses. The emigrants recovered only two.

A fortnight or so later, another train contacted them. Indians had killed three people and driven off much of their stock. They were assembling a force to recover the animals. Two men with the Savage Party's only horses joined the band. But the Indians easily repelled their attempt. They also killed a man from the Savage train. Americus wrote, "No one ever went back to bury the unfortunate man, Powell."

After that, they routinely posted a sentry. A few weeks later, they detected signs that natives were lurking about. That night, the guard cried a warning of "Fire! Fire!" Americus wrote, "The Indians had set the grass on fire by one of their number taking a bundle of dry grass on fire, and running with it through the dry grass to the windward of us."

The pioneers quickly put out the blaze, so the Indians made no follow-up attack. Fortunately, they soon joined a larger train, and had no further Indian trouble.

Neither the Army nor the few resident whites, like Johnny Grant, described any specific signs of danger in the first years of the Fifties. Still, a heightened sense of tension suggested that greater trouble was brewing. The explosion occurred in August 1854.

The small party of six wagons and twenty emigrants, led by Alexander Ward, camped for lunch at a good forage spot off the primary Trail. The train was about a day behind the main party.

Suddenly, Ward's oldest son ran into camp. Three Indians had stolen a horse. The same trio had earlier tried to trade for the animal. Ward realized how exposed they were in the brushy area where they had stopped. He hurried them back into the more open country along the main Trail. Within minutes, a Shoshone band swirled about them. Clearly, this small contingent seemed a safer target than the lead party.

The pioneers formed a defensive corral, about two miles south of today's Middleton. Then the Indians attacked, "whooping and yelling like savage demons and firing their guns."

Firing desperately, the handful of armed men beat them off. The initial engagement was fairly even. The attackers wounded one overlander, but had one of their own killed. For two hours, the whites exchanged shots with the attackers. Survivors thought two hundred warriors had assaulted them. One after another, the exposed defenders fell, dead or mortally wounded.

Finally, the Shoshones rushed the enclosure. The two younger Ward boys, William and Newton, tried to escape into the sagebrush. Warriors wounded both and knocked them senseless.

Meanwhile, the main party, under Captain Alexander Yantis, had lost some stock the day before. A search by a seven-man contingent found one butchered cow. Yantis and another man rode back to hurry the Ward party along.

They heard the shooting and fetched the other five men to form a rescue party. Unfortunately, seven men were not nearly enough. They retreated, but not before one young man was shot and killed. They did succeed in rescuing Newton Ward, who had dragged himself into the brush.

A larger rescue party arrived much too late. They found six men dead at the attack site. Four others (including the young would-be rescuer) were scattered at locations nearby. Mrs. Ward and another wife lay dead further away. They had been wantonly abused. Three young Ward children had been burned to death in a flaming wagon. They also found Ward's seventeen-year-old daughter, brutally raped, abused, and then shot.

The death toll, eighteen of twenty plus the young man, was the largest for a single attack up to that time. It would not be exceeded until the 1860 Utter Massacre. During that attack and subsequent ordeal by exposure and starvation, twenty-five of forty-four emigrants died. (Like the Donner Party, survivors desperately resorted to cannibalism). Four kidnapped children died or were never returned to their families.

Word of the Utter Massacre quickly reached Oregon. In less than two weeks, Major Granville O. Haller led a small force of Army troops and Oregon Volunteers into Idaho. Sent to protect travelers still on the Trail, they also raided several nearby Indian villages. During these attacks, they managed to shoot three innocent bystanders and wound a fourth.

The Oregon governor called for a much larger retaliatory expedition, right away. The voice of experience, Lieutenant Colonel Benjamin Bonneville, advised against such a move. During his fur trade venture, Bonneville's request for an extension on his leave had gone astray. The Army had therefore retracted his commission. He finally regained it, and saw action in the Mexican War.

In 1847, Bonneville was serving as a supply officer at Fort Vancouver. He knew a dangerous Idaho winter would blow in before the Army could assemble a larger punitive force.

Major Haller led another expedition into Idaho when the snows had cleared enough to get troops and their supply train across the Blue Mountains. Newspapers were calling for the "extermination" of the offending tribe.

Haller held a council with the Bannocks at Fort Boise. In an odd turn, four members of the guilty Shoshone band showed up. Taken prisoner after the council, one confessed his part and implicated the other three. In an even weirder turn, he then tried to escape and a sergeant shot him dead. The others were tried and sentenced to hang. Their final words suggest they had offered themselves as "sacrificial lambs" for the tribe.

Soldiers managed to kill two more of the guilty. They shot one trying to escape, while the other was caught and hung. In the process, troopers managed to shoot down two more who had taken no part in the Massacre. All told, Haller's forces seemed to have inflicted more harm on bystanders than on the guilty. That and the constant harassment of non-involved bands made the already-volatile situation worse. Then the U.S. Army withdrew units in response to the Yakima War flare-up in Washington.

A flood had damaged Fort Boise, so the HBC decided they would not rebuild. They shut down Fort Hall in 1856. Two years later, Indian pressure forced Mormon colonists to abandon the last significant white settlement in the south, an outpost in the Lemhi-Salmon river area.

Meanwhile, after much political maneuvering, the present Oregon-Idaho border was established in 1857. Two years later, Oregon became a state (the 33rd). Congressional action also tacked Idaho and part of Wyoming onto Washington Territory.

Despite the trouble in western Idaho, Johnny Grant continued to raise and trade cattle around Soda Springs. Haller had drafted him as interpreter for one of his search columns. Grant was later told that a small band of Indians had intended to kill him on his ride home from the Fort Boise area. They stopped to butcher a stray cow, so he escaped. Fortunately, Johnny's wife was sister to Tendoy, a powerful chief of the Lemhi Shoshones. That probably forestalled any further action.

Grant makes no mention of any other threats, but it is perhaps significant that he spent the winter of 1857-58 in the Deer Lodge Valley of Montana. He traded with Trail emigrants through the following summer, and then returned to Montana in the fall. "I settled then at Deer Lodge, building my first house on the Little Blackfoot, a stream which comes from the summit of the Rocky Mountains."

Johnny had about 250 head of horses and over 800 cattle. He took great pains to maintain good relations with tribes that traversed the valley in the spring and fall. In the Sixties, after his wife died, Grant sold the ranch and moved back to Canada. The Grants, father and son, had proven that cattle could thrive in southeast Idaho.

Still, by the end of the decade, the North Idaho missions and Indian tribes ran the only active cattle operations in the state. Fewer than two hundred whites lived within its borders. In the words of historians Beal and Wells, toward the end of the decade, "Idaho literally was given back to the Indians."

Two factors worked to change that situation. First, California cattlemen who faced pressure from crop agriculture had begun moving herds into Nevada. However, events in the north would have the greatest impact on Idaho's early history.

Chapter Five: Mining Makes a Territory

The mounted men moved cautiously through the willow and alder thickets along-side the stream. Occasionally, they and their pack train splashed into the shallow water to avoid a close-growing pine. The Nez Percés wouldn't harm them, but they would surely escort the prospectors off reservation land.

The party's leader, Elias Pierce, had exerted all his experience and guile to avoid Indian patrols on the main trails. His party was chasing the possibility that there might be gold in this portion of the Clearwater River watershed.

They reached a location high on the course of Orofino Creek in late September 1860. The Weippe Prairie lay about ten miles to the southwest. The men scattered along the Creek and side streams that flowed into it.

Finding a likely spot, a miner dumped a shovelful of sand and gravel into his pan. The sturdy slope-sided dish was about $2\frac{1}{2}$-inch deep, 16-inches at the lip, and 10-inches at the bottom. Since grease or oil might cling to ultra-fine gold powder and allow it to float away, he had scorched the metal in fire.

Seating himself on a chunk of driftwood, he hunched over to thoroughly wet his load. Then he stirred it to start the dense gold settling to the bottom. Immersing the pan to just below the water level, the miner shook the pan so the flow carried away dirt and debris. After five or ten minutes, he picked out the larger stones, checked for gold fragments clinging to the surface, and then pitched them. He repeated this until the pan showed only sand and small gravel.

Capt. Elias Pierce

The prospector tilted the dish away and began to carefully dip water, swirl, and flip the lightest surface material into the flow. Occasionally, he held the pan flat and agitated it to ensure that any gold sank to the bottom. He repeated the dip, swirl, and flip process in the most delicate manner, hoping to see "color" – a swirl of gold dust.

The prospector slaved along the watercourse until the sunlight faded. Then he trudged back to the campfire to warm his chilled feet and relax his aching back and hands. Finally, after days of searching, Wilbur Bassett came to Captain Pierce in some excitement. He had panned color up one of the side streams.

The men checked, and Pierce noted that they, "Found gold in every place in the stream, in the flats and banks and gold generally diffused from the surface to the bed rock. I never saw a party of men so much excited. They made the hills and mountains ring with shouts of joy."

Born in 1824, Elias D. Pierce always gave his birthplace as either Virginia or West Virginia. In 1847, he joined the U. S. Army and was shipped out for the Mexican War. Afterwards, he became a Forty-Niner in the rush to California. Like many, he experienced boom and bust there. In 1852, he was in Washington Territory trading with the Nez Percés.

Setting up near Lapwai, Pierce began dealing with the tribe for their abundant horses and cattle. He learned the language, and found that the Nez Percés only wanted to trade for cattle one at a time. He said, "I soon abandoned the idea of trading for cattle and turned my attention to horses alone. They had all been well broken and kind under the saddle."

Over the next several years, Pierce cultivated his good relations with the Indians. His eye for country convinced him that the Clearwater area "was a gold bearing region." That and talks with individual Nez Percés finally brought his party into the watershed. For over a week, Pierce's band mined the region, ending with over $100 worth of gold.

Pierce's group needed additional supplies to continue prospecting, so they left the backcountry. Their appearance surprised but did not particularly upset the Nez Percés. The tribe did not see gold mining as a threat. Transient miners didn't worry them nearly as much as white settlers.

The miners returned to Walla Walla, Washington and news of their strike spread quickly. In November, the *Portland Times* reported, "On the flats, the pay dirt is from $2^{1}/_{2}$ to 4 feet deep, next to granite bed-rock." The article also said "the pay dirt strata seemed to extend through the whole valley."

The 1860 census for Washington Territory had enumerated about 11,600 non-Indian inhabitants. Over three-quarters of them lived west of the Cascades. Fewer than a hundred whites were located in the Idaho districts. With the discovery of gold, that changed with dramatic swiftness.

In January 1861, the Washington Territorial legislature carved out Shoshone County for the region east and south of the Clearwater-Snake river confluence. This huge county encompassed most of future Idaho, plus pieces of Montana and Wyoming.

As far as they knew, the only town in that entire region was Pierce, all eight cabins of it. They ignored Franklin, near the Utah border, and made Pierce the county seat. (Everyone was a bit vague about the Utah-Idaho border.)

The rush impacted the Walla Walla area first. In March 1861, a prospector claimed, "This valley will be deserted in a few days. There are some 300 who have gone already; 83 left today. I am going to start on the 7th, in company with 50 or 60 others. He also said, "The town is full of pack animals."

The mention of pack animals was particularly significant. A couple years passed before pioneers cut even rough roads into the backcountry. Goods for the gold fields had to be loaded onto horses or mules and packed in. They faced an enormous demand. Around twelve thousand prospectors had flooded into Idaho by the fall of 1861. They arrived from Washington, British Columbia, Oregon, California, and even further afield. In fact, Idaho occupies a short list of states that were settled from the west, not the east.

To shorten the haul, the raw tent city of Lewiston formed at the confluence of the Clearwater and Snake rivers in May 1861. For most of the year, steamboats could get no closer to the gold camps. Lewiston grew rapidly as a shipping point. Unfortunately, legislators had done little to implement any law enforcement infrastructure in the new county. Lawlessness and violence thrived.

"Murders were frequent; robberies and thefts constant; gambling, drunkenness, and all their attendant evils, openly flaunted," Nathaniel Langford wrote. He had come west near the start of the Idaho and Montana gold rushes. He later played a major role in Intermountain history.

With so many chasing "color" in the Clearwater system, even relatively honest prospectors might be tempted into claim jumping, or worse. In fact, the Clearwater streams could not possibly yield claims for all who prospected the area. Luckily, in late 1861, news of even larger finds in the lower Salmon River drainage alleviated that problem.

The news quickly led to the blossoming of Florence and other camps in the region. Newspapers at the time reported, with some hyperbole, that Orofino instantly lost its allure. It was now merely a waypoint to the new bonanza. "Turn your eye where you would, you would see droves of people coming in 'hot haste' to town."

The report went on, "Flour, bacon, beans, tea, coffee, sugar, frying-pans, coffee-pots and mining utensils, &c., were instantly in demand. The stores were thronged to excess."

A letter to the *Oregonian* from the gold fields explained the excitement. The writer said, "I have seen seventy-five dollars washed out in ten hours by one man using the pan alone. ... Five men have just cleaned up seven hundred dollars, the result of ten hours work with the rocker."

Florence appeared quickly about thirty miles south of Mount Idaho. As happened further north, the huge influx of prospectors overwhelmed the town's services. Prospectors also pushed deeper into the Salmon River wilderness. Within weeks they made new finds near Warren, 20-25 miles to the southeast. As could be expected, the "banditti" followed the money into the mountains. Florence became even more lawless than Lewiston.

"Its isolated location, its distance from the seat of government, its mountain surroundings, and ... its utter destitution of power to enforce law and order" made it a criminal hotbed, Langford observed.

Even without outlaws, the country was hard and dangerous. The winter of 1861-62 proved especially severe. One newspaper report said, "We … have no doubt that at least one hundred men have perished from the cold in the upper country this winter."

The chill weather also devastated livestock herds in Oregon and Washington. These losses were probably exacerbated by the fact that some ranch hands had joined the gold rush. Seizing the opportunity, ranchers in California pushed animals north to restock those ranges and supply the miners.

"Large trains of mules and droves of cattle are now on the way from California for Salmon River and the Cariboo country," a newspaper in The Dalles reported. (Cariboo country was in British Columbia.)

The richness of the gold fields dictated whether a camp died or became a town. Most disappeared or declined with the depletion of the "easy" placer riches. Such alluvial gold could be collected with pick and shovel and washed out with pan or rocker.

Florence was one example of the boom and bust cycle. Its population reportedly exceeded ten thousand in 1862, yet the 1863 census recorded only 575.

Lewiston experienced no such peaks. Yet it remained the prime destination for steamer traffic on the Snake. A letter-writer to the *Oregonian* reported many reputable businesses there by mid-1862. He also identified "twenty-five liquor saloons, about ten gambling establishments, and about twenty places whose names might put the paper to blush."

The *Golden Age*, first newspaper in Idaho, began publication on August 1. That stamped a degree of permanence on the town. The *Golden Age* tended to be a "booster" for the area. It featured the town's services and extolled the fortunes to be made. Yet, sadly, the local crime rate captured far too large a portion of the news.

"The number of robberies and murders committed by the banditti will never be known. Mysterious disappearances soon became an almost weekly occurrence," Nathaniel Langford noted.

Road agents operated largely unhindered on the trails between the camps and Lewiston. They not only appropriated cash and pouches of gold, they often stole the victim's mount. Even small pack trains were not immune.

The *Illustrated History of North Idaho* (published in 1903) saw fit to print a summary of crimes recorded in the newspaper and other documents of the time. (They also conceded that scores, if not hundreds of other robberies and violent deaths went unreported.)

The *History* listed, mostly by name, twenty-one deaths and a dozen robbery victims. Some of the dead were victims, some were crooks. For example: "William Rowland and George Law were a couple of horse thieves operating on Camas Prairie; George A. Noble of Oregon City, was robbed of 100 pounds of gold dust between Florence and Oro Fino in December, 1862; two horse thieves, for stealing from a government train, were shot dead."

A turning point, of sorts, came in the fall of 1862. Masked gunmen accosted a pack train owned by the Berry brothers. They rode off with over a thousand dollars in gold dust. Recognizing two of the men's voices, the brothers quickly identified the third.

Pursuers soon apprehended the over-confident outlaws. According to later accounts, "The people of Lewiston were more thoroughly aroused over this crime than they had been over any other."

Citizens appointed a committee to handle the case. However, during the night, "persons unknown" dismissed the special guards and hung the malefactors from the rafters. The *Illustrated History* asserted that this summary execution "marked the decline of lawlessness in the vicinity of Clearwater."

Rich gold strikes in 1862 further changed the landscape. First, prospectors discovered gold in (future) Montana. That drew hordes of hopeful miners out of the Idaho fields. A party led by George Grimes had a more direct impact on Idaho. In early August, one of the band panned color in the Boise Basin, the rugged country around the headwaters of the Boise River.

By that fall, eight to ten thousand men had reached the Basin. Reports also said, "thousands more were on their way." Towns sprang up to exploit the fabulous riches. These included Idaho City, Centerville, Placerville, Pioneer City, and others that came later. The 1863 census recorded well over fifteen thousand people in the region.

Early Pioneer City

As noted before, southern Idaho Indians had grown more and more hostile to the Oregon Trail pioneers. And they were merely passing through. Prospectors angered them even further. George Grimes had little time to enjoy his party's discovery. A week after his gold find, he died in an Indian ambush.

Meanwhile, Shoshone attacks hit a number of wagon trains near Soda Springs, Massacre Rocks, and further west. These killed several emigrants. But authorities had little time to spare for Idaho. In the East, the Union army had suffered repeated defeats. Casualties had been horrific. A Sioux uprising in Minnesota left hundreds of settlers dead or in captivity. A handful killed on the Oregon Trail meant nothing.

Then, in December 1862, Indians ambushed a band of miners as they crossed the Bear River. When the miners arrived in Salt Lake, their leader protested to the Territorial officials. They had lost a man and some equipment. Actually, Utah had no legal jurisdiction where the assault occurred. However, Mormons in southeast Idaho had already complained about Indian forays. Thus, authorities in Utah issued warrants for the arrest of three Shoshone chiefs. They gave these to the U. S. Marshal. He, in turn, passed them along to Colonel Patrick E. Connor.

Two months earlier, the colonel had led over seven hundred California Volunteers into Utah. They built Camp Douglas east of Salt Lake City. Their main duty was to protect the telegraph and mail links to California. Connor, however, yearned for a showy battlefield win. That might earn him a transfer East, to the real action. The three warrants only spurred the colonel's existing intention to punish the restless Indians.

Connor marched north in late January 1863. He sent his cavalry and infantry over separate routes so they wouldn't clog the primitive roads. Along the way, harsh winter conditions disabled nearly a quarter of the soldiers. They had to remain in settlements along the route. Deep snow also delayed the column's two mountain howitzers.

In the morning glow of January 29, Connor and his cavalry troop stood on the heights facing west. The Bear River wound through the flat valley below. Smoke rising on the far side marked the Shoshone encampment. They had sheltered in a ravine cutting the bluffs.

Lack of a local guide had delayed the infantry. Fearing that the tribe might flee, the colonel sent four cavalry companies across the river. Hopefully, that would force the Indians into a defensive posture. A soldier commented, "That was a bad looking river, half frozen and swift."

Sporadic firing began between Army skirmishers and the defenders. Then the infantry arrived, giving Connor a total of about 200 soldiers. Impatient and over-confident, the colonel ordered a frontal attack.

A blast of shots drove them back, with stinging casualties. Chastised, Connor regrouped the infantry to lay down a steady barrage with their .58-caliber rifles. They advanced carefully. Meanwhile, cavalry squads armed with .44-caliber revolvers swept around the flanks.

Warriors fought back with bows and a mixed bag of muzzleloaders. They had limited ammunition for the few guns they had anyway. At short range, this proved no match for the high-volume fire from the attackers on the flanks. Only desperation delayed the inevitable. Finally, cavalry units advanced along the ravine's rims, driving the defenders back. The carnage lasted around four hours.

The Army suffered twenty-one dead and forty-six wounded in the clash. Connor estimated that they had killed at least 250 to 300 Indians. Local witnesses claimed 400 to 500 Shoshone dead. At least a third, and perhaps more, were women and children caught in the hail of gunfire or murdered by Connor's "take no prisoners" intent.

The Battle of Bear River – sometimes, with justification, called the "Bear River Massacre" – crippled the power of the Shoshone. National and even local critics questioned the attack's brutality. Yet Connor was soon promoted to General. After all, as one settler said of the battle, "It made the flocks and herds and lives of the people comparatively safe."

That relative quiet did not extend into western Idaho. There, Indians continued to ambush small bands of whites and to drive off stock. Finally, Major Pinckney Lugenbeel led a small force of Oregon Volunteers into the Boise Valley. In July 1863, he established Boise Barracks about fifty miles east of the original HBC Fort Boise trading post.

Even before the Army arrived, settler Thomas Jefferson Davis had "pitched a tent" along the river. Lugenbeel sited his post, soon to be called Fort Boise, not far away. Born in Cincinnati, Ohio, in 1838, Davis joined a wagon train headed for the Idaho fields in 1861. The emigrants reportedly encountered trouble on the trip and reached Elk City with only their draft animals, and very few supplies. Davis made a side trip into Oregon, then traveled to Idaho City. He moved to the Boise Valley in late 1862.

After the Army selected its site, Davis and some others began planning what soon became Boise City. One of the other founders was Henry Chiles Riggs. A Kentuckian born in 1826 about twenty miles east of Lexington, Riggs had served in the Mexican War. He went to California in 1850, then returned east to get married. He and his wife were back in the West by 1854. They moved to Corvallis, Oregon about five years later.

Riggs and his family arrived in the Boise Valley right after Lugenbeel selected a site for Fort Boise. He and a partner erected a building that housed a saloon and livery stable about a half mile west of the post. Within a matter of weeks, other civilian businesses and small farms sprang up in the vicinity. One Boise Basin prospector wrote, "The rush of miners into the country – the high prices offered for hay and provisions – make it evident that ranching and gardening in the vicinity would be very profitable."

The Volunteers proved ineffective against the Indian unrest. In August 1864, the Army transferred the First Oregon Cavalry to Fort Boise. The so-called "Snake War" would flame and flicker for another four years. These later Indian clashes took place in the newly formed Idaho Territory. All through 1861, thousands of prospectors flooded into gold fields in the region. By the end of the year, they had doubled the population of what was then Washington Territory.

Those numbers suggested opportunity to boosters in Lewiston. They saw a chance to become the capital of a new Territory. Politicos in districts west of the Cascades agreed. Those swarms of miners threatened their majority in the Territorial legislature. The catch was Walla Walla. They wanted a new border to run along the east side of the Cascades. That would free them from the political clout of the Puget Sound politicians. It might even make the town capital of the new Territory.

The agents from Lewiston and Olympia were Republicans … the party that controlled the U. S. Congress. In the 1862 elections, Walla Walla and the mining districts had voted Democratic. In the end, that proved enough to advance the Olympia-Lewiston plan.

Congress and President Lincoln created Idaho Territory on March 4, 1863. They used the current Washington-Idaho border, which kept the maximum area for Washington. But that line carefully excluded Lewiston and the Idaho mining districts. Lewistonians reveled in their status as Territorial capital.

The following June, a new treaty substantially reduced the Nez Percés reservation. This remedied the awkward detail that settlers had built Lewiston on their 1855 Treaty land. However, many chiefs did not sign the new treaty, for the very good reason that it gave away their tribal homelands. This promised trouble down the road for these so-called "non-treaty" bands.

Idaho Territory originally included all of today's Idaho and Montana, and much of today's Wyoming. Its area was greater than Texas. A census enumerated about thirty-two thousand people. Census takers still used the wrong southern border, so the count did not include the Mormon settlements north of the Utah line.

By that error, they ignored the third example of stock raising in the state. (The other two were the northern missions and the Indian herds.) Even before the creation of Idaho Territory, Mormons were grazing cattle and sheep on southeast Idaho range.

White stock raising soon began elsewhere in Idaho, including southeast of Lewiston. A pioneer recalled that, "Camas Prairie was a vast pasture growing natural bunch grass that waved in the breeze like a great sea and reached the stirrups of the horsemen as they rode over the prairie."

By the fall of 1862, one Hiram Lusk had built a log cabin a few miles north of Mount Idaho, a station on the Lewiston-Florence pack train road. The following year, John M. Crooks and Aurora Shumway bought the cabin as a headquarters for their planned cattle operation.

Crooks was born in Indiana, in 1820. He and his family emigrated to Corvallis, Oregon in 1852. Four years later, they moved to a farm near The Dalles. After prospectors found gold in the Salmon River watershed, Crooks bought cattle and moved his family to Florence. He then opened butcher shops there and in Warrens.

Born in New York State in 1825, Shumway emigrated to the west before 1854. He and Crooks had apparently met in Oregon after Crooks moved to The Dalles. The two decided there was money to be made raising their own stock to supply the mining camps. With a base on the Camas Prairie, the firm of Crooks & Shumway brought in a thousand head of cattle to graze on the bunchgrass. For the next twenty years, they would be leaders in the local stock raising industry, and also dabble in county politics.

Meanwhile, the mining fever continued. The next big strike, in southwest Idaho, arose from a doubtful but enticing legend. Earlier tales claimed that Oregon Trail pioneers traversing the region had used sinkers of pure gold on their fishing rigs. Some prospectors scrambling for claims among the throngs of Boise Basin miners in the spring of 1863 decided even such an unlikely yarn might be worth a look.

A party of twenty-nine men from the Basin rode into the area with about sixty horses and mules. By mid-May, they had marched deep into the higher ranges and camped on an upper stretch of Reynolds Creek.

The prospectors broke camp on the morning of May 18. To the south, peak piled on peak so they turned west to follow one of the many spring-fed streams flowing from a dividing ridge. Bunchgrass and other foliage had barely begun to green up in these high meadows and snow still lurked in shaded areas. Further south and west, scouts had observed "what appeared to be a large stream, judging from the topographical formation of the mountains, which were well timbered."

Once over the regional divide, the party followed watercourses down into the lower country, working south and west. Lofty mountains and ridges loomed to the left, but the western vista descended into a broad, rough plain.

Finally, outriders reported a canyon that seemed to cut deep into the high country. The column curved eastward over a low ridge and descended into a shallow, irregular bowl. From a northern gulch, a rivulet tumbled into a larger stream that flowed out of the eastern canyon. The meadows here seemed "a favorable place for camping," so they began unloading the pack train.

Oliver H. Purdy, a member of the party, said that one man couldn't wait. Instead, he tested a pan of gravel from the creek bank ... and "obtained about a hundred colors." Within ten minutes most of the miners were "busy digging and panning, and upon their return about an hour after, each man had favorable prospects to exhibit."

The miners searched the stream for ten to twelve days, claiming the more promising spots in the watershed. They called the main stream Jordan Creek, after another member of the company, Michael Jordan. They then returned to the Boise Basin, where their news set off a gold rush into the Owyhees.

Soon, even richer silver deposits were discovered in the region. Reacting to this new rush, the legislature carved out Owyhee County. It encompassed all of Idaho Territory south of the Snake River.

Pack trains charged very high rates to haul supplies into these remote mining districts. Newcomer Silas Skinner saw this as a prime opportunity. Like many sailors, he had jumped ship in San Francisco to follow the lure of gold.

With the best California and Nevada prospects taken, he continued into the Owyhee area. There, Silas tried to buy an outfit and was "stunned at the terrific prices." Local merchants set butter at $1.25 a pound and eggs at $3 a dozen (versus 20-30¢ in the East). Tools were equally expensive: $12 for a pick and shovel (perhaps $150 at today's prices).

Thus, when Skinner's prospecting efforts faltered, he decided a toll road offered more assured profits. He teamed up with Michael's brother James Jordan and another man to obtain a toll road franchise. The "Skinner Road" opened three years after the initial gold discovery. It connected Boise City to Silver City, and then on to Jordan Valley.

The *Owyhee Avalanche* expressed the area's satisfaction with the results. It said, "By this road, it is just twenty miles to Baxter's Ranch, and the only direct or even passable one to the valley and the Owyhee Crossing on the Nevada and California roads."

Skinner became known as the "Owyhee Road Builder." After a few years, Skinner ran cattle in addition to his road-building activities.

Skinner's road continued a trend happening all over Idaho, where freighters driving teams of oxen or mules had begun to supplant the pack trains. Wagon transport was more efficient, but draft animals were still very much in demand. A linked set of three heavily-laden wagons required a team of twenty oxen, more on particularly bad roads or steep grades. A single train might include anywhere from ten to twenty-five wagons.

Mule-Drawn Freight Wagon

In 1864, Julius Newberg, a man with long experience in mountain country, began construction of the "South Boise wagon road." He and two partners had received a franchise from the legislature to run a toll road from Little Camas Prairie (the Goodale's Cutoff portion of the Oregon Trail) into the Boise Basin.

By now, placer mining had begun to give way to lode mining, which required heavy machinery to extract gold from quartz ore. Rash men could sometimes break a stamp mill into components small enough for a pack train. However, the cost was prohibitive and the loads hard on the animals. They needed a wagon road.

Newberg hoped to complete the road in early summer, but that proved impossible. Their franchise agreement stipulated that they had to bridge numerous small streams as well as the South Fork of the Boise River. And the Boise required a structure strong enough to handle the heavy spring runoff.

The partners poured a small fortune into building all those bridges and cutting switchbacks on the worst grades. In return, legislators allowed them to charge substantial tolls: one team and wagon cost $4.00 (roughly two day's pay in the East for a skilled carpenter), $1 for extra teams, 75¢ for loose stock, and so on.

On October 5, 1864, the citizens of Rocky Bar were wrapping up the day. Sundown came early here. Pine-covered ridges towered a thousand feet above and crowded close to the small valley. Prospectors just in from the deep canyons sought provender for their stock, and accommodations for the night. Raucous music floated into the street.

Suddenly, a crashing clamor reverberated through the town, stilling music and conversation. A quick check found two blacksmiths hammering a tattoo on their anvils.

"What the devil are you doing?" someone surely asked.

An eyewitness reported the reason: "Three heavily laden wagons were coming in over the new wagon road just completed by that enterprising individual, Mr. Julius Newberg. Long and loud huzzahs rent the air and made the welkin ring."

Not incidentally, stockmen who had set up operations on (southern) Camas Prairie had a better way to deliver cattle and sheep to the mining district's butchers.

At key locations, entrepreneurs built ferries to provide more direct routes across major rivers. In late 1862, one such company advertised its ferry across the Snake River near the mouth of the Malheur River. It was "on the direct road leading from Walla Walla, Grand Ronde and Auburn to the Boise Mines. There is plenty of the best kind of grass for animals on this road with good camping places at convenient distances."

Freighter John Hailey no doubt read the announcement with interest. Born east of Nashville, Tennessee in 1835, Hailey emigrated to Oregon 1853. He found work at various jobs to accumulate a stake and then leased a farm in southern Oregon. John enlisted in the Oregon Volunteers as a private for the 1855-1856 Rogue River War. He rose to be a lieutenant by the time of his discharge. Hailey expanded his holdings by a land purchase and began raising cattle and then sheep.

In 1862, he herded "a number of sheep and horses" as far as Walla Walla. After selling the sheep, he added mules to his train and moved on to Lewiston. There, he began packing goods into the gold camps. Two years later, he and a partner began offering stagecoach service between Umatilla, Oregon and the Boise Basin. With that modest line, Hailey began a stage and freight empire that would eventually employ thousands of draft animals.

Across the state from the Malheur ferry, one John P. Gibson and a partner built a ferry across the Snake north of old Fort Hall. They operated for many years until a competitive ferry and a later upstream bridge made the business unprofitable. Alexander Toponce, a French emigrant, used the service on his way to Montana. He later recalled, "We went on up the river to a point near Blackfoot, where we crossed in a ferry boat, run by a man named Gibson."

Born in France about twenty-five miles west of Basel, Switzerland, Toponce came to the United States in 1846. He was then seven years old. For a decade after 1854, Alexander "whacked bulls," drove a stage, and rode briefly for an express mail service out of Fort Kearney. (Some accounts say he rode for the 1860-1861 Pony Express to California, but his *Reminiscences* clearly state that he rode express in 1857.)

Toponce chased gold in Colorado without much success before heading for Montana in early 1863. Members of the wagon train he joined must have recognized his already-considerable experience. Alexander said, "I had the honor of being elected captain of the train. I was just a little past my 23rd birthday."

After using the ferry, he said, "We started up the west bank and found a wagon train belonging to Livingston and Bell, surrounded by Indians."

Clearly the disaster on Bear River had not cowed all the Shoshones in eastern Idaho. Toponce went on, "They had stood the Indians off for eight days. You never saw a better pleased bunch of people than they were when we drove up, over 180 strong."

A month or so after this encounter, Harry Rickard and William Hickman built another ferry about thirty-five miles further up the Snake. An eagles' nest on a nearby lava rock island provided a name: Eagle Rock Ferry.

Late the same year, Reuben P. Olds started a ferry on the Snake near Farewell Bend, where the Oregon Trail leaves the river. Not only did it serve Trail traffic, it provided a good route for pack trains that followed the Weiser River into the gold country.

Lloyd Magruder was another pioneer who operated a pack train in north-central Idaho. Scion of a prominent Maryland family, Magruder had fought in the Mexican War, earning a promotion from private to second lieutenant. He soon resigned that commission and tried his hand in the California gold fields.

He prospered at first, but bad luck drove him to Lewiston in July 1862. Within a year, the hard-working and shrewd Magruder owned both a pack train and a store. In August, Magruder's train of mules headed east from Elk City on the South Nez Percés Trail. Passing through incredibly rough country, that Trail nonetheless provided the most direct route across the Bitterroots into Montana.

They arrived at the Montana gold camps in mid-September and Magruder quickly sold his loads. He began his return in early October, leading a train of eight other men, six horses, and about forty mules. The lightly loaded mule train soon crossed the Continental Divide at Nez Percés Pass. After about fifteen trail miles, they encamped on a side stream at the base of a ridge. This spot away from the main trail might have been recommended by William "Billy" Page, an experienced packer and guide who knew the Nez Percés Trail well.

Magruder and a man named Christopher Lower drew the sundown-to-midnight watch over the animals, released on pasture about a half mile up the slope. When they left camp, Lower carried an ax, supposedly to clear some intruding brush.

Lower and another man named David Renton returned to camp about midnight, according to Page's later testimony. Renton and a third conspirator, James Romain, had helped Magruder sell his goods. Either Lower or Renton had split Magruder's skull from behind with the ax.

Back at the camp, Lower, Renton, and Romain slaughtered the other innocent bystanders. Page had known about the plot, but was too greedy or frightened to warn the victims. He helped dispose of the bodies and excess equipment and weapons. Then the conspirators led most of the stock deep into the forest and shot them. They kept only enough to ride and to haul their supplies and the stolen gold.

Avoiding Elk City, they timed their arrival at Lewiston to enter after dark. While Page arranged to corral the animals out of sight, the others went to buy passage on a boat. However, with nothing scheduled any time soon, they decided to take the early morning stage to Walla Walla.

The nearest ticket office happened to be at Luna House, the hotel operated by Hill Beachy, a friend of Lloyd Magruder. Beachy had years of experience in reading men, and situations. He had left home at thirteen and served on Mississippi River steamboats as cabin boy, steward, and, eventually, pilot. However, the lure of gold drew him to California, where he ran hotels and dabbled in politics. Beachy had been early to establish his hotel in Lewiston.

On the evening of October 18, 1863, he saw a man enter the lobby, book four tickets, and leave. Although the man's face was partially covered by a scarf, something in his stance caught Beachy's eye. Beachy asked his livestock and stage business manager, Chester P. Coburn, if there'd be much gold on the morning stage. Coburn said he knew of at least $2,500 worth.

Beachy voiced his suspicions that the four planned to rob the stage. Unfortunately, the passengers carrying the gold could not afford to wait. According to the *History of North Idaho,* as the stage started off the next morning, "Beachy remarked to his companion that he thought there was no danger of a robbery, as the men seemed to have considerable gold with them."

This further aroused Beachy's suspicions. Investigation uncovered the animals and gear Page had stashed with a friend. Among these were a horse and a saddle known to belong to the Magruder train. Local authorities swore out warrants for the four.

Accounts at the time romanticized Hill Beachy's efforts to catch his friend's killers. Later stories continued that theme, but the facts speak for themselves. With a head start, the conspirators fled Portland on the San Francisco packet. With no ship ready, Beachy raced overland to Yreka, California. There, he telegraphed the indictments and full descriptions of the four to San Francisco.

When he returned the murderers to Lewiston, Beachy had to muster all his persuasive powers to head off a lynching. Still, for all of them except Page, who turned state's evidence, that only delayed the inevitable. The other three were hanged on Friday, March 4, 1864, the first legal hanging in the Territory of Idaho.

Actually, scholars have argued that the trial itself was illegal. They point out that the Territory had no legal code, and no court system. However, public outrage over the brutal murders would have rendered such legalistic nit picking, while perhaps technically valid, moot.

In Virginia City, vigilantes had already hung the notorious Henry Plummer. (The town was then in Idaho Territory.) They also executed several members of Plummer's criminal gang. The Vigilantes operated for several years after Montana became a Territory.

Vigilantes also patrolled the Boise area. In mid-1864, farmer and rancher "Billy" McConnell and two neighbors set out to track thieves who had run off four mules and five horses from the neighborhood. They returned two weeks later, with all the stock. Nothing was said about the fate of the crooks. William J. McConnell later represented Idaho in the U.S. Senate, and would be elected Governor.

These activities can be blamed at least partly on geography. From the Idaho Panhandle, high mountains impede travel east into Montana or south to the rest of Idaho. During the winter, any trip between Montana and the south could be difficult and dangerous. Thus, no matter where the Territorial Marshal had his office, he would be cut off from much of his jurisdiction.

Congress tried to correct the problem in May 1864. They created Montana Territory, giving it the same boundaries as the later state. The initial thought was to use the Continental Divide as the western border. That would have left the Bitterroot Valley in Idaho. Settlers there protested. For most of the year, they could travel east far more easily than trying to cross the Bitterroot divide. Congress agreed to move the boundary west. Idaho Territory retained a portion of Wyoming, and still suffered a north-south geographical divide.

The census administered in 1863 had counted roughly three thousand people in the towns of the Clearwater and Salmon river watersheds. Fewer than 500 lived in Lewiston. The Boise Basin and southwest Idaho held over seventeen thousand. Earlier that year, the *Oregonian* repeated (May 20, 1863) a report from the "Upper Country" that said Placerville and Idaho City were exhibiting "quite a spirit of rivalry on the subject of the location of the capital of Idaho Territory. The idea that Lewiston has any claim is ignored altogether."

The severe population imbalance – over six to one in favor of the south – clearly fueled the "spirit of rivalry." However, by the time of the 1863 census, Boise City had been founded. It assumed the lead over the Basin towns because of its better year-round weather, and role as a major transportation hub.

In the fall of 1864, voters gathered to elect candidates to the Second Territorial Legislature. Henry C. Riggs was one of those chosen. Just over a week after the session convened, Representative Riggs introduced a politically charged bill. It called for the relocation of the Territorial capital from Lewiston to Boise City.

Boise Pioneer Henry Riggs

Northerners naturally howled in protest. Yet they simply didn't have the votes to kill the measure. For years to come, resentful residents of Lewiston and other North Idaho regions fought to become part of Washington.

When Pierce's party discovered gold on Orofino Creek, Idaho was a wilderness practically devoid of whites. Scarcely three years later, it was a thriving Territory. Now, thousands sought riches in all of its out-of-the-way corners. At the same time, the seeds planted by Shumway, Crooks, and others were growing into a major stock raising industry.

Chapter Six: Idaho Meat for Hungry Miners

The sternwheeler churned eastward up the Snake. To the south, the steep slope rose over a hundred yards above the river. The ship's steam engines pounded, and sooty smoke poured from the tall stack. All business, the vessel sported no fancy grillwork or colorful paintings like a Mississippi-Missouri river packet. Occasionally, the swirling wind brushed the smoke and a few cinders over the passengers leaning on the upper deck rail.

Minutes later, they turned northeast. On their right, the hills flattened into a broad, brush-covered terrace twenty to thirty yards above the river. Wind gusts raised some surface chop, but the agitation was nothing to match what they had encountered earlier.

"The ascent of the Palouse Rapids baffles all generally received notions in regard to steamboat navigation. ... The water is lashed into billows capped with foam, and the feat of ascending them looks fool-hardy. But we take a running jump right into the centre of the rapids; and inch by inch the boat goes bravely up. The waves strike her sides as if she were thumping on the rocks. Sometimes the 'upper-tow' will carry her ahead half a length at a time, and then she will stand trembling for minutes in a place ... In an hour and a quarter we made three-quarters of a mile ... ," wrote (June 5-22, 1861) Henry Miller of the *Oregonian*. The rapids were located about a half mile above the mouth of the Palouse River.

As the boat followed the curve of the Snake toward the south, the travelers saw the mouth of the Clearwater opening out to the east. A shriek of the steam whistle announced their impending arrival at Lewiston. Only the town itself altered the scene witnessed by one of the earliest steamboat captains. He had said, "Before us spread out a beautiful bunchgrass valley, or rather a series of plateaus, reaching away to a high prairie to the southward."

A bell sounded and the great reel of paddles stilled as the sternwheeler drifted toward the landing. The paddles reversed, beating the water into frothy splashes. A final stop bell, then a deck hand slung a hawser to fix the boat at its mooring.

The passengers hurried ashore. They had paid dearly to avoid the bone-jarring stagecoach ride from Walla Walla. The Oregon Steam Navigation Company faced minimal competition on the route. This freed them to impose brutally high rates for passenger and freight traffic. They sometimes levied ten times the freight charges common on the Missouri River. Whatever their ultimate destination, the passengers' goals had to be worth the price.

Some headed for Luna House, the hotel where Hill Beachy and Chester P. Coburn had begun their investigation of the Magruder murders. After the trial, Beachy had moved to the Silver City area and started a stagecoach line. Coburn had stayed in the north. Lewiston remained a vital supply point. Of course, mining activity had declined in the Clearwater and lower Salmon fields. However, new finds in the Kootenai watershed sparked further traffic.

Vermont native Chester P. Coburn caught a boat to California in 1852, when he was twenty years old. After taking the shorter route across Nicaragua, he began mining and tending store in the gold rush area. Not striking it rich, he turned to stock raising around 1857.

In late 1861, reports circulated about exciting gold discoveries in the Florence Basin. Coburn sold his holdings and headed for Idaho. After a short stint in the gold fields, he settled in Lewiston and opened a livery stable. In 1864 he claimed a ranch southeast of town.

By the mid-Sixties, Lewiston was stable enough to support a small school with fifteen or twenty pupils. The city set up a local school district, which levied a modest tax for education. The new organization moved the school to a small frame building that had formerly housed a drug store.

The number of settlers and stockmen grew. "Numerous stations along the route to the Kootenai mines" drew stockmen to move horses and some cattle into those areas. Closer to Lewiston in 1865 "the Rice Brothers brought in a band of stock sheep, and about the same time C. P. Coburn imported one hundred and fifty head of cattle into northern Nez Percés county. … A little later Captain Ankeny and his sons brought in 500 neat cattle from Oregon. About this time, also, Thomas Moore took up what is now known as the Dowd ranch in Tammany hollow."

["Neat cattle," by the way, refers to Bovine animals that are commonly domesticated, as opposed to generally wild bison, buffalo, and certain species of antelope.]

The *Illustrated History of North Idaho* went on, "Another horse ranch was taken possession of probably as early as 1865 by Schissler & Siers, from whose brand the place came to be named the '21' ranch."

As noted above, Coburn added cattle to his ranch in 1865. He soon started a dairy business and opened a butcher shop in Lewiston.

William A. Caldwell was another who took up ranching in the area, about "twenty-two miles distant from Lewiston," in the mid-Sixties. By careful management, he built up herds of about a thousand cattle and ten thousand sheep.

Still, the truly dramatic changes in stock raising took place in the south. Julius Merrill, a twenty-three year old native of Harmony, Maine, traveled to the Idaho gold fields in 1864. His *Trail Journal* provides insight into the state of stock raising at that time. In late August, their party reached the Soda Springs area, near where the Montana road branched off.

"At the junction of the roads there is a ranch ... Ranchmen buy lame, worn-out cattle from the emigrants very cheaply. By putting them upon good feed they soon revive, are ready for market, and bring a good price," Merrill said.

By this time, Mormon and Gentile settlers had pushed deeper and deeper into southeast Idaho. In Marsh Valley, thirty-odd miles north and a little west of Franklin, the natural meadows along the various creeks furnished ideal grazing for stock.

Within a year after Merrill's passage, William Head began operating in the upper Cache Valley and others joined him in the next couple years. Around 1866, they founded the town of Preston. Historian Byron Lusk noted that Head's operation "was successful enough that he was able to trail cattle to the Montana mines three years later."

Settlement had also begun in the next major valley to the west, along the Malad River. By 1864, what would soon be Malad City had one or two rough houses. Settlers began irrigated farming, and grazed stock on the nearby foothills.

A few days after leaving Soda Springs, the Merrill train reached the Snake River. Merrill wrote, "To the emigrant who has seen nothing for months but sagebrush and sage plains, nothing could be prettier than this river bottom. Along the larger streams are tall cottonwoods and vines, while along the smaller are willows and thorns."

Near a much deteriorated Old Fort Hall, Merrill wrote, "The stage company has two mowing machines at work cutting hay. We were told they had five hundred tons in stack and were still cutting."

James Madison "Matt" Taylor started the earliest settlement further north, in the upper Snake River valley. Born in Kentucky, Matt married in Missouri in 1853, when he was about twenty-six years old. As might be expected from his name, Matt was a second cousin to President James Madison and President Zachary Taylor.

The "Panic of 1857" ruined prospects in Missouri so in 1858 Matt began hauling freight to the Colorado camp that soon became Denver. Five years later, Montana gold discoveries drew Taylor further west. His wagons carried supplies through eastern Idaho to the camps. During the summer of 1864, he and two partners bought the Eagle Rock Ferry, which traversed the Snake a few miles upstream from today's Idaho Falls.

On one of his early freighting trips, Taylor camped near what was called Black Rock Canyon, a few miles downstream from the ferry. At this point the Snake is constricted between walls of lava. Careful measurement with a tossed stone and string finally established the distance: eighty-three feet. Engineer William F. Bartlett, one of Matt's partners, had probably already outlined what it would take to bridge the river.

By the time the bridge opened in late May 1865, they had built a stage station near the bridge site. The station included a barn and corral, blacksmith shop, and general store with a simple eating space. Extremely high water in 1866 wrecked that first bridge. However, they recovered most of the timbers and rebuilt it, stronger than before. That same summer a telegraph line from Salt Lake reached Taylor's bridge. From there, construction continued on to Virginia City. Taylor's Bridge became a focal point for settlement in the upper Snake River Valley.

Still, the heaviest traffic crossed to the south, headed to the gold fields or Oregon. From near Fort Hall, the 1864 Julius Merrill party headed onto Goodale's Cutoff. That route led across the dry flats toward Big Southern Butte and on to the Big Lost River. Merrill wondered, "Why call it a river? The very boulders in its bed seem parched with the drought."

The Cutoff then turned west. Ten days later they marched out onto the southern Camas Prairie. Here, Merrill wrote, "We found some men from California, with sheep which they were fattening and selling occasionally to some emigrants who were so fortunate as to have money enough to purchase."

Of course, the stockmen's real customers were the butcher shops in Rocky Bar and the other mining towns. About fifteen miles further along, Merrill's party passed a cluster of huts erected by pioneers who had cut large piles of hay. They planned to haul it off the prairie, then assemble a pack train to reach the mining towns.

"It was said to be worth $200.00 per ton delivered at the mines," Merrill observed. Not an unlikely price, considering the number of pack animals and wagon teams moving in and out of the mining districts.

On Little Camas Prairie, the Merrill train saw more hay being cut, another large herd of sheep, and a party of emigrants who intended to start ranching in the spring. They next faced the hard climb off the prairie and over to the Snake River side. Around noon they reached Willow Creek, a tributary of the South Fork of the Boise River. Here they found a farm-ranch operation.

"Potatoes 50 cents per lb., squashes 2 dollars each and small at that," Merrill railed at the prices. "We will keep our money straight and live on bacon yet awhile."

Further along, they encountered several herds of cattle and sheep grazing in the mountain valleys. Merrill said, "They are herded here upon good fresh feed, kept fat … They have shops at Boise City and generally drive in and butcher once a week."

Merrill also commented on the many small ranches where "a few vegetables are raised." They perhaps passed the Blaylock place, located twenty to twenty-five miles southeast of Boise City. The Blaylocks grew vegetables, provided forage for stock, and served traffic along the stage route.

In the fall of 1864, James Obediah "Obe" Corder and three partners drove a cattle herd into the area from California. In 1850, at sixteen, Corder had left Indiana for the gold fields. He soon discovered he could do better raising stock. Obe and his partners delivered the herd under contract to some Boise City butchers. They built a cabin on Indian Creek so they could graze the cattle until they had to make a delivery.

Obe married the Blaylocks' daughter in March 1865 and the couple purchased her parents' waystation. They stayed on to run the station and raise cattle, melons, and peaches. Corder Station remained a fixture in the region for nearly forty years.

The Julius Merrill party arrived at the Boise Valley overlook on September 17, 1864. Merrill conceded that the view of fresh greenness thrilled them. Still, on closer inspection, he declared, "It merely seems beautiful when compared to the hundreds of miles, so barren and desolate, we have travelled over. "

One of Merrill's partners remained in Boise to practice his trade. Blacksmithing was always in great demand. Two others left immediately for Idaho City, while Merrill stayed long enough to sell their wagon and cattle. The growing town provided a ready market for stock of all kinds. Even three years later, a correspondent complained about the high cost of horses and the short supply of cattle.

Boise City, 1864

Long before the Merrill party arrived in town, William Byron gauged that demand and did something about it. He purchased five hundred cattle in Walla Walla, trailed them into Idaho, and grazed them on the abundant bunchgrass not far from town. As needed, he slaughtered a few for his butcher shop.

Like many who followed, he also discovered the excellent forage properties of a native shrub called "winterfat" or "white sage." The latter name is incorrect; winterfat is not a member of the sage family. (Unfortunately, even more so than bunchgrass, winterfat cannot tolerate over-grazing.) Byron does not appear to have started an independent cattle business.

James Wilson was one Boise area stockman who did. Wilson was born in Indiana, northwest of Louisville, Kentucky, in 1826. He grew up near Terre Haute. James and his family lived for eight years in south-central Iowa until the spring of 1862. They then emigrated to Oregon. Two years later, they retraced their steps to Idaho. Starting with just five yoke of oxen, Wilson built a very successful cattle operation. He was later considered a leader in the importation of better breeds of cattle to upgrade Idaho's herds.

Unlike Wilson, most of the early settlers came for the gold. Truman C. Catlin was one of many examples. Born about eight miles west of Springfield, Illinois in 1839, Catlin attended college for a few years. Tales of Idaho gold drew him west. After spending the winter in Oregon, in 1863 he found a job in the mines around Idaho City.

Dissatisfied with working for wages on someone else's claim, Truman tried again in Silver City and then back in Oregon. That didn't work out either, so he and two partners built up a stake supplying shingles to Fort Boise. Earlier, Catlin had taken a homestead claim about ten miles northwest of Boise City. Now, on what came to be called Eagle Island, he began irrigated farming. He also entered the cattle business in a small way. That sideline eventually grew into a major operation.

Of course, not everyone who came for the gold stayed. Julius Merrill, for example, did very well in the gold fields. After less than three years in Idaho, he went back east. In Iowa, he purchased "a rock-free farm of his own." (A welcome change from his previous experience farming in Maine.)

Even with such turnover, miners continued to throng the gold and silver fields. Idaho Territory still contained nearly nineteen thousand people, three-quarters of them in the Boise Basin. Idaho City alone had around seven thousand, more than Portland, Oregon.

In 1866, prospectors discovered the hugely productive fields around Leesburg. One prospector said, "Much coarse gold was found and nuggets of $5.00 to $50.00 were common."

Getting supplies in proved to be a challenge. Leesburg lies deep in the mountains ten to fifteen miles northwest of the mouth of the Lemhi River. The trail climbs over 4,600 feet above the river, then drops 1,800 feet into town. Pack trains couldn't even get in during the winter.

Partly as a result, Salmon City grew quickly as a jumping-off point. By the following summer, the town had a newspaper, the *Semi-Weekly Mining News.* Also by then, Leesburg contained an estimated two thousand people.

Further discoveries deep in the central Idaho wilderness, along the Snake, and even in eastern Idaho further fueled the excitement. Meanwhile, stock raisers and settlers filled the plains and valleys.

New mining fervor also gripped the Owyhee region, with similar results. The gold placers along Jordan Creek had soon been supplanted by quartz finds that assayed in silver almost ten times the value in gold. By the summer of 1864, claims had been located all around the area. War Eagle Mountain held the most promising lodes. Silver City grew apace.

Interestingly, Michael Jordan, one of the original discoverers, soon turned away from a focus on mining. He had taken note of the stock-raising potential of the foothills and plains to the west of the Owyhee high country. Within a matter of months, he invested some of his mining profits in a cattle ranch along Jordan Creek.

"The thousands of hills and mountains furnish a broad and luxuriant pasture; the hundreds of springs and small streams afford a never-ending supply of water. In the sheltered valleys, the herds find comfortable quarters and refuge during the winter," was how historian Hiram T. French later described the region.

Other ranches followed and they soon developed a thriving cattle industry. Sadly, Jordan didn't live to see that development. The following year, Indians drove off his stock and he was killed trying to recover the herd.

As traffic on the roads from California ballooned, so did the number and frequency of Indian attacks. In June 1865, the Army sited Camp Lyon about seventeen miles northwest of Silver City. Troops clashed with bands along the Owyhee River, but their efforts were not very effective.

Finally, with the Civil War over, the Army dispatched Regular units to the theater later in the year. However, even the presence of the Regulars did little to quell the unrest. Newspapers now called the conflict the "Snake War."

The crisis seemed so acute that citizens of Silver City and nearby Ruby City organized a company of volunteers to pursue the Indians. Boise City also formed a company led by David C. Updyke, whom we'll meet again later in the chapter.

In the spring of 1866, the Army moved the 2nd Battalion, 14th (Regular) Infantry to Fort Boise to reinforce the Oregon Volunteers. The Battalion's commander, Major Louis H. Marshall, was a West Point graduate and nephew of renowned Confederate General Robert E. Lee.

A newspaper, the *Owyhee Avalanche*, had begun publication in Silver City in August 1865. In late May 1866, it reported, "Another wholesale Indian slaughter has occurred west of the Owyhee just above the mouth of Jordan Creek. Fifty Chinamen were on their way to Idaho City and all but one were murdered by brutal Indians ... "

Prodded by the continuing attacks, Major Marshall had departed Fort Boise earlier in the month. After a stop at Camp Lyon, he led two Infantry companies down Jordan Creek to the Owyhee. From there, he turned south and marched upstream for a few miles. He needed cavalry to launch an effective search.

Back at Camp Lyon, Lieutenant Silas Pepoon, Oregon Volunteers, heard about the killings and "dashed to the spot" with his cavalry troop. All he could do was bury the bodies. The Indians were long gone. Marshall learned of the massacre when Pepoon and his cavalrymen joined the infantry column. This augmented force pursued the trail of an Indian band they thought might be the perpetrators.

The afternoon of May 27, Marshall and Pepoon stood on the west rim of Owyhee Canyon, a great gash in the plateau. At the base of the 800-foot drop-off, the Owyhee River twisted and turned along the cut. Directly across, about a mile away, a large Indian band moved through the brush of the canyon bottoms.

Marshall carefully assessed his quarry and figured there were about 500 Snakes in the group, perhaps 250 to 300 of them warriors. Scouts had located a ravine that cut deep into the rim, providing a stony ramp down to the river. The soldiers carefully picked their way along the route. Loose rocks and shifting gravel made the trek difficult and dangerous.

The Indians had spotted them. Already they were driving their stock over the low pass into the middle fork. By the time the soldiers deployed along the west bank of the south fork, many warriors had hidden among the rocks on the opposite side. The two forces began to exchange shots.

At one point, four Indians rashly exposed themselves. A quick volley killed two and wounded the others. Periodically, they saw the Snakes haul casualties – about five more dead and ten more wounded – over the ridge where the stock had gone. When soldiers finally got their one mountain howitzer in place, they lobbed five shells over that ridge.

After nearly four hours, Marshall shifted his forces downstream. If the troops could cross, they might flank the Indians. The Three Forks Dome crouched near the opposite bank like a giant, ragged plug of tobacco, and prevented the Snakes from following.

By now, shadows deep in the canyon had grown long. The soldiers began ferrying men and equipment across. With about half the troop on the other side, Marshall decided it was time to send over the howitzer. Disaster. Their craft capsized and the cannon vanished into the river. The major moved more men over until it grew too dark, then finished the crossing the next morning.

Marshall sent two scouts to reconnoiter the high ground rising to the south of his position. As they ascended the slope, a blast of shots killed one man and the other's horse. Miraculously, the survivor skipped to safety despite a hail of gunfire. The Snakes occupied the high ground and kept the soldiers pinned down until nightfall.

"The country is so difficult that only one man at a time can climb these Indian trails. Ten men can hold a hundred in check and prevent their ascent," Marshall said later. He ordered a withdrawal across the river under cover of darkness.

The next morning, they ascended to the plateau and returned to Camp Lyon and then to Fort Boise. Although the soldiers inflicted more casualties than they took, they had retreated from a stand-up fight and lost their artillery. Attacks on isolated ranches and stage stations increased, both in frequency and intensity.

An Oregon pioneer, C. B. Wiley, described his experiences in the Owyhees at that time. He had worked as a packer in Oregon during the summer of 1866, but then took a winter job herding cattle for a Silver City butcher. He said, "The Indians were bad. I always carried a Henry rifle and two six-shooters. The Indians killed the settlers on both sides of me, but I was lucky and kept my scalp on."

Frustrated at the lack of progress, the Army assigned the job to Lieutenant Colonel George Crook. Crook had gained tough Indian fighting experience in northern California and the Pacific Northwest. He had then distinguishing himself in the Civil War. Crook understood that the Indians had legitimate grievances. Whites had broken faith on many treaties and settlers kept intruding on Indian land. Crook condemned those offenses. Still, he saw reservation life or "Americanization" as the tribes' only hope. Otherwise, they would be wiped out by white aggression, civilian or military.

Crook took command and led his first clash against a Paiute band on December 26, 1866. That fight inflicted stinging Indian casualties and kicked off a grueling winter campaign. Yet even with the increased Army pressure, Indian bands struck at isolated homesteads. During the May after Crook took over, the *Avalanche* reported, "Last Sunday several Indians attacked Con Shea – a ranchman – on Sinker Creek."

Joseph "Joe" Wasson, co-editor of the *Avalanche*, joined Crook's force as one of the first "embedded" correspondents for an Indian war. He praised the success of the colonel's approach. Joe also said, "I believe he has the Indian character a little nearer down to a scratch than any man in the regular service."

In the end, Crook balanced relentless pressure with honest negotiation and fair dealing. Less than two years after Crook's appointment, the unrest was largely over. A year later, President Grant authorized Fort Hall Indian Reservation for the Shoshone-Bannock tribes. Many scattered bands were then relocated there.

Pioneers had other worries besides Indian attacks. In southern Idaho, that trouble developed in a manner oddly reminiscent of what happened with the Plummer Gang in Montana.

David Updyke, mentioned earlier, had built up a small stake in the Boise County gold fields. In 1864, he moved to Boise City and bought a livery stable. Soon after, he began rubbing elbows with hard cases and known crooks. Citizens came to suspect the stable was a front for criminal activity in the area.

The experience of William J. "Billy" McConnell provided some of the evidence. McConnell spotted a horse in Updyke's barn that had been stolen from his pack string some three months earlier. Updyke had no bill of sale, but claimed he'd bought it from an anonymous "drifter."

McConnell satisfied himself that a man who worked for Updyke had stolen the animal. Even then, he had to hire a lawyer to reclaim his property. (As noted in the previous chapter, he and some friends tracked and dealt with some other stock thieves themselves.)

Despite all that, the first elections in the newly created Ada County selected Updyke as sheriff and *ex officio* tax collector. The area vigilantes, who might have otherwise disbanded, stepped up their pursuit of horse thieves and other crooks. However, they did not operate in Boise City itself.

To counter them, Updyke obtained a court order for the arrest of Billy McConnell and several other settlers suspected of being vigilantes. Fearing a convenient "trying to escape" shooting, a large armed contingent met Updyke's posse of toughs. In court, they easily refuted the charges, for which there was not a shred of evidence.

William J. McConnell

Oddly enough, the next outrage of note didn't happen in Updyke's Ada County jurisdiction. In July 1865, robbers struck the stage traveling south from Montana to Salt Lake City. All the passengers were well armed, but the thieves opened fire with almost no warning as the stage passed through Portneuf Canyon. This murderous blast killed four "merchants of Nevada City in Alder Gulch." Shots also badly wounded another passenger, and savaged the shotgun messenger so badly that he lost a leg. The killers then made off with a reported $75,000 worth of gold. Although nothing could be proved, word soon surfaced that Updyke's gang had supplied guns and ammunition, and shared in the loot.

The stage driver, Frank Williams, quit his job shortly afterwards and was observed tossing money around freely in Salt Lake. Realizing his mistake, he fled east. Soon caught, he confessed to his role as spy for the robbers, and was immediately hung. The stagecoach company pursued the other robbers relentlessly. Alexander Toponce said, "J. X. Beidler, who was with the company as shotgun messenger for a great many years, told me that all of them were taken and punished."

Even beyond the suspicion of complicity, Updyke had plenty of trouble in Ada County. Among other offenses, he had misappropriated tax receipts. Commissioners let him make restitution and resign rather than press charges.

Unfortunately for him, he couldn't avoid trouble. He strongly promoted the formation of the Ada Volunteers and led them out. Dispatches from the field painted a rosy picture of energy and dogged determination. Of course, Updyke never claimed to have fought, or even seen any Indians. Still, readers could kid themselves that the "cowardly savages" were fleeing the Volunteers' onslaught.

In reality, the men camped as soon as they found a likely spot south of the Snake. They then spent the time horse racing, firing off their guns, eating, and drinking. The company started back when their supplies, or perhaps just the whiskey, ran out. They marched boldly into Boise City, claiming they had only returned because the stingy quartermaster at Camp Lyon wouldn't provide more supplies.

This farce was a fairly common debacle with such efforts. Some cynical amusement might have been the only fallout. However, some irregularities about supplies ended up in court. There, the testimony of a likable young man named Reuben "Honest Rube" Raymond made trouble for the Updyke interests. Afterwards, a notorious thug shot and killed the unarmed Rube in early April 1866.

Authorities immediately arrested the killer, John C. Clark. Fearing either a rescue or lynching attempt, they had the commander at Fort Boise confine him in the guardhouse there. Two days later, a band of well disguised vigilantes hung Clark from a makeshift gallows. They left a note:

> "Justice has now commenced her righteous work. This suffering community, which has already lain too long under the bane of ruffianism, shall now be renovated of its THIEVES and ASSASSINS. Forbearance has at last ceased to be a virtue, and an outraged community has solemnly resolved on SELF PROTECTION.

> "Let this man's fate be a terrible warning to all his kind, for the argus eye of Justice is no more sure to see than her arm will be certain to strike."

Updyke decided Boise City might be unhealthy and fled to Rocky Bar with a confederate. He couldn't resist issuing dire threats against those he felt were responsible for the lynching. A week later, locals found the two dead, hung by vigilantes.

A bill of particulars posted the following day in Boise City detailed the offenses for which they'd been executed. Updyke's part ended with, "Justice has overtaken you."

The note then listed the henchman's crimes and closed,

"All the living accomplices in the above crimes are known through Updyke's confession and will surely be attended to.

"The roll is being called."

The vigilantes and other forms of rough frontier justice did reduce some of the crime and violence. One Salmon City pioneer wrote, "In 1866, a vigilante committee was organized. As soon as this became known there was an exodus out over the mountains."

Not all the violence resulted from criminal activity. Some could be blamed on the general cussedness of men thrown together in a rough land. However, the fact that Congress created Idaho during the Civil War exacerbated the problem. As the war went on, refugees and other discouraged Southerners made their way to Idaho.

Alexander Toponce remarked, "It was a standing joke in Idaho that 'the left wing of Price's army' was located in Cassia county."

The "joke" referred to Confederate General Sterling Price. In March 1862, Price fought on the losing side of the Battle of Pea Ridge in northwest Arkansas. Inept staff work and poor decisions by Price's commander threw away a distinct advantage in numbers. Add in some bad luck, and the southern force suffered a demoralizing defeat.

That, plus other pressures, forced the Confederacy to abandon the state of Missouri to the Union. As it happened, Missouri State Guard divisions manned Price's left wing. Many chose to forsake a cause that treated their homes as expendable.

After the war, more Southerners fled the excesses of Reconstruction. Tension between North and South factions turned most elections into bitter partisan battles. Sometimes that tension flared into violence.

Like many from the state of Maine, Sumner Pinkham had strong Union and abolitionist feelings. Pinkham had been a Forty-Niner and then came to Idaho in 1862. Two years later, he was appointed Boise County sheriff. He served only a brief term. Then newly arrived Democrats swamped the voter roles and elected one of their own.

Ferdinand J. Patterson, reportedly a native of Tennessee, harbored equally strong Southern sympathies. He never hid his corrosive bitterness about their Lost Cause. "Ferd" had tried his hand in California, then in Oregon, and finally in Idaho. Reports indicate he had killed at least two men in gunfights, but got off on "self-defense" pleas. He had also skipped bail on another charge in Oregon.

In 1865, Pinkham returned to Idaho City from a business trip not long before the Fourth of July. When he asked about a celebration, no one knew of anything. That got his dander up, so he organized a parade himself. On the big day, Pinkham and a straggle of no-doubt inebriated Unionists marched through the streets, singing patriotic and anti-Secesh songs. This show incensed Patterson and the other Southern sympathizers, and angry words were exchanged.

Exactly what happened later in July is impossible to say for sure. The two sides offered wildly contradictory accounts, of course. Still, one can't avoid the impression that Patterson forced a confrontation. Pinkham had gone to relax at a hot springs resort, with saloon, a miles or so west of Idaho City. Soon, Patterson showed up.

Witnesses did agree that Pinkham stood outside waiting for a carriage back into Idaho City when Patterson exited the bar. Here, witnesses matched only two points. Patterson said the word "draw" in some (disputed) context, then taunted Pinkham as an "Abolitionist son-of-a-bitch."

Patterson certainly shot quicker, whether he drew first or not. Pinkham got off one inaccurate response and then took a second bullet. As the ex-sheriff dropped over, dying or already dead, Patterson fled with some of his cronies. He surrendered to the sheriff within a few hours.

Neither side doubted the outcome of the trial. And, indeed, a jury selected from rolls packed with ex-Southern Democrats acquitted Patterson on the murder charge. Soon after his release, Patterson moved to Walla Walla. The following February, a man shot Patterson full of holes while he visited a barbershop. The man's reason for the killing: "He threatened me." After a muddled hung-jury trial, someone let the prisoner walk away from the jail. He then disappeared from history. Local and Idaho sentiment suspected vigilante justice had reached out to punish Patterson even hundreds of miles away.

Despite crime, violence, and inflammatory politics, pioneers continued to settle in Idaho. Even before the first Territorial legislature convened, permanent settlers had moved into the lower Weiser Valley. Nancy Harris had tired of cooking and waiting tables in her parents' boarding house in Oregon. She and her beau, William Logan, eloped into Idaho.

On their way to an Idaho Justice of the Peace, they stopped a few miles upstream from the mouth of the Weiser River. They had heard that a man named Rueben Olds planned to build a Snake River ferry. It would cross near Farewell Bend, where the Oregon Trail left the Snake to begin its ascent into the Oregon mountains. William and Nancy figured a roadhouse on the flats near the Weiser could turn a fine profit serving Trail pioneers.

After the wedding, they returned and built their first rude station. Olds built his ferry in 1863 and the Logans soon began to serve, not only pioneers, but also traffic eastbound to the Boise Basin mines. A few years later, they sold the business and claimed ranch land about three miles upstream.

Also in 1863, Woodson Jeffreys and Thomas C. Galloway arrived from Oregon. Woodson had two brothers – Solomon M. and James – who joined him shortly. The Jeffreys family had emigrated from near Kansas City, Missouri to the Yamhill region of Oregon in 1845.

In 1849, Solomon ("Sol"), then only fourteen, went to California with his father and another brother. Although they did very well in the gold fields, the father died on the trip home. Solomon raised stock in Oregon for a number of years before coming to Idaho. He and Woodson soon established a cattle business, "Jeffreys Brothers," in the Weiser area. Solomon also opened a store along the stage road that ran up the Weiser River.

Their friend Thomas Galloway did not focus on the Weiser area at first, although he did claim land there. Thomas was born about forty miles southwest of Madison, Wisconsin, in 1837. The family moved to Oregon in 1852 and homesteaded in the

Yamhill region. Although he had learned the printer's trade, in 1859 Galloway followed the gold rush into the Cariboo fields of British Columbia. Two years later, he packed goods to those same gold camps.

For a time, Galloway led pack trains into the Boise Basin and prospected a bit. In 1865, he replaced a log hut he'd built in Weiser City with the first frame home in the settlement. For several years, he ran a rough hotel there. He also served as agent for express mail and freight passing through the area. After about 1868, he began a major expansion of his horse and cattle holdings.

Stockman Thomas C. Galloway

Development also continued further east. The Boise Basin gold discoveries had prompted a steady eastward flow of prospectors and freighters along the Oregon Trail. An *Oregonian* correspondent who traveled the route said, "We met on the average not less than ten pack trains per day, many consisting of from fifty to one hundred animals and not less than five, five-thousand-pound freight wagons besides the countless other vehicles and travelers."

Those travelers included Nathaniel Martin and Jonathan Smith. The two had prospected in Oregon until they learned of the Boise Basin finds. They followed the road to where the Payette River curves from the plains into the mountains. Looking over the amount of wagon traffic, they decided a ferry would be highly profitable.

The roadhouse they built in 1864 laid the basis for the town of Emmett, initially called Martinsville. Soon, farmers and ranchers began to settle north of the river. Many settlers brought a few stock with them. They quickly learned that this region provided excellent grazing.

About the same time, stockmen were driving large bands of cattle and sheep from California onto ranges in the Owyhee region. Irishman Matthew Joyce came to the U. S. around 1855, when he was twenty-five. He married soon after and farmed in Illinois until 1864. They then started west to California. Unfortunately, the rigors of his wife's pregnancy landed them on the Humboldt River in Nevada.

In three successive years, Indians burned their homestead so they moved into the Owyhees. There, on Sinker Creek, Joyce established a ranch to supply beef, pork, and dairy products to the miners. He later expanded his holdings into the Bruneau River area.

Over in south-central Idaho, James Bascom built Rock Creek store in 1865. The Ben Halliday stage line had already erected a lava-rock home station there, about twelve miles south and a bit east of Shoshone Falls. That building served mainly as a stock barn to support the stage from Utah into Boise City. It also provided a rudimentary hotel where passengers could purchase a meal and lodgings.

The general store served both the stage line and the stream of pioneers on the Oregon Trail. Bascom operated the store for over a decade. A small settlement, with its own post office, grew up around the buildings.

To the south, ranges in Nevada had begun filling up with California cattle herds. It would not be long before the ranchers moved them north into Idaho.

Far north of Rock Creek store, herds were growing in the Wood River area, and in the Lemhi-Salmon watersheds. Salmon City had, almost immediately, become more than a staging area for the Leesburg mines. Early on, two ranchers had brought beef cattle and milk cows from Virginia City to the Salmon River area. Then E. R. "Ed" Hawley and his brother trailed a considerable herd from Nebraska and released them to graze in the Lost and Lemhi river valleys.

South of Salmon City along the Lemhi River, prospectors searched for placer gold along the creeks that fed into the river. Many also built cabins and began ranching. James L. Kirtley, for example, moved to the valley from Alder Gulch, Montana in the mid-Sixties. He located a claim and ranch six to eight miles east of Salmon City. Later, they sold that property and bought another. Kirtley ranch would play a prominent role in the valley well into the next century. Other families followed much the same path to ranching on the Lemhi.

At this point, distant forces again took a hand in Idaho history, as they had with the Louisiana Purchase, the great fur company competitions, and the Civil War itself. Before the War, Texans found ready markets for their cattle in the South and via shipments from New Orleans. They lost those customers with the blockade and particularly when Union forces captured the Mississippi River in 1863. Herds grew, and stockmen allowed many cattle to go wild … but the animals continued to breed.

Meanwhile, growth in the cities of the north and northeast fueled rising demand for beef. Texas stockmen looked towards those new markets for their huge surplus of cheap animals. Thus, cattle drives to railheads in Kansas began within a year after the war ended.

Western lore rightly celebrates Montana pioneer Nelson Story. In 1866, he used his mining profits to buy Texas cattle and point them north. Story and his crew braved the natural hazards along the trail, and dodged outlaws and hostile Indians to drive the first Texas cattle into Montana Territory.

John Q. Shirley and Charles Gamble are less known, yet they too endured the same kinds of danger. Around 1865, Shirley and California stockman Andrew Sweetser began scouting locations for cattle raising in Idaho. The area around old Fort Hall seemed to have potential.

Joseph Pattee had succeeded Richard Grant as manager of Fort Hall. After the HBC abandoned the fort in 1856, Pattee turned stockman. He still found plenty of demand to trade fresh cattle for lame, just as the Grants had done. Records are sparse, but he seems to have kept the herd fairly small. It's likely he traded his surplus for flour, coffee and other supplies. In any case, the rangeland in that area was still relatively empty.

Shirley and Sweetser selected a spot in the river bottom and considered their options. Like Nelson Story, they knew that Texas had plenty of cheap cattle. The partners reportedly purchased over twelve hundred head. Then, at some point, Shirley hired Charles S. Gamble to help trail the cattle from Texas to their spread in Idaho.

Born on Maryland's Eastern Shore in 1846, Gamble moved west to St. Louis as a teenager. From there, Charles made his way to Kansas. There, he found work on a ranch and gained experience as a cowboy and all-around hand. It's somewhat unclear whether Shirley hired him in Texas, or Gamble had already come to Idaho.

About this time, Joseph Pattee decided to winter his herd in the southern Raft River region. He avoided pastures near that leg of the California Trail because moving stock had heavily grazed the forage. However, the valleys and bottomlands further from the main route still had impressive stands of bunchgrass and other forage.

It was not long before Shirley and Sweetser told Gamble to move some or all of their cattle into the Raft River drainage. They eventually shifted their headquarters to that area.

Expansions like those around Fort Hall and Raft River were happening all over Idaho. The ample supply of inexpensive Texas cattle noted above certainly helped fuel that growth. A switch to "small-scale farming and 'bonanza' wheat-growing agribusinesses" in California proved equally important. Those changes began to push experienced stockmen off more and more land.

Thus, just three years after becoming a Territory, Idaho had an emergent stock raising industry. Now located closer to the mines – their primary markets – ranchers had bands on most of the best grazing lands in the region.

Large Cattle Herd, Grazing

Chapter Seven: Stock Raising Grows

The herd moved slowly over the broken, scrub-covered plain. Gathered in the spring of 1870, they had now been on the trail for many weeks. Having left the creeks of the shallow valley behind, many miles separated them from the next water.

The trail boss guided his horse up a modest rise east of the plodding column. Piled-up ranges, made small by the considerable distance, crowded the horizon far off to the west.

Occasionally, dust raised by the cattle's hooves obscured his view. The parched soil had sucked dry all the moisture from the light showers that fell earlier. Still, the fitful breeze sometimes brought a whiff of damp sagebrush. Forty miles or so on their back trail he saw the high ridges of the Divide they had crossed from Montana. Off on the eastern horizon, the *trois tétons* still gleamed with snow.

Ahead and to the left of their line of march, a pair of truncated-cone buttes provided a familiar landmark, well known to freighters and stagecoach drivers. With a practiced eye, the trail boss judged the distance: bit over twenty-five miles north of Eagle Rock. They should reach the next good water right on time.

He lifted his hat and waved for the point riders to angle the herd to the southwest. After a moment, the right-hand point signaled back. The two began to ease the lead steers toward their right. The swing men paralleling the middle of the herd should have seen his gesture. He'd wait until the flankers and drag riders came into view so they'd understand the direction change and start pushing the slower stock. The wrangler with the remuda of extra horses could follow their lead.

Only a bloom of dust to the south marked where the cook's wagon was rushing ahead to the camping spot the boss had selected. Maybe when they got to the railhead he could learn more about Charlie Goodnight's newfangled "chuckwagon" notion. Heard tell it made life easier for the cook.

Couple more days they'd ford the Snake with the herd while cookie took his wagon across the bridge. Danged if he'd pay toll on two thousand cattle.

The herd belonged to German emigrant Conrad Kohrs. Kohrs had come to Idaho to prospect for gold, but ended up running a butcher shop in Montana instead. Between 1862 and 1865, he built a little meat shop empire. Kohrs needed cattle to supply his shops, so his herds grew also. He had bought a horse from Johnny Grant in 1864. Grant turned down Conrad's first offer to buy his Deer Lodge ranch, but agreed after his wife died in 1866.

Four years after Kohrs bought the ranch, Montana herds had outgrown their local markets. Kohrs assembled the nucleus of a drive and then followed the rivers west before turning south into the Bitterroot Valley. There he purchased enough cattle to make a decent-sized drive.

While Kohrs tended to business in Montana, cowboys drove the herd into and across east Idaho. Their route led them all the way to the extreme northeast corner of Utah. There, they turned east through Wyoming and finally loaded the cattle on the train at North Platte, Nebraska.

Much had changed in eastern Idaho since Johnny Grant moved his operation out of the Territory. Of course, he would have known about Matt Taylor's bridge because of the steady stream of freight and stage traffic. He might not have known about the Snake River ferry near the mouth of the Blackfoot River.

Kohrs' trail drive passed several new outposts. In about 1868, John N. Adams built a stage station at Market Lake, about seventeen miles north of Taylor's bridge. He cut hay for the stage stock and brought in additional horses and cattle as a sideline. His sideline soon grew into a substantial holding. About the same time, he, his brother William, and Thomas Lauder began what is credited with being "probably the first active irrigation farming in the Snake River Basin."

In the few years since Matt Taylor built his bridge, it had become a landmark known throughout the northern Rockies. Taylor himself became known enough that in 1868 voters elected him to the Territorial Council. (The Council was similar to a state Senate.) He represented the district that included what was then Oneida County.

Taylor's Toll Bridge, 1871

Matt Taylor also cut hay as an adjunct to his toll bridge and station. He asked a cousin, Samuel F. Taylor, to join them and handle a big contract cutting hay for the stage line. Sam was born in 1848, in Kentucky. The following year the family moved to Missouri. When the Civil War began, his father, Samuel F. Sr., joined the

Confederate Army. He died at the Battle of Corinth, in 1862. Sam Jr. returned to Kentucky and graduated from their Agricultural and Mechanical College (precursor to the University of Kentucky).

When Sam arrived in the summer of 1870, he found, "Nothing there then but Matt Taylor's family and what help they had around, and men that worked for the stage line; no settlers at all. The family kept a home station and fed all the travel. I took charge of the outfit and put up the hay. There was no farming done, no tame hay, no stock in the country; lots of good grass and we just had to cut the wild grass wherever it could be found."

Settlers had appeared further south, however. Nels A. Just was ten years old when his family emigrated from Denmark to Utah in 1857, arriving in one of the so-called "handcart" companies. By the late 1860s, he had worked at various jobs, including running freight into Montana. Meanwhile, his future wife, Emma, had also emigrated here from England. According to local historian Barzilla Clark, "During the winter of 1866-67, we find her cooking at the stage station at Taylor's Bridge."

Divorced with an infant child, Emma married Nels in November 1870. She was twenty years old. Late that year, Nels took up land along the Blackfoot River to run "considerable numbers of cattle and sheep." For their first home, Nels cut a dugout into the bluffs along the river.

The Justs secured a steady income selling some of their cattle under contract to the Army at Fort Hall. The year after they settled, Nels filed a water rights claim on the Blackfoot. He and the only other early pioneer then laid out a small-scale irrigation project. Just also filed a timber claim in the nearby foothills.

The further south the Kohrs herd moved, the more ranchers they encountered. They probably did their best to avoid the Shirley and Sweetser herds near Old Fort Hall.

The Montana drovers surely passed the road junction ranch Julius Merrill saw in 1864. They might also have seen another new phenomenon: herds of cattle and horses being trailed from Oregon to the same markets the Kohrs drive had headed for. They traveled too far east to see the new settlements and cattle operations at Preston, Riverdale, and Samaria. Late in the decade, John Winn and Emilius Hansen added their cattle herds to those already grazing in and around Cache Valley in southeast Idaho.

Had the Montanans made their drive two years earlier, they would have still been in Idaho Territory when they turned east. However, in July 1868, Congress created Wyoming Territory. In the process, they relocated the border to its current line, giving the new Territory all the land between that border and the Continental Divide. Idaho Territory also lost population, down over a thousand in the 1870 census from the nineteen thousand recorded in 1864.

John Hailey attributed the drop "mainly to the working out of many of the rich placer mines in Boise Basin." Born in Tennessee, Hailey had lived through the Territory's birth and growth, starting as a packer into the Basin in 1863 and later operating over two thousand miles of stage line. He would twice be elected as Territorial Delegate to the U.S. Congress (territories, of course, had neither Senators nor Representatives).

Despite the comparative depression in mining, grazing areas all around Idaho Territory gained settlers and herds during the latter years of the decade. John Pattee had decided the upper reach of the Raft River would provide a better wintering ground. After having a cabin built, he had his son-in-law move his cattle there. Unfortunately, Pattee's wife died the following spring so he sold the herd.

Grazing Land in Raft River Valley

In 1868, settlers, including cattleman Colonel Rice L. Wood, found their way west of Raft River to Marsh Creek (not to be confused with the stream flowing into Marsh Valley, further east). Wood built a home on Howell Creek in the higher ground south of Marsh Basin. The Basin would soon become a key portion of the freight route from Utah to Boise City and the mining districts.

Far north of Raft River, the Salmon and Lemhi stock operations grew in response to continuing rich finds in the Leesburg gold fields. By 1868 or 1869, the Leesburg population approached an estimated seven thousand. As usual, the legislature created a new county, Lemhi, to handle the administrative functions of this newly populated region.

Like citizens all over the state, Lemhi settlers had to deal with cattle rustling and horse theft. Two freighters walked into a small settlement southwest of Bannack Pass and reported that their horses had been stolen. They had trailed the band enough to believe the thieves were headed for the Lemhi River. Locals immediately sent for help from Salmon City. Pursuers discovered evidence that pointed to the Hawes ranch, long suspected to be a haven for rustlers. At the ranch they found the freighters' horses and Hawes himself. None of his known associates were around. The posse took the thief to Salmon City and locked him up to await a hearing.

That night, a band of men immobilized the guard and marched Hawes to where the local butcher had set up a windlass for hanging sides of beef. Three times the men lifted Hawes by his neck, letting him down just before he strangled. At that point, he was feverishly anxious to answer questions and identify his fellow thieves. Then, according to George E. Shoup's "History of Lemhi County," his questioners told him to "get out of Lemhi county and that if he or any of the rustlers ever again were seen in Lemhi they would be hanged without a word."

George E's father, Colonel George L. Shoup was among those who helped build Salmon City. Shoup was born about forty miles northwest of Pittsburgh, Pennsylvania in 1836. He lived in Illinois for a time, but in 1859 followed the rush to Pike's Peak gold. During the Civil War, he served in the Colorado Volunteer Cavalry. By the time the unit disbanded after the war, Shoup had risen to the rank of colonel.

In 1866, George packed goods into Virginia City, Montana, and opened a store. At that time, Alexander Toponce, the French émigré, had not yet switched from freight hauling to stock raising. In his *Reminiscences*, Alex said he sold eggs to the Colonel during the winter of 1867. During that same period, Shoup opened a store in the blossoming village of Salmon City. The town soon contained several saloons, a livery stable, another store, and other businesses. Shortly, Shoup was heavily involved in cattle raising and would later play an important role in Idaho politics.

Settlement also continued in the Clearwater and Panhandle regions in the far north, accompanied by a succession of changes in the array of county boundaries. Although the legislature created Kootenai County in 1867, it had no formal organization for well over a decade. That same year, the first school in Mount Idaho opened, with Miss Biancia Reed as the teacher. The year after that, Mount Idaho citizens built a new school to replace an "old log building" used before.

In the summer of 1869, the brother of Loyal P. Brown trailed a band of horses and cattle to Mount Idaho. Born in New Hampshire, L. P. Brown had arrived in Idaho in July 1862. Thirty-three at the time, he'd had considerable success in the California gold fields, owned a store for awhile, and raised stock in Oregon. He and his wife headed for the gold fields around Florence. However, he was "struck by the business opportunity" the Mount Idaho waystation offered.

He and a partner purchased the station and filed on land nearby. By 1869, L. P. had bought out his partner and expanded his interests considerably.

"A few days after arriving at Mount Idaho, I went to Elk City and took charge of my brother's store there," Alonzo Brown wrote. "He asked me to run it as long as I felt I could stay away from my family, and close it out, as it was too far away from him, and besides he had more business at home than he could look after. I kept the store a year and a half."

Despite the expansion in stock raising, mining still fueled the Idaho economy. Providing a link back to Idaho's fur trade era, Stephen Hall Meek told an interviewer, "In the spring of 1867 I took a train of twenty-two wagons, loaded with quartz machinery, from Sacramento to South Boise, Idaho, and then went to the ranch of my brother, the well-known Joe Meek, near Portland, where I spent the winter."

(Rocky Bar started out as South Boise. Stephen would have been about sixty in 1867.)

New discoveries deep in the Salmon River wilds, at Loon Creek and the "Yellow Jacket" area, encouraged new rushes. The legislature also authorized another toll road to facilitate traffic into the mining districts. This extended the Rocky Bar – Little Camas Prairie road across the high country to the Snake River plain southeast of Boise City. The *Idaho Statesman* said, "This road is a vast improvement over the old road. There are no steep hills or heavy grades and it is several miles shorter."

More and more, stock raising was becoming an economic force of its own. For example, Peter Pence trailed the first large herd of cattle into the lower Payette Valley. Pence had headed west from Pennsylvania in the late 1850s. Like many pioneers, he tried his hand at various jobs: firewood cutter, freighter, farmer, and threshing machine operator. Finally, Pence landed in Placerville, Idaho about the time of its founding in December 1862. He was twenty-five years old. Again he tried various jobs, including prospecting, but did best threshing grain in the Boise Valley.

Pence later recalled an incident in Boise City during its first days. As told in Hawley's *History of Idaho:*

> "He and his partner, returning to their mine from Idaho City, stepped into the butcher shop to get a steak. Just at that time a fight broke out in the street and Jones, the butcher, decided to interfere. Being a powerful man, he threw the fighters apart and in so doing stopped a bullet by his head, resulting in his instant death. He was left lying where he fell until the next day, when a rope was put around his neck and he was dragged away – such was the little value placed upon a man's life at that time."

In early 1867, Pence traveled to Walla Walla and invested his profits in a herd of fifteen hundred cattle, which were then moved into Idaho. That summer he paid a man named Bill Hill $1,400 for the rights to a ranch where Big Willow Creek joins the Payette River, about twenty miles downriver from Martinsville (today's Emmett). Pence later branched out into real estate, banking, and other investments. He would also serve in various public offices.

At that time, the town of Payette did not exist. There was only a primitive store to serve travelers on the Oregon Trail and the surrounding settlers. The arrival of Peter Pence and other stock raisers and settlers along the Payette River allowed them to expand their business.

As noted in the previous chapter, Thomas C. Galloway pioneered the Weiser area early, with his friend Woodson Jeffreys. He ran a hotel and acted as an express agent, and also began ranching in a small way. In June 1867, Galloway headed for Boise City by way of Martinsville, along the Payette River. He had shopping and other business he could not handle locally.

Leaving the Payette, Tom saw before him the notorious and dreaded "Freezeout Hill." The "Hill" featured a murderous series of switchbacks with many dangerous drop-offs. The name arose because heavy wagons had to lock, or "freeze" their wheels to, literally, slide down the incline. Galloway cautiously guided his rig up the slope. Fully loaded freight wagons sometimes required a dozen yoke of draft animals to ascend.

Surmounting the final hairpin, he started down the much gentler eastern slope. Coming toward him was a wagon loaded with provisions and household goods. A gentleman in his late fifties was driving.

Tom carefully stopped along the shoulder, and introduced himself. Colonel Augustus Flournoy was the name, the man replied, his courtly and affable accent proclaiming his Southern origins. Behind the wagon stood a small carriage. The colonel's oldest daughter Mary, a very nice looking young lady, drove it. His wife Anna and two teenagers sat in the back. The colonel said he and his family were headed for a homestead on the Payette River. They knew little beyond the location, but descriptions of the region had been impressive.

Galloway warned them that they faced a tricky and dangerous descent just ahead. He, being familiar with the road and its grade, would be glad to help with proper locks. He could also drive the smaller outfit with the family. The colonel accepted thankfully.

The young woman gave up her seat and they advanced to the brow of the drop-off. The travelers were surely even more grateful when they saw the daunting track they faced. Several hundred vertical feet separated their craggy perch from the flat plain, with looming ridges beyond and Squaw Butte to the north. Far below, the cottonwood trees looked like shrubs. The road, such as it was, teetered down the steep slope through a litter of rocks, ruts, and loose gravel.

Tom assembled a rude brake for the wagon, then nimbly guided the carriage down the grade behind the colonel. Judge Frank Harris, a Weiser pioneer who later related this story, said that the colonel and his family "were profuse with their thanks for the kindly assistance given them."

Moreover, "the good Colonel and his wife insisted that if the skillful driver should ever have occasion to come that way again he must make it so he could be their guest over night."

Galloway climbed the slope to his rig and continued into Boise City.

On his next trip into Boise City, Tom ensured that he could accept the colonel's invitation. The colonel hailed from Virginia, by way of Missouri, where he'd twice been elected to the state senate. Judge Harris, who knew the Galloways for over three decades, romantically summed up what happened next: "Afterwards [Tom] made frequent visits to their hospitable home until ... he carried away as his bride the young lady whom he had displaced as driver down Freezeout hill in June the year before, and they jogged along together for 51 years."

Shortly after his marriage, Thomas began to expand his ranch holdings. He raised both cattle and horses, but specialized in the latter. The Galloway spread would eventually also include mixed-crop irrigated farming.

Settlement had extended at least fifty miles up the Weiser by 1868. One of those settlers was Stephen Durbin, a New Yorker who had traveled to the Boise Basin with the 1864 Julius Merrill party. He did well as a prospector and in 1868 purchased a half-interest in a ranch near Logan's station. In time, Durbin became one of the most progressive horse raisers in Idaho, importing topnotch Clydesdales and trotters. Further up the Weiser, the John Reed family homesteaded the Midvale area while at least one white man had settled in Council Valley.

Pioneers also settled between these two spots, near today's Cambridge in the Salubria Valley. William B. Allison was born about sixty miles south of Akron, Ohio, in 1845. In 1863, the family moved to the Boise Valley while William drove a freight wagon between Omaha and Salt Lake City. During the next five years, he also freighted across southern Idaho.

William homesteaded in the Salubria Valley in 1868. For a brief time he had only one neighbor, until his father moved the family next door. William immediately began raising cattle, horses, and hogs. He also built a log home, to which he brought a new bride in late 1868.

The Owyhee Country also grew extensively during this period. Stock arrived not just from Oregon and California, but also all the way from Texas. A year after Shirley and Sweetser trailed Texas cattle into the Fort Hall region, Cornelius "Con" Shea brought the first longhorns into the Owyhees. Originally from Canada, Shea arrived in Silver City around 1864 when he was about twenty-four years old. He first worked as a blacksmith in the Owyhee mines. However, by 1867 locals knew him as "a ranchman."

Cornelius "Con" Shea

That year, a local businessman commissioned him to go to Texas and assemble a trail crew to bring a herd back. On his way, Shea encountered a drive much closer to hand. George T. Miller and Sol Walters had themselves purchased a thousand longhorns and driven them as far as Raft River. Probably figuring they'd done the hard work for him, Shea made them an offer, which they accepted.

While Miller and Walters returned to Texas to buy more cattle, Con completed the drive to the area of Catherine and Sinker creeks. Later, he made several drives from Texas himself. Thus, the *Owyhee Avalanche* reported (March 26, 1870), "Con Shea and Tom Bugbee have gone to Texas after another band of cattle."

While not exactly blasé about the dangers involved, reports are nonetheless surprisingly matter-of-fact about these drives. Raid and counter-raid between soldiers and Indians – Kiowa, Comanche, Arapahoe, and other tribes – still inflamed the plains stretching from Texas into the Dakotas. The southern tribes would not be subdued until around 1875. Shea managed to avoid major trouble with his drives.

Cattleman John Catlow gave Shea some of his early ranching experience. Born in Yorkshire, England, in 1830, Catlow came to the U. S. around 1847. He worked for five years in Massachusetts and then Illinois before heading for California. He engaged in mining there until 1864, when he moved on to Silver City.

In Silver City, Catlow had his finger in many pies, including mines and a butcher shop. The shop led him into the cattle business. He had herds of his own and also acted as agent for other stockmen. In time, he came to own extensive ranch land in southwest Idaho and across the border in Oregon.

David L. Shirk also dealt with Catlow and went on to become a prominent stockman. Shirk was from Indiana, born fifty to sixty miles west of Indianapolis in 1844. The family moved to Illinois when he was eleven. From there, he came west to Silver City in 1866. Within two years, he had proved himself a capable and reliable hand, herding cattle part of the time for George T. Miller. In early 1869, he tended a herd Miller had sold to a Silver City butcher, Phil Kohlhire.

In his reminiscences, Shirk provided a cattleman's view of winterfat, or white sage:

> "This grows to a height of from fourteen inches to four feet, and is excellent forage for horses, cattle, and sheep. I have driven cattle off the range, where white sage was abundant, in the month of January, as fat as I ever saw in the corn fed stalls of Illinois.
>
> … At that time, there was worlds of white sage. During summer, it was green in color, and bore a close resemblance to the old fashioned garden sage, but when the heavy frosts came in early winter, it became as white as snow, and stood from one to two and a half feet high. During summer, stock will not feed upon it, only after the heavy frosts does it become fit for forage."

Late that May, Shirk went to Kohlhire to settle up. The butcher said he had no cash money, but offered him a proposition. Drive a band of 2,500 sheep to a booming mining camp in Nevada. "Take charge of the sheep and sell them and get your money out of them."

Shirk agreed to the deal, although, he admitted, "The sheep business was all new to me. I knew a sheep when I saw one, but that was all. … I was absolutely without experience in handling a large band of range sheep."

He learned on the job extremely well, losing only twenty-five head on the drive. That was almost miraculous, considering the rough country they traversed and all the runoff-swollen streams they had to ford. After completing the deal in Nevada, he returned to Silver City with nearly $16 thousand.

There, he discovered that Kohlhire's creditors had forced him out of business; he was totally broke. When Shirk handed over the sheep money, less the $2,200 due him, the butcher was overcome with emotion. "I then bid him goodbye, but he was unable to speak, merely extending his hand."

"After getting through with that drive, I could hear a sheep bleat for five years. Yet, I do not know of any one engaging in the sheep business, and giving it proper attention, who did not make good. But it is a dog's life at best," Shirk observed. Shirk's experience emphasizes the point that the growth in stock raising was not confined to cattle and horses.

"We are credibly informed that there are five thousand head of sheep now on the way from Honey Lake to this and adjoining markets. They are coming over the Chico route," the *Idaho Statesman* reported in the spring of 1867. (Honey Lake is in northern California near the Nevada border.)

C. B. Wiley, the Oregon pioneer quoted earlier, said, "I put in the summer and fall herding sheep near Camp Lyons, and also sheared the band I was herding. After shearing them I drove them to Elko, Nevada, where I sold them to a butcher. I sold my saddle horse and outfit at Elko and went by way of Winnemucca to San Francisco on the train."

Wiley's comment noted a crucial new factor in the region. About the end of October 1868, the western (Central Pacific) leg of the transcontinental railroad had opened for traffic as far as Winnemucca. Then the Central and Union Pacific tracks met at Promontory, Utah on May 10, 1869.

Perhaps no other region, not directly on the new tracks, felt the impact of the transcontinental railroad as much as Idaho. As mentioned earlier, Idaho's population actually dropped somewhat in the 1870 census compared to 1864. Boise City suffered a far worse decline: from 1,658 to to 995 (roughly a 40 percent loss).

That soon began to change as the relative proximity of the rails took effect, and brought a flood of settlers into Idaho Territory. The total population increased by 84 percent over the next decade and Boise City practically doubled in size.

Stagecoach pioneer John Hailey had much to do with that growth. Two years after starting his stage line into Idaho from Umatilla, Hailey received a mail sub-contract for the route from Boise City to The Dalles. A year after that, he bought the assets of a Salt Lake to Boise City stage line. He then bought out the Oregon sub-contract, giving him rights to a continuous route from Utah to The Dalles.

Then Kelton became the key station for Idaho on the transcontinental railroad. Hailey immediately began offering stage and light freight service from The Dalles to Kelton, called the "Kelton Road." Hailey had a knack for creating effective stagecoach service. He made sure the line had well-chosen tracks through rough country, efficient way stations, and top-grade stock. Best of all for customers, his coaches had a reputation for running on time.

It seems somehow fitting that one of the earliest of the new settlers into Idaho worked on the railroad. John and Emma Turner, a young English couple, actually witnessed the "Golden Spike Ceremony." John had been a laborer on the eastern leg of the rails, the couple moving from camp to camp. They decided to continue on to Oregon.

First, they traveled to Boise City, where they could spend the winter. Years later, their daughter Adelaide Turner Hawes explained how chance acted to change their plans. Relaxing in a saloon, John overheard some surveyors talking about a valley south of the Snake where "the grass was as tall as a man on horseback, deer and antelope grazed on the hillsides in the winter, the river was full of salmon, and also beaver, otter and mink were there."

They decided to check it out and arrived in sight of the valley on September 5, 1869. In her sometimes flowery history, Hawes put stirring words in her father's mouth: "This is the Bruneau Valley – 'the Valley of Tall Grass' – the little paradise we are looking for, and here we will stay."

The Turners planted barley their first year and began to accumulate cattle. Later they would replace the bunchgrass with alfalfa. After over a half-century, both husband and wife were laid to rest in the valley. A stone monument erected by their son and daughter identified them as "The first settlers in Bruneau Valley."

That was not quite accurate, although they were indeed the first permanent white settlers. The following spring they purchased a place from John Baker, whom Hawes identified as a "squaw man." He had built a log cabin on the east side of the Bruneau River for his Indian wife and their three boys. He had even improved his homestead with a well and irrigation ditch. John and Emma Turner's success started from that homestead.

**Rancher and Later State Senator
Arthur Pence**

A neighbor of theirs was Iowan Arthur Pence. Born near Des Moines in 1847, Arthur came west around 1864. He found work where he could in the Boise Valley, but spent most of the next few years driving stage. One of the routes passed near the Bruneau Valley, which led him to explore the area further. In April 1869, he filed there on what is still known as Pence Hot Springs. Eventually, Pence built a two-room log house to prove his claim, and ran cattle in partnership with his brother Joseph C. Pence.

Three years older than Arthur, Joseph joined the Union army and saw considerable action in the Civil War, including the capture of Vicksburg. Like his brother, Joseph freighted in the west after his discharge. In 1869, in addition to his venture with Arthur in Idaho, he established a cattle business in Nevada.

Although no documented genealogical link exists between the Bruneau Pences and Peter Pence, Hawes wrote that Arthur's nephew "worked five years for his Uncle Pete Pence of Payette."

Oddly enough, Dave Shirk also appeared in the Bruneau area about this time, right after his sheep herding venture. Shirk said, "On September 30, 1869, who should I meet in Silver City, but my old friend and employer, George T. Miller, who had just returned from Texas. He had driven a large band across the plains and had located them on the Bruno [sic] River and came in for supplies."

Shirk accepted a job offer to help winter Miller's herd. Miller had not built any kind of shelter, so he and Shirk camped out. They allowed the cattle to graze near the Bruneau "and the white sage plains between that stream and Duck Valley."

The following year, two more settlers arrived in the Bruneau Valley. One was Tennessean "Captain" George W. Hill. Hill had been a Forty-Niner and then moved on to Silver City, Idaho Territory, in the early Sixties. Finally, he tired of prospecting and established a ranch in the Valley, on the south side of the river. As soon as it was a going concern, he returned to Tennessee, married, and brought his wife back to Idaho.

Benjamin F. Hawes also arrived in the Valley about this time. Hawes had come to Idaho early in the gold rush and then turned to farming and stock raising near Boise City in 1864. After five years of steady growth, his herds became too large for the Boise spread. In the meantime, he returned to Ohio and married. She came west when she could ride the railroad into Utah. (Their son Joseph became the husband of Adelaide Turner, "the first white girl born in Bruneau Valley.") In the spring of 1870, Hawes built a home in the Valley and claimed range near Big Springs.

As described in the previous chapter, California was then in a switch from cattle ranching to crop growing. That pushed stockmen into Nevada and Idaho, and fueled the expansion of Idaho's stock raising industry. Oregon would soon see a similar impact.

In 1867, newspapers there reported that many thousands of cattle and sheep had been driven out "the southern portal" and into California. Most came from Oregon, but some also started from southeast Idaho. However, Oregon's Willamette Valley soon followed California's lead and stockmen began to relocate to ranges east of the Cascades. That indirectly impacted available grazing areas further east, including Idaho.

Nonetheless, the rapid growth of Idaho herds soon turned the Territory from consumer to a supplier of livestock for outside markets.

Bruneau Valley Pastures

CHAPTER EIGHT: FILLING IN THE GAPS

Moonlight threw long ebony shadows from the willow clumps and tall cotton-woods along the nearby stream. The stagecoach pitched sideways as a front wheel dropped into a pothole, then jolted back alarmingly when the wheel ground over a stone. The driver cursed routinely while the traveler on the seat beside him reset his perch.

The discomfort up here was nothing compared to the crush of eight burly inside passengers, all heavily dressed against the nighttime chill. Yet, exposed on the top seat, one passenger had commented, "Even my good reliable blankets felt as though they had lost some of their fleece."

Thankfully, the moon-glow somewhat eased their passage through the notorious Portneuf Canyon, scene of far too many holdups and killings. Of the canyon and its skulking banditti, Nathaniel Langford wrote, "Nature seems to have endowed it with extraordinary facilities for encouraging and protecting this dangerous class of the community."

Thus, an epitaph read, "In memory of Charles Phelps of St. Lawrence Co., New York, Driver on the Overland Stage Line who was mortally wounded July 16, 1873 in an attack on his coach by highwaymen in Portneuf Canyon, Idaho, and died the following day. Age 43 years. He fell as all heroes fall, while answering to his duty's call."

In 1871, much traffic to Montana still originated at the railway station in Corinne, Utah. They had left early the previous morning, bouncing and grinding their way north into Idaho. Every ten to fifteen miles, they pulled into changing stations, where their jaded animals gave way to a fresh four-horse team.

After forty or fifty miles the stage line grudged them a half hour to eat at a home station. Basic fare included boiled beans, salt pork, sourdough biscuits, and lots of coffee. At Malad City, the landlady had enlivened the menu with beef from the nearby "rich and extensive pastures."

Constant pounding on the wooden seat had bruised the traveler's buttocks, and his back and shoulders ached from the jerks and jars of their passage. Thumps, bangs, rattles, and squeals accompanied every motion. Exhausted, he'd nodded off several times, only to pop awake in seconds, frantically clutching the side rail.

Amazingly, when the moon first rose high above, the driver had him "finger the ribbons" – drive the stage – and dozed off. For an hour or so, only the wildest bumps roused the man to regain his upright, swaying position.

Powdery dust clung everywhere, making it uncomfortable even to blink. One disgruntled stagecoach passenger remarked, "Dust, deep and thick, is the staple production of this country. Our condition is more easily imagined than described."

The morning glow began to ease into dawn when they exited the Canyon and turned north. They traversed the Indian reservation in late morning, passing the Army's Fort Hall and the homestead of Nels Just shortly thereafter. The old Fort Hall location had been susceptible to flooding and the main Virginia City road had settled further east. Thus, in 1870 the Army established their post twenty to twenty-five miles northeast of the old spot.

The stage rolled into Taylor's Crossing shortly after sunset. The station wasn't much: mainly a barn, blacksmith shop, and trading post. It also had the Eagle Rock post office with Robert Anderson as postmaster. In 1865, the Andersons had also established the private Anderson Brothers Bank (the fourth bank in the state).

Talk in the region focused on one question. How long before the railroad came north through Idaho to Montana? To lessen his dependence on tolls and station service revenues, Matt Taylor bought a thousand head of high quality heifers in Missouri during the spring of 1871.

He then had his cousin Samuel F. Taylor and Sam's younger brother Ike trail them to his range, southeast of Eagle Rock. According to local historian (and Idaho Falls mayor, and Idaho governor) Barzilla Clark, "These were the first cattle brought into this country."

To maintain the herd's quality, Matt also purchased a rail carload of thoroughbred Shorthorn bulls and had them shipped to Corinne. There they were offloaded for the drive north.

The following year, Sam built a cabin on the plain north and a bit west of Taylor Mountain. The brothers then bought another thousand head of cattle in Missouri and trailed them to their range. Sam and Ike's "SI" stock brand was the first used in the Upper Snake River Valley.

Also in 1872, Matt Taylor sold his part of the bridge and station enterprise to the Anderson brothers and went into the cattle business full time, feeling that had better prospects. The three Taylors teamed up to winter their herds on "The Island," at the confluence of Henry's Fork and the main Snake River.

Although Matt soon became "a large operator," he may have also begun expanding his holdings back in Missouri. By the mid- to late-1870s, Matt and his family lived back in Missouri. Sam, however, went on to play a role in the further development of Idaho.

In 1873, Orville Buck and his family arrived in Idaho. Both natives of Maine, he and his wife Helen had spent a decade in Connecticut before heading west. Helen's mother, Jane (Standish) Heald, was the many-times-removed granddaughter of Myles Standish, the prominent Mayflower pioneer.

The Bucks had originally planned to purchase an outfit in Corrine and follow the Trail to Oregon. However, news of good land closer to hand led them to Eagle Rock in August. Buck purchased a small cattle herd, starting a long tradition of Buck family ranching in the area.

The following spring, Buck and George Heath, an acquaintance he had met in Marsh Valley, also homesteaded on Willow Creek. There, with irrigation from the creek, the two showed that the plain was suitable for growing wheat.

Of course, while pioneers began to build herds north of Blackfoot, quite extensive operations already occupied lands further south. For example, French émigré Alexander Toponce ranged cattle in the area. Toponce, who had freighted through eastern Idaho like Matt Taylor, proved to be a born entrepreneur. Entirely without formal education, he would try his hand at anything that promised a profit.

In his *Reminiscences*, he mentioned a Salt Lake boot and shoe store called the "Big Boot" because of its huge boot-shaped street sign. Over a period of time, Toponce "acquired an interest" in the store's inventory. Then the LDS church decreed that "Mormons should patronize only Mormon stores," which the Big Boot was not.

Stymied, the owner closed the store and held his goods until the spring of 1871, when he and Toponce shipped them to Denver. From there, part of the merchandise continued to Texas, where an agent traded for nine thousand longhorns. In fact, according to a letter-writer to the *Idaho Statesman* (June 10, 1871), "thirteen thousand head of cattle left the Brazos river, Texas, on the 13th of April, *en route* for Idaho."

The writer does not identify who acquired the extra four thousand. Toponce's cattle were driven to near Denver, where he and his partner could inspect them. Toponce said, "In the spring of 1872, we trailed most of the cattle to Idaho and rented pasture on the Fort Hall Indian Reservation. We established our own ranch on 'Toponce Creek,' near Chesterfield."

The partners paid a relative pittance for nearly 1.8 million acres, well over half the Reservation. They also sold beef to the Indian Agent for distribution on the Reservation. The experienced and level-headed Toponce had no qualms about hiring Indians riders for herding and drives.

Longhorns on the Move

In a way, Toponce's Idaho cattle venture formed a bridge between his days as a freighter and his later endeavors as a land and mining speculator, race promoter, branch stage line operator, and more. He easily foresaw that the railroad would, sooner or later, preempt main-line freight and passenger service. His "take" on the wide-open railroad construction camps was equally clear-eyed. He wrote, "It seemed for a while as if all the toughs in the west had gathered there. ... It was not uncommon for two or three men to be shot or knifed in a night."

Conrad Kohrs also grazed cattle in the same general area. His cowboys routinely ran drives from Montana though east Idaho. At some point, one of his most-trusted cattle bosses claimed some range there. The location was "on the west side of Snake River," below the mouth of the Portneuf River, "some distance above American Falls."

In late fall 1872, a Kohrs partner moved about a thousand head of Texas cattle onto the range. Unfortunately, they suffered higher than expected winter losses. Kohrs decided against adding another thousand head to that spread in 1873.

The following year, two more Kohrs herds trailed through the Snake River valley. They may well have staged at the Idaho ranch. Late that summer, Kohrs sold the Snake River property.

Others eagerly took his place, sometimes via some odd routes.

"Colonel" Dudley H. Snyder and his younger brother John were prominent Texas drovers. They had trailed herds to New Mexico, Colorado, Kansas and Nebraska.

They sponsored a drive in 1872 that would have a notable outcome. The brothers had an experienced hand, John Sparks, trail a herd to where the Utah-Nevada border meets southern Idaho. He made the delivery to one John Tinnin. Tinnin may have already been associated with cattleman Jasper Harrell. Harrell, Tinnin, and Sparks would play major roles in the future of Mountain West cattle ranching. Nor were the Snyders done with Idaho.

Despite its relative isolation, national and international events still impacted the Territory. Analysts blame risky financial investing as the underlying cause for the "Panic of '73." Railroads were the "hot" industry, but speculators chased many wild notions.

The bubble was bound to burst sometime. However, the main trigger was probably the "demonetization" of silver. The dominos began falling in Europe, as Germany transitioned to the gold standard. In May 1873, the Vienna Stock Exchange crashed and banks began to fail all over Europe.

The United States switched to the gold standard in February 1873, when the Coinage Act suspended government silver purchases. It also did away with all silver coinage except for "trade dollars" used in dealing with China. As in Europe, taking silver out of circulation created a "tight money" climate. Coupled with the fallout from the Continent, U.S. banks began to fail in September.

While all that was happening, the Snyder brothers drove a herd into Wyoming. However, the financial crisis had swept west and they found no market for their cattle. After a costly wintering, they trailed the herd into Utah, but their prospective buyer defaulted. Finally, they turned the herd north. There, they secured a contract to supply beef to the Fort Hall Indian Reservation. Records indicate that "They delivered twenty-five beefs a week to the reservation, with the rest of their cattle ranging as far west as Rock Creek on the Snake River Plains."

Cattle and sheep ranches further south continued to grow. In one sense, the Panic helped populate the Territory, as victims of the recession sought new opportunities in the West. Some found land to claim while others took jobs to support the new ranch and farm economy.

The southeast Idaho settlements were now known to be in Idaho Territory. A survey in 1872 proved that the border ran south of all those Mormon colonies around Malad City, Preston, Franklin, and so on.

Shortly, a new venture would enhance Franklin's status. The Utah Northern Railroad had been formally organized in August 1871. Soon, the company began laying track north from near Brigham City, Utah.

The railroad was basically a creature of the Mormon Church. The company selected John W. Young, one of Brigham Young's sons, as president and superintendent. Also, Mormon settlers along the route performed the grading work with their own teams and equipment. (They received company stock rather than cash wages.) An experienced crew then laid the ties and rails.

To reduce expenses, they built the Utah Northern as a narrow gauge railway. Especially in mountainous country, building a narrow gauge roadbed is substantially cheaper than standard gauge. This did mean, however, that goods needed to be transferred from standard gauge cars running on the transcontinental railway.

The line connected Ogden to Franklin on May 2, 1874 and passenger service began the following month. However, the aforementioned Panic of '73 crippled the company's financing. It would be some years before the rails pushed further north. Franklin quickly became the preferred starting point for hundreds of freight wagons headed to Montana.

Elsewhere, stock raisers filled existing grazing areas and explored new ones. That included settlers and stockmen spreading up the Goose Creek watershed, further west from Raft River.

Until now, stockmen had only trailed cattle across the area from Raft River and Marsh Basin to the Bruneau Valley. In 1871, Arthur D. Norton and partner Miles Robinson imported three or four hundred head of Texas cattle and set them to grazing around Rock and Cottonwood creeks.

Born west of Rochester, New York, in 1841, Arthur Norton graduated from the University of Rochester. He studied medicine for two years, but poor health sent him to Idaho in 1867. He and his partner built a store in the Snake River Canyon, not far from today's Murtaugh.

The sale of that store financed their venture into cattle. They built a home ranch on Cottonwood Creek, a few miles west of Rock Creek Station. Their venture proved that there was more than enough bunchgrass among the clumps of sagebrush to fatten cattle.

The following year, Jasper Harrell moved a herd of three or four thousand cattle onto Big and Trout creeks, a few miles inside Idaho and twenty-five to thirty miles due south of Rock Creek Station. Harrell and his foreman, James E. Bower, knew the range in Nevada and northwest Utah well, but "knew nothing of the country to the north."

Then, according to pioneer Charlie Walgamott, the foreman decided to scout north toward the Snake River Valley. Walgamott said, "Bower rode into the valley and was surprised to find signs of cattle." He had happened upon the Norton-Robinson herd. Later, Bower talked with Norton, who told him about the proximity of Rock Creek Station on the main stage line from Kelton, Utah to Boise City.

The only male among seven siblings, Charles Walgamott came west from Iowa in 1875, when he was seventeen years old. He joined his sister and brother-in-law Charles Trotter at Rock Creek Station in August.

Speaking of the land the stockmen had discovered, he wrote, "The condition of the range in the mountains was ideal. There was an over-abundance of pure sparkling water flowing from many springs and creeks with virgin grass and vegetation in the mountain parks and coulees that would yield two to three tons to the acre if cut. Sagebrush was unknown in the mountains except on the low dry ridges, and there only in small shaggy growth"

Harrell recognized the potential right away. He "immediately commenced bringing in more cattle from Texas." His Idaho-Nevada herds would grow to be some of the largest in the west. He and the Cottonwood stockmen did not, however, have the range to themselves for long. By 1875, several large Nevada cattle operations had decided their ranges were too crowded. Many moved herds into southern Idaho, occupying land from the upper Raft River across to the upper Owyhee, and on into southeast Oregon.

The Owyhee area was already suffering its own growing pains. David Shirk accumulated enough capital in 1871 to go partners with his previous employer, George T. Miller, on a drive from Texas. In March, he and a third partner, Sol Walters, met with Miller to gather fifteen hundred longhorns, 250 of which belonged to Shirk. All helped trail the herd to Idaho, with Miller providing the chuckwagon, other equipment, and supplies.

By now, Shirk was an experienced and knowledgeable stockman. About a week after they passed through Fort Worth, they encountered a tremendous prairie storm. Shirk's account is graphic.

"About nine o'clock, and while the cattle were all lying down, snug and contented, big drops began falling, and a tremendous roar announced the approach. As the storm struck us, accompanied by wind, rain, and hail, the cattle began to drift. I was in the lead holding them back as best I could. ... The rain came down in torrents, and it was so dark that one could not see one's hand before his face save when vivid flashes of lightening lit up the surrounding gloom."

Fortunately, the cattle didn't bolt, but they did continue to move along with the storm. He went on, "After an hour of such, the storm subsided in a measure, and the flashes were less frequent. We could see nothing."

Then he and his horse stumbled off a high embankment into a rapidly rising creek. He quickly discovered that the opposite bank was equally steep.

"Feeling my way, I ventured down the stream and reached what appeared to be an island. But the water was rising rapidly. ... The flashes of lightening had ceased and I was in total darkness. Thinking I possibly might be heard, I called loudly, but the only answer was the wind and rushing of the waters.

"After an interminable period of waiting, the clouds began to break away, and day soon began streaking the horizon." Surveying the stream bottomland, Shirk concluded that "All that saved me was the cessation of the storm. ... The cattle had held together, but we were about five miles from camp, cold, wet, and hungry."

Further storms met them as they trailed the herd north. They arrived in Idaho in September and divided the herd a month later. Miller and Walters took their share to the Bruneau Valley, while Shirk headed toward range he knew further west.

Shirk said, "The next day found me behind my own herd of cattle, my own boss, void of all cares and responsibilities save those of my own making, and no one to lean against except D. L. Shirk."

Rancher David Shirk

Shirk wintered his herd on the Snake, about a mile and a half from the mouth of Rabbit Creek. The following spring, he moved them onto Reynolds Creek. Shirk sold some calves separately, and then the older animals to a larger operator. The final settling-up left him over $7 thousand ahead. His comment: " 'A very fair profit', you will say. But when one considers the risk, dangers of the drive, and the risk of losing every dollar you had in the world, not to mention life itself, the profits were not unreasonable."

Shirk arranged financing for yet another drive, then spent the winter with family in Illinois. He went to Texas in the spring of 1873 to buy just under two thousand head of cattle. When he talked to the agent, the man said, "I have up to this date contracted for 100,000 head of cattle, and have 42,000 cattle between here and the Leond River all ready for the road iron."

Shirk's herd arrived at the Bruneau Valley in October. In less than two weeks, he sold the cattle to John Catlow for cash and a six-month note. Catlow owned a Silver City butcher shop. Shirk first kept the cattle on winter range southeast of Silver City. Then he and his brother held them southwest of town until late summer. Finally, Con Shea took possession for Catlow and moved them to range along the Idaho-Oregon border.

Within a couple years, Shirk had established his own ranch in Oregon, having concluded that the Owyhee region in Idaho lacked room for the ranch he wanted.

About the same time, Shea also went into ranching for himself, although he still owned a sawmill and parts of some other businesses. He ran his cattle on Cow Creek, which rises in Idaho, and established his ranch headquarters about a mile over into Oregon. Con eventually became one of the most prominent cattlemen in Owyhee County and eastern Oregon.

As noted earlier, Miller and Walters brought their Texas cattle to the Bruneau Valley in 1871. There, they established a headquarters for the "T" ranch. According to Adelaide Hawes, theirs was the first large ranch based in the Valley. Others would soon join them. One of those was Dan Murphy, who established a headquarters near the hot springs where the Valley constricts into Bruneau Canyon. In time, Murphy would earn the sobriquet, "Cattle King of Idaho" for the many thousands he owned.

Another who found space for a ranch in southwest Idaho was Michael Hyde, a native of Rome, New York. Gold fever fired his imagination at a young age (he was six in 1849). His father finally gave him the money to go west in 1863. He took the seaborne and Panama crossing route and arrived almost broke. In California, he worked on the railroad for awhile, then found employment in the Virginia City, Nevada mines. He continued on to Silver City two years later. Mike rose rapidly in the mines there and, in 1868, had attained a foreman's position at the "Golden Chariot" mine.

One of the Golden Chariot owners was Hill Beachy, well known for his pursuit of the Magruder killers. The mine became famous as the antagonist to the "Ida Elmore" company in the ill-famed "Owyhee War." The firms had claims to silver and gold quartz ledges that ran deep into War Eagle Mountain.

When their tunnels met far down in the ridge, the confrontation escalated into an underground shooting war. The exchanges became so heavy that an eyewitness asserted that one 15-inch supporting beam had been "nearly cut in two" by bullet impacts.

Finally, the governor asked John R. McBride, Chief Justice of the Idaho Territorial Supreme Court, to investigate and try to mediate. On March 28 the governor also issued a proclamation that said, in part, "the lawless proceedings of the parties referred to, must cease and peace and order be restored" or they would feel the full weight of Territorial authority.

A Deputy U.S. Marshal rushed on horseback to Silver City with the proclamation. When Judge McBride arrived, he learned "with great pleasure, that the two parties had just agreed upon a compromise."

But soon, opposing viewpoints exchanged hot words. It is known that a Chariot supporter shot one of the Elmore owners, supposedly because the other was about to brain him with a rough walking stick. An Elmore partisan then shot the Chariot man in the arm. Beachy, his partner and manager George W. Grayson, and some other Golden Chariot men barely managed to prevent a lynching. The Elmore owner died within three hours. The Chariot man survived an amputation but died from gangrene several agonizing weeks later.

Contemporary records do not describe Mike Hyde's possible role in the Owyhee War. We do know that by 1871 he had invested in a ranch near the upper reach of Catherine Creek. He immediately began stocking it with cattle purchased from Texas drives as well as local ranchers.

Four years after his start, he brought his brother David into the business. Eleven years younger than Mike, Dave rode the railroad to Winnemucca in 1872. He then worked in the Silver City mines for three years. Hyde Brothers Cattle Company became one of the largest stock raisers in the Owyhee Country.

Richard H. Bennett also amassed his ranching stake in the mines. Born in Cornwall, England, in 1850, Richard and two brothers emigrated to the U. S. in 1868. They found their way to Silver city after three years in the Pennsylvania coal mines. Richard worked in the mines for over a decade, while also raising cattle on the side. He married in 1878 and began to pay more attention to his stock holdings. Within a few years, Bennett had a respectable herd.

The expanding herds of Miller & Walters, Catlow, Murphy, Hyde Bros., and many others provided considerable beef for the Owyhee mines. Moreover, cattlemen were now trying to upgrade their stock.

Texas longhorn cattle of the time were very hardy, hardy enough to tolerate a ranching system that made almost no provision for their health and well being. These cattle had adapted to an often-harsh environment where only the strong survived.

Stockmen had to balance that fact against some severe deficiencies. Probably the breed's greatest faults were its slow growth rate and relatively small weight, compared to "English" breeds. Even fully-grown longhorns did not pack a lot of beef. Some claimed they were more bone than meat. Finally, longhorns did not produce a lot of creamy milk to make butter and cheese.

An article in the *Owyhee Avalanche* of July 27, 1872 described one rancher's attempts to improve the herds. The reporter had visited the Cow Creek ranch of William F. Sommercamp, about sixteen miles from Silver City. He noted that Sommercamp had imported four Durham bulls from Illinois.

"They are decidedly the finest looking band that we have seen for many a year," the reporter said. "Three of the bulls are two years old and one is a year old."

After explicitly listing the bulls' pedigrees, he noted that the cattle dealers, Hoffer & Miller, and stockman Sommercamp "deserve great credit for the importation of these short-horns, which are generally the greatest favorites for fine beef and dairy purposes, because of their large size and early maturity."

He closed with the remark that, " It costs no more to raise superior beef cattle, milk cows and work oxen, than it does poor, and we are proud and pleased at the progress our stock men are making in the right direction."

Still, despite the growing and improving herds, market forces led to some oddities. The *Owyhee Avalanche* published (October 18, 1873) the following item:

> "V. Blackinger, of the War Eagle Hotel, has returned from Oregon, having succeeded in purchasing some 400 head of cattle in Powder River and Grande Ronde valleys. He left his son Frank behind to bring up the drove, which they will winter at Rabbit Creek. Mr. Blackinger will immediately build a slaughterhouse near the mouth of Webfoot gulch, and engage in the butchering business."

In other words, the normal surplus from local herds could not meet the demand at a reasonable price. Just over a year later, however, "eight hundred head of cattle from Owyhee County, Idaho, were sent to San Francisco by rail." Moreover, historian Orin Oliphant observed that in 1874 "a hundred horses, mostly brood mares from Idaho, arrived in Mohave County, Arizona."

Late that year, the railroad "finished its cattle corral at Winnemucca" to further encourage shipments from Owyhee County. If Mountain West ranchers could somehow satisfy that demand, the possibility of shipping beef East beckoned. Thus, stockmen all across southern Idaho had good reason to explore all the potentially usable range they could find.

Nor was it all about just cattle … recall Shirk's earlier experience herding sheep. The family of Robert Noble emigrated from England to Canada in 1854, when he was ten years old. Three years later, the family moved to New York state. Robert served in the Civil War until his discharge in 1865, then spent five years farming in Illinois. After four years hustling for a stake in California and then Idaho, in 1874 Noble established a sheep ranch on Reynolds Creek. In time, he would own one of the largest sheep operations in Owyhee County.

Norman S. Hubbell also established a substantial sheep ranch. Hubbell first came to Idaho for the Boise Basin rush. After knocking around for five years as a freighter, miner, and in other work, he moved on to Oregon, and did not return until 1873.

After unsuccessful attempts to establish meat markets in Boise City and the Wood river area, Hubbell went into sheep raising west of Boise. Years later, he turned day-to-day operation over to his son Walton. At that point, the flock contained eight to nine thousand head.

Like the more farsighted cattlemen, sheepmen also began to consider the pedigree of their stock. They paid particular attention to how well the animals adapted to range conditions in the Territory. One sign of progress was the following announcement in the *Idaho Statesman* (October 8, 1872) that said, "Premium List of the Ada County Agricultural Society, for the First Annual Fair, to be held at Boise City, I. T., 1872."

The Live Stock Department of the Fair had Divisions for horses and mules, cattle, sheep, hogs, and chickens. Another Department had awards for "Products of the Soil" (grains, potatoes, onions, fruits, flowers, etc.). Their third Department covered "Domestic Manufacture and Home" (butter, breads, pickles, needlework, mineral samples, oil painting, blacksmith work, boot and shoe work, etc.).

A year later, the *Statesman* included the announcement (September 23, 1873) that "Notice is hereby given that the fair of the Ada County Agricultural Society will be held at the Boise City Race Course the 2nd, 3rd, and 4th days of October."

Ranching along the Payette and Weiser rivers also expanded. Although Henry C. Riggs had helped found Boise City, he sold his livery stable there in 1871. He then moved his family to a homestead nine miles northwest of Emmett. Riggs began raising cattle there along the Payette River. He eventually had a major holding, and two of his sons operated a meat market in Emmett.

In the late 1860s, John F. T. Basye had taken up land in the area. By 1870, he had built a house and barn, and established the beginnings of a dairy operation. Starting in the spring of 1872, he and his wife drove their herd of milk cows to the vicinity of Idaho City. There, they sold milk and butter to Basin inhabitants. They'd drive the herd back to their homestead in late fall.

Irishman Daniel Regan was another pioneer in the area. He and his family located a ranch northwest of Emmett. Local historian Ruth Lyon noted that they "became successful with their livestock project, and some of the largest cattle shipments from this part of the country were made by them."

One way or another, by the mid-Seventies, cattle had begun to fill the country west of Boise and between the Snake and the hills north of the Payette. Mrs. Jacob Stroup came west from Missouri as an eighteen-year-old bride in 1873. Crossing Idaho along the Kelton to Boise route, she found it hard to adjust: "The county looked desolate, uninhabited, and to my mind was wild and terrifying."

They settled in the Washoe area, south of where the Payette joins the Snake. At first, the emptiness, and roving Indians terrified her. One of Mrs. Stroup's observations tells a lot about the state of the country when they first arrived. She said, "Mosquitoes at this time were a terrible pest. The valley was full of wild cattle that stamped and pawed of evenings, raising clouds of dust to rid themselves of the mosquitoes that literally covered their hides. I dared not venture out among the cattle, used only to seeing a man on horseback. I stayed close to my little house."

Rangeland was also filling up in central Idaho, sometimes with results that portended trouble for the future.

Pioneers had steadily expanded their operations on the southern Camas Prairie. This greatly distressed the Indians on the Fort Hall Reservation, who had been promised that they could continue to forage there. In fact, they depended upon the camas to supplement the too-often-inadequate rations provided at the Reservation. In 1871, Indian leaders reported that some whites had brought hogs onto the Prairie. As the number of porkers grew, the natives found more of their precious camas beds ripped up.

Herds had also grown further east in the Salmon-Lemhi area. By 1872, pioneers John and Sandy Barrack ranged about eighteen hundred cattle in the foothills southeast of Salmon City. The following year, a rancher took up a location in the valley of the Pahsimeroi River.

Storekeeper George L. Shoup also found himself in the cattle business in a big way. The placers around Leesburg and deeper in the mountains were running out of "easy" gold. That depleted the supply of money – gold dust – in the region. Plus, Salmon City suffered impacts from the Panic of '73 and the resulting national depression. Shoup's store was one of only two that hung on, selling miners and ranchers necessities on credit, or accepting stock in lieu of cash.

Shoup had started his cattle business with two experienced livestock handlers. The herd swelled as the economy soured, so Shoup located a ranch about six miles north and a little east of Salmon City. Within three years, the herd outgrew the limited forage in that area. Shoup found unoccupied range in the upper Pahsimeroi Valley and on the Little Lost River.

Despite the recession, ranchers and settlers had claimed much of the Salmon - Lemhi - Pahsimeroi region by 1875. The ready markets for the stock were the mining camps, even with the setbacks they had suffered. Many years later, Colonel Shoup's son commented wryly that cattle drives to the camps were "one of the diversions of Salmon City."

Salmon City, ca 1870

The lead cowboy glanced back at the band of about a dozen beeves. The boys had them pretty well bunched, right now, and their lowing seemed calm enough. The broad, dusty street spread out ahead, the surface churned and scarred by their first run. That had gone well. They'd rushed the cattle through town right to the watering place just below the one-lane toll bridge. The river was down, so the swim over had been uneventful.

Off to the right, a hotel clerk stuck his head out the door, then called to someone inside. Probably warning them about this band. On the left side, a blacksmith turned from a shoeing job and draped his arms over the rail fence. Drinkers in the saloons on and near Main Street were probably rubber-necking out the narrow windows. This could be better entertainment than a bar fight.

A Chinese man exited Shoup's general store and scurried toward their riverside enclave downstream from the bridge. Not good; could upset the herd. The cowboy waved back for a pause until the little man was out of sight. To the west, beyond the river, the Salmon River ranges formed a massive backdrop. The snow had long since melted from the tops, but soon the early storms would arrive. This might be their last drive to the mining camps for the season.

The cowboy eased to the side and called for the riders to start the rush. The cattle commenced a shambling trot. The herders wanted to hurry the stock through before they spooked at the strange surroundings. They almost made it. Perhaps the blood smell from the Main and Terrace butcher shop did it. Who could know? Wild-eyed steers scattered in every direction.

A half hour later, the cowboys and their blown horses had the band re-assembled on a meadow south of town. After a moment, the boss realized they were short one and sent men to check the bushes. Down by the Lemhi seemed likely.

Back in town, a housewife walked over to the livery stable. She asked if one of the men could come check her cellar. She was hearing strange noises. One man said it was probably just rats, but he'd come and chase them out.

The typical pioneer cellar was simply a big hole in the back yard roofed with split rails and straw. The roof was then covered with sod and grass, and perhaps a few bushes. The Good Samaritan threw back the sloping outside hatch, descended the stairs, and opened the bottom door.

Inside, he came face-to-face with a maddened, snorting longhorn. Fear lent him wings. He flew up the stairs in two giant steps and leaped aside as his angry pursuer lunged by. The son's history noted, "The steer had started to cross over the cellar and had fallen through, unseen, and no one had noticed the hole through which he had fallen."

Eventually, stock raising would become the mainstay of the regional economy.

A similar occupancy of available grazing lands took place in the north, although perhaps not to the same extent. Iowan Phillip S. Smith had emigrated to Oregon at the age of fifteen with his mother, in 1853. Soon orphaned, he tried his hand at mining in California, and then in Idaho, mostly in the north. He ran a pack train until about 1871. That year, he took up a claim on the Camas Prairie and began a mixed stock raising and farming operation. The following year, he married a Nez Percés woman.

Stockmen and settlers also pushed further north, augmenting the small stations on the trail to the Kootenai mines. Pioneers had already started cattle ranches on the high plain ten miles or so northeast of Lewiston, and in 1871-72 settlers and more stockmen followed. By 1875, the town of Genesee had sprung up.

Twenty to twenty-five miles north of Lewiston, people were moving into Paradise Valley. Almon A. Lieuallen played a major role in that growth. Born in Tennessee, Lieuallen moved to Walla Walla in 1867, when he was twenty-five. There, he developed a thriving freight outfit and a considerable stock ranch. Then, the *Illustrated History of North Idaho* (published 1903) noted, "In 1871 he brought forty thousand dollars worth of cattle to the region now embraced in Latah county, taking a pre-emption four miles east from where Moscow now stands."

Lieuallen's enterprise flourished. He homesteaded the future site of Moscow in 1875 and opened a general store there.

A year after Lieuallen arrived, I. C. Matheny trailed "a large band of horses and cattle from the Willamette Valley into the Paradise Valley." A year after that, Charles W. Palmer arrived. Palmer, a native of South Bend, Indiana, had spent two years in Nebraska before traveling further west to settle in the Valley. Besides his agricultural interests, Palmer focused on horse raising. At one point he would have as many as three thousand head.

Palmer's stock numbers were relatively unusual for a northern operator. Where stockmen in the south and in nearby Washington State often had thousands of head, those on the Camas Prairie and further north generally ran into the hundreds. Mixed stock and crop-raising homesteads were common. Collectively, however, they raised substantial numbers of cattle, horses, and sheep.

Many pioneers followed that pattern. John Rice was a native Westerner. His parents migrated from Canada to The Dalles in 1844, where John was born a year later. He moved to Camas Prairie in 1871. He settled a few miles north of Mount Idaho and began raising stock while also engaging in "general farming." Later, he ran a livery stable, and then returned to stock raising and farming.

Another settler was James J. Remington, who came from a mechanically gifted family. They included the men who established the famous Remington Arms Company, and his Uncle Lafayette. His uncle later designed and patented a device called the "Best steam traction engine," a power source much used in the agricultural and lumber industries.

In 1871, James' father settled near Cottonwood on Camas Prairie, about seventeen miles northwest of Mount Idaho. There, the family took up farming and stock raising. His parents alternated between Idaho and Oregon over the years, ending in Oregon. James, however, preferred Idaho. His holdings grew to include four hundred acres on the Prairie as well as plots along the Salmon River. On these lands he ran "goodly bands of horses and cattle, and a very large holding in sheep."

Northern stockmen received an early warning about the dangers of their open-range, *laissez faire* approach to their business. The *Illustrated History of North Idaho* said, "The winter of 1874-5 was so severe that thousands of head of cattle perished, bankrupting several stockmen."

By 1875 Idaho stock raisers occupied, to some extent, all but a handful of the worthwhile grazing regions in the state. The "neglected" spots mostly seemed to be useful only as summer range, requiring a long drive to find suitable wintering areas. Idaho stockmen now began to concentrate even more on improving and building up their herds.

> *The Big Picture.* In 1875, the U.S. comprised thirty-seven states. Colorado would join them the following year. Ulysses S. Grant was President, and the nation's population topped 44 million (not quite double what it had been a quarter-century earlier). The previous year, Joseph F. Glidden had patented a new form of barbed wire. This year, production had jumped sixty-fold. Barbed wire would dramatically change western ranching. Horse racing enthusiasts held the first Kentucky Derby at Churchill Downs.

Despite the considerable expansion of Idaho stock raising, there were those who felt the pace was too slow and not properly directed. The editor of the *Idaho Statesman* published (October 8, 1872) a column, labeled "Prosperity." It said, in part, "The difficulty with our people is, we are sending too much money out of the country, and not producing what we ought. We buy too much and sell too little; our money is sent out of the country to pay for articles we should produce or manufacture."

Even some improvements fell short, he felt: "For the last two or three years, there has been a good deal of interest manifested among stock growers, and the business has been largely expanded and improved. But … it is not one-tenth what it should be. We ought to raise $100,000 worth of stock annually to send out of the Territory for sale to our neighbors."

He went on, "It is not the difference in cost alone that we should look to, when introducing manufactories of our own. Giving employment to more people and keeping the money at home as much as possible, is the only judicious plan upon which we can become prosperous."

Some would argue that the *Statesman* wanted them to run before they had mastered walking, but the editor had a point.

With their comparative head start, the states further west found themselves with surplus stock in the Seventies. As early as 1870, a drover purchased a herd of some two thousand sheep in Oregon and trailed them across Idaho into Montana. In 1873, newspapers reported that Montana buyers were seeking cattle, sheep, and horses around Walla Walla. By 1874 and 1875, drovers were trailing thousands of cattle across Idaho to ranges and markets in Wyoming, Colorado, and Nebraska.

Trail herds back-tracking the Oregon Trail through Idaho generally selected one of two routes. The southern route reversed the Trail's southern leg: Shoshone Falls, Goose Creek, Fort Hall, and the Blackfoot River. There, they diverged from the pioneer road, going directly east toward Gray's Lake and on into Wyoming.

The other route crossed the Snake early, veered south of Boise and traced Goodale's Cutoff across Camas Prairie to the Big Lost River north of Big Southern Butte. There, rather than heading southeast toward the Blackfoot River, the herds were driven more directly east toward Eagle Rock. Although the ford north of Eagle Rock could be "somewhat precarious," it avoided the bridge tolls. Swimming the herd during higher water was particularly chancy for animals weakened by the dry trek from Big Lost River. This route rejoined the southern trail near Gray's Lake.

To avoid friction, herds trailing east across Idaho tried to bypass settled areas. However, that still led them through public rangeland that Idaho stockmen considered their own. Although a few local stockmen apparently trailed herds east, it would be a few years before they moved substantial numbers.

Still, both cattle and sheep herds were growing and harbingers of trouble had already risen. The *Idaho Statesman* reported (January 17, 1871) results from the Sixth Session of the Idaho legislature, which passed "An Act restricting the herding of sheep in Oneida county." (At that time Oneida County included all of Idaho south of the Snake River and roughly east of Massacre Rocks.)

The item provided no details, but subsequent Acts excluded sheep grazing within two miles of a cattleman's "possessory claim."

Late the following year a letter-writer to the *Statesman* (December 17, 1872) addressed the issue. Quickly dismissing a less important item, the writer, J. H. Whitson, said, "The people of Ada county, and perhaps other counties need, ask for and demand a relief that is of much more importance than the retrenchment so much talked of. It is a law 'Restricting the herding of sheep,' as in Oneida county, passed by the last legislative Assembly."

Whitson described the problems created when herders tried to have sheep and cattle share a piece of range. "The range must be divided, and the rancher has a right to that nearest him; for no man in this country is ignorant of the fact that sheep will drive all other stock away."

Agitation continued until, finally, the 1875 legislature passed a comparable "Two Mile Limit Law" applicable to Ada, Alturas, and Boise counties. Some years later, the law was extended to include the entire state. In practice, the law banned sheepmen from grazing on any block of range that had a traditional history of being used for cattle.

The *Idaho Statesman* of March 11, 1875 published a letter from some "Citizens" living in the general area of Indian and Ditto Creeks (twenty to twenty-five miles southeast of Boise). They demanded immediate application of the new law to their foothill rangeland. In part, it said:

"Resolved, That in accordance with the law, we declare sheep a nuisance, and notify all owners of sheep and their agents to remove them from Indian Creek and vicinity, according to the bounds fixed by law … "

After explaining the reasoning behind their "resolution", the writer went on, "Now, Mr. Editor, we do not pretend to claim any more right to the government grazing land than the sheep owners have … " Cattlemen, however, had prior claim on this particular range.

Moreover, "Sheep were put on our range last fall: what was the result? The cattle cleared the range quicker that it could be cleared by men and dogs. The cattle were scattered and grew too poor to stand the hard winter, and many of them died."

The battle lines had been drawn.

Idaho Sheep on the Range

CHAPTER NINE: THE LAST STANDS

In June of 1877, Loyal P. Brown had to find life good, although a few clouds peeked over the horizon. In the fifteen years since he bought out Moses Milner's way-station and began promoting the town of Mount Idaho, he had prospered greatly. Of course, he owned the townsite and collected lease payments from others doing business here. Earlier, his political maneuvering had won the county seat of Idaho County for the town. That had fueled further growth.

Not far away, his grist mill could crank out thirty barrels of flour in a long working day, and he also ran stock. But the Mount Idaho hotel, largest structure in town, was the crown jewel of his holdings. Happy customers complimented his hospitality and cuisine: "It is precisely like living at home with a good uncle. The food is choice, abundant and well cooked."

At times, he saw wagons roll onto the dusty street from the tiny settlement three miles north of town. Perhaps it hadn't been wise to deny the Grangers a lot for their new hall. They'd gone instead to rancher John Crooks, who donated some acreage. Now two or three dozen people had settled in the immediate vicinity of the hall. How much competition would the upstart Grangeville be?

Locals who wanted a good meal often parked elsewhere, perhaps by Frank Oliver's blacksmith shop, and visited Montgomery's saloon for a bracer. They knew he never served liquor at the hotel, and never would.

Vollmer & Scott and the other store in town thrived on business from the surrounding farms and ranches, as well as trade with the Nez Percés. Both firms sold freely to the Indians, who were generally peaceable and even helpful. One young pioneer said, "Some of the Indians were quite friendly. One woman, Big Lizzie by name, did mother's washing at times when mother was unable."

The bands often camped six or seven miles to the west near Tolo Lake as they moved between the Clearwater and the Salmon.

Still, everyone knew that tensions had heightened in the two years since President Grant reopened the Wallowa Valley tract in Oregon to settlers. Intense political pressure had forced the President to revoke an earlier executive order that reserved part of the valley for the Indians.

The Nez Percés there would not leave their ancestral lands to crowd into the reservation in Idaho. Their leader, "Hin-mah-too-yah-lat-kekt" or "Thunder Rolling Down the Mountain" – Chief Joseph to most whites – had so promised his dying father, Old Chief Joseph.

Pioneers in north Idaho sensed that trouble was brewing. Seeds for that trouble had been planted by the 1863 Nez Percés treaty.

Somewhat like the Shoshones, Nez Percés leadership consisted of a council of equals. No one band chief had any real power outside his own group. Thus, fifty-eight leaders signed the original 1855 treaty.

Sadly, the two sides had tragically different views of this compact. To white officials, they were magnanimously "granting" the bands most of their traditional lands in the Pacific Northwest. Conversely, the Nez Percés saw the treaty as a recognition of their sovereignty over lands they had roamed long before Europeans arrived on the continent.

Events went smoothly until the gold rushes into Idaho and eastern Washington. In 1863, white officials told the Indians that they intended to reduce the reservation to just the lands stretching from near Lapwai to around Kamiah. The tribes there would have to make room for the other Nez Percés. The fact that these "first stockmen of Idaho" would have no range for their herds meant nothing to the land-grabbers. By this time the tribes had many hundreds of cattle to go with their thousands of horses.

Naturally, the bands that would lose their hereditary domains protested. The heavily Christianized bands in Idaho found the terms agreeable. Officials made much of the notion of curbing "Dreamer" beliefs, rooted in the old Indian ways, but that was merely an excuse.

The chiefs of the bands living in the lower Snake and the Salmon-Wallowa areas refused to sign. That split the Nez Percés into "non-treaty" and "treaty" factions. Over half the fifty-three tribal chiefs refused to sign. Ominously, officials somehow scraped up fifty-one names and signature marks.

Officials had sent along a troop of Oregon Volunteers to "protect the white officials." Their captain said, "Although the treaty goes out to the world as the concurrent agreement of the tribe, it is in reality nothing more than the agreement of Lawyer and his band, numbering in the aggregate not a third part of the Nez Percés tribe."

Amazingly, the non-treaty bands managed to live peacefully with their white neighbors for over a decade. They succeeded despite continuing provocations. Historian Francis Haines unearthed records of over thirty Indians killed by whites in the years leading up to the Nez Percés War. With just one exception, he noted, "There is no record of any punishment and very few instances of the guilty men even standing trial."

Conversely, he found just two confirmed instances of a Nez Percés killing a white man. In two other cases Indians *might* have done the killing. Of the two where details were known, an Indian was tried but acquitted, perhaps on the grounds of self-defense.

This situation worsened even further in the mid-Seventies. More and more settlers moved onto the Nez Percés grazing lands. Non-treaty chiefs, Joseph in particular, demanded that authorities remove the intruders. For them, the 1855 treaty was still in force. That agreement prohibited such incursions. Officials did nothing.

Brigadier General Oliver O. Howard, commander of the Military Department of the Columbia, took all this in. He saw much potential for violence. Howard directed Major H. Clay Wood, a member of his staff, to evaluate the situation from a legal standpoint. Delivered in early 1876, Wood's brief sided with the Indians. One key point stood out: "The non-treaty Nez Percés cannot in law be regarded as bound by the treaty of 1863, and insofar as it attempts to deprive them of the right to occupancy of any land, its provisions are null and void."

The local Indian Agent, John B. Monteith, found Major Wood's conclusions most unwelcome. He was under intense pressure. The Oregon Governor had even gotten involved. Finally, in late 1876 authorities appointed a commission to examine Indian claims to the non-treaty areas. The results were predictable. Because a majority of chiefs had signed the 1863 Treaty, its provisions were binding on all bands.

This decision simply ignored the fact that "a majority" of the signatures could not be valid. Worse yet, the commissioners arbitrarily decreed that the Nez Percés chiefs were subject to the democratic processes used by whites. In reality, the bands were simply a loose confederation linked by family ties and language. Centuries of give-and-take had set the rights, prerogatives, and territories of the different bands. The idea that a so-called "majority" could impose its will on the rest was bizarre and unnatural.

Some white critics noted the injustice of the commission's ruling. Even so, Monteith directed the Army to move the non-treaty bands onto the reservation. The relevant document didn't pull any punches It said, "We recommend the employment of sufficient force to bring them into subjection."

The harsh tone of this (non)-negotiation may well have arisen from recent events in Dakota Territory. That situation had many ironic points in common with what happened in Idaho. Starting in 1874, gold miners invaded the Black Hills. As with the Nez Percés, the U. S. had signed treaties that expressly forbid such intrusions. The various Sioux tribes and Northern Cheyenne demanded that white authorities uphold those treaties.

But even stepped up Army patrols failed to stop the miners. As in Idaho, white officials tried to persuade the Indians to give up the region. The tribes flatly refused to sign away what they considered sacred ground. Unlike with the Nez Percés, negotiators found almost no takers to give the land grab any semblance of legality.

When pushed, the Indians went to war. Then, on June 25, 1876, tribesmen wiped out Custer and his Seventh Cavalry command. That was the context when the negotiators met with Joseph and the other non-treaty chiefs.

In the end, authorities demanded that the bands be on the reservation before mid-June, 1877. After the protracted argument, the Indians had only thirty days to move. That was hardly sufficient for them to assemble and travel over such rough country.

Evidence suggests that Monteith set, or recommended, the unreasonable deadline on purpose.

He felt that the bands could only be acculturated if they gave up their herds and took up farming. Stock raising brought prosperity, thwarting the Agent's ability to control them economically. Worse yet, horses provided mobility. That allowed tribesmen to travel to buffalo country and hunt. Monteith particularly opposed this ability to roam freely east of the Divide. He wrote, "Nothing can be done toward civilizing such, and by their example they keep others from settling down."

The tight deadline compelled the bands to abandon many horses and cattle. Crossing run-off-swollen rivers swept many more away. These material losses – perhaps as many as a thousand head – only sharpened the sense of outrage.

Finally, stressed beyond endurance, three young warriors took revenge on several known Indian haters. That loosed a storm of pent-up anger, fueled by years of broken promises and unpunished white crimes. By the late afternoon of June 14, 1877, vengeful warriors had killed seven settlers, wounded two others, and sent many fleeing for their lives.

Coincidentally, that was about the time General Howard rode into Fort Lapwai, having arrived in Lewiston that morning. At about 6 o'clock, a mounted courier galloped in from Mount Idaho. He carried a long letter from Loyal P. Brown to Captain David Perry, commander of the Fort's cavalry force. Brown had sent the message shortly before the outbreak started. He wrote that many of his neighbors were "very much alarmed at the action of the Indians."

After describing some of the Indians activities, he went on, "I do not feel any alarm, but thought it well to inform you of what was going on among them."

Nonetheless, he felt enough concern to recommend that Perry send "sufficient force" to handle the bands. However, since Brown had

Yellow Wolf, Surviving Nez Percés Warrior

downplayed any "alarm," Howard and Perry decided to only send observers to assess the situation. Two soldiers and the post interpreter left at dawn the next day. They hadn't traveled far when two friendly Nez Percés raced up and broke the news that the non-treaty Indians were killing settlers. Back at the Fort, translation difficulties led to some confusion, for these might be isolated revenge killings rather than a general uprising.

They were still trying to decide on a course of action when two more messengers galloped in. They had started an hour apart, but joined up along the way. Loyal Brown's first note said, in part, "The people of Cottonwood undertook to come here during the night; were interrupted, all wounded or killed. ... One thing is certain: we are in the midst of an Indian war. "

The second message, dispatched at about 8 o'clock that morning, referred to the first courier, and said, "Since that was written the wounded have come in."

After describing the casualties, Brown went on, "The Indians have possession of the prairie, and threaten Mount Idaho. All the people are here, and we will do the best we can."

He then appealed for help, urging the commander to "Hurry up; hurry!"

Howard and Perry knew they must act as fast as possible, with the force they had on hand. That, however, presented a problem. It was apparently not customary to send out their entire cavalry force at the same time. The post only had enough pack animals for one company. Howard sent the Lapwai quartermaster to Lewiston to procure more, but he had not returned by sunset.

Perry refused to wait any longer. He led companies F and H of the 1st Cavalry, over a hundred soldiers, into the gathering darkness of June 15.

With only a few breaks, the column rode through the night and following day. By the time they neared Mount Idaho, Indians had killed another settler. Not wanting the bands to escape, the troop hurried on into the late evening.

The locals had promised to augment Perry's force with twenty-five or thirty volunteers, but only eleven men showed up. The force reached White Bird Summit after midnight and stopped to rest rather than attempt the descent in the dark.

Hoping to retain an element of surprise, Perry issued orders that no fires of any kind be lit. Unfortunately, one trooper unthinkingly struck a match for his pipe. Almost immediately afterwards, they heard a "coyote" howl, with an odd trailing note. A lieutenant felt sure an Indian outpost had discovered them. One private had a more personal reaction. The quivery wail was, he said, "enough to make one's hair stand on end."

Captain Perry roused his command around 4:00 in the morning. Many in the column, including horses, had nodded off where they stood or sat, but certainly no one had gotten a decent amount of sleep.

White Bird Canyon is a huge bowl. Almost a half mile of vertical drop separates the summit from the creek at the bottom. To the west, a steep ridge rises some fifteen hundred feet above the canyon floor to wall it off from the Salmon River gorge. On the south, layers of ridges climb to nearly two thousand feet above the creek. A shoulder some fifteen hundred feet above the floor looms to the east. Beyond that, even taller mountains marched off to the horizon.

The soldiers faced a precipitous trail that meandered along dry stream beds with many side cuts, around boulders, and over sharp rocks. Often, tangled brush hid dangerous drop-offs. A misstep could easily inflict a nasty bruise, strained back, or worse.

After descending the rough trail, Perry's force debouched onto a rugged bench. Close ahead, they found a low ridge, and further off a more defined crest, split by a ravine. Soon, Perry said, "On the more distant of the ridges Lieutenant Theller halted and deployed his advance guard, at the same time sending word that the Indians were in sight."

Joseph and two other prominent chiefs led the Nez Percés. The other two were notable warriors. One them was Chief White Bird, for whom the area was named. Joseph was esteemed for his force of character and eloquence, but did not lead in battle. All still hoped to avoid all-out war. They sent a party forward to parley, but someone shot at them.

While Perry shook his force into line for a charge, the civilians raced ahead around the left. Perhaps they figured to overawe the Nez Percés with a spirited attack, or were simply carried away by the excitement. However, they had badly misjudged their adversaries, who quickly returned fire and launched a well-considered counterattack. Despite their leader's plea to press home the assault, the volunteers hurriedly aborted their helter-skelter rush and scurried back to a knoll to the left of Perry's main force.

White Bird Creek lay about 400 feet lower than the ridge and about a half mile away. Perry surveyed the valley floor. A charge would only push the Indians back into heavy cover along the creek, leaving his mounted troopers wide open to hidden sharpshooters. He decided to take a defensive position on the ridge line and let the Indians come to him.

Unfortunately for Perry's plan, the Nez Percés had no intention of attacking his line head-on. Best estimates suggest that sixty-five to seventy warriors took part in the battle. Some commentators seem surprised by the ferocity and cleverness of their attack. They saw the Nez Percés as a basically peace-loving people. White greed and injustice had pushed them into a desperate response.

Their desperation was real enough, but historical records contradict the pacific image. Recall that when Captain William Clark first met the Nez Percés in September 1805, the "great chief" of that band was off raiding enemies.

During the fur trade era, Donald Mackenzie of the Hudson's Bay Company went to great lengths to keep peace with the tribe. They even tried to promote peace between the Snake River Shoshones and the Nez Percés. The Snakes scoffed at the idea.

Right into the Seventies, tribesmen regularly fought east of the Rockies. There, they joined Crow Indians against the latter's traditional enemies, the Sioux and Cheyenne. Men like White Bird and Joseph's younger brother Ollokot earned impressive warrior reputations.

Experienced and hardened warriors attacked the white force aggressively, throwing them into confusion. Early on, a shot killed one of the command's trumpeters.

Shortly thereafter the other somehow lost his trumpet. In all the smoke and dust, Perry had no way to control his troops. They were, he noted, "like a ship at sea without a helm."

Soon, the attackers skillfully turned Perry's left flank, inadequately anchored by the civilians, and collapsed that side of his line. As the soldiers retreated up the slope, an officer had Sergeant Michael McCarthy rally a small rear guard. They gave ground slowly while the bulk of the survivors fled.

Finally, Indian probes outflanked McCarthy's little unit. During their fighting retreat up the ridge, a shot disabled McCarthy's horse. Unable to keep up on foot, he plunged into the brush to avoid the pursuing Nez Percés.

"She described me quite accurately, not even forgetting my stripes and chevrons," the sergeant later noted. The young Nez Percés woman was pointing out where he'd gone into hiding. Fortunately, "I had crawled away from the spot she watched, it seems, unobserved by her."

McCarthy crouched with his pistol cocked as two youthful warriors scanned the brush. Finally, they fired a couple shots into his original hiding spot. Perhaps they glimpsed the sergeant's blue uniform coat, which he had stripped off earlier. Then they rode away.

"This gave me hope. I had already escaped death – almost certain death – three times that morning."

McCarthy dumped his cumbersome boots, then crept up the trail to White Bird Summit. He searched for fellow escapees, but saw only questing warriors and dead cavalrymen. "It was barely two hours since the first shot was fired. How many there were I could only guess. I knew of at least twenty."

Many hours later, he stumbled into Mount Idaho. That ended his part in the Battle of White Bird Canyon, the opening clash in the Nez Percés War.

As McCarthy suspected, the Army had suffered more deaths than he had witnessed: thirty-four in total. Not a terrible toll when compared to other notable Army disasters, such as Custer's Little Bighorn debacle, or the Fetterman massacre on the Bozeman Trail a decade earlier.

However, the Battle of White Bird Canyon differed in two key ways. First, those other losing commands faced overwhelming forces. They were outnumbered ten or twenty to one. Second, in both earlier battles, the Indians lost at least sixty warriors and quite possibly twice that number. At White Bird, the Army and volunteer force outnumbered the warriors involved in the battle. Yet not only did the whites lose badly, they failed to kill even one Indian.

For the next few weeks, the Indians conducted successful raids on the Camas Prairie and Clearwater area. They drove off stock, burned crops and buildings, and picked off incautious soldiers and civilians. General Howard could do little until reinforcements arrived. Most settlers scurried into Mount Idaho, where the men built a rude fort of rails and rocks. L. P. Brown's hotel served as headquarters and hospital.

Finally, on July 10, Howard's augmented force surprised the Nez Percés band along the Clearwater River. The Army claimed victory in the subsequent Battle of the Clearwater. However, they suffered over triple the casualties they inflicted, and the Indians slipped away. Arguably, only the Army's vastly superior numbers and artillery support won them the field. They "captured" a few broken-down horses and bedraggled tipis.

The fight did convince the Indians that they should vacate the Camas-Clearwater area for the safety of their families. They knew they had to move far away, perhaps even to join their Crow allies on the plains to the east. It's not clear whether or not they thought, then, that they might have to flee into Canada.

Easily evading Howard's troops, the Nez Percés fled across Lolo Pass into Montana. There, they essentially ceased their raiding, trading instead for supplies and severely curbing young hotheads who broke the unspoken truce.

However, these tribal people had a crucial blind spot. They thought their quarrel only involved General Howard and the authorities back in Idaho. Of course, they were wrong. In Montana, Colonel John Gibbon gathered a force from as far away as Fort Benton on the upper Missouri and joined the pursuit.

At the Battle of the Big Hole, Gibbon's force of about 200 men – soldiers and civilian volunteers – totally surprised the Indians. Yet their attack claimed mostly old men, women, and children.

Probably only the arrival of Howard's pursuers saved Gibbon from the Indians' furious counter-attack. The whites lost twenty-nine men killed, plus forty wounded. The Indians lost fifty to sixty dead. Years later, a survivor carefully recited the names of the warriors lost, and lamented, "Only twelve of the fighting men were lost in that battle. But our best were left there."

After the Big Hole, the Nez Percés were forced to operate under the presumption that "all whites are enemies." The Nez Percés had also realized the Crows were too closely allied to the whites to aid them. Their only hope was to escape into Canada.

Yet it was all in vain. By early October, 1877, Chief Joseph and about 420 surviving Nez Percés were in Army custody. Only eighty-seven of the captives were males. Perhaps 250 to 300 Indians, including Chief White Bird, escaped into Canada. As part of the surrender accord, Joseph was promised that his people would be returned to the Idaho reservation in the spring. Higher authorities repudiated that agreement. The Nez Percés spent the next eight years in Oklahoma, which they called "Eeikish Pah" – the Hot Place.

Only 268 lived to return to the Northwest. About 150 – Joseph included – were assigned to the Colville Reservation in Washington Territory. He would not have been safe in Idaho. On July 9, 1886, a *Idaho County Free Press* (Grangeville) writer said, "Chief Joseph may be a 'Big Injun' in the eyes of the government, but he will die with his moccasins on, some fine day."

Interested participants in the Nez Percés campaign included a band of about fifty Bannock Indians. The Army had recruited them as scouts from the Fort Hall reservation. Later actions of their leader, Buffalo Horn, suggest that he had carefully assessed the strengths and weaknesses of the Army troops. Upon his return to the reservation, the chief must have thought long and hard about his people's situation.

Bannock Indians, 1878. Magazine Illustration from Photograph.

The years since the Bannocks and Shoshones had been relocated to the reservation were ones of hardship and bitterness. They had been urged to take up farming. But the agent failed to provide promised tools, seed, and instructions. In any case, the tribes' tradition of hunting and gathering what the Earth offered gave them little foundation for conventional agriculture. The Bannocks roamed widely off the reservation.

Moreover, as so often happened, allocations to the Indian Agents somehow vanished, either through ineptitude or corruption. Even when supplies showed up, they often fell short of the need.

General George Crook inspected the Fort Hall Agency in April 1878. He reported, "The apportionment of rations for the supply of this agency was ridiculously inadequate; the Indians complained that three days out of seven they had nothing to eat, and the agent told me the allowance had never been adequate."

The treaty placing the Indians on the reservation also reserved the southern Camas Prairie for their use. Yet, as we have seen, during those years more and more settlers and stock raisers moved into the region. As usual, native protests were ignored. Then, in 1871, settlers introduced hogs to the prairie, animals that tore up the camas beds, a major Indian food source. This intrusion also went unchallenged by authorities.

For whatever combination of reasons, the Bannocks were primed for trouble by early 1878. The whole region seemed to know it. In January 1878, the *Idaho Statesman* reported, "From all accounts an Indian outbreak is very imminent in this section of Idaho. The people are organizing companies for defence from Rock Creek station to Raft River."

Buffalo Horn may have visited or sent emissaries to the Oregon Paiutes and Umatillas. Evidence does suggest he found ways to sound out their attitudes toward an outbreak. Conditions at the Malheur Reservation in Oregon were, if anything, worse than at Fort Hall. Leaders there were hardly enthusiastic. However, anger and desperation among the rank-and-file showed some promise.

If Buffalo Horn confided his plans to anyone, that confidant never told any white. The explosion occurred on Camas Prairie. By most accounts, Buffalo Horn approached several Camas stockmen in the spring. He demanded that they comply with the treaty provisions reserving the prairie for the Indians. Rejection of his claim surely hardened the decision for war.

Cattleman William "Will" Silvey made no mention of hearing the chief's demand. He and his brother Tom ran a herd on the prairie and regularly supplied beef to the gold towns. At the end of May, Will and two other hands tended the stock while Tom made a delivery. All seemed quiet until shots from some Bannock warriors wounded both of Will's companions. Will thought he had winged one of the attackers, but the three stockmen figured they'd better flee. The Indians then plundered the camp.

Buffalo Horn took no part in this attack, but may well have encouraged it. In a council held near the prairie's southern edge, the chief persuaded part of the band to go on the warpath with him. Many chose not too, and returned to Fort Hall. A band of Lemhi Shoshones also rebuffed his urging. The chief decided to proceed, probably hoping that early triumphs would encourage more to join the fight.

Perhaps emboldened by his assessment of the Army's weak points, Buffalo Horn devised a strategy that promised such success at relatively low risk. He would avoid stand-up battles with superior forces, Army or volunteer. His warriors would stay on the move, hitting isolated homesteads and unprotected herds. Unlike the Nez Percés, he was not burdened with many non-combatants.

Buffalo Horn cannot have expected to "win" in any military sense. He had to know the Army could deploy enough soldiers to match every man, woman, and child in his band. Even if other tribes joined the fight, they lacked the guns and ammunition to sustain a long war. More likely, he hoped to make a campaign of subjugation so expensive that the authorities would deal, and listen to their justified grievances. The cost to his people might be painful. But then, so was starvation.

Captain (Brevet Colonel) Reuben F. Bernard, commander of the Fort Boise garrison, learned of the attack on the cattlemen the same evening it happened. Late that night, about sixty men of Company G, 1st Cavalry, marched for the Prairie. Infantry followed the next day.

Buffalo Horn shrewdly judged that troops from Fort Boise would be the first to respond. Thus, by the time Bernard arrived, the Bannocks had decamped from the prairie into the lava fields to the south. The chief's avoidance strategy came into immediate play. When the soldiers marched close, the Indians rode south.

Bernard reported that the Bannocks abandoned important supplies, and perhaps they did. However, leaving the cavalry column far behind, the Indians raced to King Hill. There, they killed two freighters and plundered their wagons. They continued towards Augustus "Gus" Glenn's ferry. Fortunately for the whites, a friendly Indian had learned of the Bannocks' foray and hurried ahead to warn them, here and in the Bruneau Valley.

Settlers near the ferry gathered in a two-story structure Gus had built the previous year. Intended as a home, and as a fort, it had thick lava rock walls, chinked with clay. Inside, it had a well and a huge fireplace. According to a later report, "About fifty people, members of perhaps fifteen families, dwelt there for fear of the Indians, who were raiding outlying settlements."

One participant recalled that "Only twice during this fortification were Indians sighted from the house. They did not fire on the settlers in the stone fort."

Because of their hasty start, Bernard's troops had brought inadequate rations. Rather than crossing the Snake to pursue the raiders, they turned west on the stage road toward Boise City.

After crossing the river, the Bannocks cut the ferry loose and it floated far off downstream. With the Snake between him and possible pursuers, Buffalo Horn turned west toward the Bruneau Valley. He could stage raids across southern Idaho and then link with hoped-for allies in Oregon. A few miles downriver from the ferry, they encountered three men in a two-horse wagon. After killing the men, they also shot the horses. One of those lost was John Bascom, brother to James, who built the Rock Creek store.

Many settlers fled, but one contingent in the upper Bruneau Valley forted up in a cave dug by Abram Roberson and his sons. Intended for keeping dairy products and vegetables, it provided a reasonably defensible position. The *Idaho Statesman* later reported (June 22, 1878) on this refuge:

> "The excavation consisted of a tunnel with two large rooms on the sides. When it was known that the Indians were approaching the valley, the settlers collected at this point, drew up wagons in front of the cave and dug rifle pits on the bluff above, and were thus prepared with the few arms they had to make the best possible resistance in case of an attack."

These defenses were never put to the test. The Bannocks had plenty of easier targets. They killed several whites who failed to find a place to hide.

One of those casualties was Fletcher Hawes, who was tending cattle near Big Springs about thirty-five miles south and a bit east of Silver City. Had he survived, he would have been uncle, by marriage, to Bruneau historian Adelaide Turner Hawes. Although warned about the Bannock rampage, for some reason he discounted the danger. Adelaide Hawes noted that "At the time of his death, young Fletcher was preparing a home for his bride-to-be, Maggie Black, whom he was to wed the coming fall."

Naturally, the Army called for more troops. They tried to position what they had to block Buffalo Horn's likely attempt to reach allies in Oregon. Meanwhile, whites recruited volunteers, both for defense and pursuit. Larger settlements like Boise and Silver City were safe enough, but all else was open to attack.

For about a week, Indian raiders ran off or slaughtered stock and burned structures throughout southeast Idaho. Frightened settlers took refuge in Silver City, or further afield. For much of this time, no one knew quite where the hostiles were. The Army had to wait for reinforcements to cover all the possibilities.

On June 7, a force of twenty-five or thirty Silver City Volunteers led by Captain J. B. Harper marched out looking for trouble. Long-time cattleman Con Shea rode with the force, along with two of his brothers. John Catlow was also part of the company. They camped for the night at the O'Keefe ranch, about seven miles north of South Mountain. Unbeknownst to them, they had stopped within a few miles of the major Indian encampment. According to a pioneer witness, at that very time Buffalo Horn and several other Indian leaders were dining with "their old friend, Pete Disenroff."

The rancher on his isolated spread knew nothing about the outbreak, and had invited the chiefs to share his meal. He had long been friendly with the Bannocks, hiring some to help cut and stack hay. However, a courier interrupted them and the Indians hurriedly left. "Pete later realized that the scout had brought word of the volunteers' approach."

Several days earlier, Captain Bernard had reached Rattlesnake Station, about forty miles southeast of Boise City. At the Station, he joined up with the infantry and a unit of scouts, along with a volunteer force organized at Rocky Bar. They turned south to the Snake. There, men and supplies shuttled across in boats while the horses swam. They reached Roberson's *ad hoc* fort on June 6. The scouts hunted systematically for the Indians, cutting their traces on Saturday, June 8.

That same morning, Captain Harper had the Silver City Volunteers on the trail early, generally riding up along South Mountain Creek. Scattered reports, and common sense, said that the Indians might head west over this broad, rugged saddle between the Silver City Range and South Mountain. Alternatively, they could use the saddle between South and Juniper mountains.

The land resembled a sheet of paper that had been crumpled and then spread out. Weathered peaks and hogbacks rose a few hundred feet above the broken, mile-high plains. South Mountain, over seventy-seven hundred feet in elevation, loomed off that way. Bunchgrass and sagebrush filled the basins, interrupted by scattered Juniper trees and mountain mahogany. A few Ponderosa pines shared the higher peaks with the Juniper and mahogany. Numerous small creeks drained the countryside. Strips of willow, chokecherry, cottonwood, and the occasional aspen grove crowded each stream

All this provided cover for hordes of enemies waiting in ambush, so the Volunteers proceeded cautiously. By noon, the sun, blistering through the cool but thin air, surely had some wondering when they could find a bit of shade and have lunch. The column wound up a hill, planning to scout the surrounding countryside.

Suddenly, they came face-to-face with a band of warriors, primed for battle. To their consternation, the Bannocks outnumbered them by at least two to one. Realizing their danger, the Volunteers hurried off the hillside, heading west. Guns blazed on both sides. Indians fell, but four or five volunteers were unhorsed. Shots killed two Volunteers, including Oliver Purdy, one of the discoverers of the Jordan Creek placers.

The running battle continued over another low ridge onto Iron Mine Creek. Then, abruptly, the attack eased, the attackers milling about in confusion. Sensing a break, the Volunteers urged their horses into a gallop and fled.

Who actually shot and killed Buffalo Horn is not certain, but there seems no doubt his death saved the whites from a much worse beating. A week later the *Idaho*

Statesman reported (June 15, 1878) the fate of three other downed Volunteers, "at first reported killed in the fight on Saturday." The *Statesman* was "happy to learn" that "They had their horses shot under them and took refuge in the brush until they had an opportunity of getting out of reach of the Indians. Mr. Hastings, reported missing, has also turned up alright."

With their leader and driving force dead, some of the Indians made their way back to Fort Hall. The rest continued into Oregon, where most of the remaining Bannock War action took place.

The Bannocks joined a mixed bag of Shoshones, Paiutes, Umatillas, and even some Cayuse Indians. These had made their way into the Steen's Mountain country, about seventy miles from the Idaho border. Chief Egan, an Umatilla, led this motley group as they raided ranches and homesteads in the area.

Bernard's column and the scout unit paused briefly to re-supply at Silver City. They then pushed on into Oregon. On June 22, they caught up with the Indians on Silver Creek, about twenty miles southwest of today's Burns. The warriors heavily outnumbered the troops. Unfazed, Bernard launched a surprise attack the next morning. Superior firepower drove the Indians into the hills. The hail of gunfire severely wounded Chief Egan.

Assaults and skirmishes went on for several more weeks, but by now General Howard had a large force in the field. A battle near the Blue Mountains on July 13 finally convinced the Indians their cause was hopeless. Shortly after, another Umatilla assassinated the wounded Chief Egan. After that, the Indian forces scattered into smaller bands.

Captain Bernard's column and other Army troops chased warriors throughout August and September. Meanwhile, tribesmen in the Payette and Weiser watersheds engaged in small skirmishes and ambuscades. Peter Pence recalled how he and his family endured a war of nerves during this period. When his wife and kids couldn't stand it any more, they all evacuated to Boise City. There, Peter served as captain of a band of scouts. Constant pressure finally scattered the Indian forces still in Idaho.

Although many tribesmen further west just wanted to slide back to the reservations, a few still had some fight left. Bernard reported one such clash on John Day's River in late August. By October, most of the Indians had returned to their reservations or were in custody.

Records indicate that the Bannock War killed about ten soldiers and thirty citizens, with perhaps another twenty citizens and soldiers wounded. About eighty Indians died, with possibly a couple hundred wounded.

No one made an accounting of the structures burned and livestock slaughtered. Cattleman David Shirk took the "desperate chance" of forting up at his home ranch to protect it. Most families, however, fled into towns. Shirk said, "All the homes and ranches vacated were burned to the ground, their contents being taken or destroyed."

Throughout this campaign, Captain Reuben Bernard lived up to his reputation as a skilled Indian fighter. Born in Tennessee, he had enlisted at twenty-one in the 1st Cavalry (then designated the 1st Dragoons).

From 1855 into 1862, he fought in many skirmishes against Apache Indians in New Mexico and Arizona. Twice, his unit clashed with western Confederate forces. He rose to the rank of first sergeant, and was then commissioned a 2nd Lieutenant. Transferred east, he fought through the rest of the Civil War. By the end, Bernard had risen to the rank of Brevet Colonel.

After the Civil War, he fought Indians in Oregon, Arizona, and California. By the time he led his troops out of Fort Boise for the Bannock War, he had been in nearly one hundred "fights and scrimmages." He passed that mark before the Indian forces fell apart in Oregon. He later added more to his total, again fighting Apaches in Arizona.

Indian Fighter Reuben Bernard

Bernard was not, however, quite done with Idaho.

Most people, miners and Indians alike, found the high ranges of the central Salmon River drainage almost uninhabitable. Recall that Cameahwait, the Lemhi Shoshone, had declared the Salmon River mountains "inaccessible to man or horse." Only the promise of gold lured prospectors deep into this wilderness.

Yet, with remarkable adaptability, one tribe of Shoshones made this area their home. They also moved across comparable terrain in Wyoming and Montana. These people were the "*Tukudeka*," the "mountain-sheep eaters." Calling them simply "Sheepeaters," downplays their superb stalking and shooting skills.

Although the *Tukudeka* also subsisted on fish and the usual wild berry crops, they depended mostly on hunting. Moreover, they hunted on foot. Given the topography, they had little need for horses. Wild or stray animals might be treated as prey, or captured for trade with flat-land tribes.

Features of the Southern Nez Percés Trail, which ran right through *Tukudeka* country, can perhaps suggest the extreme nature of this wild region. "As the crow flies," about forty-six miles separate Elk City from Nez Percés Pass. The Trail twists and turns over double that in covering the trip.

Packers struggled along numerous steep ascents or descents: seven of over 1,000 feet, and two others over 2,700 feet. Traveling west from the Selway River presents the greatest challenge. The route steadily rises over 4,300 feet (more than eight-tenths of a mile) in less than fourteen Trail miles. Besides the rugged country, harsh weather and natural fluctuations in game populations made life hard. The *Tukudekas* may have never numbered more than a few hundred souls.

Although Weiser Sheepeaters were blamed for killing John Reed's party of Pacific Fur Company trappers in 1814, the tribe generally got along with whites. Mountain

Man Osborne Russell encountered a *Tukudeka* band in the Yellowstone area in 1835. The group included thirteen adults and "8 or 10 children," a typical number. He found them lacking in worldly goods, but was favorably impressed.

He wrote, "They were all neatly clothed in dressed deer and sheep skins of the best quality and seemed to be perfectly contented and happy. ... We obtained a large number of elk, deer and sheep skins from them of the finest quality, and three large, neatly-dressed panther skins."

Osborne also found their weaponry impressive. "They were well armed with bows and arrows pointed with obsidian. The bows were beautifully wrought from sheep, buffaloe and elk horns secured with deer and elk sinews, and ornamented with porcupine quills and generally about 3 feet long."

The few settlers who met them judged them to be "mild mannered and inoffensive." But the influx of prospectors into the mountains had a ruinous effect on the game population. This, in turn, upset the slender balance between the Indians and their demanding environment.

Miners quickly fastened a disreputable label on the *Tukudeka*. In keeping with the behavior of other Shoshones, individuals doubtless made off with tools and other items left laying around loose. That would have been enough justification, to those who needed it, for the whites to condemn them all. Of course, some miners surely robbed the Indians of their fine furs and leather goods. The resulting conflicts made it all too easy for the miners to blame the *Tukudekas* for any mysterious killings or disappearances in the region.

These troubles came to a head late in the winter of 1879. A decade before that, prospectors discovered the Loon Creek placers. These were located thirty to thirty-five miles northwest of today's Challis. They were largely "played out" by 1879. Certainly white miners were no longer interested. Thus, only a handful of Chinese miners occupied the Loon Creek town of Orogrande that winter.

The outcome of what happened next is clear, but the details are uncertain. Someone attacked the miners while they were engrossed in gambling. The only known survivor escaped to another mining camp and reported the crime. Investigators found five savagely brutalized bodies, and many whites immediately blamed the Indians.

However, a group of whites, known to be "rough and rowdy" were also wintering in the general area. Some suspected that these men wanted the Chinese miners' gold, and committed the atrocities to cast blame on the Indians. Only the true perpetrators knew for sure, and the *Tukudeka* later vehemently denied any involvement.

Still, it didn't really matter. The victims were "only Chinamen." Authorities felt no need to launch a rigorous investigation of the white party. Besides, many preferred to believe that the *Tukudekas were* the guilty parties. That gave the Army an excuse to round them up.

At the end of May, Captain Bernard again led G company out of Fort Boise, headed for Challis. A few days later, Lieutenant Henry Catley marched about fifty mounted infantry out of the new Camp Howard, two miles from Mount Idaho. Later in June, a small contingent of 1st Cavalry soldiers and about twenty Umatilla scouts were dispatched from Oregon. Lieutenants Edward S. Farrow and W. S. Brown led this force.

Leaving Challis, Bernard's troop surmounted man-tall snow drifts, frigid and swollen streams, and jagged ridges to reach Orogrande. Little remained besides scorched timbers.

Bernard's command began searching the hideously difficult Salmon River watershed. Along the way, they lost several animals and a considerable part of their supplies. Captain Bernard wrote, "This country is made up of streams and mountains. All except the streams are set up on edge, causing a traveler to go over two sides of it instead of one."

By mid-July, the unit led by Farrow and Brown was closing up with Bernard's column. Catley was still far to the north. Like Bernard, the force from Camp Howard had encountered incredibly daunting conditions. On July 28, scouts reported Indian sign and Catley hurried his men forward. They rushed right into an ambush, and hidden Indians shot two soldiers. The troops beat a hasty retreat, carrying their severely wounded comrades.

The Indians harassed the soldiers for a couple more days. However, the column soon discarded most of its baggage, which distracted their adversary from further pursuit.

Finally, the various commands joined up. All were short of supplies and worn down by the rough travel. Bernard took his force, augmented by reinforcements under Captain A. J. Forse, to where Catley had been attacked. Meanwhile the Indians had retaliated for the Army intrusion into their homeland by killing three ranchers on the South Fork of the Salmon.

On August 19 near the earlier ambush site, hostiles fired on an advance party of Umatilla scouts. Hearing the exchange, Bernard sent reinforcements forward, and the *Tukudekas* fled. The increasing pressure forced the Indians to leave most of their belongings and supplies behind.

Bernard concluded that his opponent had very few warriors, surely less than thirty. As a result of the clash, he said, "They are now destitute of everything, and are believed by the scouts to be going toward Lemhi. The country they were in when we left the trail was so rough animals could not be got through it at all."

The physical toll had been terrible. Bernard went on, "All of our stock, except Captain Forse's horses and Farrow's captured stock, are exhausted. Many horses and mules have given out and been shot, and, unless we have rest and forage, all will soon give out."

Before advancing, Bernard exchanged dispatches with General Howard. Howard authorized him to use his own judgement about continued operations in "that fearful country." If that seemed imprudent, he should "distribute his forces to the posts where they belonged."

It was now about September 20. At any moment, Bernard's command might be caught by a heavy snowfall. That could trap them for days. He decided to return to Fort

Boise for rest and refit. Catley's force would go back to Camp Howard. As they withdrew down the trail a hidden warrior's parting shot fatally wounded one soldier.

Since their animals were in better shape, Lieutenants Farrow and Brown remained in the field. They had over twenty cavalrymen to support the Umatilla scouts, and felt they might force the band to surrender.

In late September and early October, the troops rounded up fifty to sixty dispirited *Tukudekas*. Most of the captives were women and children. Perhaps a dozen warriors turned over a pitiful array of ancient and worn firearms. After a winter at Vancouver Barracks, they were moved to the Fort Hall Reservation.

Rather grandiloquently called the "Sheepeater War," this clash ended all organized conflict between whites and the indigenous peoples in Idaho. A few scattered bands continued their free-ranging ways. However, most stayed on the reservations, trying to adapt to a new way of life. Eventually, they would adjust, and even prosper, but only after many decades of pain.

Shoshone Indians at Fort Hall Reservation

CHAPTER TEN: CATTLE DRIVES ACROSS AND FROM IDAHO

Dark overcast masked any sky glow. Heavy rain had made for a miserable night. Will Jackson tossed more wood into the firepit, then hefted the smoke-blackened coffee pot. Not much left. He filled his own cup, then poured the rest into a pan. The night riders might want some before the next batch was ready.

He kept some used grounds, but threw the remainder under the wagon. Indians sometimes came begging a cup. A batch brewed from the old grounds was good enough for them.

After a quick swish to clear the last dregs, he filled the pot from the water barrel strapped to the side of the wagon. Will next grabbed the bag of fresh grounds from the chuck box. After a month on the job, his hands found it automatically. A smart cook always stayed well ahead on grinding coffee.

Will poured plenty into the pot and replaced the lid. Finally, he positioned an s-shaped hook to hang the kettle over the fire, and then poked the coals so they flared up. He had enough time to prepare breakfast, but the hands would soon be up and wanting a hot cup.

By the time the first cowboy stood slurping his stout brew, Will had a steady boil going on the kettle of beans. He carved off a few more chunks of salt pork, then tossed the whole batch in with the beans. It had been over a fortnight since they'd butchered a yearling steer.

Had to watch the fires when a sudden rain squall hit. Luckily, the storm hadn't changed direction during the night, so the wagon's bulk blocked the worst of the wind. Intermittent gusts swirled spray past the overhead tarpaulin.

Camp Cook and His Chuckwagon

Time for the bread. Will dumped flour into a big shallow bowl and formed a crater in the middle. Then he carefully unwrapped the sourdough keg. Some cooks slept with their kegs on cold nights so the fermentation wasn't interrupted. He poured enough batter into the flour depression, then stirred replacement flour and water into the keg.

Back at his work table, he added salt, lard, and a little soda and water to the starter and began working the ingredients into a well-mixed dough. After kneading the dough thoroughly, he let it rest while he prepared the Dutch ovens. By now, the flames had subsided into a bed of glowing coals. He slathered lard into the cookers, made a level spot in the coals, and plunked the ovens down on their three stubby legs. The lard melted quickly.

Removing the ovens from the heat, Will prepared the biscuits. This entailed pinching off chunks of sourdough, and working them into balls. These he coated with the melted lard, and packed them tightly into the oven. Finished, he placed the cookers near the fire so they'd stay warm. They'd need a half hour or so to rise. Then he'd put them back over the fire and spread hot coals on the rimmed top.

Will took a moment to relax and swig some coffee himself. The low clouds engulfed the tops of the parallel mountain ranges that flanked the flat plain. Along here, the Bear River Valley varied from one to three miles in width.

Later, he'd run the couple miles back into Soda Springs and buy supplies. The boys would like it if he could get some butter at a reasonable price. Maybe the settlers had potatoes.

After cleanup, he headed back to the settlement. In his diary for July 24, 1876, Will wrote, "As we entered the town a flag was hoisted on top of a little bluff, which called our attention to the fact that this is a holiday celebrated by these people in commemoration of the landing of Brigham Young and his followers on the site of Salt Lake City."

He made his purchases, and then started along the trail of their herd. "We were unable to participate in their festivities, but we were told that the day was spent in music and dancing."

The drive for which William Emsley Jackson cooked was one of two herds belonging to G. W. Lang and a Mr. Shadley. They had purchased about four thousand head in Oregon and split them into more manageable sizes. Jackson worked on one that contained about fourteen hundred cattle.

They were part of the growing trend noted earlier. Stockmen were trailing large herds from Oregon and Washington across Idaho to railheads or rangeland further east. Regional cattlemen faced the hard reality that the Pacific Northwest had a surplus of beef. Local markets and California simply could not absorb everything. They thus faced severely depressed prices. In that context, the cost and risks of a long drive looked like a bargain.

As a matter of fact, the Shadley-Lang herd passed, or was passed by, several other drives. In Wyoming, Will Jackson wrote, "Crowded now more than ever. Three herds in sight."

The following year, the *Idaho Statesman* reported (May 31, 1877) yet another drive, "Messrs. Lang & Ryan crossed Snake river a few days ago at Kenney's Ferry and came up the Boise valley to Fouche's Ferry at Boise river, where they crossed with 3,300 head of beef cattle."

The item went on, "The cattle were bought in Walla Walla valley, and will be driven to Nebraska, where, after selling a portion of the herd, the remainder will be stall-fed for the Chicago and other eastern markets."

Besides these, drives originating in Idaho had also joined the flow. Out on the Laramie Plain, Jackson wrote, "We pass a herd of about 500 cattle from Marsh Valley, Idaho. Their destination was Laramie."

Reports disagree on precisely when Idaho cattlemen first began trailing large herds of surplus animals out of state. Certainly by the mid-1870s prospects looked excellent for Idaho stockmen as Eastern markets provided an outlet for their growing herds. Indeed, the *Oregonian* commented (August 13, 1876) that the cattle "scattered all over Idaho never looked fatter and better."

Concerning the settlers near Montpelier, Will Jackson said, "The principal occupation of the people of this region is stock raising."

Moreover, cattle operations in the Bear Lake area expanded even more the following year when two new ranchers brought in herds. Later, Chester Call and his nephew Christian Nelson moved horse bands onto the grazing areas around what would become the town of Chesterfield.

Further north, pioneers like Alexander Toponce continued to operate at a high level. Recall that he had trailed a herd into Idaho in 1872 and leased range on the Fort Hall Indian Reservation. In his *Reminiscences*, he wrote, "At times I had as high as 10,000 head of cattle on the land."

"I sold out to Sparks and Tinnin in the spring of 1879, including my unexpired lease."

Thus, stockmen now ran thousands of cattle in eastern Idaho. Unfortunately, as the land filled up, the peaceful coexistence between cattlemen and sheepmen began to unravel. The *Oxford Enterprise* reported (October 9, 1879) friction between established cattle ranchers and sheepmen who wanted to move herds onto the range there.

The arrival of new cattlemen added further pressure. Texan John Sparks was among the newcomers. Born in Mississippi, in 1843, Sparks belonged to a family of ranch developers. They would claim raw land and start a ranch. When they had it ready, they sold out and moved.

John became a skilled Texas cowboy in the late 1850s. During the Civil War, he fought Comanche Indians as a member of the Texas Rangers. Soon after the war, Sparks began leading cattle drives to many destinations. As noted in Chapter Eight, one of those expeditions took him into northwestern Utah.

In 1873, Sparks drove a large herd into Wyoming. There, he built a ranch and began to repeat the family's develop-then-sell approach. Finally, however, he decided opportunities for further expansion were limited in Wyoming. He and his older brother Tom looked west. In 1881, they brought a herd into Idaho.

After inspecting the bottomland and nearby plains several miles above American Falls, Tom established a ranch. He stayed there well into the next century. John, of course, had already partnered with John Tinnin to purchase Toponce's holdings. The Sparks-Tinnin spread quickly grew to include large expanses in southern Idaho, as well as over the border in Nevada.

Partners Frank Campbell and James Stebbins were Tom Sparks' neighbors. They too ran cattle along the northwest side of the Snake. They built the headquarters of their IL ranch west of American Falls.

Also during the latter years of the decade, several stockmen built ranches in the Gray's Lake area, twenty-five or thirty miles east of the Fort Hall Indian Reservation. Among them was Dan Brockman, who had helped Samuel F. Taylor drive the second major herd onto rangeland southeast of Eagle Rock.

The growth of local ranching must have caused some friction with cattle drives entering the area from the west. Recall that herds of Oregon cattle following the northern route headed for Eagle Rock as the preferred place to cross the Snake – either via the ford or by paying (reluctantly) the toll at Taylor's Bridge.

By the mid- to late-Seventies, bands containing two thousand to five thousand head passed through fairly regularly. Not only did they compete for forage along the way, but local animals sometimes got swept into the passing drive. Their owners were naturally suspicious about such "accidents."

And, as could be expected, "private operators" saw opportunities for themselves. According to Beal and Wells, "The upper Snake River valley was infested by outlaws."

Rustlers collected cattle and horses from all over southern Idaho. There's good reason to believe that an "underground economy" existed among the thieves, those in the west selling or trading stolen animals to operators in east Idaho. The easterners grazed the stock in hidden valleys and forest clearings. When they had enough, the crooks drove them to the same markets frequented by honest stockmen.

Trying to counter the thieves, in 1877 the Territory passed an Act that directed livestock owners to "record with the recorder of his county, his mark, brand and counter-brand by delivering to the said recorder his mark cut upon a piece of leather, and his brand and counter-brand burnt upon it, and the same shall be kept in the recorder's office."

Further, brand recorders were required to exchange records with neighboring counties so animals that strayed across county lines could be identified. Despite these measures, rustlers remained a serious drain on Idaho stockmen. (It was a statewide problem. In 1878, Owyhee cattlemen met in Silver City and initiated what became the Owyhee Cattleman's Association. Their main concerns were cattle rustling and horse theft.)

Meanwhile, a new factor contributed to the history of eastern Idaho.

Crippled by the Panic of '73, the Utah Northern Railway had been forced to suspend construction ten to fifteen miles north of Franklin (Chapter Eight). Finally, in

1878, a new company, the Utah & Northern Railway, purchased all the Utah Northern properties and assets in a foreclosure sale. They soon resumed track laying.

About the same time, Theodore Danilson opened a store near where the Blackfoot River enters the Snake. According to contemporary newspaper reports, in addition to the usual items (groceries, boots, saddlery, etc.), "He also offered a choice line of standard wines and liquors."

Danilson purchased the Blackfoot Ferry, which had been crossing the Snake River for over a decade. The ferry still carried many Oregon emigrants as well as freight and stage coach traffic. Danilson expected freight volume to grow when the railroad reached Blackfoot.

Alexander Toponce was among those who used the ferry. He had expanded his freight business after selling off his cattle ranch. He ran freight and stagecoaches to the mining camps along Wood River as well as north and west of Challis. He then reduced his involvement to just supplying wagons and draft animals for other freighters.

By 1878, Nels and Emma Just had improved their homestead on the Blackfoot River. Nels continued to sell cattle to the reservation and also sold hay to freighters passing through. At times, the Justs wintered draft animals for the freight companies. The coming of the railroad would eventually make a huge difference in their lives.

The railroad reached the growing village around Christmas of 1878 and entered Eagle Rock the following summer. There, they spanned the Snake with a steel structure about a hundred feet south of Taylor's bridge. Three years later, the Railway located its shops in the town, fueling substantial growth. The tracks reached the Montana border in the fall of 1879.

U&N Railroad Bridge, Toll Bridge in Background

Less than three weeks after the first train crossed the Snake at Eagle Rock, settler Stephen Winegar finished his house on the Egin Bench. The tiny town of Egin, about thirty-three miles north of Eagle Rock, would have its own post office about a year later. Winegar and others who soon followed had to be content with cutting hay and raising stock until a ditch could be completed to bring irrigation onto the Bench from Henry's Fork.

As the Egin settlers started their canal project in late 1879, George and Robert Smith were completing a ditch that tapped into the Snake River about twenty miles east and north of Eagle Rock. This allowed them to switch their homestead from ranching to farming.

Even without railroads, other Idaho regions continued to grow, both in terms of stock production and settlement. For example, shortly before Will Jackson joined the Shadley-Lang drive, John Shirley bought twelve hundred head in Walla Walla to add to his cattle holdings in the "Raft River regions."

Charlie Gamble, who helped Shirley and Sweetser import Texas cattle, still worked for their company. Married in 1874, he and his wife had two children over the next several years. In 1880, Gamble claimed land on Cassia Creek, a tributary that joins the Raft River near Malta. There, he began raising his own cattle.

Beyond the Albion Mountains to the west, homesteads had also sprung up in the Goose Creek drainage. At that time, John Hailey's Kelton to Boise City stage line passed through City of Rocks and then swung north and west to the Oakley stage station.

In the Seventies, individual pioneers began to move into the region around the station. Then, in 1879, William C. Martindale organized a larger party of Mormon colonists from Tooele, Utah. The town of Oakley soon grew up around the station.

During the winter, snow blocked the City of Rocks route and freighters diverted through the growing settlements of the Marsh Basin. (Most years, Hailey bridged the City of Rocks route with a twenty-mile sleigh ride.) In 1878, a home station was established in the Basin. Also around that time, James Bascom relocated there after selling his Rock Creek store. He and a partner later purchased land in the area, which they subdivided for the town of Albion.

Still in Owyhee County at that time, Albion lay over 160 miles from the county seat in Silver City. They were actually closer to Salt Lake City. Locals complained (*Owyhee Avalanche*, March 16, 1878) that, "They only see or hear the county officials when they come around to assess or collect taxes, or when they are electioneering."

By February 1879, enough settlers had entered the area to induce the Territorial legislature to create Cassia County, with Albion as the county seat. The new county encompassed roughly today's Cassia and Twin Falls counties.

By this time, as historian Byron Lusk put it, cattlemen "were beginning to notice the boundaries of adjoining ranches." The Bradley and Russell Cattle Company even tried north of the Snake across from Goose Creek. They returned their herds to the south in 1879.

Further west, Rock Creek had also expanded. Besides the stage station and store, there were two log buildings, several dwellings, and the "China House," where Chinese miners congregated.

After recovering from a bout of "mountain fever," Charlie Walgamott took a part-time job at a store owned by Herman Stricker and his partner in Springtown, down in the Snake River Canyon. He also prospected along the Snake. "I did do a little mining there," Charlie said. "But the diggings near the Falls were pretty lean."

After the partners bought out Bascom's Rock Creek store, Walgamott also clerked there, and experienced an event he chose not to include in his reminiscences.

Before Charlie arrived in Idaho, his brother-in-law Charles Trotter had made a sworn enemy. He had provided a free breakfast to a down-and-out man, but then the man offered him a horse for sale. Trotter recognized the horse as being one reported stolen in Boise. When the man, who gave his name as William Dowdell, could produce no bill of sale, Trotter had him arrested. Sent off to Boise City for trial, Dowdell was found guilty and sentenced to a term in the Idaho Penitentiary. He vowed to shoot Trotter when he got out.

Dowdell completed his sentence and reappeared at Rock Creek, working for a freight outfit that had camped nearby. The morning after the wagons stopped, the ex-con marched over to the station, presumably to carry out his threat. People there told him that Trotter hadn't made it to work. He was "confined to his bed with typhoid fever."

Unfortunately, Dowdell then visited the saloon and got liquored up. Well lubricated, he wandered outside and began taking potshots at passersby, wounding one. Inside the store, Charlie heard the shots and went to the door to investigate. A cowboy letting off steam by firing his gun wasn't that unusual.

The bullet that drilled through the door casing just missed Walgamott's head. Charlie wasn't armed, but kept a loaded revolver on a nearby shelf. No doubt frightened and angry, he grabbed the pistol and shot Dowdell dead.

Nathaniel Langford wrote, "My diary for 1877 shows that on September 17th I passed through Rock Creek by stage en route for Boise. Our coach entered the place about the middle of the afternoon."

They arrived in time for the slain man's "funeral," which the locals had taken as a chance for a drunken wake. Langford said, "No clergyman was present to conduct the exercises, and no layman was in a condition to offer a prayer or read the scriptures."

After hours of drinking and staggering about, they finally buried the body.

Langford also said, "The entire settlement manifested their approval of Wohlgamuth's [sic] timely shot by a season of general rejoicing, and a coroner's jury exonerated him from all blame."

Through the latter half of the decade, cattle ranchers spread across the rangelands south and southwest of Rock Creek. Walgamott noted that "As Mr. Harrell was augmenting his band, which became known as the 'Shoe Sole,' other companies came in, viz.: the 'Winecup' and the 'HD,' both having headquarters on the tributaries of Goose Creek and on the Nevada side of the mountain."

Jasper Harrell, of course, had been one of the first to move herds north from Nevada, in 1872.

However, the country was not really "settled." Walgamott said, "The first settlers of Snake River Valley were squatters. There being no surveys, they held their land by right of possession."

In early December 1879, Charlie found himself involved with schemers who wanted to take advantage of that circumstance. Glover and Benson, partners in a California surveying firm, concocted a scheme to survey a region "south of Snake River, from Dry Creek on the east to the mouth of the Little Salmon River on the west."

The youthful pioneer was wintering at Rock Creek with his wife (he'd married earlier in the year) when Glover and Benson showed up at his cabin. They asked him how well he knew the route south to the railroad station at Wells, Nevada.

"I told them I was not acquainted with the route farther than the Hay Stack and the Salmon," Walgamott wrote later.

"Now here, we have told Mr. Donelly that you are acquainted with the entire country and we want to employ you to drive us with your team and wagon over the route," one of the partners said. "We have also told him of the fine farming country that lies along the Salmon and adjacent streams."

Mr. Donelly, "a large, likable fellow," represented the U. S. Department of Interior. At the time, a survey could be authorized if enough settlers certified their intention to file on land in a given region. Although, Walgamott noted, "the required number of settlers were not in the country," private survey companies were not averse to faking the names and putting up the required deposits themselves.

The partners needed Donelly's help to have a survey authorized. If Charlie would play along he'd be well compensated. Fortunately, when Walgamott met the party at the store that evening the surveyors had done a fine selling job. Charlie did not have to field any potentially embarrassing questions.

The next morning, Walgamott contributed bread baked by his wife, and helped the party buy the rest of their provisions. Charlie then bought a side of bacon and some matches and said he "thought that should complete our commissary."

"Aren't you going to order any whiskey?" was the question from the other travelers. They had already bought a gallon. Walgamott ordered another gallon.

That proved to be wise. On the first day they essentially traded booze for a ranch-cooked meal. Charlie declared, "When we bade them goodbye the next morning, our kitchen had not been diminished one iota, but our distillery department showed quite a reduction!"

Cowboys they met on the second day advised them to visit the Hubbart Ranch. There, they were again received warmly and fed well. Next morning turned out to be special. The hands urged them to watch while they saddled up. Walgamott described the colorful scene:

> "Among squealing, kicking, and bucking horses, cowboys darted with open loops that when thrown brought the chosen horses to partial subjection. The horses were nerved with excitement … and, as the cinches tightened, the fight

was on. It seemed impossible for the riders to find their stirrups, but they did so with an agility that was astonishing.

"With loose reins, the cowboys raked the shoulders of their mounts, flanked them, forked them, and threw sand in their eyes. Then in defiance, the horses bellowed with rage, bucked into the air, landing on stiff legs, and going immediately into the air again at different angles, using every effort to dismount the riders, but to no avail. Both rider and horses were at their best, and when the riders drew the heads of their horses above their shoulders they gave a wave of their arms, bid us *au revoir,* and disappeared into the hills for their daily labor."

Walgamott and the others headed south, eventually driving into "a blinding snowstorm." With enough clues, Mr. Donelly figured out that nobody in the party, including Charlie, had anything more than hearsay information about their route. "But," Walgamott wrote, "he was willing to forgive us."

Finally at the railroad station, Donelly said, "I never expect to see another such display of horsemanship as we witnessed at Hubbart Ranch."

"Needless to say the hoped-for recommendation for a survey was not forthcoming," Walgamott commented dryly. His observations confirmed that large ranches had spread all across the south-central portion of Idaho, and even south into Nevada.

Similar growth occurred in central Idaho, between Challis and Salmon City. By 1876, George L. Shoup's ranch had enough surplus that he too began shipping cattle east. His hands trailed a herd of eight hundred "matured steers" to the railroad in Wyoming. They ran into lots of trouble loading the cattle onto the train. Not only were the loading facilities inadequate, but the animals were uncooperative, to say the least. Shoup's son later wrote, "These old steers were as wild, fierce, and strong as grizzlies."

Four years later, Shoup, his partners, and several other Lemhi River ranchers sent a herd of eleven hundred steers east to the Chicago market.

During this period, miners and settlers poured into the Big Wood River region to exploit the silver and lead lodes there. Miner David Ketchum wintered near some hot springs and the town of Ketchum quickly became a tourist and supply hub. The town grew fast, and soon had "two banks, two hotels, six livery stables, a weekly newspaper, and a dozen or more saloons."

Further down the valley, Bellevue sprang up. Also, stagecoach operator John Hailey bought land that included the town site of Hailey, founded the following year. Hailey had sold his stagecoach line in the early 1870s and begun raising livestock in the Boise City area. John settled his family permanently in the City, opened a butcher shop, and invested in real estate.

In 1872, voters elected Hailey as Delegate to the U.S. House of Representatives. (Delegates have no vote on the floor, but can serve on committees and vote on issues at that level.) Both political parties wanted him to fill the position for the next term but Hailey declined.

Then some former associates defaulted on loans John had guaranteed. That and some other reverses led Hailey to invest again in a stage line, in 1878. The Utah, Idaho,

Stage Line Owner John Hailey

and Oregon Stage Company had over two thousand miles of routes. John's involvement with the stage line led him to the investment in the town site. He also bought shares in several mines.

Naturally, the Wood River boom was also a bonanza for stockmen along the lower Big Wood River and Camas Prairie further west. According to the 1880 Federal Census, cattlemen held "eight to ten thousand stock cattle" on the Prairie alone. (Of course, this may have been a lower limit – what the stockmen would admit to.)

Yet even beyond the increased demand from the mines, ranchers had reason to raise more cattle. For example, George Shoup no longer had to seek out markets. The "History of Lemhi County" noted that, "Col. Shoup induced buyers to come to Lemhi and enter into contracts of buying."

Shoup made one delivery of about four thousand head in June 1882. Other ranchers in the area profited too.

North Idaho, the Camas Prairie in particular, also prospered. A traveling correspondent for the *Idaho Statesman*, W. A. Goulder, filed a report (March 4, 1876) about Prairie stock raising. Writing from Mount Idaho, he said, "I was out to see Mr. H. S. Croasdaile, who … is engaged in sheep raising. He has the largest and finest flock I have ever seen. I don't know how many thousands."

Goulder also noted that, "Messrs. Williams and Jerome, two English gentlemen have bought the place of Mr. George Sears, on the other side of the Clear Water, and will go into the business of general stock raising on a large scale."

Sears was rated "among the leading cattle men" on the Prairie. The reporter said, "Mr. Sears, who has a large herd of cattle, has gone to Pierce City to examine the market, and will probably continue in the butchering business, supplying both that camp and Elk City."

Later that year, James and Thomas Surridge took up stock raising on the Prairie. Natives of London, England, the brothers arrived in Idaho by way of California. They are credited with being the first to introduce Clydesdale horses and Berkshire hogs into the region. Along the same lines, they imported Durham bulls to upgrade their cattle holdings. They would eventually own over two thousand acres of land.

Long before their herds grew, the region had surpluses to sell. The *Lewiston Teller* reported (February 3, 1877) that agents had purchased over a thousand head of cattle to be driven to Wyoming. In the *Teller* for February 20, 1880, two stockmen said, "1,000 Head of Cattle for Sale. The band has never been culled for beef or other purposes during the last three or four years. Enquire at this office or of J. Greenfield, or W. A. Caldwell."

Newcomers kept arriving. In 1879, emigrant Henry Meyer arrived on the Prairie. Henry had almost been born in the the United States. During the 1848 political turmoil in Germany, Henry's father came to the U. S. and found work in the Midwest. After a couple years, the father was able to return to Germany, and Henry was born in 1852. Henry came to American himself at the age of twenty-one.

After searching for work in several Midwestern states, Meyer settled in California. He spent six years there, then came to Idaho and claimed a homestead about nine miles west of Grangeville. He began stock raising and small scale farming. This laid the foundation for a holding that eventually spread over a square mile of prime land.

Idaho stockmen thrived during the first years of the next decade. In part, they benefited from a hard winter in the Pacific Northwest. Reports at the time claimed losses of fifty-five to over eighty percent in various Oregon and Washington counties. Idaho herds suffered also, but to a much lesser extent.

The *Idaho Statesman* reprinted (March 25, 1882) an item from the north that said, "Several cattle buyers are making their headquarters at Lewiston, buying cattle, riding horses and outfits, and preparing to drive cattle to the Eastern States."

As a result, the May 1882 *Lewiston Teller* figured that several thousand head of cattle and hundreds of horses would be driven east from the Panhandle.

Even so, an item in the January 28, 1881 *Nez Perce News* tried to sound a warning. It said, "If the reports which reached us concerning the loss of cattle in the surrounding country are true, the present winter is doing its level best to verify the scriptural maxim that it pays to be merciful to the beasts of the field."

The writer expressed the hope that the accounts were exaggerated. He urged stockmen to put aside hay and grain for bad weather "instead of relying on Providence to give us mild winters. Providence and fortune smile on the stock raiser who has the biggest feed stacks."

The hard winter crippled the north Idaho holdings of Almon Lieuallen, one of the founders of Moscow. The *Illustrated History* said Lieuallen owned "vast herds of cattle" at one point. His heavy losses around Paradise Valley caused him to rethink his approach in 1881. Almon began to focus more on real estate development. The *History* noted that "he owned between two and three thousand acres of land in Washington and Idaho, and one-half section in California."

To encourage the growth of Moscow, Lieuallen helped promote a schoolhouse and later the first church. His foresight earned its reward. In September 1885, the Oregon Railway & Navigation Company ran the first train into town. The town grew steadily after that. Almon passed away in 1898.

Not many other Idaho stockmen heeded the warning the way Lieuallen did. In fact, most continued to expand their herds. They eagerly filled the gaps left by the harder-hit herds in Oregon and Washington.

Settlement also bloomed further south on the western side of the state. In part, boosterism by area newspapers quickened this expansion. An article by the editor of the *Idaho Statesman* provides an example (May 27, 1876). He wrote, "We left our hospitable friends Mr. and Mrs. Galloway on the Weiser yesterday, and took our route up Man's creek."

That would be Thomas and Mary Galloway. Thomas settled on the Weiser twelve years earlier and had become a very successful stockman. The roving editor described the general ten-mile course of the stream (now known as "Mann Creek") and the rich bottomland that provided "choice farming land all this distance with rolling hills on either side covered with bunch grass, offering pasturage for thousands upon thousands of head of cattle."

In fact, he said, "No section of the Territory affords better advantages or greater inducements for stock raising."

He then outlined some of the area's other pluses and named the dozen or so families that had already settled there. Finally, he concluded, "There is room for half a dozen settlers to take up Government land as good as that already taken up."

That same year, George Moser and his family became the first settlers in the Council Valley, on the upper Weiser River. They trailed a small cattle herd in from Oregon and also obtained some hogs. Soon, they were able to sell beef, pork, and butter to the mining districts. In 1878, a Council Valley post office was established and many years later the town of Council grew up around the Moser homestead.

The year after Moser settled in Council, Tom Cooper and Bill Jolly crossed the regional divide into the Little Salmon River drainage and took up horse raising in Meadows Valley. That fall, the first family settled there: Calvin and Lydia White.

Then, in 1879, the Campbell brothers arrived. In Nevada, Charles A. Campbell worked on a ranch. He later did some freighting. His brother joined him before he moved on into Idaho. Immediately seeing the potential of the valley, Charles Campbell founded the historic Circle C ranch. Those holdings would eventually grow into what present-day news reports called "probably the largest family owned spread in Idaho."

Toward the end of the decade, Boise, Payette, and Weiser valley stockmen were experiencing a boom. The *Idaho Statesman* reported (May 22, 1879) that former legislator Henry Riggs and some others had sold around four thousand head to Eastern buyers. The article said, "All these cattle were purchased in one neighborhood in the Payette Valley, not exceeding twenty mile along the river."

In 1880 and 1881, Peter Pence also found himself with a surplus of stock. Each of those years, he drove herds of feeder cattle to the railheads in Wyoming. From there, train cars took them to Omaha where local stockmen fattened them for slaughter.

In Boise City, the *Idaho Statesman* (March 18, 1882) said, "Cattle men are arriving in this city in large numbers and are being distributed to the various ranges as they arrive. Yesterday's stage brought half a dozen, who will drive from Weiser and Payette ranges."

Showing how far that area had grown, the *Weiser Leader* newspaper began publication in the fall of 1882.

Owyhee County also experienced substantial growth, especially in the Bruneau area. Thus, the *Idaho Statesman* crowed (June 16, 1877) about the stock industry south of the Snake "where several of the cattle kings of Idaho have thousands of fat cattle ready for the outside markets."

By the middle of the decade, Arthur Pence had "proven" his 1869 Bruneau Valley claim by building a two-room cabin near the upper-valley hot springs. With this as a base, he and a brother built up their cattle herd.

Then an unlikely chain of events changed his life. It began in Missouri when the mother of Mary Sydney Wells, one of four children, died and the family of Joshua Miller took her in. In about 1875 or '76, Miller received a substantial offer for his holdings. The Millers accepted and decided to relocate to California. Quite naturally, the trip included the Wells girl, who was eighteen at the time.

At Elko, Nevada, they realized that a relatively short side-trip would take them to the spread of Joshua's brother, George T. Miller. They made the visit and, as Adelaide Hawes put it: "here it was young Arthur Pence met his future wife, Sydney Wells."

Hawes provides no details about their courtship (one presumes Wells continued on to California), but they were married in October 1877. Arthur was thirty years old, Sydney about twenty. During the next two years, the Pences planted fruit trees and a large garden to go along with their cattle herd. In 1879, Pence sold off most of his cattle and focused on profitably selling fruits and vegetables in the mining districts. Some years later, he returned to stock raising, this time with sheep.

In 1877, Albert Loveridge and his wife Mary also settled in the valley. They had already experienced "boom-and-bust" time in the Nevada mines and arrived with "an old wagon, a team of horses, and $60.00" ... and a willingness to work. Like many homesteaders, the Loveridges farmed and ran a small herd of cattle. They succeeded well enough that Loveridge later bought a Snake River ferry and over four hundred acres along the river.

As the decade passed, the Bruneau herds expanded rapidly. The first large spread there, the "T" ranch, changed hands several times. By 1881, the "T" belonged to Barney Horn, who had come to the Idaho ranges from California. As for other big outfits, Adelaide Hawes wrote, "Dan Murphy at that time was the cattle king of Idaho."

Born in Nova Scotia, Daniel Murphy traveled with the Elisha Stevens party to California in 1844, at the age of nineteen. Bancroft's *History of California* stated that the group was sometimes "also called the Murphy company, from the name of a large family, afterward prominent citizens of Santa Clara County, which came with it."

Dan did some mining after gold was discovered, but later became heavily involved in the cattle business. He was among the four partners who bought out the "T" ranch, and later had his own holdings as well as an operation in association with Horn. In fact, the 1882 assessment records for Owyhee County listed "Murphy & Horn" as having the largest cattle holdings there.

When he died in late 1882, Murphy's obituary (*Owyhee Avalanche*, November 11, 1882), said, "He had amassed a very large fortune in lands in California, New Mexico and Arizona, and he probably owned more land and a greater number of cattle in Nevada than any other man in the State."

The assessment results printed in the *Avalanche* (August 26, 1882) highlighted a significant change in the region's economy. Accounting for private lands under title, ranch buildings, and conservatively valued animals, the economic worth of the Owyhee stock-raising industry exceeded the value of mining, farming, transportation, and all other economic activities. The *Avalanche* asserted that, "The above figures prove that Owyhee is not less a stock than a mining county. Indeed, this is one of the best cattle counties in the Territory."

Sheep were also a reasonable segment of the Owyhee stock business, their numbers about two-thirds those for cattle. By far the largest holdings belonged to Robert Noble. His Reynolds Creek ranch had grown substantially since 1874.

Richard Bennett was third on the list of sheep operators, at thirteen hundred head. As mentioned earlier, Bennett had slowly increased his cattle holding while he also worked and invested in the mines. In 1880, he had gone to Oregon to acquire more stock for his ranch. He decided to switch to sheep instead, and sold off his cattle.

Richard clearly had a talent for sheep ranching. Around 1884, he moved his growing family from the vicinity of War Eagle Mountain to a ranch on Castle Creek. That range is 30-35 miles west and southwest of Mountain Home. Richard almost immediately began sending herds to the new railhead in Mountain Home.

Throughout this time, cattle traffic across Idaho from Oregon and Washington swelled significantly. In 1879, the editor of the *Idaho Statesman* tried to assess (May 24, 1879) the volume. He knew from a traveler that "several immense herds of cattle" were on the trail from Oregon. Some had already reached the Snake. "There are several herds of these cattle, ranging all the way from 10,000 to 1,000 head now crossing or near the river."

Based on this, and his own observations, the editor reckoned that drovers would send as many as a hundred thousand head across Idaho during the coming season. Of

Ridin' Drag on the Drive

course, this also created problems. He wrote, "All these cattle are driven across Idaho at a heavy expense to the purchasers, and at a serious inconvenience and some damage to the country passed over." Their passage often required "much labor and care on the part of resident stockmen to prevent their own cattle from being driven off."

Toward the end of the year, the editor had clearly become fed up watching all that beef – money on the hoof – go by. Why, he wondered (*Idaho Statesman*, October 21 and 23, 1879), didn't more Idaho stockmen take advantage of this bounty? He wrote, "During the present summer several large herds of cattle have been sold in this section of Idaho to Eastern dealers and driven to Cheyenne and other points on the railroad. Those who sold got what they considered a fair price at home, but they might have realized much more by driving their own cattle to market."

Actually, his carping was somewhat misplaced. Recall that Truman Catlin had started a small cattle operation near Eagle Island in 1864. Around 1876, Catlin and a partner organized a drive of one thousand head to Cheyenne, Wyoming. Three years later, they not only drove their own cattle east, they also added to the drive from herds on the southern Camas Prairie.

In fact, official records show that Idaho ranchers drove at least fifty thousand head of cattle east in 1880. There might have been as many as seventy-five thousand. Still, the *History of Idaho Territory*, published in 1884, also felt Idaho stockmen could do more. After all, it said, "Millions of acres of bunch-grass lands remain unoccupied."

Further expansion would come, as Idaho stockmen responded to the pull of Eastern markets. The populations of many East Coast cities – Boston, New York, Philadelphia, etc. – had grown by over 31 percent. Those regions were also becoming more and more urban in character. People bought their meat at the market rather than raising their own. Chicago, St. Louis, and other mid-American cities became transshipment points, sending livestock east to local markets.

However, live animals lost weight during shipment, and some died along the way. Worse yet, neighborhood butchers had to dispose of about 40% of the carcass as waste, and portions of what he could sell had little value. No one had a good answer until, in 1878, Gustavus Swift commissioned the design of a reliable refrigerated railroad car.

Others copied his approach, and soon sides of "chilled" beef, lamb, and pork replaced shipments of live animals. Despite some initial resistance to the innovation, dramatically lower prices soon won consumers over. Cheaper meats fueled greater demand. Lower-income families that might have savored a special Sunday dinner roast began to include cuts for other meals.

More people enjoying more meat, especially beef, became a bonanza for growers, and Idaho stockmen were among those who benefited.

Thus, the Territory had large and growing herds entering the Eighties. The *Omaha Daily Republican* of February 3, 1881, claimed, without citation, that Idaho's ranges held "450,000 cattle, 60,000 horses, and 60,000 sheep."

Of course, the human population had also grown along with the herds and flocks. The 1880 Census gave Idaho's population as 32,610, almost double the number for 1870. The steady influx of people encouraged some in the Territory to dream of statehood. After all, they had a third more people than Nevada when it was granted statehood in 1864. However, that was a special case since President Lincoln and the Republican Congress wanted Nevada's pro-Union votes.

Still, the precedent to ignore population requirements for statehood had been set, and gave supporters hope. Unfortunately, they faced a much more serious challenge. Back in 1876, Congressional Democrats had agreed to statehood for Colorado. The Territory had gone Democratic in 1874, and leaders rashly assumed they could retain control, even though the region had a history of Republican leanings.

In a bitterly contested, and much-disputed election, Republican Rutherford B. Hayes edged out Samuel J. Tilden by 185 to 184 in the Electoral College. Although other specific deals actually "decided" the election, both political parties saw Colorado as a lesson. Its three electoral votes for Hayes made the back room horse-trading possible.

Thus, a candidate region had to satisfy a hard-to-achieve formula. One party must control both houses of Congress, and the Territory must support that same party. Not until 1889 was another Territory granted statehood.

While they waited, the stock raising industry would get past its "growing pains" and feel the effects of two trends. The first was the obvious fact that the amount of unclaimed land was shrinking. The second factor was the growth of irrigated agriculture, which squeezed stock raisers even more. Those impacts would, in turn, exacerbate the conflict between cattle and sheep ranchers.

Early on, the level plains along the Boise and Payette rivers had attracted farmers. Here, canals fed by simple diversion dams could water considerable acreage. Just as around Eagle Rock, large-scale projects were becoming more common. Eventually, irrigated farming would plow over the bunchgrass plains and push stockmen into the higher country.

In fact, there was clear evidence that crop agriculture was beginning to supplant stock raising in favorable locations. The Oregon Trail still carried pioneer traffic in 1882. John E. McDowell migrated from Kansas to the Kittitas Valley in central Washington that year. On July 12, their little train was just over a week into Idaho. McDowell wrote, "In camp for the night at the bridge one half mile south of Boise City. This is a beautiful place. We come over an awful rough country today. The gardens that is here beats all."

They had camped the previous night near Rattlesnake Station, so their route had brought them over the broken, arid plain and down the steep grade into the Boise Valley. The next day, eight miles further west, he wrote, "Boise is a beautiful place and this valley can't be beat for beauty and fertility. Wheat oats and barley to all destruction."

Coincidentally, the *Idaho Statesman* offered (July 18, 1882) some advice to those who chose to keep stock in the city. The writer said, "There is very little benefit from keeping cows in town. A few years ago, the grass covered the hills north of town, and cows could be driven out two or three miles and get very good feed."

136

They used Thomas J. Davis as one example of those who had once kept stock near Boise City. Davis had, along with others, founded the town. Besides his businesses, Davis acquired cattle ranches at several places in southwest Idaho. His men ranged horses all the way down into Nevada. Even so, Davis had converted many of his Boise Valley properties to fruit and vegetable farms.

The *Statesman* basically advised local owners to follow his example. One would simply wear the cattle out driving them to decent grazing. The article went on, "It would be just as well to keep them yarded up at home, and pay out the money for feed instead of herding."

By the 1880s, farms occupied much of the Boise Valley land that could be irrigated by a patchwork of small ditches. Further expansion required a comprehensive, integrated water system, one that started from a higher diversion point and carried much, much more water.

In June 1882, investors incorporated the Idaho Mining and Irrigation Company to make that notion a reality. Although financial reverses eventually doomed that company, others took its place. A quarter century would pass before the full vision could be realized, but it was clear the Valley's destiny was in farming, not stock raising.

With the range filling up, major trail drives were becoming a more immediate problem. On January 22, 1881, the *Idaho Statesman* reprinted an article from the Baker County [Oregon] *Reveille*. The article said, "On the Sweetwater in Wyoming at one station a record is kept of all stock driven over the route during the past year, and this record shows that the surprisingly large number of 170,000 head had passed through … These come from Oregon, Washington and Idaho, but the majority from the eastern portion of our state. There are other routes, which will increase this number probably 70,000."

Perhaps two thirds of those huge numbers originated west of Idaho and therefore trailed across the state. The *Statesman* observed, "The transit of these immense herds across the stock ranges of central Idaho is an evil of the first magnitude to our farmers and small stock growers, as the herds that are thus driven not only devour the grass on broad belts of the range they pass over, but also subject our citizens to much annoyance and considerable loss in stock."

Five days later, the *Statesman* had occasion to repeat this theme. "There is no greater curse to the stock growing interests of a country than the large bands of cattle that have been driven through this country for the past few years."

The earlier article offered a solution. "The only practicable remedy for this, and the only hope of the afflicted is in the advent of the railroad, which will take the cattle at or near the points where they are purchased and collected."

Fortunately, the Oregon Short Line (OSL) Railway was incorporated in Wyoming in April 1881. Because of an odd provision in the Union Pacific company charter, the OSL was created ostensibly as an independent company. However, with half its shares held by UP stockholders, its independence was merely a sham.

Track laying began in May at the Union Pacific station in Granger, Wyoming. That summer, the UP used its political connections to have U. S. Assistant Attorney General

Joseph K. McCammon negotiate a right-of-way through the Fort Hall Indian Reservation. The tribes also ceded a larger area around Pocatello Station.

While the rails advanced from Granger, builders shipped materials to Pocatello via the Utah & Northern's narrow gauge tracks. From there, crews laid narrow gauge rails toward American Falls, where they bridged the Snake River.

The OSL's standard-gauge tracks reached the Idaho border near Montpelier in June 1882. Then, in October (*Salt Lake Tribune*, October 11, 1882), they linked with the narrow gauge line at McCammon station. At that time, they had not yet laid a third, standard-width rail on the roadbed. Within a few years, the entire Utah & Northern line would be converted to standard gauge.

The coming of the railroad had a major impact on the development of Idaho, including the stock raising industry.

American Falls Railroad Bridge

CHAPTER ELEVEN: RAILS ACROSS IDAHO

Thud! Dust and smoke billowed from where the explosions slammed into the tough lava. When the cloud drifted away, Jim Kyner examined the results. The potent blasting powder – more powerful than ordinary black powder – had crumbled a considerable span of the rocky ledge.

He watched as the foreman waved hammer men onto the site. They could wield an eight-pound sledgehammer all day, and would soon break up the larger slabs. The stronger explosive cost more, but, Kyner said, "Black powder did little but heave up blocks too big to handle."

Off to the north ran the Little Wood River valley, a shallow mile-wide trough that rose to higher ranges in the hazy distance. The thin soil along this south side offered little nourishment for the sparse clumps of sagebrush, greasewood, and skimpy bunchgrass. Further south, across some twenty-five miles of rugged plain, lay the great canyon of the Snake River.

Meager as the ground cover was, it harbored plenty of rattlesnakes. They seemed to be everywhere. Fortunately, their notorious buzz provided enough warning so that, Kyner said, "In all the time we worked there, not a man or horse was bitten in my camp."

Scorpions, which "were far from rare," inflicted many more wounds, leaving "a white, hard spot the size of a silver dollar." Yet, Kyner said, "We ultimately learned to laugh at scorpion stings as if they were no worse than bees."

Wagons arrived and crewmen began pitching broken lava into their beds. Loaded, a wagon rattled toward a dumping area where they'd discard most of the chunks as being too large to form a stable base for the roadbed.

Less than a mile east along the course marked by the surveyors, another team shoveled hard-won gravel and dirt onto the grade line where a horse-drawn scraper had scoured off the scraggly vegetation. They needed a level, packed surface that rose a minimum of two feet above the surrounding landscape.

Beyond the fill crew, finished railroad grade swept by a craggy black wall, about four feet high. There, the blasting crew had knocked off the end of a massive lava slab. Railway surveying required tradeoffs among curves, cuts, and severe grades. Too many curves to avoid rocky outcrops or high ridges lengthened the rail line to be graded and laid. However, digging cuts and breaking rock slowed the crews down and added to the total cost.

Back at the forward blasting site, the foreman brought news of a common problem. The explosives had indeed shattered the higher slabs of the ridge, leaving a craggy surface of lava. However, some of the blasts had not cleared the rock below the grade line. Unfortunately, Kyner noted, "A railroad track laid directly on such unyielding stuff would ruin the rolling stock in no time. No locomotive could stand the punishment."

Teams with sledge hammers and steel drill bits moved onto the lava surface. They must pound holes deep enough so another set of charges would shatter the rock for at least a foot below the grade level. The crew could then fill the corridor with gravel, sand, and dirt.

Hacking and filling grade for the Oregon Short Line Railroad had proven far more difficult, and costly, than Kyner had anticipated. The contract offer had allowed him to choose where to start, so he'd selected a stretch a few miles west of Shoshone. The section was "to the unaided eye, a simple enough task, but what difficult, unyielding stuff that lava rock turned out to be!"

The countless ledges and ridges made for slow work, and shipping costs proved to be a constant drain. Even basic food supplies were expensive. Kyner figured that, "For every dollar that I spent in the purchase of case goods, more than two dollars was spent in getting it to camp."

When he took the grading contract in the summer of 1882, he had been assured that "end of track," with the main supply depot, would be completed to near his selected stretch within a month. Five months later, the new, hopeful town of Shoshone still waited for the track.

By the time the trains arrived, and he completed the contract, Kyner was $63 thousand in debt, "a sum so vast to me – and to most others in the Eighties – as to seem cast in astronomical figures."

Nor was he alone. Kyner said, "The work throughout all that country was so hard and so costly that contractor after contractor was going broke."

Fired by youthful Abolitionist feelings and the purported glamor of war, James H. Kyner lied about his age and joined the 46th Ohio Infantry in October 1861. Of his time in training camp, he said, "No boy of fifteen finds it difficult to fit into such a life. Within a day or two I felt as much at home as many of the older men who had been there longer."

Six months later, at the Battle of Shiloh, a Confederate musket ball smashed his right leg below the knee. Although it entailed more risk, surgeons listened to his plea to remove as little of his leg as possible. Kyner took his "handicap" matter-of-factly. The only concession he made was to always ride a buckboard.

After the war, he had tried his hand at farming, sold insurance in Nebraska, and served in the legislature there. At that time, railroads were the "hot" industry. Kyner's frankly pro-railroad legislative views landed him first a Union Pacific grading contract in Nebraska and then the OSL job.

Beyond the work itself, the Idaho job posed a crucial physical test. A hammers man challenged his authority on some minor point and Kyner brushed him off. The man angrily called him a coward. Kyner dove off the buckboard and knocked the man flat with one blow. He then proceeded to punch him senseless. Kyner later wrote, "From that time I was boss, while pick handle justice reigned."

Conceding that track-laying delays contributed to his Idaho losses, the company did provide a voluntary, but totally inadequate, $9 thousand reimbursement. More importantly, they awarded him a grading contract in the Indian Creek area, fifteen to twenty miles west of Boise City.

After the horrors of the lava ridges along the Little Wood, this new contract was like a dream. "When I went to look it over I almost danced with delight."

"I greatly enlarged my outfit," Kyner said, "and during a long period of time had so many horses at work there that it took three tons of oats a day to feed them ...

"Hay, by good fortune, we did not need, for among the sagebrush and greasewood the bunch grass grew, and by night-herding the horses, we took advantage of that. They worked all day and ate that bunch grass during most of the night, sleeping on their feet for the most part after four o'clock or so in the morning."

Kyner paid off his debts with several thousand dollars to spare, and left Idaho with his larger company. His connections brought further contracts in Colorado, Wyoming, and other plains states. He only returned to Idaho after vast changes had taken place. In contrast to the previous "parched and sagebrush-covered" expanse, he said, "Irrigation ditches have turned the desert dust into fruitful soil."

His memoir, *End of Track,* contains many interesting observations about Idaho in that earlier era, by no means all negative. Concerning Idaho's capital, he said, "Boise, to those of us accustomed to the desert, was almost Paradise."

He also said, "It may seem hard to believe that I fed my men on venison until they turned against it. ... The deer were easy to get, for as cold weather came they left the higher land about the Sawtooth Mountains and dropped down into the valley of Wood River.

"Trout, too, were endlessly plentiful – fine Rocky Mountain trout, speckled brown. ... We had many wagonloads of trout from Wood River."

While Kyner's crews were grading near Indian Creek in early 1883, the OSL diverted its track layers from the main line at Shoshone. Management figured they could generate revenue with a branch line north to the booming silver mines in the upper Wood River area. The tracks reached Hailey in May. (They were extended to the smelter in Ketchum the following year.) Work on the main route resumed in early June.

Not only did the branch serve the mines, it greatly encouraged the region's stock-raising industry. Thus, the company's hopes were realized, for "this railroad became profitable immediately. The freight consisted primarily of livestock and mineral products."

Shoshone thrived as a junction point. Kyner was told by those who knew all kinds of western camps and towns "that Shoshone was in those days quite the toughest of the lot. Certainly if any other place was tougher it was very tough indeed. Stabbings and shootings were common occurrences. A cemetery among the sagebrush near by was well populated by men who had died with their boots on."

The town turned more peaceable as the main line pushed west and "end of track" moved on. The railroad's impact was quickly apparent.

The north side of the Snake about thirty miles west of Shoshone had excellent pasturage. That prompted homesteading along Clover Creek and other streams. One of those settlers was David B. Bliss, who established a horse ranch there in 1879. Soon, the scattered settlement had a saloon and a small store, and three years later, a larger store built by Bliss's son-in law. When the railroad arrived, pioneers quickly coalesced along the tracks and Bliss soon became a local railroad headquarters. A post office was authorized there in October 1883.

Bliss became a vital watering station for steam locomotives that had just completed the long eastbound climb out of the Snake River canyon. Soon, stockyards provided a gathering point for cattle and sheep to be shipped on the railroad.

Steam Locomotive, ca 1885

Gus Glenn's ferry became the next convenient stopping place. The town was near water, and it brought business from the south side of the Snake. It is from the arrival of the Oregon Short Line, in the spring of 1883, that the actual town of Glenns Ferry dates its establishment.

Overall, the ferry lost Oregon Trail traffic to the railroad and it was abandoned by the end of the decade. Other ferries, however, benefited from the presence of the railroad, because of what Charlie Walgamott called "that great crack in the earth, [the] Snake River Canyon." Pioneers on the south side had few other options to reach the railroad.

Tom Starrh built a ferry near the mouth of Goose Creek (about four miles west of today's Burley) in 1880. Starrh Ferry ran until Ira Perrine spurred the construction of Milner Dam in 1904. Walgamott himself started a ferry above Shoshone Falls. It's not clear when he sold the business, but the ferry remained commercially viable until the Perrine Bridge opened in 1927.

Around thirty public ferries carried traffic across the Snake between American Falls and Farewell Bend, on the Oregon border. Many of them were established in the 1880s. All but a handful operated well into the next century.

Local markets like these and the Hailey/Ketchum branch were, in one sense, "gravy" for the OSL. The UP created the railroad mainly to secure a Pacific Coast link that was not dependent upon the rival Central Pacific. Rumors at the time suggested that the CP might send traffic over the Southern Pacific Railroad. That could close the transcontinental traffic to competitors. The CP and SP made a legalistic show at being separate entities. They were, however, one intertwined company for all practical purposes.

Promoter and developer Robert E. Strahorn deserves a big part of the credit for the rapid impact of the railroad in Idaho. Pennsylvania-born, Strahorn started out as a self-taught journalist. He had covered, and fought in, the war against the Sioux in 1875-1876.

A year after that, he published a hype-heavy book about the resources and wonders of Wyoming. Impressed, Union Pacific hired him to publicize all the empty western lands the UP was stretching to serve. This was shortly after his marriage in September 1877. Robert insisted that his new wife, Carrie Adell, be allowed to go with him. The company agreed. The couple traveled west to collect data, and impressions, of the UP domain. Robert then wrote pamphlets and articles to promote settlement.

Research for such promotion was, however, something of a cover story. Robert's "real" job was far more important. Carrie Adell later wrote, "His confidential arrangement to carefully examine various routes and regions with reference to railway extensions and possible tonnage was a most laborious task."

They had completed surveys in several western states when the OSL enterprise began. Then a group of major players formed the Idaho & Oregon Land Improvement Company. Its president was Alexander Caldwell, who had previously represented Kansas in the U. S. Senate. Strahorn was vice president and general manager. Although founded as an independent company, it had strong ties with the UP.

The surveyor's word was law on where the track would be laid. Strahorn had to select locations along the route that could provide business for the railroad. Of course, they also had to have a water source to service the steam trains. The Improvement Company profited by claiming the acreage around the selected spot.

It was taken as a matter of course that officials could benefit personally from the venture. In Hailey, the manager of the company that claimed the land allowed Strahorn to select a prime lot for himself.

Bliss and Glenns Ferry became railroad towns because the tracks followed the old Oregon Trail through their locations. Out on the plains to the west, the survey line began to diverge from the Trail. Thus, the route passed about eight miles west of Rattlesnake Station. That station served the old Oregon Trail, the Kelton-to-Boise stage route, plus traffic from the Boise Basin mines and Goodale's Cutoff across south Camas Prairie.

Strahorn makes no mention of any inducement from the land owner, but locating a rail town so near such an important traffic junction made perfect business sense. The new town quickly drew commerce to itself and appropriated the "Mountain Home" name and post office that had been assigned to the old stage stop four years earlier.

The railroad company's main priority was to connect with its partner in Oregon as quickly and cheaply as possible. People in Boise City sensed this, but hoped for the best. The *Owyhee Avalanche* summarized some of the issues. The article said (June 24, 1882), "There is some uneasiness in Boise among real estate owners for fear it will pass south of that place. … It looks … as though the road will run below Middleton, passing Boise about fifteen miles to the south."

The writer had a good handle on the situation. The steep grades between the Boise Valley and the higher plains to the south and west thwarted a direct approach. (Forty years later, construction of a main line link required crews to dig an eighty to one hundred foot deep cut through a quarter-mile of ridge.) The track would indeed bypass Boise City, the largest market in Idaho.

The road from Boise to Silver City had to cross Indian Creek, and a station had been built there. The stageccoach company called it simply "Fifteen Mile House." The *Idaho Statesman* praised it (September 13, 1883), noting that outbound travelers found "the welcome early breakfast" there. "Coming to Boise, it is the last place of changing horses, and the last opportunity for a meal in the 'desert' before driving over the intervening sage land to the green paradise on the Boise."

Steam engine limitations dictated the railway route in two ways. They labored on severe climbs, and they had a huge appetite for water. Thus, the surveyed route for the OSL followed Indian Creek through this expanse.

Kuna Depot near Fifteen Mile House offered the ideal combination of water and business. The existing road allowed for a relatively short stage trip between the railroad and the capital. The *Owyhee Avalanche* reported (September 15, 1883), "We hear that passenger trains are now running to Kuna, within fifteen miles of Boise City."

The *Avalanche* might have been somewhat misinformed. Trains were running into Kuna on the 15th, but reportedly the first passenger train didn't arrive for another ten days.

Railroad planners built another watering stop on Indian Creek about ten miles from Kuna. However, "Pard" – Carrie Strahorn's affectionate name for her husband – saw no obvious commercial possibilities there.

Early one spring morning in 1882, the Strahorns clattered north out of Boise City in a light wagon. In the back, they had stored a hamper of provisions, some equipment, and several blankets. Ostensibly they planned a tour of the mining districts. This misdirection, plausible because the mines were an important market for the railroad, would hopefully throw off watchers who followed Robert's every move. They, Carrie said, "were determined to profit by his enterprise."

Pard verified that no one was following them and then turned west. Carrie observed, "The whole air was full of budding life and birds were twittering in their new-made nests."

Some hours later, they had left the newly green trees, brush, and grass along the Boise River. Now they had to bounce and jolt around tangles of greasewood and sagebrush. Pard knew generally where surveyors had marked the rail line, but they had to search patiently for quite some time to locate the widely spaced stakes. The posts marched across Alkali Flats and cut the Boise River upstream from where Indian Creek flowed into it.

Pard parked the wagon along the proposed line but some distance from the river. The location should be safely out of the flood plain. It seemed singularly unpromising to Carrie. "The ground was as white with alkali as the winter robe of the mountain tops."

After hitching the horses at the rear of the wagon and feeding them a ration of oats, Pard grabbed some equipment and began assessing the surrounding area. The more Carrie saw of it, the less she liked it. She wrote, "Not a tree nor a sign of habitation on the town site, only the white, desolate glare and clouds of choking, biting dust that consumed the very flesh. It seemed like a place deserted by God himself, and not intended for man to meddle with."

Cottonwoods and willow thickets along the distant river provided the only relief from the stark gray desert vegetation. Unable to hear the sounds of the river or the birds in the shrubbery along its banks, Carrie found the silence and desolation oppressive. "What a forbidding place to build a home; my face was already sore from the poison ash, and my heart sank in a flash of homesickness."

She tried to read a book while Pard tramped around through the brush. Finally, unable to concentrate, she retrieved the town plans and artist's conception they had brought along. She remarked,

"There was pictured so enticingly the commercial streets, the residence locations, the parks, the places for churches and schools, the railroad and its switches, the depot and hotel, the wagon roads leading in various directions, and even the shade trees were there, and it all looked so complete that I fairly strained my ears to hear the toot of the engine and the ringing of bells. A lift of the eyelids and the dream vanished, leaving a wide chasm between the dream city on paper and the reality."

Undeterred, or probably unaware of his wife's reservations, Pard returned to their camp site and said cheerily, "Well, this is the spot."

The tracks reached Caldwell Station in September of 1883. By then, a crude depot had been built and many other structures were under construction. In early December, the new *Caldwell Tribune* printed its first issue. Within a year, the town of Caldwell had grown dramatically, with something like 150 buildings of various kinds. Locals planned a branch line to the Boise City market, but an economic downturn killed it.

Beyond Caldwell, the railroad again generally followed a branch of the Oregon Trail that led toward the Snake River ford near the mouth of the Boise River. Starting in about 1864, farmers had settled the area four or five miles east of the ford. The region offered rich soil, plenty of water for irrigation, and was far enough from the rivers to escape the periodic flooding. A considerable horse ranch – reportedly with over sixteen thousand head – occupied the land near the Snake.

Oregon Short Line tracks entered the area late in 1883 and crews built a siding four to five miles east of the river. Literally within a few weeks, entrepreneurs Albert and Frank Fouch moved the Fouch General Merchandise Store there.

The station here probably used the new standard railroad time right from the start. In an earlier era, cities and towns kept their own local time. Their reference might be a clock tower at city hall, a prominent church, a factory, or even a local jewelry store that carried watches. Accuracy, of course, depended upon the skill and reliability of the timekeeper … and whether or not the sun was visible.

Sun time also varies with the location. Thus, when it's noon in Boise, it's 12:02 p.m. in Idaho City, about 18 miles further east. Not too bad, but sun time has advanced to 12:15 in Pocatello. However, Pocatello *station* would not have been on sun time back then. It would have been on OSL (i.e., Union Pacific Railroad) time.

Early on, schedule glitches based on local time conflicts caused quite a number of disastrous train wrecks. By the latter part of the century, railway companies ran their schedules on the time at their headquarters, or perhaps their busiest terminal. This only added to the chaos.

Chicago's Union Station can serve as a hypothetical example. (Ignore the alphabet soup of railway names.) Our intrepid 1882 traveler boards a CB&Q Railroad at Burlington, Iowa. We'll suppose he bought a First Class ticket, so his luggage is checked through. When night falls, he sleeps soundly in his Pullman accommodation. He alights at Union Station right at noon, Chicago time. They're running late. His watch shows hometown time: 11:46 a.m.

To change railways, he has six choices, four of them on Chicago time. Luckily, he's not booked on the Michigan Central Railroad, which is in a separate terminal. Their next train leaves at 12:17 p.m. so he could probably make it if he really had to. His ticket for the PFW&C Railway says the train departs Union Station at 12:15 p.m. No problem, right?

Actually, he's missed both connections. The Michigan Central runs on Detroit time. It's currently 12:18 by their clock, and that train just pulled out. The PFW&C runs on Pittsburgh time. Their clock is at 12:30 and they left a quarter hour ago. That was why larger terminals had several big clocks showing the different railway times. It's also why thick printed railroad guidebooks were much in demand.

To alleviate the chaos, railroad officials in the U.S. and Canada created a set of multiple standard time zones. These are what we use now, except their "Intercolonial" zone, for eastern Canada, is called the "Atlantic" zone today. On "The Day of Two Noons," November 18, 1883, railway timekeepers all over North America made the switch. Some people squawked, but larger towns followed their lead within a year. Federal installations generally went along too, but the government didn't make the zones "official" until 35 years later.

When the little Idaho siding near end-of-track got its first station clock, it would already show the standard time. The siding would be named Parma the following year.

Four miles northwest of Parma, the grade came within a mile of the Snake River. The tracks then turned north to generally follow the river to where the Oregon Trail marked a way over the mountains in Oregon.

Less than three miles north of the turn, however, the Snake curved east to hug the base of the bluffs on the Idaho side. Thus, builders had to construct two bridges, at "Bridge Island" on the Snake, to carry the tracks across into Oregon.

Judge Frank Harris, who arrived in the Weiser area in 1880, wrote, "Another delay was necessary and a mushroom town sprang up there called St. Paul, which was somewhat of a lively place until the bridges were completed. Then it disappeared as rapidly as it was built and not a vestige of its existence now remains."

The tracks stayed in Oregon until the path of the river moved closer to the bluffs on that side. Then, yet another bridge brought the OSL back into Idaho. The next major bridge crossed the Payette River. Again, the coming of the railroad had an immediate impact. James Hawley's *History of Idaho* said, "The City of Payette, the county seat of Payette County, owes its origin to the building of the Oregon Short Line Railroad."

David S. Lamme had come to Idaho from Illinois in 1864 when he was twenty-two. For the next two decades he prospected and mined. Then, in May 1883, he happened to be passing near the mouth of the Payette River and observed advance parties of the railroad. Hawley says Lamme "saw the engineers surveying the route," but more likely it was the grading crew – most of the survey work would have been completed the previous year.

Judge Frank Harris

Sensing an opportunity, Lamme bought some land near the right of way and opened a general store, calling his outpost "Boomerang." Two months later, a railroad tie contractor set up camp near the river mouth and opened another general store in Boomerang. Once the railroad was completed, more settlers arrived and soon the little village changed its name to that of the river.

Beyond the Payette, the tracks followed the winding course of the Snake toward the Weiser River. At that time, the village of Weiser City had only been in existence since 1880. Washington County was created in February of the previous year, but the new county had no towns worthy of a name. Then "Lower Weiser" boosters, with a bit of voter fraud and skullduggery, won a hotly contested election to secure the county seat for their area. Since there was no town, county officers worked from their homesteads.

Solomon M. Jeffreys had been among the earliest pioneers along the Weiser River. Besides going into the cattle business, he also opened a store on land near the north bank. Now Jeffreys donated five acres near his store to the county. A short while later, a settler "built a small hotel, and thus began what is now Weiser." Jeffreys became one of the first commissioners for Washington County.

Weiser City construction picked up in 1881, fueled in part by news about the Oregon Short Line Railway. Thus, when the tracks came marching down the Snake River valley, Weiser was a fair-size town. The *History of Idaho Territory* (published in 1884) offered the following description.

> "There are three stores of general merchandise, two drug stores, three hotels, two blacksmith shops, two jewelry stores, three livery stables, one large establishment dealing in saddles, harness, hardware, etc., two stores dealing in stoves, tinware, etc., six saloons, one brewery, one large flouring-mill, with a capacity of fifty barrels per day, a good school house, a commodious hall, a good Court House and jail, and many smaller buildings and enterprises."

There was one catch, however. The village was located about a mile away from the railroad. The OSL decided that was too far and had Strahorn lay out a town site. "New Weiser" was located near the right-of-way, but south of the Weiser River. Despite angry words from "Old Weiser" inhabitants, several structures were built there, including a hotel.

A compromise of sorts occurred the following year, when the railroad relocated the depot to the bank of the Snake River just north of the Weiser outlet. Town and depot were still a mile apart, but at least now they were on the same side of the river. Ironically, the town suffered a devastating fire five years later, and most of the businesses moved nearer the depot during the subsequent rebuilding.

Just under eight miles from the Weiser River bridge, the rail line entered the constricted gorge that forms the entrance to Hell's Canyon. Here, the grade had to be blasted and filled between the steep mountainsides and the turbulent waters of the Snake River. Still, the tracks ran to opposite the mouth of Burnt River by February of 1884.

By then, Idahoans were already enjoying their new-found freedom of movement. From Silver City, the *Owyhee Avalanche* exulted (February 2, 1884), "The long looked for railroad is now opposite us, and is stretching its length along the plains of the Snake River in a westerly direction."

The article averred that "the Oregon Short Line to Granger and the Union Pacific thence to Omaha" offered the best way to travel. It went on, "Persons desiring to go east from here or Ada County, can take the cars either at Weiser City or Caldwell and have a quick, safe, and pleasant ride to Omaha, without changing cars, no sharp curves, no night changes, and no failures to make connections."

By this time, numerous railroads served Omaha. One line ran north to Duluth. There, passengers might board a Great Lakes steamer with destinations in Canada and all the way to Lake Erie. To the south, travelers could ride the rails through St. Louis to New Orleans and Atlanta. Several railway companies offered connections to Chicago, Pittsburgh, and every major city on the East Coast.

Ironically, links from Idaho to the west had to wait because construction errors delayed completion of the final bridge across the Snake. Not until November 1884 did the Oregon Short Line rails meet the Oregon Railway and Navigation Company tracks at Huntington, Oregon.

At that point, two transcontinental railways crossed Idaho. A little over a year earlier, the Northern Pacific had completed tracks across the Idaho Panhandle. The Oregon Railway and Navigation Company had actually laid rails north of Lake Pend Oreille by January 1882. From there, high mountains slowed progress. But the west and east segments linked up in September 1883.

Before the NP finished the through line, northerners began planning branch or alternative routes. A group from Lewiston, Grangeville and the Camas Prairie founded one such company in late 1881. Pioneer stockman John M. Crooks was among the investors. Besides branch lines, they hoped to find a lower pass across the Bitterroots. That could draw the main line to the Clearwater River.

148

Branch lines reached the Palouse region within a year or two. They would boost the north Idaho economy just as the OSL did in the south. The Camas Prairie, however, waited almost a quarter century for train service.

Oddly enough, rail traffic in southern Idaho became a two-way street for livestock. Market-ready cattle moved east, while ranchers with overstocked ranges in states east of the Rockies shipped herds into Idaho. They hoped to find open grazing land, but that opportunity was very short-lived. In any case, settlers poured into Idaho.

Alexander Duffes, born in Utica, New York, prospered as a builder and merchant for many years in Ontario, Canada. In the Eighties, he sold off his business interests and traveled west to explore the Pacific Northwest. Then, in 1885, he returned east, riding the Oregon Short Line. Somewhere in his travels, perhaps in Portland, he met Caldwell businessman James McGee.

McGee urged Duffes to scout the land around the watering station about nine miles southeast of Caldwell. Water, open land, and the railroad clearly favored development. However, the spot's proximity to Boise City was its real plus.

In April, the branch rail line project that was to start from Caldwell had finally called it quits. An alternative route from the closer station would reduce trackage from thirty to less than twenty miles. Moreover, there were fewer streams to be bridged.

Encouraged by what he saw, Alexander and his wife homesteaded a quarter section near the station. Duffes and his family moved into their new Nampa home in November 1885.

The Idaho Central Railway Company was incorporated in June 1886. The directors planned an ambitious program of major lines, but never actually built anything except the spur to Boise City. In September, Duffes and McGee formed the Nampa Land and Improvement Company and laid out additional town lots. Negotiations with the railway company continued through the winter.

The *Owyhee Avalanche* observed (May 14, 1887), "There can be little doubt now that Boise City is to have a railroad from Nampa, if surveying the route counts for anything. We are glad of it, and hope that the building of the road will add greatly to the building up of our capital, and the prosperity of her citizens."

Railroad construction started from the Nampa station in June 1887, and crews completed the line to the Boise Bench in early September. By staying up on the Bench, builders avoided the abrupt fifty to sixty foot drop to the river plain. However, the center of town lay over a mile away, on the east side of the river. Residents called their new rail link "The Stub," initially in derision, later with a perverse kind of pride.

Soon, they built a road from town to the depot, which required bridges over the Boise and a side stream. A few warehouses and a small hotel went up near the depot, but no one really wanted to pick up and move. Six years later, a spur off the Stub brought tracks down from the Bench and across the river to a new depot on the edge of town. The railroad district became an immediate magnet for growth.

The coming of the railroad had brought substantial change to Idaho even before the capital city joined the system. That included profound changes to the stock raising industry.

CHAPTER TWELVE: LIVESTOCK BOOM

The buckaroo circled the fringe of the loose band of cattle. The roundup crew had gathered over a hundred head from the high plateaus southwest of Bruneau Canyon and mustered them where the curved edge of a low bluff formed a natural amphitheater. To his right, the ground crew tended the fire, keeping several branding irons hot. The tenders watched carefully. The gusty June breeze could blow embers into the dry brush.

The rider flapped a two-foot-long *tapaderos*, his stirrup toe protector, to shoo a cow back into the group. Sun flashed off the silver inlay of his spurs, his saddle, and the horse's bridle.

Looking over the herd, he spotted an unbranded calf. He twitched the reins and applied slight knee pressure to direct his mount toward it. These calves were older, heavier, and more skittish than the spring-caught youngsters. The crew kept the gather loose so riders could move through it to ease the calves outside without spooking the rest.

Soon, the buckaroo had the calf and its mother out in the open. Deftly, he maneuvered to create some separation between the two. The horseman angled his mount and slung a loop towards the animal's head. Forty feet, fifty feet, the supple riata reached out. As the loop unerringly snared the head, the roper looped a quick dally around the saddle horn. Careful there; the rawhide rope would remove a thumb or finger caught in the bight when the calf hit the end.

The rider played the animal like a fish, drawing rope around the dally as he closed in. He let the line slide when the calf made another run. At times, friction produced a faint wisp of smoke from the wooden horn. Finally, a heeler rode over and flicked a loop around the hind legs.

The buckaroos stretched their captive between them and the ground crew quickly dumped it on its side. While one man earmarked the animal, another applied the branding iron. Freed, the calf trotted to where its mother waited. The roper turned his horse back to find another.

The term "buckaroo" is an Anglicized form of the Spanish/Mexican "vaquero" – ba-KER-o, "b" and "v" both sounding like the English "b". It denotes a cattle herder whose distinctive dress, equipment, and methods developed among the riders of the Great Basin – on ranges in Nevada and bordering areas in Utah, Idaho, and Oregon.

Nineteenth Century western herders – cowboys, buckaroos, and vaqueros – shared many attributes, including pride in their work, and especially their individuality. Cowboys and buckaroos both adapted techniques from Spanish and Mexican vaqueros. Each has subtle, distinctive features or practices.

Cowboys in the southwest and the regions north of Texas brought other traditions with them from the eastern states. The melding of those traditions with selective borrowings from the vaqueros led to a much greater difference between the cowboy and the vaquero. Buckaroo adaptations more clearly show their *Californio* – California vaquero – lineage.

The "typical" buckaroo, as much as there ever was such a man, wore a flat-brimmed hat with a low, flat-topped crown. Of course, many vaqueros wore the classic sombrero, which the buckaroos never seem to have adopted. Cowboys more commonly wore a hat with a rolled brim and high rounded crown. These often had indentations on the front or even a broad crease down the middle. (Still, just to confuse the issue, buckaroos did, and still do, wear such hats.)

Buckaroos also inherited a fancy neckerchief, often made of silk, from the *Californio*. Cowboys tended to wear a simple cotton bandana. Buckaroos might fasten the kerchief with a silver-inlaid slide. Cowboys mostly used a simple knot. Other apparel offered relatively few differences between cowboys and buckaroos, although the latter might be somewhat more creative in their design. Some *Californios* displayed more elaborate ornamentation on their clothing, perhaps some decorative stitching, fancier buttons, and so on.

Cowboys generally preferred spurs with short shanks and small rowels. Decorations, if any, would be simple "generic" marks, such as playing-card suits. Buckaroos, like vaqueros, liked big rowels, held away from the boot on a long shank. These might be embellished with intricate scenes traced in silver.

The horse's tack, especially the saddle, offered other points of distinction.

Cowboy Cutting a Cow from the Herd

Buckaroos and vaqueros preferred a simpler and lighter single-cinch saddle. Buckaroo saddles differed from those of the vaquero in a number of stylistic and structural details. Cowboys almost universally preferred a double-cinch saddle.

Another obvious difference appeared in the *tapaderos*, the leather shields attached to the stirrups. These prevent branches from jamming between stirrup and boot. Cowboy "taps" simply wrapped around the toe, with no flaps below the stirrup. Buckaroo taps had long flaps hanging down – as much as twenty-eight inches below the stirrup. Vaqueros had short flats or none at all, like cowboys.

Charles Walgamott described many of these features in his reminiscences, although he did not use the term "buckaroo." He referred to them as "Snake River Valley cowboys." After noting their preference for single-cinch saddles, he said, "Every cowboy was jealous of his rig, and often the saddle, bridle, spurs, and blanket were more valuable than the horse he rode. Often a bridle bit inlaid with silver, and bridle reins made by hand of rawhide or hair were highly valued."

"Those were the days of the 'Gay Vaqueros'," Adelaide Hawes recalled. "Of silver-mounted saddles, and bridles with Spanish bits, of bright shirts and big red-silk handkerchiefs, of long tapaderos, silver-mounted spurs, rawhide reatas that would reach a calf sixty to seventy feet away."

Her final statement is significant. Their ropes and roping techniques were a key distinction between buckaroos and cowboys.

Like vaqueros, buckaroos employed ropes made from thin strips of rawhide. These riatas were quite long – sixty to eighty feet, sometimes even more. The cowboy's rope seldom exceeded thirty to thirty-five feet and was fashioned from hemp or some other plant fiber.

Properly made fiber ropes are stronger than braided rawhide, so the cowboy roper could make a quick, vigorous catch. Thus, he would make his shorter throw, tie off "hard and fast" on the saddle horn, then bring his horse to a stop. The resulting shock was hard on both animals, sometimes throwing the calf off its feet. (This strenuous action may, to some extent, account for the cowboy's preference for the double-cinch saddle.)

As described in the representative scene above, the buckaroo employed more of a finesse approach. Again like vaqueros – whose roping skills are legendary – buckaroos generally had a greater repertoire of throws. Not simply "rope tricks," these were casts that might be needed at some point: into a tight corner, at a sharp angle, whatever. In general, cowboys stuck to the basics, although some individuals could certainly match buckaroo skills.

Buckaroos and vaqueros used the sliding dally technique to relieve the strain on their rawhide ropes, which might otherwise break. Buckaroo, cowboy, or vaquero … all ropers rightly fear the backlash of a snapped rope, which has been known to maim a man's eyes.

Livestock pioneers in Idaho, arriving from the East or Southwest, could not avoid observing vaqueros at work with their distinctive style. Some have estimated that, during the Nineteenth-Century heyday of stock raising in the Great Basin, as many as half the herders were Hispanic, especially in Nevada. According to Adelaide Hawes, cattle king Dan Murphy "ran thousands of head of cattle and hired Spanish help almost entirely."

As noted in Chapter Ten, Murphy's operation included considerable range in Nevada. Michael Hyde, once associated with the Golden Chariot mine, had a similar large holding. The *History of Idaho Territory* noted that, in addition to Hyde's land in Idaho, "He is also the owner of 5,300 acres of hay lands in … Nevada, all under fence. This is probably the most extensive ranch in Nevada. This ranch is principally used for feeding beef cattle. They are grazed in Idaho during the summer and driven to Nevada in the fall, where they are fed for the San Francisco market in winter."

Moreover, the *Owyhee Avalanche* reported (June 9, 1883), "Mike Hyde is constantly adding to his possessions, both in land and cattle. He recently purchased from Wm. Paine on Catherine Creek his ranch, for which he paid $1,500 and from Mr. Epperson of Bruneau his band of cattle, consideration $7,000. Mr. Hyde is now probably the largest land and cattle owner in Owyhee County."

Two years later, the paper reported, "We understand that Hyde Bros. has sold 1300 head of stock cattle and beeves to an eastern gentleman. The cattle are now being gathered for delivery."

Of course, the *Avalanche* could also give advice. On October 27, 1883, it said: "In as much as it is currently reported around the county, that there are horse, cattle and other thieves infesting our borders, we would recommend to the various horse and cattle men in this territory as well as the states of Oregon and Nevada, the propriety of having their brands and ear-marks advertised. It will aid the owners of horses and cattle in finding their animals, and have a tendency to discourage people from driving horses and cattle away that do not belong to them."

By now, little open land remained. David Shirk ran into this problem at the beginning of 1884. His herd "had increased at such a rate" that his range was getting over-crowded. He said, "I began to make every effort available to acquire title to more land by filing on all rights that the law afforded."

His statement referred to the various ways the Federal Land Office allowed settlers to claim public lands at nominal cost. Shirk acquired most of his new range in Oregon.

Crowding on the range, the ever-present rustlers, and other common interests brought together stockmen from Owyhee County and the adjoining ranges in Oregon and Nevada in July 1883. Their purpose was to organize a regional stockmen's association. Comparable efforts would soon occur all over Idaho.

Another "old-timer," Richard Bennett, also sought more and better range. In late 1886, he sold the Castle Creek property and moved his growing family to a ranch near Mountain Home. Over time, Richard created the R. Bennett and Sons Livestock Company. The *Illustrated History of the State of Idaho* (1899) said, "He is accounted one of the leading and most successful sheep-raisers of this part of the state, and his opinions on such matters are received as authority."

Old-timer or newcomer, people who wanted prime land now had to buy it. In about 1877, Levi Harris relinquished his mining interests in Nevada and took up a farm and stock spread in the Duck Valley area. However, in 1886, he and his family had to leave when the government expanded the Duck Valley Indian Reservation. They moved to the Bruneau Valley and bought land and stock from George Hill.

Captain George W. Hill had been one of the original white settlers in the Valley, claiming a homestead on the south side of the river. The Harris family took up where he left off, adding their own stock to the purchased herd. According to Hawes, they became "one of the most substantial and respected families of the valley."

Joseph Rosevear also came late to Owyhee County. Born in Cornwall, England, he had chased gold in Australia and again in Nevada, with returns to England in between. He and his family finally settled in America, first in Kelton, Utah, and then in Kansas. Rosevear was about forty five when he drove twelve hundred head into Idaho in 1887. They found open land at the extreme headwaters of the Bruneau, about five miles from the Nevada border. A few years later, Rosevear moved to near Glenns Ferry, hoping to avoid the mounting encroachment of sheep herds. Ironically, he and his family eventually went into the sheep business themselves.

Other pioneers also settled on lands near the Nevada border, one of them being Dow Dunning.

After thirty-five miles on the trail from Bruneau, Dow topped a small rise and reined in his horse. On his right, 500-foot bluffs formed a rough wall that rose from the irregular plain onto the Bruneau-Owyhee plateau to the west. To the south, the plains continued to climb slowly toward the broad saddle between Poison Butte to the southeast and the north-south line of bluffs. About three-quarters of a mile east was the deep ravine that led Wickahoney Creek north to its confluence with Big Jack Creek and on to the Bruneau River.

Dunning urged his horse forward. Here and there, cattle marked with his "87" brand grazed contentedly on the bunchgrass. The stream winding across his route ahead was what made his homestead valuable, despite its isolation. The steady flow from Wickahoney Springs, part way up the bluffs, provided a reliable supply of water for their garden and stand of apple trees. His hay crop would improve further when he extended the ditch system.

Dow waved to his two small daughters as he rode toward their dugout, cut into a slope near the stream. Someday, they'd get enough ahead to build a real house. He'd need a stone mason for that. No useful timber grew anywhere near them on these high plains. His wife Maggie emerged from inside, moving with some effort. Older wives and grandmas who saw her swore the new arrival would be a boy, but who knew?

Dow Dunning and his brother George had come to Owyhee County from Michigan in the late 1870's. They first raised stock along Reynolds Creek, then moved to Little Valley near the Bruneau, where they also cut and sold hay. George never married, but was considered a reliable worker in a variety of jobs. Although not a trouble-hunter, he was also known for his gun skills, once serving briefly as a deputy sheriff. Later, the association of big Wyoming ranchers hired his gun for the infamous Johnson County War. Dunning turned against them when he learned that their plans called for a wholesale slaughter of alleged rustlers – settlers and small ranchers.

Dow married Maggie in October of 1886, when he was about twenty-seven and she about twenty-three. He took up the Wickahoney Springs homestead, about twenty miles north of the Duck Creek Indian Reservation, in 1887 (hence the "87" brand).

The diminished amount of open grazing land that pushed Dow Dunning onto his isolated ranch naturally heightened tensions on the range. Old-timer memories suggest that far more confrontations happened than the few that actually made the news.

Cattlemen even clashed with other cattlemen. David Shirk, whom we met earlier, had a shootout with a man who had jumped his ranch claim. He was acquitted of a murder charge when it became clear that a nearby "cattle king" had paid the intruder to "get" Shirk.

Oregon had another case just across the border from Owyhee County. A vaquero known only as Spanish Charley had located his home ranch twenty-five to thirty miles northwest of Silver City. Charley was herding his considerable band of horses when someone informed him that sheep had been moved onto his home spread. He hurried back and confronted the sheepman, Jake Mussell. At the subsequent trial, Mussell claimed he had shot Spanish Charley in self defense, and there were no witnesses to say otherwise. The jury acquitted him, but the legal costs put Mussell out of the sheep business.

By the latter part of the decade, estimates placed the number of cattle in Owyhee County at over one hundred thousand head. No comparable figures exist for sheep, but it's possible they matched or even exceeded the cattle numbers.

The late Eighties brought another sign that stock raising in Idaho was now a mature endeavor. Recall that, in 1864, pioneer James Wilson had established a very successful ranch not far from Boise City. As that operation grew, he imported top-grade shorthorn cattle to improve the quality of herds. Around 1882, when he was about 56 years old, James promoted his son William to manage the James Wilson & Sons stock company.

William E. Wilson was born in Oregon and brought to Idaho when he was less than a year old. Now his father handed him the reins for day-to-day operations. At the time, William lived in Mountain Home. When James Wilson died in 1899, he owned over a thousand acres of land.

Another old-time cattleman, Truman C. Catlin, also had a son working for him. However, Truman continued to run the main operation himself. The son apparently handled only the Eagle Island property. Catlin even owned cattle in Montana. That herd suffered during the disastrous winter there, but his Idaho properties allowed him to recover. Catlin often shipped cattle east from Idaho in carload lots.

Further north and west, Peter Pence began to look beyond the Payette River cattle business. Oregon Short Line tracks would soon arrive in the area. At least

Cattleman Truman C. Catlin

Pete would no longer have to drive cattle across the Territory to reach outside markets. He knew the town of Payette would grow when the railroad arrived. He moved his family into town before 1885. There, Pence opened a meat market and a hotel, and owned other real estate.

Pete continued to operate the ranch. It was during this period he began raising sheep along with cattle. Around 1884, Pence sold a major block of cattle to enlarge a ditch bringing water to the ranch. He then extended the ditch to sell water to farms north of the river. Over the next two decades, Pence invested in other ranch properties as well as Boise City real estate.

Another original settler, Thomas C. Galloway, also anticipated the impact of the railroad. He had acquired ranch property along the river and in a mountain valley to the northeast. As the tracks approached, Tom sold the valley ranch and a vast herd of horses. He then invested in property around Weiser, and also in Boise City. For a time, he and his family lived in Boise so the children could attend the better schools there. In 1882 and 1884, Thomas served on the Territorial Council (equivalent to a state Senate), so it made sense for him to live in the capital anyway.

The approach of the railroad turned "Weiser Bridge" into Weiser City, an actual town. Galloway prospered along with the town, but retained his stock ranch for many years. Like Pence, he also became involved in irrigation projects.

Of course, newcomers continued to settle. One such was James A. Gerwick who arrived in the Weiser area in 1887, at age twenty-seven. He must have had a decent stake because he immediately went into the sheep business. At times, his operation would run as many as five thousand head.

Hawley's *History of Idaho* emphasized the importance of the railroad to stock raising, particularly sheep. He wrote, "The high price for transporting wool and the impossibility of putting the lambs on a market precluded any great attention being given the sheep business in Idaho until after the building of the Oregon Short Line."

However, "with the advent of the railroad soon came great herds of sheep."

Although some ranchers had substantial sheep holdings before the railroad arrived, census numbers bear out Hawley's assertion. In 1880, cattle outnumbered sheep by more than three to one. A decade later, herds of both had grown dramatically, but sheep then outnumbered cattle. A reasonable projection of this growth suggests that sheep numbers probably caught up by about 1887.

Railroads had a totally different effect in the north. There, they tipped the balance away from stock raising. Because the Panhandle receives more rain, agriculture does not generally require extensive irrigation systems. Even so, farms remained fairly small, aimed at local markets. Settlers relied on products that could "walk to market," mostly cattle and horses. Then, in the late 1880's, the Northern Pacific completed a branch line into Genesee. Soon, grain and fruit production dwarfed the stock industry in the Palouse region.

Unfortunately, growers on the Camas Prairie had to wait another two decades to have a rail line. There, Cottonwood became a prominent gathering place for stock to be trailed out of the region.

One of those who gathered stock at Cottonwood was Jacob L. Eckert. Born in Ohio, Eckert spent many years in Kansas, first as a cowboy, then five years as a ranch foreman. He came to the Camas Prairie in 1882, at the age of thirty-seven.

Eckert began almost immediately to upgrade his herds, bringing in Shorthorn and Galloway stock as well as Percheron horses. He also broke out land and began raising grain on the prairie. Jacob fed most of the grain to his stock, essentially upgrading his feed mix along with the animals themselves. This also saved the cost for transporting and milling the grain.

Irishman James Madden also came to Camas Prairie during this period. Madden had immigrated to the United States as a young man and taken up farming in California, first as a hand and then with his own place. Twice, high water ruined his prospects, so he and his family moved to Idaho in 1884. Madden managed to claim enough land for a ranch, where he began with a small herd of cattle. That didn't work out, so the following year he turned to raising sheep. Finally, hard work and luck earned him notable success in the sheep business and made him a wealthy man.

As these new pioneers arrived, some of the "old guard" began to pass on. In 1863, the firm of Crooks & Shumway had pioneered stock raising on the Prairie. John Crooks later provided the land for Grangeville and survived the Nez Percés War. In 1881, he invested in a company formed to bring a railroad to the Prairie.

By then Crooks was over sixty, and seems to have divested himself of his ranch property. He still owned considerable Grangeville real estate upon his death in 1884. Aurora Shumway seems not to have done quite as well financially. However, he too lived through the Nez Percés War, and later served as a Probate Judge. Shumway passed away in Grangeville four years after Crooks.

On the other hand, Loyal P. Brown, Mount Idaho businessman, rancher, and promoter, was still active in the area. The Grangeville newspaper, the *Idaho County Free Press,* reported (June 18, 1886), "Over one thousand head of horses will be shipped from Camas Prairie this summer to Montana and other eastern markets. A band of cattle, belonging to L. P. Brown, passed through Grangeville on Saturday morning the tenth instant. They were taken near Cottonwood somewhere to be herded."

However, like many other stockmen, Brown had also diversified into sheep. The *History of Idaho Territory* noted that "He has 6,000 or 7,000 fine and grade merino, cotswold, etc."

Two years after that *History* was published, the *Free Press* said (June 25, 1886), "A band of 3,800 sheep, the property of L. P. Brown, passed through town last Monday bound for the summer range on Craig mountain. The flock was sheared and dipped at Mt Idaho."

Brown was also the first president of the Idaho County Stock Growers' Association, which had been organized in July 1885. According to its charter, the Association's goals were "to advance the interests of stock growers and dealers in live stock in said county and for the protection of the same against frauds and swindlers and to prevent the stealing, taking or driving away of horned cattle, sheep or other stock from the rightful owners thereof, and to enforce the stock laws of Idaho Territory."

As it had done just over a decade before, the winter weather of 1886-87 warned stockmen that they needed to change their way of doing business. In April 1887, one pioneer living a few miles west of Cottonwood sent off a letter that described the weather in February.

He wrote, "The snow was five feet deep at my place. Near the new public road it was three feet deeper. The only way to get out was by means of snowshoes. ... Our neighbor, Mr. Cooper, did not feed his sheep at all and did not lose even eight per cent. He has 300 spring lambs in his flock now."

Other stockmen in the northwest were not so fortunate. Many in Montana and Wyoming were wiped out. In July 1887, the *Free Press* said, "In Montana, stockmen are congratulating themselves that they only lost fifty per cent of their stock last winter, while here our cattlemen are kicking and cursing because a few of them lost ten per cent."

Again, the warning was largely ignored in Idaho. In fact, stockmen were pleased at the business opportunity. The Conrad Kohrs ranch near Deer Lodge, Montana lost about two-thirds of its herd. Kohrs purchased the bulk of his replacements in the Boise and Payette valleys, then moved on further west. He said, "I restocked my herds with steers from Idaho, Oregon, and Washington, and others adopted the same method of recuperating."

Most areas in Idaho suffered much less than the states east of the Divide, although the Lemhi and Upper Salmon River valleys felt some effect. Colonel George Shoup's son recalled that, "The severity of this season was not so severe in this section, but amply so."

In her memoir, Abigail Duniway does not mention a rough winter in the region. Abigail Jane Scott had chronicled graves along the Oregon Trail when the family moved to Oregon in 1852. Unfortunately, a farm accident disabled husband Ben Duniway, and Abigail had to support the family. She ran a millinery shop and then published a weekly newspaper. She became famous for her advocacy of women's suffrage

Abigail succeeded well enough that she also found time to lecture all over the Northwest. However, her efforts in Oregon and Washington had been notably unsuccessful. In the early 1880s, her husband and son claimed a homestead in Idaho's Pahsimeroi Valley, east of Challis. She joined them there in 1887 and they ran a livestock ranch for seven years. They apparently came through the 1886-1887 winter without too much damage.

In general, areas further south saw relatively less of an impact. Eastern Idaho, for example, was booming and reports from the period don't mention any particular problems during that winter.

By this time, ranches and settlements were filling in all across the region. South of the Lemhi Valley, Dave Wood turned from mining to raising stock along Birch Creek some time in the early 1880s. Initially, he ran both cattle and sheep, but the Wood Livestock Company would later be known mostly for its substantial sheep bands.

In 1885, money from some Salt Lake City investors funded creation of a stock ranch on the Little Lost River, fifty-five to sixty miles northwest of Eagle Rock.

Settlers and ranchers had also spread north of Eagle Rock. Mormon pioneers led by Thomas E. Ricks founded Rexburg and built the first log houses there in the spring of 1883. A year later, colonists arrived in the general area that would become Rigby. By about 1886, area ranchers had imported over four thousand sheep.

In this same period, two homesteaders settled east of Eagle Rock. One of them, John Empey, went into stock raising as well as farming. At this point, relatively little had been done to develop irrigation canals and ditches to allow extensive crop agriculture. Still, the combination of stock raising and an expanding farm base fueled growth in the town.

Samuel F. Taylor certainly envisioned a rosy future. In 1884, voters elected him Oneida County sheriff. At that time Oneida County included most of Eastern Idaho. Sam also served as a director on the first school board in Eagle Rock. In 1885, he established a livery stable which quickly became the leading such business in the village. Taylor grew grain and hay for stock on his three hundred and sixty acre spread southeast of town.

The first newspaper appeared in Eagle Rock about that time. The editor/owner, William E. Wheeler, had first based his publication in Blackfoot. Then, in 1884, he moved everything to Eagle Rock and rechristened it the *Idaho Register.*

Large cattle drives still ran through the area during this period. Two years earlier, a local correspondent estimated (*Salt Lake Tribune*, July 15, 1882) that perhaps 75 thousand Oregon cattle would pass through Eagle Rock during the year. At that point, the Anderson Brothers, who then owned the old bridge, had collected tolls for "some 15,000 head of cattle and 30,000 head of sheep."

A year after the move, the *Register* published (April 4, 1885) an article prepared by Robert Anderson, in which he said "Large numbers of cattle have been driven from Oregon during the past season."

By then, of course, Oregon Short Line tracks had been completed across Idaho. Soon, cattle drives from Oregon largely ceased. Even so, local and regional drives continued to and through Eagle Rock, although the town's population dropped precipitously when the railroad moved its shops to Pocatello in 1887. Fortunately, the village survived and began to recover as regional farming and ranching increased. That growth resulted in heavy shipments of cattle and sheep.

The *History of Idaho Territory* had highlighted the potential for such growth in 1884. In fact, the writers considered the area under-utilized. They said, "The country is well watered by numerous small streams; the winters are mild, and thousands of acres of the best natural grasses lie unused and wasted from one year to another. ... All the foot-hills and high up in the ranges the ground is covered with bunch grass as thick as it can stand, and watered by a thousand springs and brooks in all directions."

One deterrent might have been the continued presence of outlaws: rustlers, horse thieves, and men on the run from the law. They could hide all too easily in the dense thickets along the river and the rough foothills to the east, and were often blamed for mysterious disappearances.

Still, criminals did not have it all their way.

In June 1884 three heavily armed men, guiding twenty-five horses, splashed across the Teton River. Clouds of mosquitos swirled about them from the marshy ground and sloughs along the stream. The men swatted and flailed about to protect their faces and eyes until they approached the Rexburg settlement, a half-mile south of the river. To the southeast, not far beyond the cluster of log cabins, the land rose steadily to an imposing bench that overlooked the plain.

Horses on the Move

The town was too new to have a hotel, so the leader asked Brigham Ricks, brother of Thomas, if they could get supper and a place to sleep. Their shoulders sagged and their faced reflected tiredness. Brigham allowed as how he could accommodate them at his home, but they'd have to make beds on the floor.

The western sky still retained a twilight glow when Thomas entered and said, "Brig, your cows are in the corn."

Outside, Tom told his brother that a sheriff and posse from Montana had ridden into town. They had trailed the horses, which were stolen, all the way from Deer Lodge. It was too dark to do anything right away, but the posse planned to arrest the men first thing in the morning. Back inside, Brigham tried to think of a way to send his wife and children to safety. But the men watched him closely.

Not until morning could he get his family out. Around 6:30, he told the men that they should come across the lot to his brother's house for breakfast. The lawmen had taken up key spots by the houses and nearby stable. Their views commanded the yard between the two homes.

About a half hour later, two men strolled out into the yard. They were past the woodpile when a lawman yelled from the stable, "Hands up!" Startled but desperate, the two fled back towards Brigham's house. A hale of shots rang out, and one man stumbled and fell. The other scrambled into the house. Trapped but game, the fugitives inside began exchanging shots with the lawmen. Gunsmoke swirled and drifted among the structures, with an occasional spray of wood chunks from a near miss.

Finally, the firing from inside stopped and a gun sailed into the yard. Moments later, one rustler came out with his hands held high. He'd had enough, and his companion had been hit hard. As the pursuers secured their prisoner, the man who had stumbled stirred and also surrendered.

The wounded man, a Texan, soon died and a young man from the posse buried him. Gathering up the recovered horses, the Montanans headed back toward Deer Lodge with their two prisoners. Later, word reached Rexburg that the posse hadn't troubled themselves with taking the two back for trial. A handy tree along the Snake solved that annoyance.

In another instance, the *Idaho Register* reported (October 24, 1885), "Horse thief caught at Jackson Hole with 17 head of High and Stout's horses."

160

In time, the rustling problem diminished as increased settlement gave the criminals fewer places to hide. Two newcomers who settled in the area were Charles W. Berryman and George B. Rogers.

Older by a year, George Rogers was born in 1842, about thirty miles west of Madison, Wisconsin. Gripped by gold excitement after 1862, he tried his hand mining in California, British Columbia, Idaho's Boise Basin, and Montana. Finally, around 1870, he joined with Berryman in the freighting business.

Charles Berry was also born in Wisconsin, 8-10 miles from Dubuque, Iowa. He too tried his luck in the mines in 1862, first in Oregon and then the Boise Basin. A pack train provided much greater success for him until Indians stole everything. He went back to the mines in the Boise Basin and then bought claims around Virginia City, Montana. He had better luck than Rogers. After visiting family in Wisconsin, he returned west and started the partnership with Rogers.

The firm of Berryman & Rogers thrived for over a decade. However, the railroad cut into their profits and in about 1883 they sold the business. They then bought property northwest of Blackfoot and began raising cattle and horses. Two years later Rogers had a fine home built in Blackfoot. Over the years they purchased more land to grow hay and grain for their stock.

About that same time, H. G. Rand established his War Bonnet Ranch on land south of the Blackfoot River. The operation did very well. By the end of the decade he and a partner would be running twenty-five to thirty thousand head. They are credited with bringing the first Herefords into eastern Idaho, in 1887.

Down near Franklin, Samuel C. Parkinson was building up his herds. Like many others, Parkinson had been a successful freighter, but around 1885 he turned to raising cattle and horses. He too saw the value of high-quality stock and imported thoroughbred horses as well as pedigreed Holstein and Durham cattle. Within a few years Parkinson added sheep to his holdings, eventually running ten to twelve thousand head.

Ranchers probed into every valley and upland plain, looking for promising land. Writing about the years before the mid- to late-Eighties, James H. Hawley, frontier lawyer and later state Governor, said, "Eastern Idaho, except for a few of the older and easily settled valleys, was for fifteen years in reality one big cattle ranch."

Nor were areas further west being neglected. Partners Lonegan and Burke added to their own holdings by buying out the "IL" brand, which ran stock on the west side of the Snake above American Falls. After the acquisition, the Lonegan-Burke "70" brand ran cattle on blocks of land located from north of the Blackfoot all the way south to the Raft River. They competed for grazing space with the Armour Cattle Company and the Idaho Land and Cattle Company, both reportedly large operations.

Many consolidations took place during the decade. The most impressive of these transactions occurred in mid-1883. John Sparks and John Tinnin purchased a substantial part of Jasper Harrell's holdings for the then-astronomical sum of $900 thousand. A Chicago stockman's journal reported the deal and said, "They have now 70,000 head of cattle, and they will brand 17,000 calves this fall. They are undoubtedly the largest of the cattle kings" in the region.

Three years later, the March 1886 *Albion Times* said the Sparks-Tinnin ranch had "in the neighborhood of 100,000 head of cattle and their range takes in the entire western portion of the county, from Rock Creek to Owyhee county. Their summer range extends into the mountains of Nevada, while their winter range is principally on Warm Creek, Shoshone Valley and Snake River."

The Raft River Land and Cattle Company ran at least seven thousand head. That firm had purchased the holdings of John Q. Shirley in 1883. (Shirley, of course, had helped bring Texas cattle into Idaho in 1866.) Also, the firm of Sweetser Bros. & Pierce had grown substantially and was "breeding thoroughbred Hereford bulls to thoroughbred Durham cows and raising their own bulls for the range."

From its modest beginnings, the Arthur D. Norton ranch near Rock Creek had grown to three or four thousand head, and he had taken up range further west. (Norton had apparently bought out his 1871 partner, Miles Robinson.)

Ranching saved the Rock Creek store and community. By March 1883, with the railroad completed as far as Shoshone, stagecoaches and freight wagons from Kelton, Utah no longer ran through Rock Creek station. Fortunately, local business grew to offset the loss of long-distance traffic.

Charlie Walgamott related a story that speaks to the community's continued importance and, at the same time, to the depredations of rustlers and horse thieves. Texan George Goodhart had come to Idaho in the late 1850s. Although still in his teens, he was already known to be a fine tracker, marksman, and rider. After acting as a scout and guide during the Bannock War of 1878, Goodhart found steady employment as a messenger, guide, and tracker, including work with various law officers.

On one occasion, he rode east from Rattlesnake Station to pick up the mail from end-of-track. The stage station was located about seven miles northeast of today's Mountain Home, while the Oregon Short Line was advancing west from Glenns Ferry. After he had the bundles, he cut the trail of a half-dozen horses with three riders. Goodhart sensed something fishy about the way the men avoided the railroad right-of-way, where they might be seen.

Goodhart delivered the mail and then rode toward Boise City. Soon, he met three men who were looking for a thief who had stolen some horses from the Boise race track. They asked if he had "seen a man with five head of horses." They also said that the owner and the sheriff had offered a substantial reward for the thief's capture.

Goodhart knew immediately that these men were hopeless trackers. Needless to say, Goodhart contacted the sheriff as soon as he reached Boise City, and arranged a suitable agreement on the reward money. Accompanied by a deputy, with fresh horses, he headed east. They met the three searchers, who were sure the thief must have gone west, not east.

Goodhart offered no opinion. They continued east, although the deputy wondered if they "were looking in the wrong direction." Further along, George said, "Let us leave the stage road and get a little south and I think we will strike their trail."

When they found the trail, Goodhart read the signs so the deputy would understand that they had three horse thieves to deal with. With pauses to rest and feed their horses, the two followed the fugitives up the Snake, once visiting a ranch to exchange their jaded mounts. Finally, they crossed the river by way of Starrh Ferry, across from Goose Creek. The ferryman said the three men had talked of taking the Albion road toward Corinne and Salt Lake City.

The tracker soon discovered the men had doubled back to the west. They were most likely headed for Nevada, probably with a stop at Rock Creek store. At Rock Creek, as Walgamott told it, "George glanced at the horses in the barn and saw the five head of stolen horses. This part of the reward was sure, for the horses were virtually in his possession, but to capture the men might be different."

Inside, the only customer besides the three fugitives was a man George knew. He said, "Hello, Tom, we are on our way from Fort Hall to Tascora, and if Mr. Stricker will give us quarters we will stop for the night. I have swallowed a peck of dust along the Oregon Trail and I think we had better all have a little drink."

When Goodhart tossed his money on the counter, Stricker pushed it back and said, "Travelers always have a drink coming on their arrival at the Rock Creek store."

That was all the pretext George needed. He said, "That tastes just like another; you gentlemen at the table, can you quit your game long enough to take a social drink with us?"

The three rose and bellied up the the bar, whereupon Goodhart quick-drew his gun and told them they were under arrest. After the thieves were secured, George and the others "all drank to each other's health." Rock Creek continued to serve local ranchers for another thirty years or so.

Besides the A. D. Norton ranch, the *Albion Times* also identified at least three other Cassia County firms that ran anywhere from five to twelve thousand head of cattle and horses. Moreover, in 1887, the Russel and Bradely Cattle Company sold seven thousand cattle in one lot to another outfit that was trying to expand its holdings.

In fact, the *Idaho Statesman* asserted (October 9, 1886) that the business "has grown to wonderful proportions of late years. Where 1,000 head was formerly considered a large band, now bands of 5,000, 10,000 and even 20,000 head are not uncommon."

Of course, a similar statement could have been made about the sheep business, which was also booming. Nonetheless, in 1887, the legislature extended the "Two Mile Limit" law to encompass the entire state. Two factors drove this extension.

One was the erroneous, but widely accepted notion that cattle would not feed where sheep had grazed. Modern husbandry has shown that mixed cattle and sheep grazing can actually be more productive, if properly managed.

However, if stock are allowed to over-graze a plot, they will deplete all forage plants, regardless of their normal preferences. (Cattle heavily favor grasses, while sheep are more likely to include broad-leaf non-grasses, called "forbs," in their diet.) Moreover, sheep are basically more efficient eaters. Their lips, teeth, and tongues can cut closer to the ground and more effectively strip leaves off browse plants. A flock may literally leave nothing behind for cattle to eat.

The second factor driving the ban was more complicated, given the fact that some stockmen – like L. P. Brown up north – raised both. Established ranchers who ran just one or the other mostly got along. They might argue over rights to a given patch of range, but that sort of friction was, as noted above, also true between neighboring cattlemen.

Owyhee cattleman, and regional historian, Mike Hanley explained: "It was the tramp cowman and tramp sheepman who caused the friction. They ... mooched off those who had put together an outfit. Cattlemen and sheepmen alike fought these itinerant individuals."

The Two Mile limit law was just one more tool in that fight. Some ranchers found another solution to the land holding problem. They put up barbed wire fences. As noted in Chapter 8, in 1874 Joe Glidden had invented the first practical form of barbed wire. After a slow start, even stockmen embraced the notion and production skyrocketed to meet the demand. Down in the Texas Panhandle, in 1882, a ranch company fenced off a quarter million acres.

Barbed Wire Fence

Within a few years, other ranches dwarfed that land grab: a million acres for one Nebraska spread, 3 million in New Mexico, and 3 million for one in Texas. Big operators could afford massive amounts of wire and thousands of posts. They fenced off huge gulps of public lands all over the West. Often, they didn't bother with details like gates, and strung wire right across well-used roads. Small ranchers and farmers, trying to prove up a modest claim, sometimes found themselves caught inside a cattle king's giant enclosure.

It became a national scandal, so in 1885 Congress made it illegal for private individuals or companies to fence public lands. However, enforcement was lax to non-existent. Some have estimated that by 1887 cattle barons had over 10 million acres illegally fenced in.

Cowboys found themselves with a new job: protecting the strands from fence cutters. Of course, cutters might be cooperative bands of farmers and ranchers ... or rustlers. Men died on both sides when the shooting started, although no verifiable deaths occurred in Idaho. Fences were cut in many parts of the Territory, however. Also, frustrated farmers sometimes not only tore down fences, they then slaughtered any cattle that happened to be nearby.

In 1885, land-use questions and other issues, including the ever-present rustling, led to an attempt to form a broad-based stockmen's association. The *Owyhee Avalanche* reprinted (March 28, 1885) an article from the *Shoshone Journal.* The item read, "The first annual meeting of the Idaho Cattle Growers' Association will be held at Shoshone, on Wednesday, April 1, 1885, and members of all associations of stock growers in Idaho are cordially invited to be present. All stockmen desiring to become members are requested to be present or send their names to the secretary, or hand them to any member of the executive committee."

The first president of this group was George L. Shoup, from the Salmon-Lemhi area. Ten months later, stock raisers created a more inclusive group called the "Idaho Territorial Stock Growers' Association." The *Owyhee Avalanche* reported (January 23, 1886) that the organizational meeting took place on January 11th and that "the by-laws adopted are in nearly all respects like those" of the earlier organization.

The *Avalanche* later noted (April 10, 1886) that their first annual meeting "was well attended by stock men from Wyoming, Nevada, and Utah, and also from the various stock owners in the counties of this territory."

Among other business, the Association passed several resolutions. One urged Congress to redress "the want of quarantine laws against importing diseased cattle into this territory." Another stated:

"Whereas, there is to-day a large portion of the range country badly overcrowded, and a tendency is exhibited by certain parties to destroy the value of both ranges and herds by the unwarranted introduction of more stock upon the ranges; therefore, be it Resolved, That the members of this association will not work at the round-ups with men who recklessly place cattle or other stock upon ranges already fully occupied, and when the rights of range tenure have been previously fully recognized."

This seems to be a shot aimed at the "tramp" stockmen, although some of the established stockmen were equally guilty. A year later, a roundup foreman recounted his experience in gathering stock for the Shirley & Hitt ranch. The *Avalanche* reprinted (May 14, 1887) the *Cassia County Times* item. It said, "He says he never before saw the like of dead cattle along Snake river and Mud Creek. The whole atmosphere is impregnated with the stench from the remains of cattle. This was all caused by the overstocking of that portion of the country … This is downright cruelty on the part of stock men and there should be some law to prohibit it."

During the early Eighties, national and international speculators, gripped by get-rich-quick fever, poured money into the American cattle market. Stockmen all over the west responded by expanding their herds. With the inevitable over-production, beef prices plunged. The only way to survive seemed to be to produce even more.

Even under normal range conditions, such a cycle was not sustainable. Shortly, Mother Nature would drive home that lesson.

CHAPTER THIRTEEN: NATURE DELIVERS A LESSON

The rider clicked his mount into a trot. Those wisps of clouds streaming over the ranges ahead looked ominous. Behind him, the plain stretched off to the southeast along the course of the Pahsimeroi River. Massive ridges and peaks blocked the view in every other direction, forming a kind of expansive cul-de-sac. The narrow Salmon River canyon lay just a few miles ahead. At least he didn't have to reach that.

They topped a small rise and the ranch appeared. Sensing the home stable, the horse increased his pace further. That was definitely snow swirling in from the northwest. The rancher had sent his few hands ahead while he checked one last side valley. Weather during this new year of 1888 had turned very cold, but so far his cattle were holding up.

The rancher's mount turned toward the barn, a log structure with a rough shake roof. The ranch buildings formed an inverted "L," with the barn on the right edge of the yard, bunkhouse north of that, and his four-room home to the west. A lean-to alongside the home faced the bunkhouse. That held the kitchen and eating area.

A cowboy ran over and opened the barn door. Before entering, the rancher assessed the incoming storm. Billows of snow were rolling in, against a solid backdrop of thick gray clouds. A bad one.

After rubbing down his mount and providing a bucket of oats, the rancher trudged across the yard to his home. Bitter wind slapped powdery flakes into his eyes. Icy threads found their way down his neck.

When he entered the kitchen, his wife handed him a mug of steaming coffee. The rancher rubbed snow off his thick mustache and took a grateful slurp. He met her gaze. No need for words. This was the one they had feared would come, sooner or later. Fortunately, they had laid up plenty of supplies from the stores in Salmon City. But how would the stock do?

The winter of 1888 should have delivered another warning to Idaho stockmen. It was extraordinarily cold. Boise City's *Idaho Statesman* reported (January 15, 1888), "Water pipes have become frozen and burst in various parts of the town."

Two days earlier, it had said, "The unusual cold snap of the past two weeks has been very severe on jack rabbits, and we learn that hundreds of them have frozen and starved to death. After all, cold weather has its compensation."

Later in the month, the *Idaho Register* in Eagle Rock reprinted (January 28, 1888) a somewhat jocular item from the *Oxford Enterprise* that showed how people were supposedly coping with the harsh weather. "The water in wells 14 feet deep has been frozen solid. Coal oil is sold by the yard, beer by the foot, and the hottest kind of rotgut whiskey by the stick."

Still, sheer cold was not the killer. Cold combined with severe blizzard conditions created the truly lethal combination. A rancher on the Little Lost River lost a substantial part of his herd to the cold and blowing snow.

The *Idaho Statesman* again sounded its warning (January 24, 1888). It said, "The *Statesman* has repeatedly told the stock men to raise feed enough to carry their stock through a hard winter. This winter forces upon every reasonable man the most positive proof of the necessity of such a course."

The Hyde Brothers company, one of the largest cattle owners in Owyhee County, lost heavily in the 1888 winter. David decided to move out of the large-scale stock business. He moved to the Bruneau Valley and bought a store that had been built there four years before. David also claimed a homestead in the valley and planted a large fruit orchard. As the bad memories faded, he also returned to stock raising, although on a much smaller scale.

Mike Hyde also cut back on his stock raising activities. He founded, or helped found, the town of Oreana and opened a saloon there. (Oreana is about thirty-five miles west of Mountain Home.) He was also the first Oreana postmaster.

The "warning" winter did not seem to hurt smaller operators as much. Thus, Matt Joyce's ranch on Sinker Creek apparently survived without serious loss. It is, however, perhaps significant that at some point Joyce bought a spread on the Bruneau River where he could winter his herds. During the summer of 1893, Matt was hurt in an accident and died the following September. The family carried on as the Joyce Brothers Ranch.

In fact, most Idaho stockmen considered their losses not all that bad. Many did nothing in response to the warning. In their minds, they figured "it is more profitable to lose their stock, or a portion of them, than it is to put up hay and feed them."

Thus, by and large, stockmen continued to expand their herds, not cut back. A roving correspondent for the *Statesman* reported (September 16, 1888) his own count of stock on the ranges north and east of Mountain Home. He found nearly fifty thousand cattle, about thirty-five thousand sheep, and eight thousand horses.

The correspondent obtained his numbers by direct interviews with stockmen in the region. He confidently asserted that they were "more reliable" than " the assessor's tally." To support that view, he said, "We have been told by gentlemen who have busied themselves on the range that there were bands that had not been assessed for years."

Owyhee County itself had over one hundred thousand assessed cattle by 1889.

On the Salmon, Col. Shoup had enough surplus that he could sell blocks of a thousand or more at a time. The *Idaho Statesman* reprinted (June 24, 1888) an item from the *Challis Messenger* about one such sale. The item said, "The purchase price is $13 per head, which is good news to the growers of cattle as it shows that the market value of range cattle is ruling stronger, that the lowest point is now passed and that, during the next few years, from good to high prices will be realized."

Herds grew all over the state. Born in Michigan, Charles Bomberg moved to Genesee in about 1888 and opened a meat market. He and a partner raised cattle on a ranch that came to include over five hundred acres. Yet even that was not enough to meet demand. To support the town's rapid expansion, they built "a large market building" and established a regional cattle emporium.

Beyond the established ranches, newcomers even sometimes found nooks to move into. In 1882, Andrew Jackson Fletcher had established a stock ranch on the southern Camas Prairie along Chimney Creek (about ten miles west of today's Fairfield).

Late in 1888, his brother James and family passed through the Prairie and wintered southeast of Boise City. The following spring, they returned to Chimney Creek. There, they settled on some unclaimed land, and began raising cattle. Eligah "Lige" Fletcher, who was fourteen when the family settled on Camas Prairie, later became a prominent sheep raiser on public land between the Prairie and Mountain Home.

By now, stockmen had become as concerned about quality as they were about quantity. The *Idaho Statesman* headlined (September 18, 1888, "Greatest Sale of Thoroughbred Cattle and Thoroughbred Horses Ever Offered in Idaho."

The article said, "The breeds of cattle are Holsteins, Short Horns, Jerseys and Ayershire. Thoroughbreds and choice grades, consisting of cows, bulls and heifers. The Holsteins raised are sired by Imported King. King weighs over 2200 pounds and is as perfect in form as any creature ever brought to the United States. ... The Horses comprise the best line of trotting stock. Several studs and fillies are sired by Black Walnut, imported from Kentucky. Some by Main Slasher, imported from Maine and others by Doctor Steven's Hambletonian Saxy, who was imported from Kentucky."

Less than a year later, the *Statesman* publicized (June 13, 1889) a sale from the Hot Springs Herd, "the largest herd of thoroughbred cattle in the Northwest." The owners had imported 125 registered shorthorns from Kentucky. With those, they set up "at Hailey Hot Springs a permanent breeding and dairy farm from which Idaho and neighboring States and Territories could select the very best type of home-grown, robust, pure-bred cattle with which to grade up native herds."

About the same time, Loyal P. Brown pushed the same trend on the northern Camas Prairie. In the fall of 1887, he had purchased a band of purebred Herefords in Iowa. Their arrival in Mount Idaho the following spring was reported to be "the first cattle of this kind brought to the prairie." Although Brown remained active in Prairie affairs, he began selling off outlying parcels of real estate in the early 1890s. He passed away in 1896.

Stock imports did, however, pose a risk from the spread of diseases. Bovine pleuropneumonia was probably the most dreaded of these contagions. In 1889, the Idaho legislature created a livestock board to regulate livestock traffic. The board would lay out detailed rules to prohibit the importation of diseased animals. It would also set standards and procedures for quarantines. That clearly meant they must lay out guidelines for the destruction of infected animals

To "soften the blow," the law also set up a county-based indemnity fund to compensate owners whose stock had to be destroyed. Creation of the board was part of a nationwide campaign, which would eventually subdue most of these infectious diseases.

Of course, the other great scourge for the stockmen was rustling and horse theft. The *Owyhee Avalanche* reprinted (June 2, 1888) an item from the *Cassia County Times* that advised stockmen to "furnish Mr. F. C. Ramsey, stock inspector for this county, with a list of their marks and brands. Outside parties have had a habit of claiming everything on the range unclaimed by parties present at the rodeo, and if Mr. Ramsey has your marks and brands he will probably save a large number from being driven away. He keeps a record of all stock on the range and now has a large list of estray stock but does not know to whom they belong."

Two years later, the *Avalanche* reprinted (September 13, 1890) an item from the *Mountain Home Mail* that said, "Idaho stockmen lose thousands of dollars worth of stock every year by having it stolen. It will probably startle many of our readers to learn that over $20,000 worth of horses have been stolen in this county in the last five months. At least 500 head of the best horses in the county – for a thief always takes the best – have been stolen."

In the north, the *Idaho County Free Press* published (May 24, 1889) an announcement that the Idaho County Stock Growers' Association was offering a one hundred dollar reward for the arrest and conviction of anyone who illegally marked or branded cattle or horses.

Chester P. Coburn no doubt endorsed that intention. After nearly a quarter century in the cattle business near Lewiston, he still looked for opportunities. While he retained property in Lewiston, in 1890 he also claimed land south of the Camas Prairie. For

the next eight years, he ran cattle there. About the time he sold out, rustlers made off with $3 thousand worth of his stock. Although he never recovered any of the loss, Coburn still managed a comfortable retirement back in Lewiston.

Even as ranching thrived despite disease, rustlers and occasional weather problems, other pioneers spread beyond the already-settled areas. A long hiatus had dismissed the name Pierre's Hole into history. Newcomers called it the Teton Valley. Late in the decade, Mormon colonizers established the towns of Driggs and Victor there.

Cattleman Chester P. Coburn

Also about that time, settlement spread northeast from Egin Bench. As more irrigated farmland opened up along Henry's Fork, the town of St. Anthony began to grow. Just a few years later, the legislature created Fremont County, with St. Anthony as the county seat.

A key change in Eagle Rock fueled further growth in that area. Recall that Matt Taylor had sold his toll bridge interest to the Anderson brothers in 1872. By now, the span handled mostly local business, because long-haul traffic went largely by rail. In 1889, the county commissioners denied an extension of their franchise and then turned the bridge into a public thoroughfare.

The commissioners hoped to spur settlement on the west side of the river, previously discouraged by the constant toll cost to travel in and out of town. It worked. Within a month, pioneers began settling on the thousands of acres to the west, and planning for new irrigation ditches.

John M. Taylor came to Idaho in 1882, after graduating from the University of Missouri with dual Bachelors degrees in science and civil engineering. For a few years, he worked with his brother Samuel F. (who was fifteen years older) in the cattle business. John then spent several years working as a civil engineer for the Union Pacific Railroad. He returned to Eagle Rock in 1889. His engineering expertise proved invaluable for many new irrigation projects.

During this period, Sam shifted more from cattle ranching to breeding top-grade horses. One of his trotting horses later made a splash on the Eastern racing circuit. The sports page of the *New York Times* reported (July 27, 1894), "Ryland T. Surprises the Talent in the Races on the Grand Circuit." "The talent" – racing aficionados – had never seen that much speed from the bay gelding, which was "bred in Idaho" and carried the "SI" brand. Taylor also owned farm acreage where he raised hay and grain to supply his breeding operation.

In 1889, developers surveyed a town site around Pocatello Station. The village of Pocatello received incorporation papers in late April. As a key junction point for railway traffic in two directions across Idaho, the area had grown quickly to a population of over two thousand. In an 1893 flurry of county creation, the town became the county seat for Bannock County. By the end of the century, Pocatello had more than four thousand people.

Similar developments happened all over the state. Settlers on the high plains around Mountain Home found it impractical to draw water from the Snake River, far down in its rugged canyon. Instead, irrigators built a set of storage reservoirs to catch runoff from the ranges north of town. These would eventually irrigate several thousand acres of farmland.

Projects along the Boise, Payette, and Weiser rivers served to expand the reach of irrigation systems in those areas. Because north Idaho is not generally as dry as the south, pioneers there built fewer large-scale canal and ditch projects. However, some areas had many smaller ditch systems to irrigate one or a few farms.

As the end of the decade approached, citizens of Idaho Territory looked around at what they had accomplished. Railroads with branch lines spanned the region, and new towns had sprung up along them. Older towns had better schools, newspapers, courthouses, and other marks of a settled community. Very progressive, for a Territory.

James H. Hawley later wrote, "All over the territory, people began to cherish the hope that they would soon have a state government, under which they could elect their own officials and not be dependent upon non-residents appointed by the president for the administration of their affairs."

After much agitation in 1888, Idahoans issued a joint Legislature-Council memorial to the U.S. Congress. The resolution asked for passage of an "enabling act." That would authorize the Territory to convene a constitutional convention, to prepare for statehood. Nothing specific came of that.

Still, the following April, supporters in the U.S. Senate advised Idaho Governor Edward A. Stevenson to go ahead on his own. He did, calling for a constitutional convention on July 4, 1889. However, without a go-ahead from Congress, the Territorial legislature could provide no money to finance an election for delegates.

At the end of April, cattleman George L. Shoup took over as governor. He issued a proclamation that reaffirmed Stevenson's call. However, he offered a clever way to get around the lack of funds for an election. His said, "If for any reason the citizens of any county prefer to elect their delegates by some other equitable method, I am satisfied that the delegates so chosen will be recognized and admitted to seats in the convention. The manner of choosing delegates is of less importance than that they should be representative men, of character and ability, whose work will be satisfactory to Congress and the people."

Most counties split the ticket and allowed the two major parties to elect or appoint delegates. (Where uneven numbers were involved, the odd seat went to the majority party in the 1888 elections.)

Sam Taylor was among the delegates selected. The county had elected him to the (last, as it turned out) Territorial Council. Thus, his selection to the convention was probably a foregone conclusion.

With a few sometimes-heated exceptions, the *ad hoc* selection of delegates worked surprisingly well. Leaders then used a similar low/no-budget approach to ratify the constitution. It passed easily: over twelve thousand for versus less than two thousand against.

At that time, the Territory had a legal prohibition against polygamy and "celestial marriages." The proposed constitution included a similar provision. That law disenfranchised Mormon Church members, who would have surely voted against it had they been allowed. However, even that block vote would not have changed the outcome.

Despite some grumbling about the hurried and unorthodox preparation, Congress passed the Idaho statehood bill. President Benjamin Harrison signed it into law on July 3, 1890. The 1890 Census found the new state's population to be 88,548. George Shoup became the state's first governor, then the legislature made him and William J. McConnell the first U. S. Senators. Voters reelected Shoup to a full term five years later.

Unfortunately, 1890 was not a good year for the new state's economy. The winter of 1888-89 was considered "truly mild." However, the very dry spring and summer that followed stunted the growth of forage. Then 1889-90 turned out to be "one of the four worst winters" recorded for the Pacific Northwest in the Nineteenth Century.

As had happened in Montana and Wyoming three years earlier, many Idaho stockmen suffered huge losses. North Idaho was spared the worst of it, although ranchers in the Palouse region apparently lost livestock. But the brutal weather devastated southern Idaho. In the western Owyhee area and parts of Oregon, some ranchers were virtually wiped out. David Shirk and his brother suffered a forty percent loss, even though they had made some provision for winter feeding.

George Shoup and his partners had also provided for cattle on the properties they owned along the Salmon, and this limited their losses. However, a herd they had running on leased land suffered eighty percent fatalities. As Shoup's son wrote, "Numerous other range cattle owners who neglected the warnings and past lessons of nature lost in proportion, and again the ranges were much devoid of range cattle, and numerous owners never recovered from the losses inflicted."

After that, Shoup restricted his herd size to what they could feed from forage put aside on his own ranch properties. Of course, since George spent the decade serving in the U. S. Senate, ranch management fell on son George E. and his associates.

Eastern Idaho did not report such severe losses as those recorded along the Salmon. However, it is known that the hard winter hurt the War Bonnet Ranch.

Ranchers in south-central Idaho suffered perhaps the worst.

The horseman gently reined in his buckskin. He had camped for the night with two buckaroos who were looking for work. The rancher didn't know yet whether or not he'd need more hands, but gave them a small stake anyway. They could ride the fifteen miles east to buy grub at Rock Creek station.

They'd drifted in from the Bruneau Plateau. Over there, cowboys had found dead range horses in the branches of juniper bushes. The poor creatures had struggled into the meager shelter of the limbs reaching above the deep snow.

So far, he hadn't seen much to alarm him. He found a half-dozen clean-picked carcasses in all those miles of rolling plains. Not really an unusual number for any winter. They'd all heard the grim reports out of Nevada. Down there, people were digging water wells for the first time because piles of dead animals had fouled the streams.

He turned the buckskin and they trotted northeast toward the higher ground. Finally, they ascended a gentle slope onto the low tableland and stopped. Miles to the east, heavy snow cloaked the tall peaks. Warm spring winds had melted the snow here on the broken foothill plains and thinned the drifts on the lower ranges off to the south.

The rancher peered around. The stony soil had dried out and the bunchgrass was greening up. By rights, he should be able to see at least a dozen cattle from this higher level. He saw two in the distance, and both looked gaunt and weak.

The rancher nudged his mount forward and they circled a big sagebrush. Only the clop of hooves and the whisper of the breeze at his back broke the silence. He carefully walked the buckskin through a shallow ravine and up onto another elevation. He stopped again at the highest stretch.

Finally, off to the northeast, a flurry of activity caught his eye. Birds, many birds. He urged his horse into a canter, watchful of the rocky ground. They slowed for a knee-deep rift, then continued across another low mesa. The rancher's horse shied abruptly as a coyote, its belly distended, ambled across their path. The rider cursed softly. A minute later, he pulled his mount up sharply as a twisting stream bed came into view.

The recent thaw had exposed an uncountable number of animal carcasses. The gully might have protected the cattle from the driving flurries and chill wind, but it had then become their graveyard. During the worst of the storms, the snowfall had probably drifted flat across here, with no sign of the depression or its frozen charnel house.

Now and then one turkey vulture hissed at another, but mostly the scavengers, winged or four-legged, ignored each other. A gorged vulture, its monstrous appetite sated for the moment, made a run and boosted into the air. Up this close, the horseman almost gagged from the fetid odor of rotting corpses.

The narrative above represents a combination of horrific scenes that played out all over southern Idaho. The *Idaho Statesman* reprinted (April 8, 1890) a *Blackfoot News* item that said, "The dead cattle around town are beginning to tell of their resting places by their appeals to the olfactories for removal."

In the Lost River region, the stench was reportedly so nauseating a circuit-riding judge issued a court order to force county officials to immediately dispose of the bodies. The Sparks-Tinnin cattle herds were among those that lost heavily, over half in Cassia County and across the border in Nevada. That spring, after the round up, Sparks, Tinnin, Jasper Harrell, and his son Andrew Harrell met to discuss what could be done to rebuild. Sparks and the Harrells had other resources, but John Tinnin was broke.

In the end, Sparks paid Tinnin $45 thousand for his interest in the ranch. Thereafter, the properties belonged to the Sparks-Harrell Company. The Company soon procured three thousand cows to restock the range.

Although the severe weather hit cattle the hardest, sheep also suffered.

The Gooding brothers, Frank R. and Fred W., emigrated to the U.S. from England in 1868. Frank was eleven, Fred was eight. Nine years later, Frank went to California to farm, and then in 1881 moved to Ketchum, Idaho. There he supplied wood and charcoal for the  smelter. The following year brother Fred also landed in Ketchum and opened a butcher shop.

In 1888, the brothers individually went into sheep ranching. Fred's flock incurred heavy losses in the hard 1890 winter. Fortunately, his good credit allowed him to recover quickly. In later years, he "had as many as thirty thousand sheep on his ranch at one time."

Frank Gooding's herd apparently suffered less damage. He too prospered and would soon be "regarded as the most successful sheep-raiser in the state." He served several terms as President of the Idaho Wool Growers' Association.

Losses in the Bruneau area were likewise heavy, especially for those who depended upon the high plateau south of the river. Only a remnant of the Murphy holdings remained. They were moved to Nevada and never returned.

During the worst of the winter, the *Owyhee Avalanche* reprinted (February 1, 1890) an item from the *Winnemucca Silver State* about the twin evils of over-grazing and failure to set aside winter feed. The *State* said, "This winter teaches stockmen a lesson which they should always remember. It shows the folly from a business standpoint of letting cattle run at large in the snow when the range is pastured bare and trusting to luck to take them through. In no other country is such shiftlessness exhibited."

The *Avalanche* editor didn't belabor the point, but said simply, "The above remarks are applicable to the stockmen of Idaho, at least of this county."

Although many ranchers tried to follow this good advice, it took time and there were obstacles. The only practical place to grow hay was on relatively level ground. Mowing on steep hillsides or cut-up range with horse-drawn equipment was slow and hazardous. That put stockmen in competition with farmers who wanted the better land to grow higher-value crops. Transporting hay from distant pastures was also slow and costly.

Plus, even with the best of intentions, stockmen had to deal with inescapable changes that man and nature had wrought on the open range. There is no question that ranchers over-grazed the range in Idaho and the Great Basin in the years 1875-1920. Moreover, historical accounts suggest that Idaho received less and less rain and snow during that period. Together, those factors visibly altered the range ecology.

As noted in the previous chapter, cattle prefer native grasses and sheep lean toward broadleaf forbs. In Idaho, that meant various kinds of buckwheat, yarrow, and biscuit-root. Neither animal targets shrubs, and both actively avoid "big sagebrush."

With grass and forb seed supplies depleted by overgrazing, sagebrush and other shrubs invaded the empty ecological niches. Thus, sagebrush rapidly moved onto the higher foothills and valleys, where it had not been common before.

Still, despite the setbacks in stock raising, Idaho grew rapidly after statehood. Its population topped one hundred thousand in less than two years. In the north, agriculture and the new University of Idaho, which began classes on October 3, 1892, fueled the growth of Moscow. Early the following year, Cottonwood signaled its expansion by the publication of its first newspaper.

Oddly enough, not all these newcomers came by railway train. A report from Boise City in the *Idaho Statesman* (September 16, 1891) said, "Five emigrant wagons drew up on Ninth street yesterday opposite the opera house. ... They had some loose stock with them." After resting and making a few purchases, the little wagon train turned north, planning to take up homesteads northeast of Lewiston.

Grangeville also expanded in the early Nineties. The town got its first two banks, a second flour mill, a much larger schoolhouse, and two churches. In 1894, a telephone system connected the town to Lewiston and several new businesses opened their doors.

Further south, in Caldwell, the private College of Idaho began teaching classes in 1891. The friendly rivalry between the College and the University as to who came first was largely moot. Both started with preparatory classes because they found no students ready for college work. In 1892, Boise City developers bridged the river to provide better access to the "South Boise" development across the river. Two years later, the city had to build a new public school to augment a structure that had earlier been criticized as being wastefully large. To the east, Albion Normal School opened and taught its first classes.

Pocatello also grew rapidly, as did the Snake River Valley further north. Years of work had greatly improved the Nels and Emma Just homestead along the Blackfoot River. Yet, while stock raising provided reasonably steady income, Nels wanted to do more. He claimed more land in 1885, but still had much to learn about building a reliable ditch.

Finally, by the end of the decade, his system could irrigate three hundred acres of land. Nels had also planted many acres of trees. With his hard-won knowledge, Just helped organize a canal company to put water on land further north.

Some of that water would serve the town of Shelley. John F. Shelley began the town in 1893 by establishing a post office to serve the many homesteaders who had taken up land in the area. The following year, he opened a general store and stable.

Eagle Rock had also grown, with all the new homesteads to the west. Still, plenty of unoccupied land remained, which attracted the attention of speculators in Chicago. They hoped to foster a land rush, which they could cash in on. However, the name "Eagle Rock" did not convey the impression they wanted to create with their planned advertising campaign. With relatively little opposition, a referendum in July of 1891 changed the name to "Idaho Falls."

With more irrigation systems coming into use, the economic base of the region had begun to change from ranching to crop agriculture. (That included growing potatoes, but the spud was many years away from the economic power it would become.) Still, ranching held major sway in the early- to mid-Nineties.

Englishman Charles H. Berett came to the U.S. in 1849, at the age of twelve. Orphaned on the trip to Utah, he set out on his own three years later. He traveled through southeast Idaho and to the Salmon River at a time when Old Fort Hall was the only white settlement in the region. After "knocking around" the Pacific Northwest, he returned to Utah in 1862 and took up farming.

Then, in 1890, Berett came back to Idaho and purchased a ranch about eight miles from (then) Eagle Rock, on Willow Creek. In addition to an extensive horse herd, he raised dairy cows. It was said that "the butter from his dairy has an enviable reputation."

On the Raft River, even after the hard winter, the Sweetser Bros. & Pierce Company had around fifteen thousand head on their range. Andrew Sweetser and his brother, of course, were among the earliest stockmen in this part of Idaho. Since then they had expanded their operations into Nevada and Oregon.

In 1890, Andrew Sweetser even encouraged a second-generation stock raiser. He "sold" 320 acres of rangeland along the Raft River to his son Lewis for one dollar. Lew had met two brothers at Yale University and they formed a partnership to run the Bar-Y (Y for Yale) ranch.

A year later, an influenza epidemic swept through Chicago, where the parents of Lew's partners lived. They sent young Edgar Rice Burroughs to join his older brothers at the Idaho ranch. The sixteen-year-old loved Western life. He even learned to tame wild broncos. Ed's youthful experience in the West did not directly influence his famous Tarzan of the Apes stories. However, its impact shows in many of his other works.

Another second-generation example evolved near Mountain Home. Around 1882, James Wilson had made his son, William, manager of the James Wilson & Sons stock company. William successfully led the operation through the hard 1890 winter. A few years later, he started his own ranch. He acquired land along Bennett Creek, about fifteen miles northeast of Mountain Home. William moved his family there in 1894. Raising mainly cattle, he ran a productive ranch there for over forty years.

Some areas recovered quickly from the bad winter, or perhaps escaped the worst impact. James W. Webster was born at Franklin, Idaho, about two years after its founding. His father played a prominent role in the local business community and the Mormon church.

As a young adult James split time between helping with his father's varied interests and ranching. In 1892, he and a partner established their own sheep operation. Within a few years, they began shipping "from fifty to ninety carloads of sheep" every year.

Across the state, the *Owyhee Avalanche* reprinted (May 28, 1892) a *Weiser Signal* story that showed the growth there. The item said, "Three train loads of cattle were shipped from Weiser this week, and it kept Jim Coakley and Beck Jenney busy painting big legends on cloth to tack on the sides of the cars, setting forth from whence the fat beeves came, and that this was also a great prune, timber, grain, fruit, cattle, horses, sheep, agricultural, wool, mining, farming and grazing country."

About that same time, one of the most notable Idaho stock raisers visited Omaha, Nebraska. A local reporter wrote, "Miss Kittie Wilkins, the 'horse queen' of Idaho, has been in the city for a few days. ... She is at the head of one of the largest horse raising ranches in the world, and is not only the manager, but also saleslady of all the horses produced. Her ranch, which comprises several thousand acres, is located near Mountain Home, in the famous Valley of Bruneau, Idaho, and upon it every detail which pertains to the rearing of the horse has been perfected."

According to local historian Adelaide Hawes, the Wilkins family came to the Bruneau area in 1880. Born in Oregon, Katherine "Kitty" Wilkins would have been about twenty-three.

They had been running a hotel in Tuscarora, Nevada. Then it burned down, the second business the family had lost to fire over the years. Kitty's father John decided they could do better ranching.

They raised both cattle and horses, but it soon became clear that Kitty had a special affinity for horses. By the end of the decade, she was primary manager of the horse ranch. Their Diamond brand led to another colorful sobriquet for her: "The Queen of Diamonds."

Kitty made a concerted effort to upgrade the herd from its wild stock beginnings. Eventually, they became renowned for their premium horses. As early as 1890, the famous King ranch in Texas purchased 750 Diamond Ranch horses.

Very well educated in Catholic schools and quite attractive, Kitty caused a sensation wherever she went. In December of 1891, the *St. Louis Republic* reported, "Miss Kittie Wilkins, of Idaho, has been spending a few days in the city. This is not exactly a society item, but it is of far

Kitty Wilkins, Horse Queen of Idaho

more interest to some people than any society item that could be printed. Miss Wilkins is a horse trader, and what she does not know about a horse is not worth knowing. She has just been to New Orleans and is going East. She went to New Orleans with three cars of horses and sold them."

Historian Hawes, who knew Kitty personally, wrote, "Contrary to public belief she did not don male attire. Engaged in whatever kind of work necessary to her undertaking, she wore feminine clothes. When demonstrating her horses she rode a sidesaddle and wore the usual feminine riding skirt of those days. When riding the range she always rode a sidesaddle."

Kitty shipped horses all over North America for over a quarter century. With thousands of horses being readied for customers, Kitty hired only the best riders. Then their work made them better. Those who survived attained a well-deserved reputation as being among the best in the world.

In 1883, buffalo hunter, scout, and impresario William F. Cody introduced the spectacle that evolved into "Buffalo Bill's Wild West and Congress of Rough Riders of the World." They toured the U.S. and Europe, and inspired a host of imitators. Knowing good horseflesh, the showman snapped up some of Kitty's best mounts. Moreover, it wasn't long before some of her top hands found new jobs with Cody's extravaganza. As professional rodeo events grew in popularity, riders from the Diamond began following that circuit.

Despite the successes of Sweetser, Wilkins, and others, the hard winter of 1889-1890 hugely altered Idaho stock raising. First, stockmen obviously had reason to plan for more cultivation and storage of winter feed. That also generally dictated smaller herds.

The second change was an accelerated transition to more sheep raising. Some cattlemen began raising both or switched completely to sheep. Plus, newcomers began driving bands onto rangeland emptied by winter-kill.

As noted above, the hard winter had not hit sheep as hard as it did cattle. Recovery or expansion also required less capital. J. D. C. Thiessen, who had a ranch near Lewiston, began the switch even before the catastrophe. He had begun running cattle and horses in about 1886. Three years later, he sold his two hundred cows and bought nearly two thousand sheep. By the end of the Nineties, he would have around twelve thousand head.

Sheep herds also increased along the Payette. By the early 1890s, Boise City and Emmett pioneer Henry Riggs had begun to assign more ranch responsibility to his son Boise Riggs. Boise became a successful rancher in his own right. Another son, Samuel, expressed their early attitude toward sheep. He said, "In 1892, when times were getting hard and sheepmen were *over-running the range*, I took off by pack train to seek work in the mines of Boise Basin." [My emphasis.]

But down in Owyhee County, a news item reported (*DeLamar Nugget*, May 19, 1891), "Robert Noble, Owyhee County's big wool man has just sold ten thousand mutton sheep at three dollars per head."

This was out of a herd totaling over fifty thousand. A decade earlier, Noble's herd numbered only seventy-five hundred. Similar large numbers had also appeared in southeast Idaho.

Naturally, stockmen with smaller financial reserves recovered more slowly from the killing winter. Then a crucial outside event aggravated their problem. Another worldwide economic depression and financial crisis – the "Panic of '93" – hit. By the end of the year, over six hundred banks had failed. By the following summer, nearly two hundred railroads were bankrupt. The Panic dried up sources of capital.

The War Bonnet Ranch was one casualty of this panic. They held their last real roundup in 1894, and then dissolved the company. (Any actual connection with today's War Bonnet Roundup is tenuous at best. That professional rodeo event didn't start until 1911.)

Another event in 1894 also had a major impact on agriculture and ranching in Idaho. Joseph M. Carey, Wyoming Senator, sponsored a bill, naturally called the Carey Act, intended to promote water projects in the so-called "arid states," including Idaho. The Act granted these states specific rights to public lands "not to exceed 1,000,000 acres." (The amount rose to two million in 1901).

The details and nuances of the Act are less important than the results. Over the next twenty to thirty years, vast blocks came under irrigation. Without water, much of that land had been suitable only for stock raising. (Some was barely worthwhile even for that). Every acre converted to farming was one less acre for stockmen. Naturally, that caused even stronger competition for the dwindling supply of rangeland.

Of course, the conflict started long before Carey Act irrigation projects began. An item from the *Idaho County Free Press,* highlighted (March 7, 1891) the problem, "The sheep and mule men along Salmon River have been dancing war quadrilles and ghost schottisches since early winter which culminated in an outbreak a few days ago. They rolled rocks down the mountains at each other for two or three days, and we believe it ended in all hands being arrested and taken to Lewiston."

In 1892, threats of violence forced a Lemhi Valley sheepman named Porter to move his flock out of the region. Such pressure continued for a number of years. Valley night riders bombed the sheep sheds of one openly defiant herder, crippling many animals. He too left the area.

The following year in Cassia County, sheepmen and cattlemen took turns poisoning the others' herds. The level of violence climbed in March 1894, when someone, allegedly cattlemen, shot sheepman Hugh Fleming. It was a fact that cattlemen in the American Falls area had argued with the Fleming Brothers sheep operation about grazing their flocks on what had traditionally been cattle range. Their warnings had been ignored and now a brother was dead.

The *Idaho Statesman* reported (April 3, 1894), "It is now learned on good authority that more than a dozen well known citizens are implicated in the affair, and it is only a question of a short time when they will be placed under arrest."

Indeed, within a couple days, the Pocatello sheriff arrested four cattlemen suspected of the killing. Less than a week later, a court dropped the charges on the grounds of insufficient evidence. The lack of action outraged area sheepmen, but there was nothing they could do. Their anger simmered and the stage was set for worse to come.

Chapter Fourteen: Range Conflict Heats Up

February 2, 1896, about 9:00 p.m. The two cowboys picked their way quietly amongst the low ridges and cuts of the south-central Idaho rangeland. The moon wouldn't rise for another ninety minutes and they didn't want their horses to stumble on the rough terrain. Suddenly, they heard the "tinkle, tinkle" of a hobbled horse somewhere close by.

They investigated and spotted a sheep camp. The sheepmen had pushed well over the deadline, the informal boundary between cattle and sheep country. The young men conferred quietly. The more assertive Jackson Lee Davis – generally known as "Diamondfield Jack" – wanted to "cut it in smoke" to warn these interlopers to get out. That was, after all, their job with the Sparks-Harrell cattle outfit, which claimed this range and its luxurious bunchgrass. Better paid than the average buckaroo, Davis and his saddle mate, Fred Gleason, had been hired as so-called "outside men" to intimidate and discourage the encroaching sheepmen.

Gleason demurred, perhaps reluctant to blindly blaze away in the dark. Then, by accident or design, Jack's horse "spooked," and his rifle discharged into the air. While Gleason galloped away, Davis circled the encampment and fired into it. The sheepmen, brothers Joseph and Loren Wilson, dove for their rifles and shot wildly into the darkness. After about a dozen shots each way, Jack rode off. The exchange made a lot of noise and killed one unfortunate horse in the sheep camp.

Davis and Gleason spent the next day at Brown Ranch, a subunit of the Sparks-Harrell spread. The ranch was located in Idaho, five to ten miles northwest of today's Jackpot, Nevada. The two cowboys worked in the barn, shoeing a horse. Gleason chatted with another cowboy and mentioned the sheep camp they had shot up. His account probably had more credibility than if Jack had told the story.

Davis hardly looked the part of a hardened tough. Of average height and slender build, he was about twenty-five years old. Sun and wind had given him the ruddy complexion of any other cowboy, and weathered his thick mustache to a sandy color that contrasted with his dark hair. His deep-set blue-gray eyes avoided direct contact and projected no sense of wildness or menace.

Charlie Walgamott, who had pioneered in southern Idaho for over twenty years, wrote, "Jack Davis was very companionable, good in his manners, extremely fond of children, and kind-hearted almost to a fault, but he was a great talker."

Knowing Jack's propensity to embellish or even possibly invent shooting affairs, listeners couldn't be sure anything he said wasn't just another tall tale. People did concede that Davis was gun-handy, and a few were willing to believe that some of his claimed past exploits might be real.

Jack had signed on the previous summer and began warning sheepmen to stay off Sparks-Harrell range. No shots were fired, but months of verbal jousting finally produced a reaction, in November. Bill Tolman, a sheepmen known to Jack only by name, rode across the deadline and braced him with a rifle. They argued until Davis spotted an opening, quick-drew his .45 caliber revolver, and winged his opponent in the shoulder.

After getting Tolman to where his fellow herders could help him, Jack discreetly rode south into Nevada, out of the county sheriff's jurisdiction. He had not re-entered Idaho until the day before the nighttime exchange with the sheepmen on February 2nd.

After their easy day around Brown Ranch, Gleason and Diamondfield Jack rode south on February 4. Starting around sunup, they drifted toward another Sparks-Harrell site. All-out range war had not yet erupted, so they felt no need to ride out and see whether or not Davis's fusillade had chased the sheepmen away.

Although some light snow fell, the area was experiencing a classic Intermountain phenomenon, a mid-winter thaw. A resident said of February 4th that, "The roads were soft at that time."

The cowboys had lunch at the closest Sparks-Harrell ranch in Nevada, about fifteen miles south. The foreman who saw them there testified that their horses had not been ridden hard, a key observation. They continued south ten miles further and spent the night at Middlestacks ranch, another Sparks-Harrell unit. They would ride deeper into Nevada the next morning.

Jack and Gleason should have probably gone back to check on the sheepmen. Herders had pushed at least two other flocks well west of the deadline. That same morning, J. W. Davis Hunter carried a cart load of firewood from his sheep camp

Sheepherder with Flock and Wagon

to a site further east. He supplied some fuel to John Wilson and Daniel Cummings, two Mormon sheepherders camped on Deep Creek. They were not quite twenty miles northeast of Brown Ranch.

Hunter later testified that the flock was under control, their two dogs were tied to the sheep wagon wheels, and the men were preparing breakfast. Hunter had then headed north past Goat Springs.

Also on the 4th, two cattlemen rode south from near Rock Creek. The older man, James E. Bower, pointed ahead to where a hard-riding horseman had topped a distant rise. He remarked to his companion, Jeff Gray, that he thought the rider might be a cattleman who many suspected of collaboration with the sheepman. The young cowboy agreed that it might be. The rider perhaps didn't want the two horsemen to get close enough for positive identification, since he could be headed for a sheep camp.

The range south and west of Rock Creek is quite broken and rough, and the rider quickly disappeared into a swale. As a Sparks-Harrell superintendent, Bower needed to know about sheepherder intrusions across the deadline.

Many threats against him personally had been reported, and rumors abounded that the sheepmen planned a major push. He'd had business in Albion a few days earlier and had now ridden well into the company's grazing area along Soldier and Deep creeks.

As Bower and Gray passed Goat Springs, a two-wheeled cart rattled by on the stony road. After a quarter century living in Cassia County, Bower knew a substantial number of local people, at least by sight. The driver was a stranger, and the superintendent strongly suspected he was an intrusive sheepman.

Further along, they noticed that the cart tracks came from the direction of two sheep camps in view from their vantage point. The hard rider's tracks no longer showed on the road. Bower wondered if he had cut across country to visit a camp. As Bower and Gray moved closer, they noted that the nearer camp had some activity. The other looked empty.

As they rode up, a man stuck his head out of the sheep wagon. The time was between 11 o'clock and noon. The sheepman invited them to dismount and Bower asked, "Are you getting dinner?"

When they entered the wagon, they saw another sheepman near the bed at the rear. On their right, the small cook stove radiated heat. Typical of most such wagons, sideboards projected out from the wagon body, making convenient tabletops or sitting areas. Hoops running from sideboard edge to edge held a tight canvas top. Gray sat nearest the door and Bower plunked down beside him. Bower did not recognize either man, which made it likely they came from outside Cassia County.

Bower calmly lit up the corncob pipe he had purchased at the Rock Creek store just that morning. After a moment, he asked quietly, "Do you think it is right to come in here with your sheep?"

"We have as much right in here as anyone," the closer man said, referring to the fact that most of the range was public land.

"I don't think you have," Bower said. He made no reference to the law that barred sheep from "traditional" cattle ranges. "You don't pay any taxes in this county."

"We do pay taxes here," the sheepman claimed.

"I think you are mistaken about that," Bower said. Possibly the owner of the sheep had told these herders he did pay taxes. The cattlemen was confident the animals were not on the county rolls. "I think you are tramps in this country ..."

"You are a lying son of a bitch," the argumentative sheepman said angrily. He jumped up and grabbed Bower's collar and shoulder as the rancher rose. The sheepman's rush knocked Gray out of the wagon bed.

Gray saw that the sudden attack had thrown Bower back over the wagon's end gate. The older man seemed dazed, but had tried to retrieve his revolver from a shoulder holster.

Gray hesitated until the other sheepman grabbed a rifle and started to point it toward the front. Gray drew quickly and snapped off a quick shot. The man dropped the rifle and stood still. Meanwhile, the other sheepman had twisted Bower's pistol away. Luckily, the cattleman had grasped an arm so the attacker couldn't turn the gun on him.

"I'll fix both of you," the sheepman growled.

The attacker ignored Gray's shouted order to drop the gun, so Gray fired once, then again when the man didn't react. Still not sure if he'd stopped the assault, he raised the revolver for another shot when Bower called out, "Hold on."

The sheepman had relaxed his grip and a little blood dripped from his chin onto Bower. As they helped the man toward the bed, he said, "I am hurt pretty bad."

"I don't think you are," Bower replied. The facial injury looked like no more than a superficial wound. They lowered the sheepman onto the bed, where his frightened compatriot sat silently at the head.

While Bower went after the horses, which had run off, Gray stayed with the sheepmen. Before they mounted, Gray ejected the empty cartridges and reloaded. Brower suggested they alert the other sheep camp, just in case. Gray said, "No, they have heard or seen us and we may get into more trouble."

Gray then returned to Rock Creek. Two days later, he told long-time rancher Arthur D. Norton about the shooting. Jeff figured there'd be trouble over the incident and he might need some protection.

Bower hurried southwest from the sheep camp to Point Ranch. In his later deposition, Bower said, "I expected trouble on the road, because so many threats had been made against me, that I believed if I had been recognized as one of the parties to the difficulty a mob of the sheep men would follow me and kill me."

When he stopped at the ranch, he discovered that his watch chain had been broken, and realized he had also lost his corncob pipe. After a short time there, he rode on toward Brown Ranch, which was deep in the Salmon Falls Creek canyon. He arrived at Brown Ranch the afternoon of the day that Diamondfield Jack Davis and Fred Gleason drifted south into Nevada from there.

Bower caught up with Davis and Gleason two days later and they rode into Wells, Nevada together. The superintendent caught the train to Reno the next morning. Bower later said, "I saw no mention of the affair in the papers for over two weeks, and that made me feel certain no one had been badly hurt."

Davis and Gleason checked into the Hardesty House hotel. Over the next week or so, emboldened by liquor, they bragged about "shooting up" a sheep camp that had intruded into cattle country. Davis stayed in Wells for a week or so. He then drifted further to the southwest to visit ranches where he had worked before. Naturally, Jack being Jack, the "shooting scrape" grew with every telling. At least one listener formed the notion that he had actually killed two men.

On February 16, events began in Idaho that would haunt Diamondfield Jack for years to come. Early on the morning of the 4th, Edgar "Ted" Severe, another sheep-man, had become concerned about an impending snowstorm. He drove his band from a spot relatively near the Wilson-Cummings camp to a more sheltered area. When the weather improved, he returned, arriving nearby on February 16, 1896.

The lack of activity at the other camp, and the scattering of their flock worried Se-vere. The herd might have dispersed after some alarm, but normally one would expect the sheep dogs to be out reforming the band.

After settling his own flock, Severe decided to check the other camp. As he ap-proached it, he noticed the two dogs tied to the wagon. Severe later said, "They barked, or tried to bark."

Inside the wagon, the horrified Severe found the long-dead bodies of Wilson and Cummings. Because Wilson had been poised over Bower, the close-range shot had ranged through his body, tearing first a lung and then his liver. He had died probably within hours, if not sooner. Bower and Gray didn't even know that Cummings had taken a bullet in the midriff, but he also died within a day or so.

It took awhile to notify authorities in Oakley and relay the news to the sheriff in Albion, the county seat. Thus, not until the 18th did Sheriff Harvey Perkins and the Cassia County coroner arrive at the murder scene. In the meantime, Davis Hunter had released the dogs and taken them to his encampment for food and water.

The coroner thought the men had been dead for ten days to two weeks. Davis Hunter recalled that he had dropped off firewood at the Wilson-Cummings camp on the morning of February 4th. That verified the coroner's maximum time. Still, such estimates are notoriously imprecise.

Some blood had dripped outside the wagon box and there was a bloody handprint on the canvas wall. Unfortunately, the sheriff had no knowledge of the barely infant practice of fingerprint identification, so this evidence was useless.

Searchers found three empty .44 caliber shells near the wagon, which matched slugs found at the crime scene. The coroner carried these to his home as evidence, but managed to lose all but one of them by the time of the trial.

Between the front wheels of the wagon, they found a little-used corncob pipe. Oth-er sheepmen verified that the two Mormon victims did not smoke. Investigators also mis-handled this crucial piece of evidence, allowing a spectator to wander off with it. It returned to a county officer after passing through a second sheepman's hands.

Cummings had lived long enough to scrawl a quick note which, according to witnesses at the crime scene, said "If I die, bury me. Take care of my sisters." The sheriff and coroner also lost track of this evidence. At the trial, jurors would see only a random piece of paper with unreadable marks or smears on it.

They also found some dried up, but uncooked bread dough in a baking pan. The sheriff speculated that this could be part of the breakfast the men were preparing when Hunter passed through around 8:00 o'clock.

In his later deposition, James Bower said, "After the bodies of Wilson and Cummings were found, my first impression was to tell the whole matter as it occurred, but excitement was running high and so many threats had been made that I was satisfied that if I did so that both Gray and myself would be murdered."

Excitement certainly was "running high." It's not clear from records of that time, or the later testimony, when officials fastened on the 4th as the murder date. The available evidence proved only that the shootings took place no earlier than about 9 o'clock on that day. It could have been as late as February eighth.

Given later events, one has to wonder if authorities focused on the 4th after they discovered the only possible hole in the alibi of Diamondfield Jack Davis. (The date was correct, of course, but the reasoning was bogus.) Multiple witnesses confirmed that Davis and Gleason had left Idaho on the 4th and hadn't been back since.

However, no witness could verify their whereabouts from sunup until about 1:00 that afternoon when they finished dinner at the Boar's Head Ranch. The distance from Brown Ranch to the murder site and on to Boar's Head was about fifty-five miles. On February 4th, the likely route was soft

Diamondfield Jack Davis

and slippery, with patches of snow in shaded areas. It also included five to six miles of hills and cuts without roads or well-worn stock trails.

Experienced horsemen estimated that such a ride would take eight to ten hours under wintry conditions. Nevertheless, against all reasonable expectations, investigators decided that the five to six hours gap would have allowed Davis and Gleason to gallop to Deep Creek, stop and shoot Wilson and Cummings, and then hurry on into Nevada.

The details mattered less than the fact that their old nemesis had exerted the most pressure on sheep camps west of the deadline, wounded Tolman, and had now, they were sure, murdered Wilson and Cummings. Intense anger flamed in sheep country.

"Rumors reached the cattle country of Rock Creek that an uprising of the east side would invade the cattle country, with the intention of destroying the entire population," Charlie Walgamott wrote.

Down in Nevada, Davis and Gleason had talked big about their dust-up at the campsite where a horse was killed. But that brag had now morphed into an admission of guilt about the murders of Wilson and Cummings.

On March 20, 1896, officials in Albion issued a warrant for the arrest of Davis and Gleason. In no time at all, Diamondfield Jack and his alleged accomplice had rewards on their heads of $4,600. (That amounted to over twelve years salary for an ordinary cowpoke.) They would elude Idaho authorities for almost a year.

Much happened in the state while Davis was away. Even before he had found work with Sparks-Harrell, Idaho had passed legislation to exploit the irrigation opportunities provided by the 1894 Carey Act. That included creating the office of State Engineer.

In 1896, investors formed the American Falls Canal & Power Company to construct canals in that area. (Red tape and money problems delayed construction for a number of years.) Also by that time, the Great Feeder Canal was delivering water to new farms north of Idaho Falls. (The Great Feeder was not a Carey Act project.)

On the other side of the state, the Payette Valley Irrigation & Water Power Company had completed another canal project. During early 1896, the rather unusual town of New Plymouth came into being. Organizers planned the town around the irrigation system. They laid out a horseshoe shape with its flat end pointed north.

Each colonist purchased shares that came with a town lot for his dwelling along one of the curved streets. The title also included a block of irrigated farm land. A certain amount of sub-dividing provided for small stores and public buildings. However, plans called for most colonists to plant vegetables and fruit trees on ten- to forty-acre plots around the outer edge of the horseshoe. By the summer of 1896, colonists had crops growing.

This period also saw key educational milestones. On June 11, 1896, the University of Idaho granted its first four college degrees: bachelors in Arts, Philosophy, and two in Civil Engineering. Just eight days earlier, Lewiston State Normal School (today's Lewis-Clark State College) held a dedication for the first structure built expressly for the school. They had begun teaching classes using rented space early in the year.

That same summer Albion State Normal School completed the first building for which the state provided funds. They had begun teaching classes two years earlier in a structure erected using volunteer labor.

The year 1896 also produced a major milestone in government and politics. Recall that, around 1887, women's suffrage advocate Abigail Scott Duniway had moved to a ranch in Idaho's Pahsimeroi Valley. Two years later, suffrage supporters in Idaho sought her help for their campaign to include a women's suffrage provision in the proposed state constitution. She answered the call, but their effort failed. However, she did secure "an unofficial pledge" to advance a suitable constitutional amendment, basically "when the time was right."

Six years passed while the new state of Idaho assembled its organizational structure and body of laws. Meanwhile, suffrage advocates built support and judged the political climate. Finally, they felt confident enough to call their first full state convention. A second convention met on July 2, 1896. That fall, Idaho voters approved a women's suffrage amendment to the state Constitution. Idaho was the fourth state to approve voting rights for women.

Civilized influences were hardly supreme, however. On August 13, 1896, a hot Thursday afternoon, three riders moseyed into Montpelier. The streets were mostly empty. Had the operator of a local jewelry shop looked out, he might have recognized the men. He had hired them a couple weeks earlier to put up hay at the ranch he owned east of town. The riders first shopped for a few supplies at the general store, then mounted and walked their horses toward the bank.

Near the hitching posts there, they dismounted. The two men deep in conversation in front of the bank paid little attention. Suddenly, two masked men confronted them with drawn revolvers. Inside, the apparent leader, a chunky man with blond hair, held four of the citizens with their faces to the wall. His accomplice, a taller and darker individual, demanded money from the assistant cashier behind the teller's cage.

When the cashier said he had none, the tall robber called him a "Goddamn liar" and smacked him with his pistol barrel. The leader heatedly told him to leave the man alone and just get the money.

The tall man stuffed bills from the cash drawer and vault into a sack. He also dumped gold and silver coins into a bank money bag. During this time, the cashier closely studied the features of the horse holder outside. The man had not donned a mask.

The accomplice walked out and loaded their loot onto his own mount and a sorrel pack horse. Without rushing, the leader joined the other two and they rode out of town.

When the robbers' hoof beats subsided, the head cashier hurried to tell the law. Unfortunately, only a part-time deputy sheriff, who didn't carry a gun and had no horse, represented "the law." Game enough, the deputy grabbed a "penny-farthing" – a bicycle with giant front wheel and tiny rear – and gave chase. Hopelessly outclassed, he at least discovered that after leaving town the thieves had galloped toward the Wyoming border.

When the sheriff and his regular deputy arrived, they organized a posse and set off in pursuit. However, as Montpelier Canyon narrowed around them, the civilians realized they were riding into ideal terrain for an ambush. They turned back.

Nothing deadly happened to the pursuers. However, the officers soon discovered that the outlaws had switched to fresh mounts, which they had clearly hidden away beforehand. Investigation suggested the haying job had been a cover while the robbers scouted escape routes and places to stash extra horses.

Suspicion first focused on a known outlaw who worked out of Star Valley, Wyoming. However, he was much older than any of the Montpelier thieves. Eventually, authorities caught and convicted the man with no mask, Bob Meeks. Meeks was a known member of Butch Cassidy's so-called "Wild Bunch." Although local officials lacked enough evidence for an arrest warrant, they had no doubt that the blond leader had been Butch himself.

Meanwhile, stock raising grew all around the state as established ranchers adjusted to the new realities and fresh faces appeared. Thus, in 1896, A. J. Knollin ran around seventy thousand sheep on the hills north of Soda Springs.

Around Blackfoot, the firm of Berryman & Rogers had greatly expanded their farm and ranch holdings. Toward the end of the decade the *Illustrated History of the State of Idaho* named them "the richest stock breeders and dealers in Bingham county." They imported the best horses, reaching out to England, as well as top cattle breeds. The *Illustrated History* credited them with producing "a grade of beef cattle that is unsurpassed anywhere." With their profits they invested in real estate and opened a store in Utah. They also moved into banking.

In the north, unusual national trends led to a special situation. Herding the indigenous people onto reservations had seemed like a reasonable solution to "the Indian problem." In most cases, relocation forced the tribes onto tracts nobody cared about. At least, not at first.

Then, settlers began to fill up the country west of the Mississippi. New homesteaders turned greedy eyes on the Indian lands. This was especially true in northern Idaho, where the Nez Percés had managed to retain very desirable holdings.

Land grabbers found allies in the national "do-gooder" community. The latter's goal had always been "assimilation." In fact, many actively sought to eradicate Native American cultures. Thus, Indians should act like white farmers and become "stout yeomen" of the soil. They were not encouraged to emulate white stockmen. Stock raising might allow them to retain some vestiges of their traditional culture. And, not incidentally, help them accrue wealth, and independence.

In February 1887, Congress enacted the "Dawes" or "Severalty" Act. Selected reservations would no longer be communal tribal property. Instead, individual Indians would own them, in various-sized allotments. The law's clear intent was to force most Indians onto small farm holdings. It paid almost no heed to stock grazing.

Once the allotments had been distributed to the Nez Percés, the remaining "excess" land was sold to the Land Office. Whites could them claim plots as 160-acre homesteads.

Red tape and uncertainties about Nez Percés family lineages delayed implementation of the Dawes Act in Idaho until November 1895. As in other orchestrated land rushes, eager settlers gathered for the opening, with some "sooners" sneaking in early to claim choice spots.

The following year, many more pioneers took up reservation land. One of them was Jacob Eckert, who had purchased a ranch north of Cottonwood in 1882. He became, according to the *Illustrated History of North Idaho*, "one of the heaviest property owners in the county." With the increased acreage from the reservation claim, he turned to more crop raising.

During all this period, Cassia County officials searched for Davis and Gleason. In addition to the rewards offered, there seemed to be ample money for an extensive manhunt, both locally and in the West generally.

Then and for years afterwards, rumors asserted that much of this money came from the Mormon church. Such claims have never been substantiated. Fugitives who fit Jack's description were examined, at considerable travel cost, in locations as near as Santa Rosa, California and as far away as Oklahoma.

The bevy of local investigators included William E. Borah, a Boise lawyer with political ambitions. Born in Illinois, Borah passed the Kansas bar examination in 1887, at the age of twenty-two. Finding business slow in Kansas, he moved west to Idaho in 1890. By the time of the Wilson-Cummings killings, he had established a large practice, and was considered a "comer" in Republican politics.

Borah posed as a cattleman in search of ranch property. Cowboys for the Sparks-Harrell and neighboring outfits talked freely to him. An unemployed hand who held a grudge against Sparks-

Attorney William E. Borah

Harrell provided the payoff. He learned that a local cowboy had received letters from Gleason and Davis. Hoping for some of the reward money, the hand stole them and tipped off Borah. During the trial, he became the prosecution's "star witness."

Gleason was in Deer Lodge, Montana and Jack was confined in the Territorial Prison at Yuma, Arizona. Davis had gotten into a fracas with the law and been sentenced to a year for aggravated battery.

Hardly a model prisoner, he had twice been locked in solitary confinement. Once, he escaped, the other time he fought with another prisoner. Officials were probably happy to turn him over to the Cassia County Sheriff and two deputies in March, 1897. Gleason was also returned to Idaho at about the same time.

The trial of Diamondfield Jack Davis for the murders of Wilson and Cummings was scheduled to begin on April 8, 1897. In view of the earlier threats and the simmering anger in sheep country, James Bower faced a tough decision. As he later put it, "After Davis and Gleason were arrested, I desired to speak and relate the whole matter." However, he kept quiet because he still feared a violent reaction and "did not believe it possible for innocent men to be convicted of a serious crime."

Bower had told John Sparks the truth, so the cattle baron knew his outside men were innocent. Without mentioning Bower and Gray, Sparks hired arguably the best lawyer in Idaho, if not all the West, to defend Davis and Gleason.

Born in Dubuque, Iowa, in January 1847, James Henry Hawley spent the years between 1862 and 1864 in the Boise Basin mining districts. He then moved to San Francisco to study at City College. He also read law at a firm in the city. Hawley resumed mining in Idaho in 1868 but continued his legal studies. He was admitted to the Idaho bar in 1871.

In addition to his extensive private practice, he served terms in both houses of the Territorial Legislature. In 1878, voters in central Idaho elected him to be county District Attorney. Hawley also served two appointive terms as U. S. Attorney for the Territory.

Attorney James H. Hawley

By the time of the Davis trial, Hawley was the best known and most respected lawyer in the state. As either prosecutor or defense attorney, he had handled scores of high-profile cases. Hawley's team included Cassia County attorney Kirtland I. Perky. Perky had previously been an associate of the nationally famous William Jennings Bryan.

However, contemporaries felt the prosecution was equally strong. One of those helping the local District Attorney was William E. Borah. Borah was already well known in Idaho for his eloquence and legal ability. (His national fame in the U. S. Senate would come later.) The other Special Prosecutor was Orlando W. Powers. Powers was a former justice of the Utah Territorial Supreme Court. Some considered him the best criminal lawyer in Utah.

Like any competent defense team, Hawley and his partners examined the prosecutors' case. They had no trouble devising a solid defense. However, a jury selected from the precincts around Albion would surely contain mostly sheepmen and farmers. There might be a miner or two, but even one cowboy or cattleman was unlikely. Nevertheless, the defense team did not request a change of venue.

Hawley's team was confident the prosecution had no evidence to prove guilt "beyond a reasonable doubt." Still, no one knew Idaho law and politics better than Hawley. He was shrewd enough to realize that a change of venue might not improve the jury makeup all that much. The nearest alternative county seats were all in settled areas with few cattlemen in the closest precincts. They apparently decided the chance was not worth the likely bad publicity a request would bring.

Naturally the trial began with the description of the crime that had been committed. (Historian David H. Grover provides much detail on the trial and its outcome in his book *Diamondfield Jack: A Study in Frontier Justice.*) To convict Davis of murdering Wilson and Cummings, the prosecution supposedly had to prove the classic triumvirate: means, motive, and opportunity.

The two sheepmen died from wounds inflicted by .44 caliber slugs. Did Davis have the means to deliver those wounds? Jack was known to carry a .45 caliber revolver. However, two witnesses said that Davis had been target practicing with Gleason the day before and might have run out of ammunition. It is possible to fire .44 cartridges from a .45. Jack could have borrowed some from Gleason, who was shooting that caliber.

As to motive, Jack's job was to threaten sheepmen who crossed the deadline. Several sheepmen testified that he had told them he would shoot if they ignored the warnings. Witnesses from Nevada also related the big talk Davis and Gleason had made down there. Perhaps worst of all, Davis had bragged to a Nevada storekeeper: "I'm getting forty dollars a month for shooting sheepherders."

However, the prosecution found no witness to say Davis even knew the two victims were on the range. It was enough that they were there, and that Jack had warned others. The corncob pipe and smeared "note" were introduced into evidence, but prosecutors made no effort to tie them to anything.

An even weaker link in the prosecution's case was "opportunity," and that's where Hawley attacked. Davis and Gleason simply could not have made the alleged fifty-five mile ride in the period they were out of sight, under the conditions of the time.

Even under better circumstances, such a ride would have exhausted their mounts, and several witnesses testified that the horses showed no signs of hard riding. Moreover, two witnesses noted that Gleason's horse was somewhat lame to start with, due to hard usage a couple days earlier.

The prosecution countered with their star witness, who gave his name as Frank Smith. He made many claims, including one that the men's horses had been ridden hard. In cross-examination, Hawley ripped the witness to shreds. "Smith" admitted his real name was Brummet and that he had gone as Charley Hill and Jim Gordon, in addition to Smith, at various times.

He also conceded that he had been angry that Sparks-Harrell had fired him. Other witnesses testified that "Smith" had vowed to make the company regret firing him. He had even threatened to kill Davis if he got off.

The defense had totally discredited the prosecution's star witness. Moreover, the county's case was clearly based on suppositions, "could have been" arguments, and badly tainted physical evidence. There were some instances of conflicting testimony, but those were minor. The defense felt sure they had proven Jack's innocence, or at least done enough to raise "reasonable doubt."

After little more than three hours deliberation, the jury returned a guilty verdict. This result "stunned" the defense team, and a week later the judge passed sentence. Diamondfield Jack Davis would hang on June 4, 1897.

This same district court next tried Fred Gleason on a lesser "aiding and abetting" charge. Except for the testimony about Jack's threats to various sheepmen, the evidence was the same as that used for the Davis trial. (Apparently, nothing much was made of the fact that Gleason, not Davis, carried a .44 caliber revolver.) Further emphasizing the local vendetta against Davis, Gleason was acquitted. Prosecutors considered trying Gleason for the murders themselves, but eventually dropped the case.

Of course, knowledgeable observers knew that Jack's date with the hangman would be postponed. Hawley's team had grounds for months, if not years of appeals and counter-claims. Much would happen in Idaho during Hawley's struggle with the appeals process.

In southeast Idaho, John Allsop played an important role in opening up arid lands to agriculture and stock raising. Born in Salt Lake City in 1855, Allsop came to Idaho in 1884. After working at various locations, he settled near Grace in 1897. (Grace is located not quite ten miles southwest of Soda Springs.) Flowing west and south from that location, the Bear River descends into Black Canyon, which runs 150 to 300 feet below the regional plain.

Allsop began raising stock and helped initiate the Last Chance Irrigation Canal Company, which he would serve first as a director and then president. He ran "a large number of cattle of a superior quality" and began growing forage and other crops on his acreage as water became available.

New owners and capital also enhanced settlement further north, and Idaho Falls would have telephone service in less than two years.

In southwest Idaho, Owyhee County saw much less transition to general crop farming. The dry, broken landscape did not lend itself to canal building and irrigation.

Thus, Dow Dunning's Wickahoney Springs ditch system provided only enough water for a garden and a grove of apple trees. He had no way to get water onto most of his rangeland. There is no known record of how the severe 1889-1890 winter affected Dow's ranch. However, not until 1895 did he finally have the wherewithal to build a stone home on his spread. That soon became a stage stop on the road into Nevada.

As noted in the last chapter, David Shirk suffered heavy losses in 1889-1890. He and his brother had tried to grow enough hay to get them through. Unfortunately, their holdings allowed little provision even for irrigated forage crops, and their supplies fell short. However, with hard work and persistence, the family recovered and prospered. Shirk owned over a thousand acres by 1899. In 1897 Shirk bought a home in Berkeley, California, where the family spent the winter months. The place had enough acreage so David could haul a load of horses and mules back to finish for market during the winter.

Coincidentally, another early Owyhee Country cattleman, Con Shea, also made a permanent move to California about that time. Around 1883, he had purchased a winter home in Santa Rosa. Soon after that, the family apparently remained in California while Con traveled to Idaho and Oregon to oversee his ranch and business properties. Shea sold his ranch holdings in 1897.

Even the lower Bruneau Valley, where the river provided more water, saw limited crop agriculture. An *Owyhee County Commercial Directory,* published in 1898, said, "Considerable fruit and grain is raised in the valley, but the principle production is hay, of which about 10,000 tons is cut annually. There is also considerable attention given to stock raising and wool growing, and the cattle and horses produced in the valley compare favorably in quality with any raised in the West."

The reference to top-notch horses referred in large part to Kitty Wilkins' Diamond Ranch operation. Kitty and the local schoolteacher were the only two women listed in the *Directory* chapter for the Bruneau area.

A Pennsylvania newspaper reprinted (August 8, 1895) an article about her from the *Denver Republican.* The item said, "Miss Kitty C. Wilkins, the famous horsewoman of Idaho, has been in Denver for a couple of weeks. ... For the past nine years she has been selling horses and making money out of the business where many others have failed."

There were many years when the Diamond Ranch sent several thousand horses to markets in the South and East. Kitty was their only salesperson, visiting points from New Orleans all the way up the coast to Boston.

The influential *Idaho Statesman* often covered her comings and goings. An article published on April 30, 1897 made some interesting observations about her and the horse business. The reporter said, "Miss Wilkins explained that they formerly employed Mexicans exclusively, but this class of riders have left the country. The American is not so generally a good roper. ... Miss Wilkins has the reputation of being a perfect judge of horses. There is no man in Idaho who is her equal and few anywhere who are as good as she."

After the Panic of '93 eased, the Owyhee region saw a resurgence of lode mining. Prospects were favorable enough to justify rail service for the area. Building proceeded throughout 1897, including construction of a major railroad bridge across the Snake River. The line was completed to Murphy by August 1898. Stagecoach and wagon service then handled the long climb into Silver City.

In fact, the last years of the century saw much construction of branch lines in Idaho. That included the Pacific & Idaho Northern Railroad (P&IN) out of Weiser and up along the river. By this time, the ranges in the Weiser and Payette valleys supported substantial herds. The *Illustrated History of the State of Idaho* (published in 1899) asserted that the Payette ranges alone held eighty-five thousand sheep and ten thousand head of cattle.

That same year the P&IN reached the Salubria Valley, where William Allison had built a ranch in 1868. Just over a decade later, Allison was elected to the Territorial legislature. While there, he introduced the bill that created Washington County. (But, as we have seen, Lower Weiser – later Weiser City – got the county seat.)

In 1893, Allison served a term in the state House of Representatives. By the time the railroad reached Cambridge Station, Allison owned over five hundred acres of land. Afterwards, that expanded to over eight hundred. He became one of the largest livestock raisers in the area.

Up north, surveyors for the Northern Pacific Railway pushed closer and closer to the towns on Camas Prairie. Rails would soon run along the Clearwater River, but for various reasons would not mount the Prairie for almost another decade.

In the meantime, despite Hawley's diligent and skillful efforts, legal events had run consistently against Diamondfield Jack. All through the summer and fall of 1897, the two sides engaged in a kind of "dueling affidavits" exercise.

Some of the issues included jurors who perhaps admitted they pre-judged the case, the cartridges (would a .44 case bulge or burst when fired in a .45 caliber revolver?), and the time required for the alleged ride to and from the murder scene. (Under good summer conditions, test riders took over five and a half hours, and totally spent their horses.)

None of that worked, except to buy time. The judge disallowed Hawley's call for a new trial in January 1898. The defense's next step was to appeal to the Idaho Supreme Court. Hawley based his appeals on several procedural and technical points, plus many substantive issues that the defense felt clearly established "reasonable doubt" as to his client's guilt.

On June 15, 1898, the Supreme Court totally rejected the appeals, with a detailed point-by-point reiteration of the prosecution's circumstantial case. In essence, they accepted a totally improbable, and realistically impossible scenario.

Aside from the riding itself, Jack could not have made even one mistake in the route over rough, slippery, and unmarked terrain. At the end, he'd have to find a sheep camp he didn't even know existed. The prosecution never connected Davis to that particular camp in any way. If Davis just wanted to plug a sheepman, there were at least two camps closer.

At the camp, he then supposedly fired three borrowed .44 bullets from his .45 caliber revolver. "Iron man" Jack gets two killing hits despite having just ridden two to three hard hours on horseback. He probably shoots from the back of a lathered horse, since he could hardly afford the time to dismount. Still, he stops to eject the empty shells. Jack then rides like hell to the Boar's Nest, where he sits down and has lunch. Pretty amazing.

As historian David Grover put it, "Reasonable doubt had gone down the drain."

Hawley now filed an application with the state Board of Pardons, a panel consisting of the governor, secretary-of-state, and attorney general. They agreed to hear his case for a pardon during their meeting in mid-October, which happened to be not long before the new hanging date, October 21.

Hawley in Boise and Perky, still investigating in Cassia County, had long since begun to "smell a rat." The evidence, or lack thereof, had convinced them their client was truly innocent. This despite that fact that, as Perky wrote, "He is the most disagreeable client to manage I ever came in contact with."

Moreover, other people in Cassia County began to believe that justice had not been done in the Davis case. Many began to say so publicly. Someone else had shot the two sheepmen, and Hawley suspected that John Sparks knew who. However, Sparks continued to protect Gray and Bower. They still feared a lynch mob might come after the two.

Davis Hunter, with his firewood cart, had been the last person known to have seen Wilson and Cummings alive. During the trial, he had described passing Bower and another man after he left the sheep camp. That placed Bower and Gray fairly close to the scene of the crime. In September, Hawley virtually demanded that Bower tell what he knew.

Just eight days before the scheduled hanging, the cattleman admitted what had happened on February 4th. Under oath, he described the events that had ended with the "self-defense" shooting of the two sheepmen.

Toward the end of his deposition, Bower said, "After the Supreme Court had decided against Jack Davis's motion for a new trial and he had been resentenced, I realized that an innocent man was about to be hanged for a crime in regard to which he had not the slightest knowledge, and then resolved to make public my knowledge of the affair."

When the Board of Pardons met, they not only had in hand Hawley's original material, they now had the Bower deposition. A sworn statement from Gray confirmed the story. The Board also had several clemency petitions from Cassia County citizens. Of course, the prosecution had been busy too and presented counter-petitions urging the Board to deny a pardon. Overwhelmed, the Board granted a reprieve until December 16, so they could call more witnesses and hold hearings

At this point, the *Idaho Statesman* published (October 23, 1898) a long article about the Diamondfield Jack case. It made several legitimate complaints about the behavior of "cattle king" John Sparks. He had knowingly concealed the truth and deceived Jack's lawyers. However, the article was also heavy on innuendo and inflammatory language.

Cattle Baron John Sparks

The writer didn't address the question of why two long-time residents and solid citizens would put themselves in danger for a piece of riff-raff like Jack Davis. If this ploy was allowed to succeed, the article closed, "All that will be necessary hereafter is for an assassin to find some one to make a flimsy affidavit for him."

The December meeting didn't settle anything except to extend Jack's reprieve to February, 1899, and call for further review. Then, incredibly, the Pardon Board totally discounted all the new evidence at their January meeting. The hanging date was set for February 1, 1899. Davis almost certainly helped torpedo his case with an angry, rambling tirade to the Board. Basically, Jack was being punished for what he was, not for what he did.

This latest setback called for desperate measures. Getting no relief from the U. S. District Court in Boise, Hawley now lodged an appeal with the federal Court of Appeals in San Francisco. Fortunately, a judge there ordered a stay of execution while the appeal was considered. Hawley received the stay in Boise the day before the scheduled hanging in Albion.

There was no time to lose. Hawley sent a partner carrying three copies of the stay on the train to Minidoka Station, where they had arranged for two riders to meet him with three horses. (The primitive telephone line into Albion was notoriously unreliable, and subject to sabotage.) One after another, the three arrived at the county seat late that night. Hawley had bought yet more time for his client.

Hawley also led the defense for Jeff Gray and James Bower. (Gray had once worked on the Spark-Harrell ranches, so Sparks paid for both men's defense.) Gray's trial was basically routine. On February 21, the jury accepted his self-defense claim and ruled him "not guilty" of murder.

The court scheduled Bower's trial for much later in the year. Fortunately, he did not have to spend the time in jail. Sparks and Arthur D. Norton posted his $10 thousand bail. Norton had already testified that Gray told him about the shootings two days after they happened. By this time, Norton owned several ranches, perhaps two thousand acres in total. Irrigation on some of that land improved hay and feed grain production.

The result of Gray's trial made hardly a ripple in the public consciousness. Bower's acquittal, after a trial even more perfunctory than Gray's, drew even less notice. By this time, dramatic outside events had captured people's attention.

About a year earlier – while the Idaho Supreme Court considered Hawley's first appeal to them – the battleship *U.S.S. Maine* blew up, or was blown up, in Havana harbor. After *pro forma* diplomatic exchanges with Spain, Congress declared war in April. The administration called for the mobilization of National Guard units all across the country.

Officials mustered Idaho guardsmen and other volunteers into the First Idaho Regiment. In early May, Regimental units from the north gathered in Lewiston to await transportation to Boise. Before they left, citizens feted them and wished them well. Celebrants included Chester P. Coburn, old-time pioneer and veteran of the Nez Percés War. He made a stirring speech to the troops and presented them with a battle flag.

By early August 1898, the Regiment had landed in the Philippines. They were just in time to act as a reserve force in the final clash with Spanish troops. The Spanish-American War officially ended on December 10, 1898. The peace treaty then transferred sovereignty over the Philippines from Spain to the U.S.

Naturally, Filipino revolutionaries soon turned their fight for independence against the Americans. On February 5, 1899, Idaho troops actively engaged Filipino insurgents, and suffered their first casualties. Action continued from there, so Idaho's attention was focused on dispatches from the front and other war-related news.

For example, on February 22nd, the day after the Jeff Gray verdict, the front page of the *Idaho Statesman* headlined a possible national scandal. Columns of text described the testimony of Major General Nelson A. Miles before the Commission examining the conduct of the war. (Miles accused the meat packing industry of foisting tainted beef off on American soldiers.)

The *Statesman* buried the Jeff Gray acquittal item on page 2. Given their earlier hostile comments about Diamondfield Jack, the editorial response was remarkably tepid. The editor said, "The verdict of the jury in the Jeff Grey case was eminently correct, from whatever point of view the jurors may have considered the matter."

Hawley surely also found the war news distracting. His eldest son was a lieutenant with the First Idaho. Even so, he sought more creative ways to fight for Jack Davis. Early in 1899, Idaho law had been changed to require that all executions take place at the state penitentiary in Boise. Authorities transferred Jack to the prison in Boise.

Prosecutors, especially Borah, suspected that Hawley might somehow use the new law to get Davis off, or have his execution canceled. Borah sued on behalf of Cassia County to have him returned to county jail. He had, after all, been convicted under the old law. In late December, the Idaho Supreme Court agreed and Jack spent Christmas back in the Albion jail.

The threat of execution still hung over Diamondfield Jack Davis, but Hawley had plans for yet more maneuvers in the new century.

CHAPTER FIFTEEN: A NEW CENTURY

After the mules drank their fill, Ira Perrine tied them to a scrubby tree not far from his wagon. He always welcomed the campsite at The Cedars after the dry trek east from the Rock Creek area. To the west, the waters of the Snake River rumbled and grumbled into the gap where the canyon narrowed. Teams could not easily reach the river level for another fifty miles downstream.

North of his campsite, the rocky islands whose trees gave the spot its name provided a band of green to relieve the starkness of the sagebrush plains. Downstream, a jumble of great black rocks split the river again. A narrow skirt of gravely soil around the obstruction provided footing for some shrubbery and willow thickets.

Many times he had camped here on trips to deliver strawberries and other fruit to the Normal School at Albion. However, this journey in 1900 had a different purpose. Perrine had started his rough measurements in the broad plain beyond the double-humped hill that rose about six miles north and a bit east of Rock Creek. The arid, broken countryside alongside the river canyon made the work slow and tedious.

Carefully, he examined both banks. What were the highest points where they could anchor a dam? Fortunately, the rocky north side was higher than where he stood, so he only had to determine the best place on the south. Poking and prying along the edge, he located the best headland. Satisfied, Perrine studied the nearby flats. If necessary, he could grub out any brush that might block his line of sight.

He picked a spot, then walked to the wagon and retrieved the tripod and spirit level. His eye for country told him his prediction was probably correct. The instrument would prove it. He planted the tripod solidly, then worked the leveling screws until the bubble was perfectly centered. Next, he measured how high the viewer was off the ground and recorded that.

Perrine sighted back along his path to where he had planted the ruled stake. He noted the elevation, made the calculation, and said triumphantly, "I knew it!"

Of course, Ira was not a professional surveyor and his equipment was rather jury-rigged, but he had some room for error. The potential dam site was at least twenty-five feet higher than the bench that overlooked the plains between Rock Creek and the Snake River canyon. His findings contradicted the opinion of the county surveyor in

Albion. That official had said the only way to get water into the area would be to divert it at American Falls – too far away to be practical.

Born in Indiana, Ira Burton Perrine came to Idaho in 1883, when he was twenty-two. He started out in the Wood River mines, but quickly decided he could do better selling milk and butter to the miners and villagers. Seeking a milder winter range for his twenty-five dairy cattle, he moved them south in October 1884.

He had been told that Charles Walgamott and his wife had a cabin near Shoshone Falls, so he stopped there to ask for advice. Although it was late, Charles and Lettie fed him and provided a place to sleep for the night. Charlie said, "Next morning we drove the cattle to the Blue Lakes and with very little trouble worked them down the Indian trail to the valley below."

From that small start, Perrine built a fine farm and ranch. His Blue Lakes holdings eventually expanded to a thousand acres. He came to own property in Shoshone, part-nered or funded various businesses there, and raised and shipped horses and purebred sheep. He also dabbled in mining investments and explored possibilities for electric railway transportation. Still, his best venture was at Blue Lakes, where he grew award-winning fruits and vegetables. In diverting water to his farmland, he learned a lot about dams, canals, and irrigation.

> *The Big Picture.* In 1900, the U.S. comprised forty-five states. The nation's population topped 76 million, over triple what it had been a half-century ear-lier. In November, William McKinley was re-elected President. Less than a year later, an assassin murdered him and Theodore Roosevelt succeeded to the office. The Spanish-American War had given the U. S. Puerto Rico and the Philippines as major protectorates. Citizens owned an estimated ten million bicycles, while there were only about eight thousand registered automobiles.

Irrigation projects interested many Idahoans. The Carey Act only increased that interest. Even before that, the United States Geological Survey had been tasked to study promising spots along the Snake River. In 1890, they had commissioned Arthur D. Foote to survey potential reservoir and irrigation sites. Foote, of course, had played a major role in planning water projects along the Boise River.

Foote did not show The Cedars in his formal report. However, he did suggest infor-mally that it might be a candidate. Perrine had formed the same notion while searching for a bridge site for an Oregon Short Line branch railroad. After his solo survey, he began to look for backers to help finance more work. He also contacted State Engineer D. W. Ross. Ross later said that Perrine's notions about the site "recalled to my mind the opinion expressed years ago by Mr. Foote."

In June of 1900, Perrine filed water rights claims for both sides of his favored spot. (He had to make separate filings because the diversion points were in different counties.) He also recruited several well-off backers, including Stanley B. Milner of Salt Lake City. When the State Land Board endorsed the plan, Perrine, Ross, and two other men completed preliminary surveys on both sides of the river. These showed that a dam at The Cedars could provide irrigation for over a quarter-million acres, mostly on the south.

The survey results led to some adjustment of Perrine's initial water rights. Then, in October, Perrine and his backers incorporated the Twin Falls Land & Water Company. Milner was president and general manager, while Perrine was vice-president.

Ross encouraged the Land Board to approve the company's project. However, one roadblock remained. Their plan included areas that were part of a proposed national park along the Snake. That would block the transfer of the land to the state under the provisions of the Carey Act. Fortunately, the park proposal was set aside the following year.

Thus, during the summer of 1901, a team completed the detailed project survey. The surveyors included Walter G. Filer, a New Jersey-trained engineer who worked with Milner's mining interests in Utah. However, construction would not really begin on Milner Dam until two years later. They encountered problems in funding the complex dam and canal system. Plus, Perrine wanted to build a hydroelectric power plant fed by Shoshone Falls.

Perrine and his partners were not alone. The American Falls Canal & Power Company had basically limped through the end of the Nineties. Lingering after-effects of the Panic of '93 hampered their search for capital. Administrative uncertainties about the Carey Act were also a concern. But finally the state settled most of the details. The *Idaho Statesman* reported (February 23, 1901), "All having been adjusted agreeably to the state and the company, but one more detail is necessary prior to the pushing of the canal, the filing of the bond, and that will be concluded this morning."

Projects outside the Carey Act process also moved ahead. Not long before Perrine secured his water rights, the New York Canal Company began sending water to its patrons along the Boise River.

In 1900, two major canal companies in East Idaho agreed to a joint project. Together, they upgraded the dam that diverted water to systems on the east and west sides of the Snake. At about the same time, a settlers' cooperative founded the New Sweden Irrigation District. The District covered extensive acreage west of Idaho Falls. It was reportedly the first such district in the upper Snake River Valley.

Reflecting these changes, in October 1900 Idaho Falls acquired a hydroelectric utility. The city has been in the municipal power business ever since.

Still, these advances did not signal a retreat of the livestock industry. One pioneer who lived north of Idaho Falls described the fine stock range there. He said, "There is about five million acres of land which will always be available for this purpose as it lies above the water supply for irrigation."

In 1900, Sam Taylor still had a flourishing livery stable in Idaho Falls. As noted earlier, he also raised hay and grain on his ranch southeast of town. There, he had erected what the *Illustrated History* called a "roomy and elegant" home. However, Sam had to know the "handwriting was on the wall" for the livery business. Within five or six years, automobiles became common on the town's streets.

Along the Wood River, ranches covered all the best land as the century turned. John Hailey now also owned a horse and cattle ranch about ten miles south of Bellevue. He had sold off his stagecoach business as railroad lines became common around the Territory. (John had also been elected again as Territorial Delegate to Congress in 1884. That may have played a role in his decision.) In 1899, Hailey was appointed Warden of the Idaho State Penitentiary.

Further south along the Wood River, the Gooding brothers now ran many thousands of sheep on their ranches. Frank had become quite a wealthy man. In 1898, voters elected him to the state Senate. There, members selected him as President *pro tempore*. In 1904, he was elected to the first of two back-to-back terms as Idaho Governor. During his terms, Gooding called for more effective rules to protect livestock from contagious diseases. He also reorganized the livestock inspection office and appointed the first college-educated State Veterinarian.

Ranching in North Idaho had begun a transition to more mixed-crop farming, Even so, many settlers still had profitable herds of cattle and sheep. Loyal P. Brown had, of course, passed on. However, his son owned a ranch a couple miles north of Grangeville where he had "a good band of cattle."

German emigrant Henry Meyer had expanded his holdings west of Grangeville. He owned nearly seven hundred acres, where he ran cattle, but now owned even more hogs. Meyer had replaced his simple homestead hut with an eleven room home. It was said to have "all [the] modern conveniences." He had served a term on the Idaho County Commission and, in 1902, missed going to the state legislature by just two votes.

During that election one of Idaho's earliest pioneers, Thomas C. Galloway, succeeded in his bid for state office. He served in the House in 1903-1904. By then, Tom owned over fourteen hundred acres of land around Weiser, some of it within the city limits. In late 1901, Galloway represented Idaho as a Delegate-at-Large at the Annual Convention of the National Live Stock Association. A few months later, he was elected President of the Washington County Stock Raisers Association.

Over in the Boise Valley, Thomas J. Davis, one of the founders of Boise City, had also done well. He owned much real estate as well as shares in several city firms. His fruit orchards in the Boise Valley provided a steady income. Thomas had also expanded his rangeland and livestock holdings. The *Idaho Statesman* reported (March 2, 1898), "Thomas Davis yesterday shipped seven carloads of beef cattle to the Union Meat Company of Portland."

County Fair Livestock Shelter

Like many other long-time stockmen, Davis took pains to upgrade the quality of his animals. In 1900, his purebred Hereford stock – a bull and a cow – won first prizes at Boise's "Intermountain Fair," precursor to today's Western Idaho Fair. All in all, Davis was one of Boise's wealthiest residents.

The Wilkins family was also among Idaho's more well-off citizens. Their ranch in the Bruneau Valley and ranges to the south ran thousands of livestock. Kitty Wilkins still handled the horse operation, and business was good. People saw the automobile as a novelty, a toy for buyers who could afford the latest.

It almost seemed like Kitty spent all her time selling horses in the East. The *Idaho Statesman* covered (September 10, 1900) a visit to Boise that they noted as being her first stay in three years. A reporter asked if she had any stock to exhibit at the Intermountain Fair. She said she did but, "We are so busy shipping horses that I have not men to spare for bringing them down. ... We have a contract with Irwin & Grant of Kansas City to furnish 22 carloads of horses every two weeks."

The 1900 U. S. Census showed the importance of the Idaho's livestock industry. It counted over three million sheep, 360 thousand cattle, and 170 thousand horses.

Sales of mineral products – mainly lead, silver, and gold – still produced the largest clearly-identifiable revenue source, at about $11 million. (That would be about $400 million at today's metal prices). Categories used for agricultural production lead to some uncertainties in assessing that area. Livestock-related income might have exceeded that for mining, or was at least a very close second. The total would include revenue from hay and other forage crops, as well as cattle sales, wool, dairy products, and so on. In comparison, crop production other than hay and other forage was valued at about $4.7 million. (Of that, only about $442 thousand came from potato sales.)

Meanwhile, James Hawley continued to fight for the life of his client, Diamondfield Jack Davis. Hawley challenged the conviction on several counts, including some constitutional issues. Elements of the package eventually made it all the way to the U. S. Supreme Court. That held off action on Jack's sentence until December, 1900. Unfortunately, the result was yet another denial. Hawley appeared to have exhausted his repertoire of legal maneuvers.

The lawyer refused to give up. Motions and appeals bought more time, but Hawley finally had to go back to the Pardon Board. By now, sentiment in Cassia County had turned overwhelmingly in Jack's favor. Also, two of the three members of the prosecution team wrote letters stating their belief that Davis was innocent. Only William Borah opposed a pardon. The Board pushed a June hanging date back to July 3, 1901 so they could hold further hearings.

However, they dithered in setting a schedule, and had to issue another stay. Incredibly, they waited until the day of the execution to take that action. News of this reprieve could be handled by telegraph as far as Minidoka. Once again Hawley had to hire riders, two of them with relays of horses, to rush copies to Albion. Hoping for some word, the sheriff had held off the execution. He and the locals – and, obviously, Davis – were greatly relieved when the riders arrived, with three hours to spare.

The Board's decision produced yet another mind-boggling twist in this bizarre case. They had order a test where one hundred .44 caliber cartridges were fired from a .45 revolver. Some of the shells ruptured and all swelled to the point that they could no longer be inserted into a .44 pistol.

The one shell submitted as evidence in the case still fit into a .44 chamber. Result: Jack couldn't be the killer because he carried a .45. Neither the Bower-Gray confessions nor all of Hawley's legal pleadings seemed to play a role. The Board conceded that Jack was probably not a murderer. So … they commuted his sentence to life imprisonment! True to their brinksmanship, they issued the commutation the day before Jack's latest hanging date.

This singular piece of double-think frustrated Hawley on two levels. Obviously, the result did not provide true justice for his client. Also, Hawley, in the words of historian David Grover, "had a near-obsession about the importance of the law." To him, this miscarriage of justice pointed to major flaws in Idaho's legal system.

Officers transferred Davis to the state penitentiary to serve out his sentence. Meanwhile, the attorney prepared another appeal to the Idaho Supreme Court.

Hawley argued that the High Court should reverse the entire process because of those flaws. Suppose, for the sake of argument, Jack Davis walked into court with Wilson and Cummings, somehow alive after all, at his sides? Under current law, no lower court had the power to overturn the conviction. Incredibly, the Court agreed. But they said his hypothetical case would never happened, even "one time in a thousand years." They rejected the appeal and referred Hawley back to the Board of Pardons.

The legal peculiarities had kept Jack under threat of hanging far past the point where any application of "reasonable doubt" should have set him free. However, there were other forces at work. One, of course, was Jack's public persona as a boastful, aggressive gunman. That surely drove the original conviction and fostered pockets of resistance to a pardon. The opposition included, but was not limited to, the *Idaho Statesman*.

Writers for the *Statesman* had a political ax to grind. The leading newspaper in the state, it was staunchly Republican. The party had staked out a strong "law and order" position. This stance proved very popular in the long run. However, it was not enough to win the 1900 elections for Governor, Secretary of State, and Attorney General. Thus, the Pardon Board consisted of a Democrat and two "Democrat/Silver-Republicans."

So the *Statesman* hammered away on its hard-line theme. A pardon for Davis would prove that the administration was "soft on crime." They assured readers that Republican officer-holders would never cave in to those pleading for a pardon.

John Sparks himself made a supporting statement to the Pardon Board. Sparks had recently been elected as Governor of Nevada. (He ran as a "Silver Democrat.") The *Statesman* had not refrained from personal attacks before, so their response to this news seemed rather low-key. They simply noted his presence and opined (November 18, 1902) that "justice would be completely defeated" by a pardon for Jack.

Two days later, the newspaper expressed another thread of their antagonism. They said, "It is impossible to believe that the plot will be at last successful." Of course, by then they knew Hawley would probably succeed. All along, the *Statesman* had claimed that the campaign to free Jack was all a "plot." To them, it was just another attempt by a "cattle king" to get his own way. And by now, many people had turned against the power and prestige of the big cattlemen.

For a quarter century, the clout of the cattle industry had been second only to mining in Idaho. Cattlemen had promoted and nurtured the "Two Mile Limit" Law. Their well-financed legal teams had co-opted the courts to favor their activities. During those heady days, the *Statesman* had not just supported them, it had been a positive booster.

But times had changed.

In 1880, Idaho cattlemen sent large herds to Midwestern and Eastern markets. Mining was still king, but some stockmen were making fortunes. In that year's Census, about one in ten working Idahoans had fairly direct links to the livestock industry. That included more than just the stockmen and their cowboys. Hostlers, blacksmiths, feed growers, and other related occupations also had a stake. Furthermore, accounts suggest that even more than that fraction were so involved. Many settlers listed themselves as "farmers" even though they also raised cattle or sheep. Often, sales of beef cattle or wool earned more cash income than crops.

By 1900, as noted above, the livestock industry had almost caught up with mining in economic value. However, around half, or less, of that revenue came from cattle sales. The rest came from wool, sheep, and dairy products. Moreover, only about one in twenty Idahoans had direct links to the livestock industry. And many of those were sheep raisers and tenders. After all, there were more than eight sheep for every head of cattle in the state.

Newspaper accounts were now as likely as not to write disparagingly of the "cattle barons." Many viewed their attempts to prolong their hegemony with suspicion.

In December 1901, the *Statesman* reprinted a critical article from the *Lewiston Tribune*. A cattleman had brought suit against a sheepman under the Two Mile Limit Law. He won, but the *Tribune* writer noted that many doubted the constitutionality of the act. (That despite a favorable ruling by the Idaho Supreme Court.) The correspondent concluded, "The cattlemen are learning of the opportunity thus presented of saving their range from the sheep and are commencing actions in several cases like the one just mentioned."

Cattlemen did not restrict themselves to legal means. In 1901, raiders scattered a flock in the Teton Valley and killed $3,500 worth of the sheepman's rams. Authorities arrested several men. However, only one came to trial, and he got off. That encouraged another equally destructive raid in the Valley.

Sheepman did not accept these attacks passively. The *Statesman* for June 20, 1902 contained the headline, "Cattle Poisoned – Heavy Loss Sustained by a Wood River Stockman." One James Ainsworth had found fifteen head of his herd poisoned. Another one hundred head were missing. Two other small cattlemen had "lost six head of cattle by poisoning within the last week. No clue to the perpetrators has yet been discovered."

Unrelated, but similar acts of violence exacerbated the turbulent, uncivilized picture that such range clashes projected. One such incident took place at Mike Hyde's saloon in Oreana. (Oreana is located on the plains about eighteen miles east and slightly north of Silver City.)

A placer miner known as "Meadow Creek" Johnson liked to ride into town now and then for a few drinks. Hyde's place was easiest to reach from his cabin. On this occasion, he walked in on a fight. An aroused buckaroo grabbed a club, probably a broken chair leg, and started to attack. Not willing to back down, Johnson drew his gun and shot the attacker dead.

One can't escape the notion that Diamondfield Jack had become a symbol of this old "Wild West" milieu. Idahoans in the new century wanted to shed that image. "Law and order" politics and antipathy toward old time cattle barons can explain some of the *Statesman's* venom. Yet even the commutation angered them. They did not just want Davis punished, they wanted him dead. Perhaps the extra symbolism pushed the writers over the edge. Smashing an iconic symbol comes easier than executing an innocent human being.

Such a vengeful attitude would have been difficult to maintain had they actually met the "new" Jack Davis. His demeanor in jail had, in fact, gained him many friends. That even included the editor of the *Albion Times* and two successive sheriffs. Once beyond the bragging stories, people found Davis easy-going, companionable, and quite likable. Good with his hands, he made hair ropes and trinkets for children who visited the jail. He even grew flowers in his cell.

Twice he had come within hours of death by hanging, yet he faced his fate with equanimity and even a modicum of humor. When he left Albion after the Board commuted his sentence, many locals came by to express their support, some with small presents and even a gold watch.

However, *Statesman* writers did not interview Jack. Their attacks never ceased. One article screamed about "the great offense of pardoning Jack Davis." A week or so later an editorial diatribe referred to "the unholy conspiracy to bring about the defeat of justice in the Davis case."

By this time, the members of the Board of Pardons were all lame ducks. Two had been defeated by Republicans, while the Attorney General had not run for re-election. On December 17, 1902, they voted two-to-one to finally set Jack free.

The next day, a carriage met Diamondfield Jack Davis at the prison. On the way into town, he stopped at a high-class bar. There, Hawley, now Mayor-elect of Boise, met him for a few congratulatory drinks. After an overnight stay at the Overland Hotel, Davis caught a train out of Idaho, never to return.

Coincidentally, as Jack – a symbol of the state's wild past – departed, a harbinger of its modern future came to fruition in south central Idaho. A variety of factors had placed the Milner Dam venture in limbo. Most notably, they needed new financing. Determined to see the project through, Ira Perrine successfully wooed new investors. Even as the Pardon Board was reviewing Jack's case in early December, old and new investors hammered out an agreement to reorganize the Twin Falls Land & Water Company.

After that, Walt Filer and a former associate of his, Frank H. Buhl, ran the main Company. Perrine and Milner kept control of the hydropower plan. While Davis sought old friends in Nevada, the Idaho Land Board reviewed a new submission for the water project. The Board and company signed a formal contract on January 2, 1903. Actual construction began some time after June.

That same summer, the Company began selling acreage in the tract to be irrigated. Initial sales disappointed everyone and some investors sold off their interests. Then Ira Perrine put together a company that contracted with the Buhl-Filer interests to sell the parcels.

Milner Dam, 1905

Their sales efforts focused on the area slated to become the new town of Twin Falls. Workers completed Milner Dam in November 1904. By the end of the year, lots and homesteads were selling briskly. The first house had even been built in the town.

Water began flowing into the canal system during the spring of 1905. In August, Twin Falls celebrated the arrival of a branch rail line. In little over a month, residents witnessed the first major livestock shipment – four thousand sheep – from their railway station. Less than two years later, the state partitioned Cassia County to create Twin Falls County. The new village became its county seat.

More water projects followed. Soon, a new generation of pioneers swarmed into Idaho. The population doubled from about 162 thousand in 1900 to over 325 thousand in 1910. Most came to settle on new farms. However, some took an interest in livestock, especially the booming sheep industry.

For example, in 1903 the Robert Sproat family moved from Scotland to a spot not far from Mayfield, Idaho, about twenty miles southeast of Boise. His wife's family had moved to that area in 1886. (John McMillan, Sproat's brother-in-law, had been selected as postmaster for the waystation there. He renamed it for his ancestral home, Mayfield, Scotland.)

John and his brother Thomas established the McMillan Sheep Company. Their business prospered. The brothers would be instrumental in the construction of the Idanha Hotel, still a noted pioneer landmark in downtown Boise.

Sproat formed a partnership with his oldest son Hugh and they purchased a band from Thomas McMillan. They herded their sheep along Ditto Creek and did well, although they too had to endure the ill will of area cattlemen.

The notoriety of the Diamondfield Jack saga within the state did seem to cool tempers somewhat. (The case apparently got little national attention.) Both sides were now more inclined to use the courts for redress or intimidation.

The last known Idaho range war killings occurred in May of 1904. Joseph A. Myers, a reclusive oldtimer, operated a sheep ranch on the Snake River. His spread was "in the vicinity of Pittsburg Landing." (Pittsburg Landing is located twenty-five to thirty miles southwest of Grangeville.)

He had refused low-ball offers by area cattlemen to buy his place, and local cowboys began to harass him. They reportedly tore down his fences, ruined his alfalfa crop, and killed some of his sheep. Then two cowboys showed up to give him more grief. Finally fed up, he shot both, one fatally.

When the sheriff arrived, Myers went along quietly, probably figuring he was safer in jail anyway. According to accounts, a mob took him away from the officer on the way back to Grangeville, and lynched him.

The following year, Congress made the beginnings of a solution to cattlemen-sheepmen strife. On July 1, 1905, they established the U. S. Forest Service to manage forested public lands. Their act capped years of groping for the proper way to handle the nation's common property and potential resources.

From 1812 on, the General Land Office (GLO) was responsible for such areas. The Office mostly surveyed tracts so they could be sold off for revenue. Over the years, Congress also gave away parcels to help fund schools and other improvements. In 1849, Congress created the Department of the Interior and put the Land Office in it. Then, in 1862, the Homestead Act moved more acreage into private hands. At the same time, Congress established the Department of Agriculture to serve those new farmers.

All those measures still left vast expanses in the public domain. The Department of the Interior had neither the manpower nor any effective regulatory mechanism to protect that land from exploitation. Public forests proved to be especially vulnerable. Private "timber pirates" logged off huge tracts and left them barren and prone to destructive erosion. After many false starts, that crisis finally led to the Forest Reserve Act of 1891, which allowed the President to set aside forests for special protection. Yet even that Act had little in the way of "teeth" until six years later.

Cattle and sheep raisers rather "went along for the ride" in a lot of this. Politicians, and ordinary people, paid little attention unless disputes over specific grazing areas erupted into violence. However, as new reserve rules went into effect, stockmen demanded some say in how they were implemented.

Unfortunately, the Interior Department lacked the expertise to handle the job properly. Creation of the Forest Service, in the Department of Agriculture, put the job in more qualified hands. Much of the basic policy for managing public lands was set during this period. Subsequent actions further refined the rules. They applied both to the USFS and the later Bureau of Land Management within the Interior Department.

The resulting system of grazing fees and allotments did finally reduce conflict on the range, although the process took some time. Violent flare-ups occurred in several western states for at least another decade. Fortunately, Idaho was relatively quiet.

By 1910, with the inclusion of required hay and other forage, livestock (including dairy) was the number-one income segment in Idaho. It led manufacturing or crops, and far surpassed mining. Wool was a substantial fraction of the livestock segment.

Growth in the wool industry brought a major influx of Basques, who found work as sheepherders. Basques arrived in Idaho as early as 1870-1880, but their numbers grew slowly at first. The 1900 U.S. Census for Idaho recorded only a handful. That jumped to nearly a thousand a decade later, and continued to grow. By 1920, Boise alone had over a dozen Basque boarding houses.

In time, many Basques sought better-paying employment. Some became ranchers themselves. Today, Boise's Basque community (largest in the U.S. by some reckonings) has its own cultural centers and museum. Various Basque associations host festivals to celebrate their history and culture.

Idaho's 1910 wool output ranked 6th in the nation, even though the state ranked 44th in population. Overall, Idaho ranked 32nd in the total value of livestock products. Only in the last few years has the value of Idaho's manufacturing sector surpassed its agricultural production.

Still, say "Idaho" to most people, and they tend to think, "potato." The quality of the state's potatoes, coupled with highly effective long-term marketing, makes this understandable. Plus, Idaho does lead the nation in potato production. (Amazing, considering that the state's population now ranks 39th.)

In 2008, potato farmers received about $800 million for their annual crop. During that same period, livestock sales and dairy product shipments were valued at over $3.1 billion. That placed Idaho in the top ten among all states. The state is also in the top ten for U. S. wool production. However, the total income from that commodity is quite small. (The U.S. now produces less than 1 percent of the world's wool.)

Of course, cattle raising practices have changed dramatically. Back then, it seemed enough to shoo the animals out onto the range, and then hold the traditional roundup. Stockmen (and women) now purchase billions of dollars in hay and other forage, plus various supplements to enhance the field crops. They pay close attention to the animals' health, and spend tens of millions of dollars on veterinary care. They trace their stock's breeding history in great detail.

Yet much has also not changed. They still have a strong work ethic and a powerful commitment to the land. If anything, their sense of community has only grown as the group itself has shrunk. Of course, the vagaries of weather and markets are still much the same. Today as always, stock ranchers persevere.

It is satisfying that "the first stockmen of Idaho" still have a role in the modern industry. Today, the Fort Hall Indian Reservation is home to about ten thousand head of cattle. Many of those are non-Tribal bands on leased range. Still, Shoshone-Bannock cowboys do a fair amount of the required herding. Tribal members also raise various forage crops. Up north, the Nez Percés have a healthy mixed economy on the reservation. That includes fishing and various forms of modern agriculture, livestock as well as crops. They have also started programs they hope will re-establish the tribe as a center for breeding and raising fine Appaloosa horses.

As part of the state's Centennial celebration, the Idaho State Historical Society prepared a list of "Idaho Century Farms and Ranches." Across more than the decade following, the ISHS added to the list. The criteria state that the farm or ranch must have been "owned and operated in Idaho by the same family for at least 100 years, with 40 acres of the original parcel of land maintained as part of the present holding."

As of 2004, the list contained over 340 farms and ranches. Among them are nearly a hundred ranches established during the Territorial period. The pre-statehood list also includes 175 farms, many of which also raised livestock.

One of the earliest ranches that we know much about was that recorded in 1865 by Matthew Joyce, on Sinker Creek. When he died in 1893, his sons ran the spread as the Joyce Brothers Ranch. Only four "Century" holdings pre-date Matt's claim, all among the Mormon settlements in southeast Idaho. (Those tended to be mixed farm and ranch operations.) As of 2010, Paul Nettleton, Matt Joyce's great-grandson, and his wife Pat still operated the Joyce Livestock Company.

In 1867, Peter Pence trailed the first large herd of cattle into the Payette Valley and settled another Century ranch. Peter later brought irrigation to farms and ranches along the river and played a major role in the development of the city of Payette.

Rancher Peter Pence

Widowed in 1906, Peter turned management of the original claim over to his two youngest sons before 1910. They ran it as the Pence Brothers Ranch. Peter had extensive banking interests, serving as Vice-President of banks in Payette and New Plymouth. He also served a term in the state House of Representatives. He passed away in January 1922.

His great-grandson, Thomas F. Pence, Jr., runs the Century Ranch today. Like many modern ranchers, Pence hosts in-season bird hunting to help make ends meet. Tom also helps run the "Big Nasty Hillclimb" on his property. The Big Nasty is said to be the largest motorcycle event in Idaho. It draws competitors from all over the world.

A year after Peter Pence brought cattle to the Payette River, William B. Allison settled on the upper Weiser River. He soon began expanding his holdings. As noted earlier, he owned over five hundred acres by the time the railroad reached Cambridge. In 1899, the *Illustrated History* said that his son Alexander was "aiding him in conducting the farm." Census records show that Alexander had charge of the "home farm" ten years later.

William died in 1914. He had reached high rank in the Masonic Lodge, so a minister conducted the funeral service at the Cambridge Masonic Hall. The Pacific & Idaho Northern Railroad ran a special train for those who wanted to attend. The newspaper said, "The attendance at the funeral and the procession to the cemetery was the largest ever seen in Cambridge."

The ISHS compilation shows 1870 as the start year for the relevant Century Ranch, the "George and Margaret Allison Westfall Ranch." William settled in the area two years earlier, so this suggests how quickly he expanded his holdings.

Andrew Sweetser, with John Shirley, trailed Texas cattle into Idaho in 1866. Later, they moved their operation to the Raft River area. Within a few years, Andrew and a brother partnered with James M. Pierce to form the Sweetser Bros. & Pierce Cattle Company. By the mid-1880s, the partnership was one of the major cattle companies in Cassia County.

Long before that, Sweetser Bros. & Pierce had acquired a ranch near Malta. That holding eventually passed to a next generation of Pierces. Officially claimed in 1871, the property appears in the Century list with Dale O. and Jean Pierce as the owners.

A year before the Sweetser Bros. & Pierce claim, Nels and Emma Just settled along the Blackfoot River and began raising livestock. Nels worked incredibly hard, and they prospered. In 1898, Nels invested in another farm, improved it, and later sold the property at a considerable profit. News items from 1910 testify that he was still busy with land development as well as cattle raising. He died in March 1912. Emma passed away in November 1923.

Nels and Emma raised four sons and a daughter. The daughter, Agnes, was the only one of five female children that survived more than a month. She later became a noted Idaho article writer, columnist, and poetess. In November 1906, Agnes married Robert Reid and the couple bought the old homestead property along the Blackfoot. They raised five sons. Today, Reid descendants (grandsons of Nels and Emma Just) run four Century ranches along the Blackfoot. Plans are to pass those ranches along to two more generations of Reids.

Thus, livestock pioneers have left a rich legacy for the state, both in terms of economic impact and an intimate kinship with the land. They have endured and adapted to depressions, new rules and regulations, and changing life expectations. Their longevity offers the best proof of all that they are good stewards of the range.

Ask any older rancher. All hope an interested son or daughter can carry the bequest deep into the new century. Younger ranchers who have already accepted the baton feel the weight of all that history. Times change. Let's hope the enduring values exemplified by these pioneers and their successors don't.

Ranch Headquarters, ca 1888.

AFTERWORD

Most of the Idaho pioneers mentioned in this history spent their working lives in the Territory and State. Of course, some of the earliest "players" on the Idaho stage did not. Yet a few of those actually kept at least a tenuous link with the area throughout their lives.

Thus, Meriwether Lewis probably had a financial interest in the Missouri Fur Company, which sent trapper parties west of the Continental Divide. His suicide or murder, take your pick, cut that short. William Clark remained Superintendent of Indian Affairs, based in St. Louis, until his death in 1838. He had a connection to the West through trapper and trader reports.

Wilson Price Hunt's direct link with the fur trade ended with the publication of his journal in 1821. However, as a St. Louis merchant, he surely discussed the trade for many years after that. Washington Irving's description of St. Louis in the 1836 book *Astoria* irked Hunt. He felt the author spent too much time on the "rough element." Hunt died in 1842, as larger numbers of emigrants began to travel the Oregon Trail.

John Jacob Astor focused on his investments after he closed out his fur trade business. He had interests in railroads, insurance, hotels, and more. However, rentals on New York City real estate became his "cash cow." At his death in 1848, he was by far the wealthiest man in the United States. In fact, gauged by the national economies of their respective times, Astor ranks as the third or fourth richest American ever.

A couple years after Snake Brigade leader Donald Mackenzie left Idaho, the HBC moved him to their Red River Colony. (The colony included about half of today's Manitoba, plus land that is now below the border.) He rose to be Governor of the colony and retired in 1835. Mackenzie then bought land in far western New York State. He died in January 1851, a few months after being injured in a riding accident.

Fur company partner Andrew Henry returned to his mining interests after 1824. He died in January 1832. Some reports suggest his estate had been wiped out by defaulted loans he had co-signed.

Astorian Robert Stuart moved to Detroit after Astor closed the Mackinac fur trade post. There he bought land and built a nice home. At some point, he had re-worked the journal he kept during his trek back from the Pacific Coast. That revised account provided background for Irving's *Astoria*. In 1841, the Michigan Governor made Stuart

State Treasurer. Part of his job was to clean up reported "irregularities" in the new (1837) state's finances. After his retirement from that job, Stuart became an agent for Eastern investors. He passed away suddenly one evening while on a business trip to Chicago. That was in 1848, the same year Astor died, and when Congress created Oregon Territory.

Former Snake Brigade leader Peter Skene Ogden worked for the HBC until 1854. Everyone lauded his triumph in freeing the white hostages from the Whitman Massacre. Ogden always said that the Company's backing was what made it possible. Protecting company interests became harder and harder as Americans poured into Oregon Country. Already ill when he retired in August 1854, he died a month or so later, having moved to Oregon City.

William H. Ashley focused on Missouri politics after selling the Rocky Mountain Fur Company. In 1829, he ran unsuccessfully for a U. S. Senate seat. Two years later, Missouri's Representative to Congress was killed in a duel. Ashley was selected to replace him. Voters re-elected him twice until he declined to run again. He did run for Governor of Missouri in 1836, but was defeated. Ill health may have hampered his campaign. He died in 1838.

Mountain man, legislator, and U. S. Marshal Joe Meek retired soon after his service in the Cayuse Indian War in 1856. While relaxing on his farm in Oregon, he yarned about his life to historian Frances Fuller Victor. She published the memoir as *The River of the West* in 1870. Joe passed away five years later.

Army officer, explorer, and failed fur trader Benjamin L. E. Bonneville went on to other posts after his stay at Fort Vancouver. He retired in 1861, but the Army recalled him for Civil War duty. Bonneville retired again in 1866 with the rank of Brevet Brigadier General. He lived in Fort Smith, Arkansas until his death in 1878. In 1911, the Idaho legislature created Bonneville County, named in his honor.

Fort Hall founder Nathaniel J. Wyeth returned to the ice business in New England after ending his fur trade venture. He payed off his debts within a few years, and then did well enough to branch out into other lines of business. Wyeth was reportedly a wealthy man when he passed away in 1856. That same year, the Hudson's Bay Company abandoned Fort Hall.

Like Joe Meek, trapper Osborne Russell entered Oregon politics soon after he arrived there from Idaho. In 1843, he helped organize the Provisional Government of Oregon. Not long after that, he was selected to be a judge under that jurisdiction. Russell ran for governor of the Provisional Government, but was defeated. He moved on to California in 1848. Osborne died there in 1892.

Pioneer stockman John Francis "Johnny" Grant moved his children back to Canada after his wife died in 1866. He soon remarried. Grant dictated a memoir to his wife shortly before his death in 1907. Johnny spoke candidly about some of his youthful mistakes. However, he also admitted that he'd left some out. Johnny said, "Some passages might not be justly suited to the taste of my fair readers."

Suffragette and one-time Pahsimeroi ranch wife Abigail Scott Duniway moved back to Oregon in 1894. She lived there the rest of her life. After the 1896 success in Idaho, Abigail still faced a long, discouraging battle in Washington and Oregon.

Washington did not approve women's suffrage until 1910, and Oregon took two years longer. Abigail passed away in 1915.

Rancher and Boise City founder Henry C. Riggs returned to Boise some time after 1900. He thus moved back into the county named for his daughter, Ada. To ease the care-giving burden on wife and family, he took up residence in the Idaho Old Solders' Home. (Recall that he was a veteran of the Mexican War.) He died there in 1909.

Wealthy stockman and Boise City co-founder Thomas J. Davis loved music, played the violin, and served in the Boise City band in the early days. His wife, the former Julia McCrumb, was renowned as a gracious hostess and civic improvement booster. When she died in 1907, Thomas donated the land for a riverside park to honor her name. Today, Julia Davis Park is the crown jewel of Boise's extensive system of public spaces. Thomas survived his wife by less than nine months, passing away in June 1908.

Boise Pioneer Thomas J. Davis

"Stagecoach king" John Hailey retired comfortably at his home in Boise after his term as Penitentiary Warden. Then, in 1907, the legislature created the Idaho State Historical Society. They asked Hailey to be its first Secretary and Librarian, and he accepted. In 1910, John published a *History of Idaho*. In part, he wanted to correct "the many misstatements published about Idaho in early days, and particularly concerning the character and conduct of the good people of those days." John held the Society position until his death in April 1921.

Freighter, stock raiser, and all-around entrepreneur Alexander Toponce eased out of the Idaho freight business in 1883-1886. He lived in Corinne, Utah for awhile, serving one term as mayor there. Toponce invested in real estate, ran a sawmill, and owned sheep in Wyoming. Always busy, he also went after whatever else might earn a buck. In 1914, he sold some old hydropower sites he had claimed in Idaho. Alex was then seventy-five. Five years later, he completed his *Reminiscences*, an account of his many years pioneering in the Mountain West. After he died in May 1923, his wife found a publisher for the account.

North Idaho merchant and rancher Chester P. Coburn remained in Lewiston for his retirement. Two years after he presented a flag to Idaho troops headed for the Philippines, he helped start the Nez Perce County Pioneer Association. Coburn was elected as the Association's first Vice President. He passed away in October 1911.

Idaho Falls founder and stockman James M. "Matt" Taylor went back to Lafayette County, Missouri some time in the 1870s. He stayed there after that. Census records indicate he later dealt in real estate. We know little else about his life there. Taylor supposedly died around 1908.

Second-generation rancher William Wilson, son of James, lived in Elmore County for the rest of his life. Widowed in 1918, he and three sons ran the ranch until at least the 1930s. William passed away at Glenns Ferry in 1940.

Eagle Island developer and cattleman Truman C. Catlin maintained his stock operation well into the new century. Thus, the *Idaho Statesman* reported (September 23, 1900), "T. C. Catlin recently sold three cars of cattle in Omaha that netted him $62.50 a head over all expenses of shipment and sale." (Adjusted for inflation, that is a fine price!) He cut back his cattle operation in 1917. That was partly because, he said, all his cowboys had joined the Army. He kept a small herd of dairy cattle and converted the Eagle Island property mostly to mixed crop agriculture. Even at age eighty, he had not given up the reins to his son. James Hawley wrote that Truman "still takes pleasure in riding the range, which he says he can do with the best of them." Catlin died in June 1922.

Cattleman and Weiser developer Thomas C. Galloway passed away in June 1916. The Weiser mansion he had built in 1899-1900 is now on the National Register of Historic Places. He reportedly sold eight hundred horses to finance the place. (Today, it is a bed & breakfast furnished in period decor.) His namesake, Thomas C. Galloway, Jr., graduated from the University of Idaho in 1907. He then went on to a highly successful medical research career. We are told that Thomas, Junior – who died in 1977 – hosted reunions at the family ranch for a half century.

Weiser pioneer Solomon M. Jeffreys mostly got out of stock raising in the 1880s. Besides his store and real estate holdings, he also invested in Weiser River canal projects. He later served on the Weiser City council and as Treasurer of Washington County. In 1904, he traveled to Portland, Oregon for surgery. Unfortunately, the operation was not successful and he died there.

Cowboy and stockman Charles S. Gamble, who had helped import Texas cattle into Idaho, ranched along Cassia Creek for 15-20 years. He then moved into the tiny village of Malta and opened a hotel. Charles and his wife ran the hotel for a number of years, and were able to retire comfortably by about 1910. Charles passed away there in 1921.

Another cowboy and stockman, David L. Shirk, chose to move out of state for his retirement. He kept up his seasonal "commute" from Berkeley, California to his Owyhee Country property until 1914. He then sold the ranch. In 1920, Shirk took some time to record his memories of what life on the frontier had been like. He wrote in a style intended simply as an account for family. Later, Shirk's daughter Lila gave Martin Schmitt permission to publish *The Cattle Drives of David Shirk*. David died in July 1928.

Stockman Cornelius "Con" Shea moved permanently to Santa Rosa, California after he sold his ranches in Idaho and Oregon. He became a wealthy landowner there, and a Director of the Savings Bank of Santa Rosa. The 1906 earthquake that destroyed San Francisco also hit Santa Rosa hard. Shea's family came through all right. However, the quake wrecked a lot of downtown property Shea owned. Local newspapers noted that he planned to rebuild with reinforced concrete. Con passed away in May 1926.

In the early years of the new century, horse breeder and Idaho constitutional delegate Samuel F. Taylor was elected a Justice of the Peace in Bingham County. However, he resigned in 1905 to look after his farm and ranch interests, including property on the Big Lost River near Mackay. Voters in that district sent him to the state House of Representatives in 1909. Two years later, doctors told the family that Sam's wife needed to live at a lower altitude, with a warmer climate. They thus moved to Ontario, Oregon, a couple miles south of Payette, Idaho. There, Sam dealt in real estate for awhile before retiring. Widowed before 1930, Taylor died in Ontario in 1936.

Stockman, Governor, and U. S. Senator George L. Shoup tried for re-election to the Senate after his second term. However, the make-up of the Idaho legislature had changed and Shoup was defeated. He retired from public life in 1901 and died three years later. A statue of Shoup represents Idaho in the National Statuary Hall Collection in Washington, D. C.

In 1905, stockman and grower Arthur Pence helped organize the Bruneau State Bank. He also joined in creating a Bruneau Valley school district. Arthur then became almost a permanent member of the school board. In the new century, Arthur served a term in the state Legislature and two terms in the state Senate. He then owned relatively small but high-quality herds of cattle and horses. Arthur's sheep flocks made him, according to H. T. French, "one of the large factors in that industry in the southern half of the state." By around World War I, Pence dealt exclusively in sheep. He passed away in 1935.

Pioneer clerk and businessman Charles Walgamott and his wife moved to Montana some time before 1890. He did come back for at least one job. It also seems likely he visited or had other jobs off and on during the years he was in Montana. Charlie moved back to live in Twin Falls around 1917. Three years later, he was working as a car salesman. In 1926, he published his memories, and stories he had collected, as *Reminiscences of Early Days*. He added to that from historical newspaper articles he wrote in 1930. Charlie published the revised compilation as *Six Decades Back* in 1936. Walgamott died in April 1937.

Cattleman Arthur D. Norton had other interests besides his extensive ranch properties in south central Idaho. He also served two years on the University of Idaho Board of Regents. Norton lived to see irrigated farming begin in the Rock Creek area, and the arrival of the first train in Twin Falls. He died after a long illness in May 1906.

As noted earlier, the Hyde brothers cut back and went their own ways after the hard winter of 1888. Dave moved to the Bruneau Valley and operated a ranch there. He sold the property in 1909 and began full-time management of the hotel he had built in the town of Bruneau. He remained with the hotel until his death in June 1922. Mike went to Oreana, where he operated a saloon for many years. He passed away in early 1925.

Sheep authority Richard Bennett passed his Elmore County ranch along to his three sons when he died in May 1917. They recast the business as Bennett Brothers Livestock Company. Like their father, they mostly ran sheep; however, they also had cattle, horses, and hogs. In 1925, one brother went off on his own with one of the shared ranch properties.

Prominent sheep raiser Robert Noble sold his ranching interests in 1906, when he was sixty-two. He then moved from Reynolds Creek into Boise. From his new base, he bought a share of the Idaho Trust & Savings (IT&S) Bank. Noble also invested in real estate in Boise, Caldwell, and Nampa. His holdings included two hundred and forty acres planted in fruit orchards. He became President of the IT&S Bank in 1912. Noble passed away two years later.

John Sparks had sold his Nevada cattle interests about the time he ran for Governor there. As Governor, he traded range disputes for labor-management strife in the mines. Even so, voters re-elected John in 1906. Unfortunately Sparks made some unwise mining investments. He was essentially bankrupt when he got sick and died in May 1908.

German emigrant and stockman Henry Meyer became a Director for the Bank of Camas Prairie and for a supply company in Grangeville. He finally also succeeded in politics, serving a term in the state House of Representative starting in 1915. Unlike some citizens of German heritage, Henry suffered no estrangement with his neighbors during World War I. After he died, the *Idaho County Free Press* noted (November 19, 1925) that his was one of the largest funerals "in the history of Idaho County" and that "stores and banks closed during the funeral hour."

Starting in 1909, stockman and stage station operator Dow Dunning served two consecutive terms in the Idaho House of Representatives. He followed that with a term in the state Senate. Between 1910 and 1920, the family moved from Wickahoney to a place with milder weather west of Caldwell. He ran unsuccessfully for the U. S. House of Representatives in 1922. By 1930, Dow had moved his family to Boise. He passed away there in 1936.

North Idaho cattleman Jacob Eckert owned a large home in Lewiston along with his ranch property near Cottonwood. He also owned a thousand acres of land in Kansas. In 1903, Jacob bucked a heavily Democratic vote to be elected as a Republican to the Idaho Senate. Voters again sent him to the state Senate in 1911. He passed away in 1925.

Charles W. Berryman, of the Blackfoot firm Berryman & Rogers, divided his time among the company's interests in stock raising, retail trade, and real estate for many years. However, by 1910, he saw himself primarily a banker, working for one of the largest banks in Blackfoot. By 1920, Berryman was President of the bank. He passed away in 1925.

George Rogers, the other half of Berryman & Rogers, served in the first session of the state Senate after Idaho became a state. He also spent two years as a Commissioner for Bingham County. In 1897, President William McKinley appointed Rogers Receiver of the U. S. Land Office in Blackfoot. Before 1910, he moved his family to Boise. There, he engaged in real estate development. He died in 1926, a year after Berryman.

Wealthy sheep owner and Governor Frank Gooding ran for a U. S. Senate seat in 1918, but lost. He succeeded two years later, and was re-elected in 1926. Gooding sponsored legislation meant to lower transportation costs in the intermountain states, including Idaho. Often called the "Long and Short Haul Bill," the act passed the Senate in 1924. Intense pressure by the railroad lobby led to defeat in the House, however. The idea was very popular and resurfaced in the Senate even after Gooding's death in office, in June 1928.

The horse business of "Queen of Diamonds" Kitty Wilkins got one last surge during World War I. The Army bought thousands of animals. Although some demand continued after the War, Kitty began to phase out the Diamond Ranch operation within a few years. She then retired to a mansion in Glenns Ferry. Kitty passed away there in October 1936.

Jackson Lee, aka "Diamondfield Jack" Davis never did discover any diamonds. However, after leaving Idaho, Jack proved to have a knack for finding rich gold claims. He returned impressive dividends to men who had staked his searches and helped finance several towns among the gold camps. For a few years, he moved as an equal among the "movers and shakers" of Nevada mining, and politics. But his wealth and fame faded with the mines. Jack was making do with odd jobs when he stepped off a curb in Las Vegas and a taxicab hit him. He died a few days later, on January 2, 1949.

Citizens elected lawyer James Henry Hawley to be Idaho Governor eight years after he closed the Davis case. Hawley launched a legislative blitz during his term. Besides many new laws, he urged lawmakers to write eight amendments to the Idaho constitution. They did, and all passed during the next election. Two changes provided for voter Initiatives and Referenda. Hawley failed in his re-election bid. He lost by fewer than nine hundred votes out of over 100 thousand cast. In 1915, he became President of the Idaho State Historical Society. Five years later, he published a four-volume *History of Idaho*. Hawley remained President of the Historical Society until his death in August 1929.

Ira Burton Perrine threw himself into promotion and sales once the land around Twin Falls had water. He also opened a grand hotel in town and helped organize a bank. As automobile traffic grew, he was among many who pushed for construction of a bridge across the Snake River canyon at Twin Falls. The "Twin Falls-Jerome Intercounty Bridge" opened for traffic on September 15, 1927. (The name "I. B. Perrine Bridge" came later.) Perrine passed away in October 1943.

As suggested during the discussion of Century Ranches, most of the pioneers who came to Idaho after 1860 put down roots here. Today, many prominent Idahoans trace their ancestry back to those early settlers.

Relaxing at the Chuckwagon,c a 1904

IMAGE SOURCES

Sources List and [Shorthand]

Bureau of Land Management [BLM]

Permission from Bailey's C4 Ranch, Sweet Idaho. Photographer Kami Bailey. [C4]

Denver Public Library, Western Collection [Den]

Elmore County Historical Research Team, Mountain Home, Idaho (1985) [EL]

Hiram Taylor French, *History of Idaho: A Narrative Account ...* , Lewis Publishing Co., Chicago and New York (1914). [Fr]

Idaho City Historical Foundation [ICHF]

An Illustrated History of the State of Idaho, The Lewis Publishing Company, Chicago (1899). [ILST]

Lemhi County Historical Society [LC]

Library of Congress [LoC]

W. J. McConnell, *Early History of Idaho*, The Caxton Printers, Caldwell, Idaho (1913). [McC]

McClurg Museum, Westfiled, New York. [McM]

National Archives [NA]

National Park Service [NPS]

Nevada Historical Society [Nev]

Oregon History Project [OHP]

Personal collection ... [PC]

"Savings Bank of Santa Rosa," *Sonoma County Homes and Industries,* Reynolds & Proctor Publishing, Santa Rosa, California (1898). [SR]

U. S. Forest Service [USFS]

Utah State Historical Society [Ut]

Page Number, Subject, [Source]

BIBLIOGRAPHY: BOOKS, JOURNAL ARTICLES, ETC.

Reference Description	Chapter Usage
Mildretta Adams, *Owyhee Cattlemen,* Owyhee Publishing Co., Homedale, Idaho (1979).	4-8, 10, 12-15
Ramon F. Adams, *Come an' Get It: The Story of the Old Cowboy Cook*, University of Oklahoma Press, Norman (1952).	7, 10
Albion State Normal School: Historical Sketch, Idaho State University Manuscript Collection, Pocatello (2006).	14
The Albion Valley: History, City of Albion (2002).	7, 8, 10, 12, 15
John N. Albright, *Grant-Kohrs Ranch National Historic Site, Historic Resource Study,* National Park Service, http://www.nps.gov/grko/hrs/hrsi.htm (March 6, 1999).	4, 5, 7, 8, 10, 12
Kent Alexander, *Legends of the Old West,* Friedman/Fairfax Publishers, New York (1994).	10
Frederick Allen, *A Decent, Orderly Lynching: the Montana Vigilantes,* University of Oklahoma Press, Norman (2004).	5
J. Cecil Alter, *Jim Bridger,* University of Oklahoma Press, Norman (1962).	3
Stephen E. Ambrose, *Nothing Like It in the World: The Men Who Built the Transcontinental Railroad, 1863-1869,* Simon & Schuster, New York (2000).	7, 11
Stephen E. Ambrose, *Undaunted Courage: Meriwether Lewis, Thomas Jefferson, and the Opening of the American West,* Simon & Shuster, New York (1996).	1, 2
Jay E. Anderson, Kristin T. Ruppel, James M. Glennon, Karl E. Holte, Ronald C. Rope, *Plant Communities, Ethnoecology, and Flora of the Idaho National Engineering Laboratory,* Environmental Science and Research Foundation, Idaho Falls (June 1996).	12
Lavina Fielding Anderson (ed.), *Chesterfield: Mormon Outpost in Idaho*, The Chesterfield Foundation, Bancroft, Idaho (1993).	10

Annual Report of the Commissioner of the General Land Office for the Year 1887, Government Printing Office, Washington, D.C. (1887).	13
Susan B. Anthony, Ida H. Harper (eds.), *The History of Woman Suffrage*, Vol IV: 1883-1890, The Hollenbeck Press, Indianapolis (© Susan B. Anthony, 1902).	14
Jesse Applegate, "A Day with the Cow Column in 1843," *Transactions of the Fourth Annual Reunion of the Oregon Pioneer Association for 1876*, Salem (1877).	4
Leonard J. Arrington, *History of Idaho*, University of Idaho Press, Moscow (1994).	6, 12
William H. Ashley, *William H. Ashley Papers*, Missouri Historical Society, St. Louis, Missouri (2009).	3
"Astor to Dorr, New York, July 7, 1813," *John Jacob Astor Papers*, Baker Library, Harvard University Graduate School of Business Administration, Boston.	2
"Astor to Gallatin, New York, June 1, 1817," *Albert Gallatin Papers*, New York Historical Society, New York City.	2
Robert G. Athearn, *Union Pacific Country*, University of Nebraska Press, Lincoln (1876).	11
Louie W. Attebery, *The College of Idaho, 1891-1991: A Centennial History*, The College of Idaho, Caldwell, Idaho (1991).	13
John Read Bailey, *Mackinac, formerly Michilimackinac: a History and Guide Book*, Tradesman Company, Grand Rapids, Michigan (1909)	2
Laurie Baker, *The City of Eagle: Yesterday and Today*, City of Eagle, Official Website (May, 2007).	6
John Ball, *Autobiography of John Ball*, The Dean-Hicks company, Grand Rapids, Mich. (1925).	3
Hubert Howe Bancroft, *History of California*, The History Company, San Francisco (1886).	10
Hubert Howe Bancroft, Frances Fuller Victor, *History of Washington, Idaho, and Montana: 1845-1889*, The History Company, San Francisco (1890).	5, 6, 7, 11-13
Demas Barnes, *From the Atlantic to the Pacific, Overland*, D. Van Nostrand, New York (1866).	8
Merrill D. Beal, *Intermountain Railroads: Standard and Narrow Gauge*, Caxton Printers, Caldwell, Idaho (1962).	10
Merrill D. Beal and Merle W. Wells, *History of Idaho*, Lewis Historical Publishing Company, Inc. New York (1959).	All
Richard J. Beck, *Famous Idahoans*, Williams Printing, (© Richard J. Beck, 1989).	15
James H. Beckstead, *Cowboying: a Tough Job in a Hard Land*, University of Utah Press, Salt Lake City (1991).	14
Peter W. Bernstein, Annalyn Swan (Eds.), *All the Money in the World*, Random House, Inc. in collaboration with Forbes magazine (2007).	3

220

John Bertram, et al, *Rock Creek Station and Stricker Homesite: Idaho Historical Site Master Plan,* Idaho State Historical Society (2001).	6, 12
John Bidwell, "The First Emigrant Train to California," *Century Magazine,* New York (1890).	4
John Bieter, Mark Bieter, *An Enduring Legacy: The Story of Basques in Idaho,* University of Nevada Press, Reno (2000).	15
David L. Bigler, "Bartelson-Bidwell Party" *Utah History Encyclopedia,* University of Utah Press, Salt Lake City (1994).	4
Archie Binns, *Peter Skene Ogden: Fur Trader,* Binfords & Mort, Publishers, Portland (1967).	3, 4
Annie Laurie Bird, *Boise: The Peace Valley,* Caxton Printers, Ltd., Caldwell, Idaho (1934).	2, 4, 5, 10, 11
Judy Boyle, "Sweet Victory," *Range Magazine,* Carson City, Nevada (Summer 2007).	15
John Bradbury, *Travels in the Interior of America, in the Years 1809,1810, and 1811,* Sherwood, Neely and Jones; London (1819).	2
Waldo W. Braden, "William E. Borah's Years in Kansas in the 1880's," *Kansas Historical Quarterly,* Vol. 14, No. 4 (November, 1947).	14
L. E. Bragg, *More Than Petticoats: Remarkable Idaho Women,* The Globe Pequot Press, Guilford, Connecticut (2001).	12-14
George Francis Brimlow, *The Bannock War of 1878,* Caxton Printers, Ltd., Caldwell, Idaho (1938).	9
Cornelius James Brosnan, *History of the State of Idaho,* Charles Scribner's sons, New York (1918).	15
Alonzo Brown, *Autobiography of Alonzo Brown,* Yale University Library (1922).	5, 7
Dee Brown, *The American West,* Touchstone Books, Simon & Shuster Inc. (1994).	6
Business Directory of the Pacific States and Territories for 1878, L. M. McKinney, Publisher, San Francisco (1878).	10
"Butch Cassidy," *Wyoming Homestay & Outdoor Adventures,* Cody, Wyoming (2010).	14
Robert Campbell, Drew Alan Holloway (Ed.) *A Narrative of Colonel Robert Campbell's Experiences in the Rocky Mountain Fur Trade from 1825 to 1835,* Ye Galleon Press, Fairfield, Washington (1998).	3
The Carey Act in Idaho, Idaho State Historical Society, Boise (2004).	14
W. L. Carlyle, E. J. Iddings, *Lamb Feeding and Sheep Husbandry in Idaho, Bulletin No. 77,* Idaho Agricultural Experiment Station, Moscow, Idaho (1913).	15
Donald L. Carr, *Into the Unknown: the Logistics Preparation of the Lewis and Clark Expedition,* Combat Studies Institute Press, Leavenworth, Kansas (2003).	1
Robert C. Carriker, *Father Peter John De Smet: Jesuit in the West,* University of Oklahoma Press (September 1998).	4

Gorton Carruth, *What Happened When*, Penguin Books, New York (1989).	1-4, 8, 12, 13, 15
Christopher Carson, Milo Milton Quaife (Ed.), *Kit Carson's Autobiography*, University of Nebraska Press, Lincoln (1966).	3, 4
Albert Castel, "A New View of the Battle of Pea Ridge," *Missouri Historical Review*, Vol. 62, No. 2, Historical Society of Missouri (January 1968).	6
H. M. Chittenden, *The American Fur Trade of the Far West*, University of Nebraska Press, Lincoln (1986).	2, 3
Barzilla W. Clark, *Bonneville County in the Making*, Self-published, Idaho Falls, Idaho (1941).	5-8, 10, 13
Malcom Clark, *Eden Seekers: The Settlement of Oregon, 1818-1862*, Houghton Mifflin Company (1981).	2-4
Marion Clawson, *The Bureau of Land Management*, Praeger Publishers, Santa Barbara, California (1971).	15
Lawrence Clayton, Jim Hoy, Jerald Underwood, *Vaqueros, Cowboys, and Buckaroos*, University of Texas Press, Austin (2001).	12
Collister Neighborhood Association, *Collister Neighborhood Plan*, Boise City Council (September 2007).	13
John Colter Biography, Grand Teton National Park (official website).	2
O. C. Comstock, "Sketch of the Life of Hon. Robert Stuart," *Report of the Pioneer Society of the State of Michigan*, Vol. III, Robert Smith Printing Co., Lansing (1881 issue, reprinted 1903).	2
Cort Conley, *Idaho for the Curious: A Guide*, Backeddy Books, Cambridge, Idaho (1982).	4-7, 9-15
"Construction: Pacific States," *Electrical World*, Vol. LXIV, McGraw Publishing Company, Inc., New York (1914).	10
Hank Corliss, *The Weiser Indians: Shoshoni Peacemakers*, University of Utah Press, Salt Lake City (1990).	3, 6, 7, 9, 14
Ross Cox, Edgar and Jane Stewart (eds.), *Adventures on the Columbia River*, University of Oklahoma Press, Norman (1957).	2
Medorem Crawford, *The Report and Journal of Captain Medorem Crawford* . . . . 1862. Sen. Exec. Doc. 17, 37th Cong., 3d sess., (January 8, 1863).	5
Crofutt's Transcontinental Tourists' Guide, George A. Crofutt, Publisher, New York (1872).	8, 9
Dick D'Easum, *The Idanha: Guests and Ghosts of an Historic Idaho Inn*, Caxton Printers, Ltd. (1984).	6, 15
Dick d'Easum, *Sawtooth Tales*, The Caxton Printers, Ltd., Caldwell, Idaho (1977).	2, 5, 6
Harrison Clifford Dale, *The Ashley-Smith Explorations and the Discovery of a Central Route to the Pacific*, Arthur H. Clark Company, Cleveland, Ohio (1918).	2, 3
James W. Davis, *Aristocrat in Burlap*, Idaho Potato Commission, Boise (1992).	15

John W. Davis, *Wyoming Range War: The Infamous Invasion of Johnson County,* University of Oklahoma Press, Norman (2010).	13
W.A. Dayton, *Important Western Browse Plants,* USDA Misc. Bull. 101 (Washington, D.C.: GPO, 1931).	6
Byron Defenbach, *Idaho: The Place and Its People,* American Historical Society, New York (1933).	11-15
Marguerite L. Diffendaffer, *Council Valley, Here They Labored,* Worthwhile Club of Council, Council, Idaho (1977).	5,7, 8, 10, 13-15
Arif Dirlik (ed.), Malcolm Yeung (Asst.), *Chinese on the American Frontier,* Rowman & Littlefield Publishers, Inc., New York (2003).	12
B. W. Driggs, *History of Teton Valley, Idaho,* Louis. I. Clements and Harold S. Forbush (eds.), Eastern Idaho Publishing Company, Rexburg (1970).	3
Ellen Druckenbrod, *Abigail Scott Duniway & Idaho's Woman Suffrage Movement,* Boise Public Library, Boise, Idaho (2005).	12, 14
Abigail Scott Duniway, *Path Breaking,* James, Kerns & Abbott Co., Portland, Oregon (1914).	4, 12, 14
M. Alfreda Elsensohn, Eugene F. Hoy (Ed.), *Pioneer Days in Idaho County,* Caxton Printers, Caldwell, Idaho (1951).	5, 9, 10, 12-15
Encyclopædia Britannica from Encyclopædia Britannica 2007 Ultimate Reference Suite (2008).	1, 3-5, 7, 11, 13
John English (ed.), *Dictionary of Canadian Biography,* University of Toronto (© 2000).	2, 3
W. A. Ferris, Leroy R. Hafen (ed), *Life in the Rocky Mountains,* Old West Publishing Company, Denver (1983).	3
Mark Fiege, *Irrigated Eden: The Making of an Agricultural Landscape in the American West,* University of Washington Press, Seattle (1999).	10
William E. Foley, *Wilderness Journey: The Life of William Clark,* University of Missouri Press, Columbia (2004).	1, 3
Carolyn Thomas Foreman, "Colonel Pinkney Lugenbeel," *Chronicles of Oklahoma,* Vol. 24, No. 4, Oklahoma Historical Society, Oklahoma City (1946).	5
"Fort Lapwai," *Idaho Museum of Natural History Digital Atlas,* Idaho State University, Pocatello (2002).	5
Altha E. Fouch, "The David Fouch Family and Their Oregon Trek," *Fouch - Fouché - Foutch Family Historian,* Vol. 2, No. 1, Bellevue, Washington (1996).	11, 13
Philip L. Fradkin, *Stagecoach: Wells Fargo and the American West,* Simon & Schuster, New York (2002).	5, 6
Gabriel Franchére, Hoyt C. Franchére (ed. and translator), *Adventures at Astoria, 1810-1814,* University of Oklahoma Press (1967).	2
J. V. Frederick, *Ben Hollady, the Stagecoach King,* Arthur H. Clark Company, Glendale, California (1940).	6

John C. Frémont, *Report of the Exploring Expedition to the Rocky Mountains ... The Senate Of The United States*, Government Printing Office, Washington, DC. (1845).	4
Hiram Taylor French, *History of Idaho: A Narrative Account ...* , Lewis Publishing Co., Chicago and New York (1914).	6-15
Mary Jane Fritzen, *Eagle Rock, City of Destiny*, Bonneville County Historical Society, Idaho Falls, Idaho (1991).	3, 7, 8, 10, 13-15
Mary Jane Fritzen, *Taylor's Bridge and Founders of Eagle Rocks*, Bonneville County Heritage Association, Idaho Falls, Idaho (2005).	6-8
Thomas C. Galloway, "Points of a Good Jack," *The American Agriculturist for the Farm, Garden and Household*, Vol. 48, Orange Rudd Company, New York (1889).	15
Patrick Gass, Carol Lynn Macgregor (ed.), *The Journals of Patrick Gass*, Mountain Press Publishing Company; Missoula, Montana (1997).	1
Joseph Gaston, *Centennial History of Oregon, Illustrated*, The S. J. Clark Publishing Company, Chicago (1912).	10
T. T. Geer, *Fifty Years In Oregon*, The Neale Publishing Company, New York (1912).	4
James R. Gentry, *A Centennial History of Bliss, Idaho: 1883 - 1893*, North Side News, Jerome, Idaho (© by Bliss Centennial Committee, 1983).	11
Jim Gentry, *In the Middle and On the Edge: The Twin Falls Region of Idaho*, College of Southern Idaho (2003).	10, 15
Rafe Gibbs, *Beacon for Mountain and Plain: Story of the University of Idaho*, © Regents of the University of Idaho (1962).	14
Halbert Powers Gillette, *Rock Excavation: Methods and Costs*, Myron C. Clark Publishing Company, New York (1907).	11
Ray Hoard Glassley, *Pacific Northwest Indian Wars*, Binfords & Mort, Portland, Oregon (1953).	9
Joseph F. Glidden, *Improvement in Wire-Fences*, Patent No. 157,124, United States Patent Office, Goverment Printing Office (November 24, 1874).	8
"Golden Jubilee Edition, 1884–1934," *Idaho Falls Post-Register* (September 10, 1934).	4, 8, 10, 12-15
George Goodhart, as told to Abraham C. Anderson, *The Pioneer Life of George Goodhart*, The Caxton printers, Caldwell, Idaho (1940).	7
W. A. Goulder, *Reminiscences : Incidents in the Life of a Pioneer in Oregon and Idaho*, T. Regan Publisher (1909).	4, 5
Leo W. Graff, *The Senatorial Career of Fred T. Dubois of Idaho, 1890-1907*, Garland Publishing Company, New York (1988).	10, 12, 15
John Francis Grant, Lyndel Meikle (ed.), *Very Close To Trouble: The Johnny Grant Memoir*, Washington State University Press, Pullman (1996).	4, 7
"John Grant Biographical Sketch," *Provincial Archives of Alberta*, Archives-Canada.ca (online resource).	4

Dale M. Gray, "War on the Mountain," *Idaho Yesterdays*, Vol. 29, No. 4 (Winter 1986).	8
Jerome A. Greene, *Nez Perce Summer, 1877: The U.S. Army and the Nee-Me-Poos Crisis*, Montana Historical Society Press: Helena (2000).	9
David H. Grover, *Diamondfield Jack: A Study in Frontier Justice*, University of Nevada Press, Reno, Nevada (1968).	13-15
Eugene H. Grubb, W. S. Guilford, *The Potato: A Compilation of Information from Every Available Source*, Doubleday, Page & Company, Garden City, NY (1912).	15
Kristina Guest and Mike Crosby, "The Shoup Ranch," *Patchwork: Pieces of Local History*, Salmon High School, Salmon, Idaho (May 1988).	10, 12, 13
Bill Gulick, *Outlaws of the Pacific Northwest*, Caxton Press, Caldwell Idaho (2000).	5, 6
R. W. "Rib" Gustafson, *From San Antone to Bannack*, Stoneydale Publishing Company, Stevensville, Montana (© 1999 by R. W. "Rib" Gustafson).	7
LeRoy L. Hafen (ed), *Mountain Men and Fur Traders of the Far West*, University of Nebraska Press, Lincoln (1982).	2, 3
John Hailey, *History of Idaho*, Syms-York Company, Boise, Idaho (1910).	7, 12, 13
Francis Haines, *The Nez Percés: Tribesmen of the Columbia Plateau*, University of Oklahoma Press, Norman (1955).	1, 2, 4, 9, 14
J. Evetts Haley, *Charles Goodnight: Cowman and Plainsman*, University of Oklahoma Press, Norman (1949).	6, 7
Mike Hanley, with Ellis Lucia, *Owyhee Trails*, Caxton Printers, Caldwell, Idaho (1973).	5-9, 12, 15
Burton Harris, *John Colter: His Years in the Rockies*, University of Nebraska Press, Lincoln (1993).	2
Frank Harris, "History of Washington County and Adams County," *Weiser Signal* (1940s).	6, 7, 11, 12, 14, 15
John Harrison, *Columbia River History*, Northwest Power and Conservation Council, Portland, Oregon (2000).	6
J. M. Harrison, *Book of Information and Settlers' Guide for the Pacific Slope*, C. A. Murdock & Co., San Francisco (1875).	7, 8
Arthur A. Hart, *Basin of Gold: Life in Boise Basin, 1862-1890*, Idaho City Historical Foundation (© 1986, Fourth printing 2002).	6
William Hathaway, *Images of America: Idaho Falls*, Arcadia Publishing, Mount Pleasant, South Carolina (2006).	15
Adelaide Hawes, *Valley of Tall Grass*, Caxton Printers, Caldwell, Idaho (1950).	7-10, 12, 13, 15
James H. Hawley, *History of Idaho: The Gem of the Mountains*, The S. J. Clarke Publishing Company, Chicago (1920).	4-15
James H. Hawley, *Eighth Biennial Report of the Board of Trustees of the State Historical Society of Idaho*, Boise (1922).	15

James H. Hawley, *Ninth Biennial Report of the Board of Trustees of the State Historical Society of Idaho*, Boise (1924).	12
James H. Hawley, *Tenth Biennial Report of the Board of Trustees of the State Historical Society of Idaho*, Boise (1926).	8, 13
Kathleen Hedberg, *Cassia County, Idaho*, Caxton Printers (© Cassia Cnty Commissioners, 2005).	6, 8, 10, 13-15
George Woodman Hilton, *American Narrow Gauge Railroads*, Stanford University Press, Stanford, California (1990).	12
A Historical, Descriptive and Commercial Directory of Owyhee County, Idaho, Owyhee Avalanche Press (January 1898).	5-9, 12-15
History of Idaho Territory: Showing Its Resources and Advantages ..., Wallace W. Elliot & Co., San Francisco, California (1884).	8, 10-12
Ruby El Hult, *Steamboats in the Timber*, The Caxton Printers Ltd., Caldwell, Idaho (© Ruby El Hult, 1952).	12
Wilson Price Hunt, Hoyt C. Franchére (ed. and translator), *Overland diary of Wilson Price Hunt*, translated from the original *French Nouvelles Annales des Voyages* (Paris, 1821), Ashland Oregon Book Society (1973).	2
James Hunter, *Scottish Highlanders, Indian Peoples*, Montana Historical Society Press (1996).	1, 2
Idaho Century Farms and Ranches, Idaho State Historical Society (2004).	6, 15
"Idaho Territory: Alturas County," *United States Official Postal Guide*, Callaghan & Company, Publishers, Chicago, by authority of the Post Office Department (January 1886).	12
An Illustrated History of the State of Idaho, The Lewis Publishing Company, Chicago (1899).	5-15
An Illustrated History of North Idaho, Western Historical Publishing Company (1903).	4-15
Michael J. Ingham, *Lower Payette River Subbasin Assessment and Total Maximum Daily Load*, Idaho Division of Environmental Quality, Boise (1999).	12
Washington Irving, *Astoria, or Anecdotes of an Enterprise Beyond the Rocky Mountains*, G. P. Putnam and Son, New York (1868).	2, 3
Washington Irving, Edgeley W. Todd (ed.), *The Adventures of Captain Bonneville U.S.A., in the Rocky Mountains and the Far West*, digested from his journal. University of Oklahoma Press, Norman (1961).	3
Donald Jackson (ed.), *Letters of the Lewis and Clark Expedition with Related Documents*, Second Edition. Urbana: University of Illinois Press (1978).	1
William E. Jackson; J. Orin Oliphant and C. S. Kingston (eds.) "William Emsley Jackson's Diary of a Cattle Drive É," *Agricultural History*, Vol. 23, No. 4; Agricultural History Society (October, 1949).	7, 10
Julie Roy Jeffrey, *Converting the West: A Biography of Narcissa Whitman*, University of Oklahoma Press, Norman (1994).	3
Randall A. Johnson, "Captain Mullan and His Road," *The Pacific Northwesterner*, Vol. 39, No. 2 (1995).	5

E. W. Jones, "Some Wonders of Idaho," *Southern California Quarterly*, Historical Society of Southern California, Los Angeles (January 1886).	6
Terry G. Jordan, *North American Cattle-Ranching Frontiers*, University of New Mexico Press, Albuquerque (1993).	4-8, 10, 12
Alvin M. Josephy, Alvin M. Josephy, Jr., *The Nez Perce Indians and the Opening of the Northwest*, Houghton Mifflin Books, New York (1997).	9
Rick Just (Ed.), *Water Man: The Life and Letters of Nels A. Just*, Cedar Creek Press, Boise Idaho (© Rick Just, 2005).	7, 10, 13, 15
Charles J. Kappler, *Indians Affairs: Law and Treaties*, Vol. 1, Government Printing Office, Washington (1903).	12
William Kittson, David E. Miller (ed.), "William Kittson's Journal, 1824-1825 Snake Country Expedition," *Utah Historical Quarterly*, Vol. XXII (April 1954).	3
Maury Klein, *Union Pacific: Volume I, 1862-1893*, Doubleday, New York (1987).	11
James H. Kyner, as told to Hawthorne Daniel, *End of Track*, Copyright © 1937 by The Caxton Printers, Ltd. reprinted by arrangement, University of Nebraska Press, Lincoln (1967).	11
N. P. Langford, *Vigilante Days and Ways*, Montana State University (1957). Original publication in 1890.	5, 6, 8, 10
Zenas Leonard, Milo Milton Quaife (ed.), *Narrative of the Adventures of Zenas Leonard*, written by himself, University of Nebraska Press, Lincoln (1978).	3
Meriwether Lewis and William Clark, Gary E. Moulton (ed.), *The Definitive Journals of the Lewis and Clark Expedition*, University of Nebraska Press, Lincoln (2002).	1
Fred Lockley, Mike Helm (ed.), *Conversations with Bullwhackers, Muleskinners, Pioneers...*, Rainy Day Press, Eugene, Oregon (1981).	4, 6-8
E. S. Lohse, *Idaho Native American Prehistory and History*, Idaho Museum of Natural History, Pocatello..	4
Leander V. Loomis, Edgar M. Ledyard (ed.), *A Journal of the Birmingham Emigrating Company ... in 1850*, Legal Printing Co., Salt Lake City, Utah (1928).	4
Cyrus C. Loveland, Richard H. Dillon (ed.), *California Trail Herd*, Talisman Press, Los Gatos, California (1961).	4, 7, 8
Edith Haroldsen Lovell, *Benjamin Bonneville: Soldier of the American Frontier*, Horizon Publishers, Bountiful, Utah (1992).	3, 4
Byron DeLos Lusk, *Golden Cattle Kingdoms of Idaho*, Master's thesis, Utah State University, Logan (1978).	4, 6-8, 10, 12-15
John C. Luttig, Stella M. Drumm (ed.), *Journal of a Fur-trading Expedition on the Upper Missouri: 1812-1813*, Missouri Historical Society, St. Louis (1920).	2
Ruth B. Lyon, *The Village That Grew*, printed by Lithocraft, Inc, Boise (Copyright Ruth B. Lyon, 1979).	8, 11-13

Carol Lynn MacGregor, *Boise, Idaho, 1882-1910: Prosperity in Isolation,* Mountain Press Publishing Company, Missoula, Montana (2006).	1, 3, 5, 10, 11, 15
John F. MacLane, *A Sagebrush Lawyer,* Pandick Press, New York (1955).	14, 15
Axel Madsen, *John Jacob Astor: America's First Multimillionaire,* John Wiley & Sons, Inc., New York (2001).	2, 3
Brigham D. Madsen, *Chief Pocatello: The "White Plume,"* University of Utah Press, Salt Lake City (1986).	5
Brigham D. Madsen, *The Northern Shoshoni,* The Caxton Printers, Caldwell, Idaho (1980).	9
Michael P. Malone, Richard B. Roeder, and William L. Lang, *Montana: A History of Two Centuries,* Revised Edition, University of Washington Press, Seattle (1991).	5
Charles F. Martin (ed.), *Proceedings of the Annual Convention,* Fort Worth, Texas, National Live Stock Association, Denver (1900).	14
Charles F. Martin (ed.), *Proceedings of the Fifth Annual Convention of the National Live Stock Association,* December 3-6, 1901, P. F. Pettibone & Co., Publishers, Chicago (1902).	15
Merrill J. Mattes, *Colter's Hell & Jackson's Hole,* Yellowstone Library and Museum Association and the Grand Teton Natural History Association in co-operation with the National Park Service (1976).	2
Dean L. May, *Three Frontiers: Family, Land, and Society in the American West, 1850-1900,* Cambridge University Press, Cambridge (1994).	6, 11
W. J. McConnell, *Early History of Idaho,* The Caxton Printers, Caldwell, Idaho (1913).	3-6, 8, 9, 13
John Dishon McDermott, *Forlorn Hope: The Nez Perce Victory at White Bird Canyon,* Caxton Press, Caldwell, Idaho (2003).	9
John E. McDowell, Haydn Marc Lewis (ed.), *There's a Long, Long Trail Awinding... (Overland Diary of John E. McDowell),* linked into Trails Project site, U.S. Department of Education (1995).	10
Joseph M. McFadden, "Monopoly in Barbed Wire," *Business History Review,* Vol. 52, No. 4 (Winter, 1978).	8, 12
George A. McLeod, *History of Alturas and Blaine Counties, Idaho,* Hailey Times Publishing, Hailey, Idaho (1930).	6, 10, 11, 14
Lucullus Virgil McWhorter, *Hear Me My Chiefs! Nez Perce History and Legend,* The Caxton Printers, Ltd: Caldwell, Idaho (1984).	9
"Notable Oregonians: Joseph Meek - Trapper, Lawman," *Oregon Blue Book,* Oregon State Archives, Salem (2011).	3, 4
Julius Merrill, Irving R. Merrill (ed.), *Bound for Idaho: The 1864 Trail Journal of Julius Merrill,* University of Idaho Press, Moscow (1989).	6, 7, 10
Gregory Michno, *The Deadliest War in the West: The Snake Conflict, 1864-1868,* Caxton Press, Caldwell, Idaho (2007).	6
Donald L. Miller, *City of the Century: The Epic of Chicago and the Making of America,* Simon & Schuster, New York (1996).	10

Nellie Ireton Mills, *All Along the River: Territorial and Pioneer Days on the Payette,* Payette Radio Ltd., Montreal, Canada (1963).	6-9, 14, 15
Rebecca Mitchell, *Historic Sketches: Pioneer Characters and Conditions of Eastern Idaho,* Bert P. Mill, Idaho Falls (1905).	7, 8
Eugene P. Moehring, *Urbanism and Empire in the Far West, 1840-1890,* University of Nevada Press, Reno (2004).	5, 11, 12
Julie R. Monroe, *Moscow: Living and Learning on the Palouse,* Arcadia Publishing, Mount Pleasant, South Carolina (2003).	8, 10
Rae Ellen Moore, *Just West of Yellowstone,* Great Blue Graphics, Laclede, Idaho (© 1987, Rae Ellen Moore).	15
Dale L. Morgan, *Jedediah Smith and the Opening of the West,* University of Nebraska Press, Lincoln (1964).	2, 3
Samuel Eliot Morison, *The Oxford History of the American People,* Oxford University Press, New York (1965).	1, 3, 4, 9, 10, 13-15
Charles Morton, "The Third Regiment of Cavalry," *The Army of the United States,* U.S. Army Center of Military History (2002).	4
John Mullan, *Report on the Construction of a Military Road from Fort Walla Walla to Fort Benton,* Ye Galleon Press (May 1989).	5
Robert Newell, *Memorandum of Robert Newell's Travels in the Territory of Missourie,* Champoeg Press, Portland, Oregon (1959).	3, 4
Roger L. Nichols (ed.), *The American Indian: Past and Present,* 6th Edition, University of Oklahoma Press, Norman (2008).	9, 14
Walter T. K. Nugent, *Habits of Empire: A History of American Expansion,* Alfred A. Knopf, New York (2008).	4
Bill O'Neal, *Cattlemen vs. Sheepherders,* Eakin Press, Austin, Texas (1989).	14, 15
Pearl M. Oberg, *Between These Mountains: History of Birch Creek Valley, Idaho,* Exposition Press, New York (1970).	10, 12
Peter Skene Ogden, David E. Miller (ed.), "Peter Skene Ogden's Journals of His Expedition to Utah," *Utah Historical Quarterly,* XX, Utah State Historical Society, Salt Lake City (April 1952).	3
Peter Skene Ogden, T. C. Elliott (ed.), "Peter Skene Ogden's Journal - Snake Expeditions," *Quarterly of the Oregon Historical Society* (1909-1910).	3
Richard Oglesby, *Manuel Lisa and the Opening of the Missouri Fur Trade,* University of Oklahoma Press, Norman (1963).	2, 3
J. Orin Oliphant, *On the Cattle Ranges of the Oregon Country,* University of Washington Press, Seattle (1968).	3-10, 12-14
Diane Olson, *Idaho State University: A Centennial Chronicle,* Idaho State University, Pocatello (2000).	15
"Omaechevarria vs. State of Idaho, 246 U.S. 343 (1918), Omaechevarria vs. State of Idaho No. 102" *U. S. Supreme Court,* Washington, D.C. (March 18, 1918).	8, 10, 12
James L. Onderdonk, *Idaho: Facts and Statistics Concerning its Mining, Farming, Stock-Raising, Lumbering, and Other Resources and Industries,* A. L. Bancroft & Company, San Francisco (1885).	1, 3, 10, 12

Joel Palmer, *Journal of Travels over the Rocky Mountains, 1845-1846,* reprinted, Reuben Gold Thwaites (ed.), in Early Western Travels, Vol. XXX, Arthur H. Clark Company, Cleveland (1906).	4
"Notable Oregonians: Joel Palmer - Pioneer, Writer," *Oregon Blue Book,* Oregon State Archives (2009).	4
Richard M. Patterson, *Butch Cassidy: A Biography,* University of Nebraska Press, Lincoln (1998).	14
Edwin H. Peasley, *Twelfth Biennial Report of the Board of Trustees of the State Historical Society of Idaho,* Boise (1930).	14
Keith C. Petersen, *Educating in the American West: One Hundred Years at Lewis-Clark State College, 1893-1993,* © Lewis-Clark State College, Confluence Press, Lewiston, Idaho (1993).	14
Marcus Petersen, *The Fur Traders and Fur Bearing Animals,* The Hammond Press, Buffalo, N. Y. (1914).	1, 3
Stacy Peterson, "Silas Skinner's Owyhee Toll road," *Idaho Yesterdays,* Idaho State Historical Society (Spring 1966).	5
Elias D. Pierce, as told to Lula Jones Larrick, J. Gary Williams and Ronald W. Stark (eds.), *The Pierce Chronicle,* Idaho Research Foundation, Inc., Moscow, Idaho (1975).	5
Gifford Pinchot, *Forest Reserves in Idaho,* Forest Service Bulletin No. 67, U. S. Department of Agriculture, Government Printing Office, Washington, D.C. (1905).	15
Elizabeth Lee Porter, "Iowa to Oregon, 1864," *Covered Wagon Women,* Vol. 5, Kenneth L. Homes, David C. Duniway (eds.), University of Nebraska Press, Lincoln (1997).	5
John L. Powell (ed.), "Great Feeder Canal Company," *Records Collection, MSS 31,* Arthur Porter Special Collections, BYU-Idaho (January 23, 2002).	14
"Adams to Prevost, Washington, Sept 29, 1817," *Diplomatic Instructions, All Countries,* 8:149, RG 59, National Archives, Washington D.C.	2
Progressive Men of Bannock, Bear Lake, Bingham, Fremont and Oneida Counties, Idaho, A. W. Bowen & Co., Chicago (1904).	5, 8, 12-15
Sandra Ransel, Charles Durand, *Crossroads: A History of the Elmore County Area,* Elmore County Historical Research Team, Mountain Home, Idaho (1985).	6, 8, 10, 12-15
"Red River Settlement," *The Columbia Encyclopedia,* Sixth Editon, Columbia University Press, New York (2008)	2
John E. Rees, *Idaho: Chronology, Nomenclature, Bibliography,* W. B. Conkey Company, Chicago (1918).	5, 6, 9, 10
Agnes Just Reid, *Letters of Long Ago,* Fourth Edition, Cedar Creek Press, Boise, Idaho (1997).	7, 15
Richard Reinhardt, *Workin' on the Railroad: Reminiscences from the Age of Steam,* University of Oklahoma Press, Norman (2003).	11
James P. Ronda, *Astoria and Empire,* University of Nebraska Press, Lincoln (1990).	1, 2

Frank A. Root, William Elsey Connelley, *The Overland Stage to California,* Nabu Press (1901, facsimile 2010).	14
Mark H. Rose, Bruce E. Seely, Paul F. Barrett, *The Best Transportation System in the World,* The Ohio State University Press, Columbus (2006).	15
Alexander Ross, T. C. Elliott (ed.), "Journal of Alexander Ross, Snake Country Expedition, 1824," *Quarterly of the Oregon Historical Society,* Vol. 14 (Dec. 1913).	2
Alexander Ross, Kenneth A. Spaulding (ed.), *The Fur Hunters of the Far West,* University of Oklahoma Press, Norman (1956).	1, 2
Jerry C. Roundy, *Ricks College: A Struggle for Survival,* Ricks College Press, Rexburg (1976).	13
William Pat Rowe, *"Diamond-Field Jack" Davis On Trial,* thesis: Master of Arts in Education, Idaho State University, Pocatello (1966).	14, 15
Robert H. Ruby, John Arthur Brown, *A Guide to the Indian Tribes of the Pacific Northwest,* University of Oklahoma Press, Norman (1986).	1, 5, 9, 10
Carl P. Russell, *Firearms, Traps & Tools of the Mountain Men,* University of New Mexico Press, Albuquerque (1977).	2, 3
Osborne Russell, Aubrey L. Haines (ed.), *Journal of a Trapper,* University of Nebraska Press, Lincoln (1965).	3, 4, 9
Don Russell, *One Hundred and Three Fights and Scrimmages; the Story of General Reuben F. Bernard,* Stackpole Books, Mechanicsburg, PA (2003).	9
Rufus Sage, *Rocky Mountain Life, or, Startling Scenes and Perilous Adventures in the Far West,* Wentworth & Company, Boston (1857).	4
Arthur C. Sanders, *The History of Bannock County, Idaho,* Tribune Company, Pocatello, (1915).	8
Abigail Jane Scott, "Journal of a Trip to Oregon," *Covered Wagon Women,* Vol. 5, Kenneth L. Homes, David C. Duniway (eds.), University of Nebraska Press, Lincoln (1997).	4
H. W. Scott (ed.), *History of Portland, Oregon,* D. Mason & Co., Publishers, Syracuse, New York (1890).	6
Stephen W. Sears, "Trail Blazer of the Far West," *American Heritage Magazine,* Vol 14, No. 4 (June 1963).	2
Raymond W. Settle (ed.), *The March of the Mounted Riflemen,* University of Nebraska Press, Lincoln (1989),	4
Edgar "Ted" Severe, Virginia Estes (ed.), "The True Story of the Wilson-Cummings Murder," *A Pause for Reflection,* J. Grant Stevenson, Provo, Utah (© Cassia County Company of the Daughters of the Utah Pioneers, 1977).	14, 15
Donald H. Shannon, *The Boise Massacre on the Oregon Trail,* Snake Country Publishing, Caldwell, Idaho (2004).	4
Donald H. Shannon, *The Utter Disaster On The Oregon Trail,* Snake Country Publishing, Caldwell, Idaho (1993).	4
David L. Shirk, Martin F. Schimdt (ed.), *The Cattle Drives of David Shirk,* Champoeg Press, Portland, Oregon (1956).	7-9, 12-14

"Shirk Ranch", *Cultural Resource Inventory: Sheldon National Wildlife Refuge and Hart Mountain National Wildlife Refuge,* U. S. Fish and Wildlife Service, Portland, Oregon (February 1885).	14
George Elmo Shoup, "History of Lemhi County," *Salmon Register-Herald* (Series, May 8 - October 23, 1940).	4-10, 12, 13
"George Laird Shoup Biographical Sketch," *George Laird Shoup Papers, Manuscript Group 8,* University of Idaho, Moscow (1994).	7
Robert C. Sims, Hope A. Benedict (eds.), *Idaho's Governors: Historical Essays on Their Administrations,* Boise State University (1992).	5, 13, 15
Eugene Virgil Smalley (ed.), *History of the Northern Pacific Railroad,* G. P. Putnam's Sons, New York (1883).	3, 7, 8, 11
Spokane and The Spokane Country - Pictorial and Biographical - Deluxe Supplement, Vol. II. The S. J. Clarke Publishing Company, 1912.	11
Harold K. Steen, *The U. S. Forest Service: A History,* University of Washington Press, Seattle (1976).	15
James Stephenson, Jr., *Irrigation in Idaho,* Experiment Station Bulletin 216, U. S. Government Printing Office, Washington, D. C. (1909).	13, 15
Carrie Strahorn, *Fifteen Thousand Miles by Stage,* C.P. Putnam & Sons, New York (1911).	11
Robert E. Strahorn, *The Resources and Attractions of Idaho Territory,* Idaho Legislature publication, Boise City (1881).	10
Reminiscences of Mr. and Mrs. Jacob Stroup and Mrs. G. W. Brinnon, Pioneers of Washoe, Payette County, manuscript donated to Idaho State Historical Society (May 1937).	8
Robert Stuart, Kenneth A. Spaulding (ed.), *On The Oregon Trail: Robert Stuart's Journey of Discovery,* University of Oklahoma Press, Norman (1953).	2
Orlan J. Svingen (ed.), *The History of the Idaho National Guard,* Idaho National Guard, Boise (1995).	9, 10, 14
John Taliaferro, *Tarzan Forever: the Life of Edgar Rice Burroughs, Creator of Tarzan,* Scribner, New York(1999).	13
David Thompson, *David Thompson's narrative, 1784-1812,* Champlain Society, Toronto (1962).	2
George A. Thompson and F. Janet Thompson, "The Americus Savage diary," *A Genealogical History of Freeman, Maine 1796-1938,* Vol. 3, Heritage Books; Bowie, Maryland (1996).	4
Dan L. Thrapp, *Encyclopedia of Frontier Biography,* University of Nebraska Press, Lincoln (1991).	9, 10, 12
Alexander Toponce, *Reminiscences of Alexander Toponce,* University of Oklahoma Press, Norman (1971).	5-8, 10
John Kirk Townsend, *Narrative of a Journey across the Rocky Mountains to the Columbia River (1839),* reprinted, Reuben Gold Thwaites (ed.), in Early Western Travels, Vol. VIII, Arthur H. Clark Company, Cleveland (1905).	3
"John Kirk Townsend (1809-1851)," *The Oregon History Project,* Oregon Historical Society (2002).	3

D. S. Tuttle, *Reminiscences of a Missionary Bishop*, Thomas Whittaker, Publisher, New York (1906).	7
Mark Twain, *Life on the Mississippi*, Signet Classic (2001).	6
United States Department of the Interior (eds.), *The Federal Land Policy and Management Act of 1976: As Amended*, U.S. Department of the Interior, Bureau of Land Management, Washington, D.C. (2001).	15
John D. Unruh, Jr, *The Plains Across*, University of Illinois Press, Urbana (1979).	4
Robert Marshall Utley, *Frontier regulars: the United States Army and the Indian, 1866-1891*, Macmillan Publishing Company, Inc. (1973).	7
Frances Fuller Victor, *The River of the West*, Classics of the Fur Trade Series, Winfred Blevins, (ed.), Mountain Press Publishing Company, Missoula (1983).	3, 4
Eugene M. Violette, *A History of Missouri*, D. C. Heath & Company, New York (1918).	2, 3
Thorton Waite, "On the Main Line at Last," *The Streamliner*, Vol. 11, No. 1, Union Pacific Historical Society, Cheyenne, Wyoming (1997).	11
Thornton Waite, *Union Pacific: Montana Division*, Brueggenjohann/Reese and Thornton Waite Publishers, Idaho Falls (1998).	15
Charles S. Walgamott, *Six Decades Back*, The Caxton Press, Caldwell, Idaho (1936).	8, 10-15
John W. Walker, Linda Coffey, Tim Faller, "Improving Grazing Lands with Multi-Species Grazing," *Targeted Grazing: A natural approach to vegetation management and landscape enhancement*, Karen Launchbaugh (Ed.), American Sheep Industry Association (2006).	12
Julia Conway Welch, *The Magruder Murders*, Falcon Press Publishing, Helena, Montana (1991).	5
Julia Conway Welch, *Gold Town to Ghost Town: The Story of Silver City*, Idaho, University of Idaho Press, Moscow (1982).	5, 6, 8, 14, 15
Merle W. Wells, *Gold Camps & Silver Cities: Nineteenth Century Mining in Central and Southern Idaho*, 2nd Edition, Bulletin 22, Idaho Department of Lands, Bureau of Mines and Geology, Moscow, Idaho (1983).	5, 10
Merle Wells, Arthur A. Hart, *Idaho: Gem of the Mountains*, Windsor Publications, Inc., Northridge, California (1985)	2, 5, 13, 15
Narcissa Whitman, "Narcissa Whitman Journal," published in Myron Eells, *Marcus Whitman, Pathfinder and Patriot*, Alice Harriman Company, Seattle (1909).	3
J. Patrick Wilde, *Treasured Tidbits of Time: an Informal History of Bear Lake Valley*, © J. P. Wilde, Montpelier, Idaho (1977).	14
Rounsevelle Wildman, "The Governor of Idaho," *Overland Monthly*, Overland Monthly Publishing Company, San Francisco, California (June 1896).	13
Walter Williams (ed.), *A History of Northeast Missouri*, The Lewis Publishing Company, Chicago (1913).	7

R. Michael Wilson, *Great Stagecoach Robberies of the Old West*, a TwoDot® Book, Globe Pequot Press, Guilford, Connecticut (2006).	6
Oscar O. Winther, *The Great Northwest: a History*, Alfred A. Knopf, New York (1955).	5, 13
Oscar O. Winther, *The Old Oregon Country: a History of Frontier Trade, Transportation and Travel*, Stanford University Press, Stanford, California (1950).	5, 6
Otto Wolfgang, "How the Wild West Was Fenced In," *The Cattleman*, Vol. LIII, No. 3, August 1966.	12
John Work, T. C. Elliott (Ed.), "The Journal of John Work," *Quarterly of the Oregon Historical Society*, Vol. X, No. 3 (1909).	3
World Almanac and Book of Facts, 2008, World Almanac Books, New York (2007).	4, 7, 8, 10, 13, 15
John B. Wyeth, *Oregon, or A Short History of a Long Journey... (1833)*, re-printed, Reuben Gold Thwaites (ed.), in Early Western Travels, Vol. XXI, Arthur H. Clark, Cleveland (1904-07).	3
Nathaniel J. Wyeth, Don Johnson (ed.), *The Journals of Captain Nathaniel J. Wyeth's Expeditions to the Oregon Country 1831-1836*, Ye Galleon Press, Fairfield, Washington (1984).	3
George C. Young, "Thousands of Herefords Carry the Circle C Brand" *Idaho Power Company Bulletin* (July 1965).	10
James A. Young, B. Abbott Sparks, *Cattle in the Cold Desert*, University of Nevada Press, Reno (2002).	4, 8, 10, 12-15
Ben Ysursa, *Idaho Blue Book, 2003-2004*, The Caxton Printers, Caldwell, Idaho (2003).	14, 15

Bibliography – Newspaper Articles

Henry Miller, "Letters from the Upper Columbia," *Oregonian,* Portland, Oregon (June 5-22, 1861).

"The Mines of Idaho," *Oregonian,* Portland, Oregon (June 7, 1862).

"From the Upper County," *Oregonian,* Portland, Oregon (May 20, 1863).

"Still They Come," *Idaho Statesman,* Boise (August 26, 1865).

"The First Train for Idaho," *Owyhee Avalanche,* Silver City, Idaho (April 14, 1866).

"Battle of Three Forks," *Owyhee Avalanche,* Silver City, Idaho (June 2, 1866).

"Philip Collier – Butcher Shop," *Owyhee Avalanche*, Silver City, Idaho (June 9, 1866).

"Indian attack on Sinker – Skirmish," *Owyhee Avalanche,* Silver City, Idaho (May 11, 1867).

"Cattle Stolen," *Owyhee Avalanche,* Silver City, Idaho (July 20, 1867).

"New Billiard Table," *Owyhee Avalanche,* Silver City, Idaho (May 2, 1868).

"Proceedings of an Agricultural Meeting," *Idaho Statesman,* Boise (June 15, 1869).

"Texas, Cattle," The *Owyhee Avalanche,* Silver City, Idaho (October 09, 1869).

"Idaho – Its Conditions and Prospects," *Idaho Statesman*, Boise (July 2, 1870).

"From Texas – Con Shea," *Owyhee Avalanche,* Silver City, Idaho (September 24, 1870).

"From Texas – Kohlheyer," *Owyhee Avalanche,* Silver City, Idaho (October 29, 1870).

"Sheep Restriction Act," *Idaho Statesman,* Boise (Jan 17, 1871).

"Texas Cattle Coming," *Idaho Statesman,* Boise (June 10, 1871).

"The New Road to Kelton," *Idaho Statesman,* Boise (June 24, 1871).

"Sommercamp Visit," *Owyhee Avalanche,* Silver City, Idaho (July 27, 1872).

"Prosperity," *Idaho Statesman,* Boise (October 8, 1872).

"Letter: Sheep Restriction," *Idaho Statesman,* Boise (Dec 13, 1872).

"Agricultural Fair," *Idaho Statesman,* Boise (October 8, 1872), (September 23, 1873).

"Blackinger Cattle," *Owyhee Avalanche,* Silver City, Idaho (Saturday, October 18, 1873).

"Cattle Raising," *Idaho Statesman,* Boise (February 28, 1874).

"Feeding Cattle in the Winter for Early Beef," *Idaho Statesman,* Boise (March 21, 1874).

"Thoroughbred Cattle," *Idaho Statesman,* Boise (June 11, 1874).

"Cattle Stealing," *Idaho Statesman,* Boise (February 23, 1875).

"Con Shea Sawmill," *Owyhee Avalanche,* Silver City, Idaho (January 1, 1876).

"Marks & Brands Adopted by Stock Owners in Owyhee County," *Owyhee Avalanche,* Silver City, Idaho (January 11, 1876).

W. A. Goulder, "Businesses in Mount Idaho," *Idaho Statesman,* Boise (March 4, 1876).

W. A. Goulder, "Northern Idaho Stockmen," *Idaho Statesman,* Boise (March 4, 1876).

"Weiser Area Survey," *Idaho Statesman,* Boise (May 27, 1876).

Roustabout, "Resources of Owyhee," Owyhee Avalanche, Silver City, Idaho (November 18, 1876).

"Utah Northern Railroad," The Helena Independent, Helena, Montana (Dec 12, 1876).

"Shot and Killed," *Idaho Statesman,* Boise (September 20, 1877).

"Cattle for Sale in Northern Idaho," *Idaho Statesman,* Boise (October 6, 1877).

"Married: Pence-Wells," *Owyhee Avalanche,* Silver City, Idaho (October 27, 1877).

"Wedding: T. Regan," *Owyhee Avalanche,* Silver City, Idaho (January 4, 1878).

"Eastern Owyhee," *Owyhee Avalanche,* Silver City, Idaho (March 16, 1878).

"Alturas County, Stock Raising," *Idaho Statesman,* Boise (Sept. 28, 1878).

"Sale of [Payette] Cattle," *Idaho Statesman,* Boise (May 22, 1879).

"Our Cattle Market," *Idaho Statesman,* Boise (October 23, 1879).

"1,000 Head of Cattle for Sale," *Lewiston Teller,* Lewiston, Idaho, (February 20, 1880).

"Stock Association," *Blackfoot Register,* Blackfoot, Idaho (October 16, 1880).

"Blackfoot: A Review … " *Blackfoot Register,* Blackfoot, Idaho (January 1, 1881).

"The Cattle Trade," *Idaho Statesman,* Boise (January 22, 1881).

"Driving Stock East," *Idaho Statesman,* Boise (January 27, 1881).

"Store Winter Feed," *Idaho Statesman,* Boise (February 5, 1881).

"Cattle Shipped from Winnemucca," Owyhee Avalanche, Silver City, Idaho (February 26, 1881).

"5000 Cattle from Oregon to Wyoming," Idaho Statesman, Boise (February 28, 1881).

"Walla Walla Stock Losses," *Idaho Statesman,* Boise (March 1, 1881).

"Blackfoot: What It Has Been and Is Going to Be," *Blackfoot Register,* Blackfoot, Idaho (April 2, 1881).

"Large Cattle Drive Through Hailey," *Idaho Statesman,* Boise (July 2, 1881).

"Cattle Buyers in Weiser and Payette," *Idaho Statesman,* Boise (March 18, 1882).

"Cattle Buyers in Lewiston," *Idaho Statesman,* Boise (March 25, 1882).

"The Oregon Short Line," *Owyhee Avalanche, Silver City, Idaho,* Silver City, Idaho (June 24, 1882).

"Eagle Rock Notes," *Salt Lake Tribune,* Salt Lake City, Utah (July 15, 1882).

"Town Cows," *Idaho Statesman,* Boise (July 18, 1882).

"Cattle, Sheep and Horses in Owyhee County," *Owyhee Avalanche,* Silver City, Idaho (August 26, 1882).

"Cattle Breeding and Farming," *Owyhee Avalanche,* Silver City, Idaho (October 28, 1882).

"Death of Dan Murphy, the Nevada Cattle King," *Owyhee Avalanche,* Silver City, Idaho November 11, 1882.

"Cattle and Sheep Law," *Owyhee Avalanche,* Silver City, Idaho (February 24, 1883).

"The Shirley Ranch," *Blackfoot Register,* Blackfoot, Idaho (March 24, 1883).

"Regional Cattlemen Meet," *Owyhee Avalanche,* Silver City, Idaho (Saturday, July 07, 1883).

"By-Laws of the Idaho Stock Growers Association," *Owyhee Avalanche,* Silver City, Idaho (July 14, 1883).

"Con Shea Writes from Santa Rosa," *Owyhee Avalanche,* Silver City, Idaho (October 13, 1883).

"Advertise Your Brands," *Owyhee Avalanche,* Silver City, Idaho (October 27, 1883); Issue 11; col C

"Oregon Short Line Railroad," *Owyhee Avalanche,* Silver City, Idaho (February 2, 1884).

"Cattle-Raising and Growing in Nevada," *Nevada State Journal,* Reno (August 9, 1884).

"The Stock Business," *Idaho Statesman,* Boise (January 31, 1885).

"Cattle Growers Meeting Announced," *Owyhee Avalanche,* Silver City, Idaho (March 28, 1885).

"Eastern Idaho," *Idaho Register,* Idaho Falls, Idaho (April 4, 1885).

"Southern Idaho," *Idaho Register,* Idaho Falls, Idaho (April 4, 1885).

Stephen Hall Meek, "A Sketch of the Life of the First Pioneer," The *Golden Era,* San Francisco (April 1885).

"Lemhi and Birch Creek Valleys," *Idaho Register,* Idaho Falls, Idaho (July 4, 1885).

"Hyde Bros. Sale, Shoshone Shipping Point," *Owyhee Avalanche,* Silver City, Idaho (September 19, 1885).

"Alturas Thoroughbred Cattle," *Owyhee Avalanche,* Silver City, Idaho (January 09, 1886).

"Territorial Stock Growers' Association," *Owyhee Avalanche,* Silver City, Idaho (January 23, 1886).

"Overgrazing Resolution: Idaho Cattle Growers' Association," *Owyhee Avalanche,* Silver City, Idaho (April 10, 1886).

"Locals News Notes," *Idaho Register,* Idaho Falls, Idaho (May 29, 1886).

"Sheep vs. Cattle and Horses," *Idaho Statesman,* Boise (June 22, 1886).

"Agricultural Fair and Cattle Show," *Idaho Statesman,* Boise (July 1, 1886).

"Bennett Ranch Sold," *Owyhee Avalanche,* Silver City, Idaho (September 11, 1886).

"Improvements at Payette," *Idaho Statesman,* Boise (March 24, 1887).

"Idaho Cattle are All Right," *Idaho Statesman,* Boise (March 29, 1887).

"Cattle Deaths from Overgrazing," *Owyhee Avalanche,* Silver City, Idaho (May 14, 1887).

"Wilkins Horse Shipment," *Owyhee Avalanche,* Silver City, Idaho (June 18, 1887).

"The Last [Narrow Gauge] Train," Idaho Register, Idaho Falls (July 23, 1887).

"Cold Weather Delays Shearing," *Idaho County Free Press,* Grangeville, Idaho (October 28, 1887).

"Raising Stock," *Idaho Statesman,* Boise (January 24, 1888).

"Sheepmen Have Right to Public Lands," *Owyhee Avalanche,* Silver City, Idaho (March 10, 1888).

"The Division of Idaho," *Idaho Statesman,* Boise (April 3, 1888).

"List of Marks and Brands," *Owyhee Avalanche,* Silver City, Idaho (June 2, 1888).

"Shoup Cattle Sale," *Idaho Statesman,* Boise (June 24, 1888).

"Stock in Alturas County," *Idaho Statesman,* Boise (September 16, 1888).

"Sale of Thoroughbred [Stock]," *Idaho Statesman,* Boise (September 18, 1888).

"Steen Mountain Homicide," *Owyhee Avalanche,* Silver City, Idaho (October 20, 1888).

"Nevada ranges too crowded," *Owyhee Avalanche,* Silver City, Idaho (April 27, 1889).

"Boise City Stock Yards," *Idaho Statesman,* Boise (May 7, 1889).

"Great Sale of Short Horn Cattle," *Idaho Statesman,* Boise (June 13, 1889).

"Hailey-Bellevue News," *Idaho Statesman,* Boise (Sept 6, 1889).

"Good for the Rancher," *Idaho Statesman,* Boise (January 18, 1890).

"Must Stock Feed for Stock," *Owyhee Avalanche,* Silver City, Idaho (February 1, 1890).

"Dead Cattle Around the Town of Blackfoot," *Idaho Statesman*, Boise (April 8, 1890).

"The Lost River Country," *Idaho Statesman*, Boise (July 9,1890).

"500 Horses Stolen," *Owyhee Avalanche*, Silver City, Idaho (September 13, 1890).

Andrew Jenson, "The Bannock Stake of Zion: Parker Ward," *The Deseret Weekly*, The Deseret News Co., Salt Lake City, Utah (1891).

"That Big Cattle Steal," *Idaho Statesman*, Boise (January 27, 1891).

"Sidney Dillon," *Idaho Statesman*, Boise (June 4, 1891).

"Emigrants," *Idaho Statesman*, Boise (September 16, 1891).

"South Boise Bridge," *Idaho Statesman*, Boise (October 27, 1891).

"Kittie Wilkins, Selling Horses," *St. Louis Republic*, St. Louis, Missouri (December 17, 1891).

"Cattle Ranchers and Settlers," Idaho Falls Times, Idaho Falls (April 28, 1892).

"Cattle Shipped from Weiser," *Owyhee Avalanche*, Silver City, Idaho (May 28, 1892).

"Railroad Transfer of Sheep," *The Standard*, Ogden, Utah (Nov 11, 1892).

"Mike Hyde in from Oreana," *Owyhee Avalanche*, Silver City, Idaho (July 1, 1893).

"Wool Growers Organize," *Idaho Statesman*, Boise (September 26, 1893).

"A New Trotting Champion," *The New York Times* (July 27, 1894).

"Idaho Falls: Great Farming Country," *Idaho Register*, Idaho Falls, Idaho (January 4, 1895).

"57 Cattle Shot," *Salubria Citizen*, Salubria, Idaho (July 19, 1895).

"Cattle Killing Cases," *Idaho Statesman*, Boise (August 8, 1895).

"She Can Lasso a Wild Horse," *Evening Democrat*, Warren, Pennsylvania (August 8, 1895).

"Big Haul in [Rustled] Cattle," *Idaho Statesman*, Boise (September 12, 1896).

"Statesman Defends Its Davis Position," *Idaho Statesman*, Boise (November 30, 1898).

"For Murder Most Brutal," *Idaho Statesman*, Boise (April 9, 1897).

"All the Evidence In," *Idaho Statesman*, Boise (April 16, 1897).

"Miss Wilkins Returns to Her Home on the Bruneau," *Idaho Statesman*, Boise (April 30, 1897).

"Special Rates from Silver City and DeLamar to Boise," *Idaho Statesman*, Boise (June 16, 1897).

"Cattle Thieves in Idaho," *Idaho Falls Times*, Idaho Falls, Idaho (August 26, 1897).

"Cattlemen's convention," *Idaho Statesman*, Boise (February 18, 1898).

"Thomas J. Davis News," *Idaho Statesman*, Boise (March 1898, Oct 1900).

"Local Brevities: John Sparks," *Idaho Statesman*, Boise (May 10, 1898).

"Jack Davis Reprieve Criticized," *Idaho Statesman*, Boise (October 23, 1898).

"Jeff Gray Affidavit," *Idaho Statesman*, Boise (December 2, 1898).

"Jeff Gray Trial Results," *Idaho Statesman*, Boise (Feb 22, 1899).

Alex Hyslop, "Terrifying Tale of a Killer Steam Engine," *Pocatello Tribune*, Pocatello, Idaho (March 20, 1900).

"T. C. Catlin News," *Idaho Statesman*, Boise (September 1900, June 1902).

"Horse Queen in Boise," *Idaho Statesman*, Boise , Boise (September 10, 1900).

"American Falls Carey Act," *Idaho Statesman*, Boise (February 23, 1901)

"Two Mile Limit Court Case," *Idaho Statesman*, Boise (December 23, 1901).

"Washington County News," *Idaho Statesman*, Boise (March 1, 1902).

"The Public Ranges," *Idaho Statesman*, Boise (May 4, 1902).

"Cattle Poisoned," *Idaho Statesman*, Boise (June 20, 1902).

"The Only One of Her Kind," Denver Post, Denver, Colorado (September 18, 1902).

"Sparks Supports Davis," *Idaho Statesman,* Boise (November 18, 1902).

"Jack Davis Plot," *Idaho Statesman,* Boise (November 20, 1902).

"Hawley Condemns Vendetta," *Idaho Statesman,* Boise (November 29, 1902).

"Stockmen Organize," Idaho Statesman, Boise (February 3, 1903).

"[Sam Taylor] Will Resign," Idaho Falls Times, Idaho Falls, Idaho (March 14, 1905).

"Solid Block of Concrete: Santa Rosa Will Have Substantial Structure," *Santa Rosa Republican,* Santa Rosa, California (July 16, 1906).

"Taylor Moving to Ontario," *Idaho Register,* Idaho Falls (July 14, 1911).

"Benjamin W. Driggs Answers Last Call," *Deseret News*, Salt Lake City, Utah (Oct. 2, 1913).

"W. B. Allison Passes Away," *The Midvale Reporter,* Midvale, Idaho (October 8, 1914).

"T. C. Galloway dies," *Oregonian,* Portland, Oregon (June 11, 1916).

"Payette's Oldest Pioneer Called," *Payette Enterprise*, Payette, Idaho (February 2, 1922).

"Three Pioneers of Idaho County Answer Last Call," *Idaho County Free Press,* Grangeville, Idaho (November 19, 1925).

"Key Dates in ... Idaho Water Development," *Idaho Statesman,* Boise (Jan 16, 2006).

Arthur Hart, "Kuna History," *Idaho Statesman,* Boise (November 18, 25, 2008).

Arthur Hart, "Meet Kitty Wilkins, the Horse Queen of Idaho," *Idaho Statesman,* Boise (February 10, 2009).

INDEX

242

133, 153-155, 167, 178, 192, 226, 235, 236

Pacific Northwest 2, 3, 13, 19, 21, 26, 33, 37, 39, 43, 68, 105, 122, 131, 149, 171, 175, 224, 225, 231
Joel Palmer 39, 100, 230
Ferdinand J. "Ferd" Patterson 71, 72, 230
Arthur Pence 86, 132, 156, 214, 236
Peter Pence 81, 86, 116, 133, 155, 156, 208
Ira Burton Perrine 142, 197, 198, 199, 204, 216
Elias D. Pierce 47, 48, 60, 130, 162, 175, 209, 218, 230
Sumner Pinkham 71, 72
Potatoes 34, 64, 97, 122, 175, 201, 207

Railroads. *See* Transportation
Ranching 53, 62, 64, 74, 81, 83, 87, 90, 91, 94, 96, 97, 101, 124, 126, 134, 159, 162, 169, 170, 173, 175, 176, 178, 200, 214, 215, 227
    Ranchers 50, 59, 73-75, 78, 86, 94-98, 102, 104, 115, 119, 123, 127, 129, 130, 135, 136, 149, 154, 156-158, 161, 163, 164, 166, 167, 172, 174, 178, 183, 187, 207-209, 212, 213, 237, 238
    Ranches 41, 46, 50, 55, 62-64, 66, 68, 72-75, 77-82, 84, 87, 90-92, 94-98, 100, 104, 115, 116, 123-126, 128, 129, 132-134, 137, 142, 145, 152-158, 161-168, 172, 173, 175-178, 180-189, 192, 193, 195, 198-201, 206-209, 211, 213,-219, 225, 226, 232, 236, 237
Henry C. Riggs 53, 60, 97, 132, 178, 212, 218
Rivers & Streams
    Bear River 24, 27, 31, 36, 38, 43, 52, 57, 122, 192
    Blackfoot River 77, 78, 102, 125, 161, 175, 209
    Boise River 18, 21, 32, 51, 56, 64, 144, 145, 198, 199, 218
    Bruneau River 73, 86, 154, 167
    Clearwater River 8, 9, 34, 38, 47-49, 51, 60-62, 80, 104, 110, 111, 148, 193
    Columbia River 2, 16, 31, 33, 222, 225, 232
    Cow Creek 94, 96
    Goose Creek 92, 102, 126, 127, 142, 163

Lemhi River 2, 20, 66, 74, 79, 129
Mississippi River 3, 28, 58, 74
Missouri River 1, 4, 12, 14, 15, 62
Owyhee River 27, 67
Pahsimeroi River 98, 166
Payette River 73, 81, 82, 97, 147, 155, 208, 226
Portneuf River 27, 28, 30, 32, 34, 69, 88, 91
Raft River 75, 79, 83, 92, 93, 112, 126, 161, 162, 175, 176, 209, 218
Reynolds Creek 54, 94, 97, 134, 154, 214
Rock Creek 73, 74, 91-93, 112, 114, 126-128, 162, 163, 172, 182, 183, 185, 197, 214, 221
Salmon River 2-4, 6, 22, 24, 49, 50, 54, 74, 80, 99, 101, 108, 117, 119, 128, 132, 158, 166, 175, 179, 218
Snake River 10, 15-17, 27, 30, 38, 55, 57, 63, 64, 72, 77, 81, 89, 91-93, 102, 109, 124-128, 133, 138, 139, 142, 145-148, 152, 162, 170, 175, 193, 197-199, 206, 216
Teton River 28, 159
Weiser River 38, 58, 72, 132, 147, 148, 208, 213
George B. Rogers 161, 188, 215
Alexander Ross 21-23, 231
Rustling 79, 124, 161, 164, 169
    Rustlers 79, 80, 124, 153, 154, 159, 160, 162, 164, 169
Settlement
    Homestead Act 206
    Homestead 36, 66, 73, 82, 86, 89, 97, 125, 126, 131, 132, 153, 154, 158, 167, 175, 200, 209
    Homesteaders 133, 158, 175, 188
    Settlers 3, 35, 36, 48, 51, 53, 54, 59, 62, 63, 65, 66, 68, 69, 72, 73, 78, 79, 81, 82, 85, 86, 92, 98, 100, 101, 104, 106-108, 110, 112, 114, 118, 122, 123, 126, 128, 129, 132, 142, 147, 149, 153-156, 158, 170, 188, 199, 200, 203, 216, 225, 238
Cornelius "Con" Shea 68, 83, 94, 115, 192, 213, 218, 235, 236
Sheep: *See* Livestock
David L. Shirk 84, 86, 93, 94, 97, 116, 153-155, 172, 192, 213, 218, 231, 232
John Q. Shirley 74, 75, 78, 83, 126, 162,

244

Made in the USA
Columbia, SC
02 July 2021